CHRISTIAN THEOLOGY
The Spiritual Tradition

The Sussex Library of Religious Beliefs and Practices

This series is intended for students of religion, social sciences and history, and for the interested layperson. It is concerned with the beliefs and practices of religions in their social, cultural and historical setting. These books will be of particular interest to Religious Studies teachers and students at universities, colleges, and high schools. Inspection copies available upon request.

<u>Published</u>

The Ancient Egyptians   Rosalie David

Buddhism   Merv Fowler

Christian Theology: The Spiritual Tradition   John Glyndwr Harris

Gnosticism   John Glyndwr Harris

Hinduism   Jeaneane Fowler

Humanism   Jeaneane Fowler

Islam   David Norcliffe

The Jews   Alan Unterman

Sikhism   W. Owen Cole and Piara Singh Sambhi

Zoroastrianism   Peter Clark

<u>In preparation</u>

The Doctrine of the Trinity: God in Three Persons   Martin Downes
You Reap What You Sow: Causality in the Religions of the World
   Jeaneane Fowler
Hindu Goddesses   Lynn Foulston
Jainism   Lynn Foulston
Taoism   Jeaneane Fowler
Zen   Merv Fowler

<u>Forthcoming</u>
Bhagavad Gita (a student commentary)   *Confucianism*
The Protestant Reformation: Tradition and Practice

Christian Theology

The Spiritual Tradition

JOHN GLYNDWR HARRIS

sussex
ACADEMIC
PRESS

BRIGHTON • PORTLAND

2 4 6 8 10 9 7 5 3 1

Published 2001 in Great Britain by
SUSSEX ACADEMIC PRESS
Box 2950
Brighton BN2 5SP

and in the United States of America by
SUSSEX ACADEMIC PRESS
5824 N.E. Hassalo St.
Portland, Oregon 97213–3644

British Library Cataloguing in Publication Data
A CIP catalogue record for this book is available from the British Library.

Library of Congress Cataloging-in-Publication Data
Harris, J. Glyndwr (John Glyndwr)
Christian theology : the spiritual tradition / John Glyndwr Harris.
p.   cm. — (The Sussex library of religious beliefs and practices)
Includes bibliographical references and index.
ISBN 1–902210–22–0 (pbk. : alk. paper)
1. Theology, Doctrinal.   2. Spirituality.   I. Title.   II. Series.
BT75.2.H375 2001
230—dc21   99–085967

Typeset & designed by G & G Editorial, Brighton
Printed by T.J. International, Padstow, Cornwall
This book is printed on acid-free paper

Contents

Foreword by D. Byron Evans

This book deals with the relationship between theology and spirituality. It treats this intriguing theme by surveying first the various trends and schools of thought throughout church history, in relation to their intellectual and social context. It is the work of a scholar who is able to clarify the complex history of this relationship from his depth of knowledge and understanding.

Students of theology, and others, will welcome this book because it is inviting to read, accessible and lucid in its exploration of the leading and basic concepts of both theology and spirituality. The survey, from the first chapter to the last, is profound in its detail and assured in its guidance; the final chapter is one that should be read by all who are concerned with the future of Christianity and the challenges it faces. In a secular age such as ours, with its proliferation of strange religious cults seeking spiritual enlightenment, this book enables both the religious and the non-believer to appreciate and think about the relationship between theology and spirituality.

In a wide-ranging survey, the new spiritualities of power, world wide, such as Liberation Theology and Black Spirituality are given their places. In terms of spirituality, the writer points the reader to the wider context by drawing on broader human experiences and reflections. The influence of the Swiss theologians Hans Urs von Balthasar and Karl Rahner, both influenced by Karl Barth, comes through in the references to theological aesthetics and the concern with the spirituality of art and beauty. The author will agree that "the transcendent beauty of God is seen in the kenosis of the cross, and union with God is to share the eternal sacrifice which is at the heart of the Blessed trinity" (*The Blackwell Encyclopedia of Modern Christian Theology*, 1995. ed. Alister McGrath).

Professor D. Byron Evans, D.Litt., D.D., Dean, Greenwich School of Theology, in association with Potchefstroom University for Christian Higher Education, South Africa

Foreword by Paul Ballard

Spitituality is in. After the Death of God and secularisation it has come
as a suprise to find that religion is not dead but very much alive. New
Age and post-modernism have produced a critique of the apparently all
conquering rationalism of modernity. "There are more things in heaven
and earth" than perhaps was being allowed for. Perhaps humanity needs
to dwell in a more personal and feeling universe. However, this counter-
action has also meant a disintegration. Meta-narratives, grand designs,
are suspect. Rather we all have to create our own meaning out of our
personal experience, producing a pluralism of universes and a con-
sumerist or even DIY model of religion. One can have faith in what
appeals and there are little or no criteria of judgement concerning right-
ness or truth. So spirituality becomes an all embracing term for personal
orientation, the way we mould our lives or the way our lives are
moulded around that which is placed at the heart of our own world of
meaning.

In such a context Christianity is at a double disadvantage. First, in
our society, it is too clearly associated with the past and too often has
accommodated itself to the retreating modernism. So the new spirituality is seen as a way of breaking loose from the dead hand of rational and
ordered religion. In this sense Christianity has to try to recover its deep
and long tradition of spirituality in order to compete in the contemporary world. This is seen, for instance, in the sometimes quirky quest for
Celtic spirituality and the popularity of retreats.

Secondly, however, Christianity offers a meta-narrative. It claims to
make sense of the universe in the light of faith in God, creator, saviour
and sanctifier. It offers revelation and exists in community. This feels,
in the present climate, oppressive and demanding. Yet there are many
who do in fact find in Christian faith precisely that spiritual centre that
gives shape to their lives in a confusing and diverse world.

This book takes these challenges on. It is a brave attempt to state the
nature and forms of Christian spirituality as it has manifested itself

through the centuries. Dr. Harris brings to his task a long and rich career in theology and education. There is immense learning and great erudition. An almost impossible task has been undertaken to provide a guide through and immense and infinitely various tradition. The reader should find this a welcome introduction to the heart of Christian believing and its story from the emergence of the New Testament and early Christian thought to the ecumenical diversity of the world Church as it enters into the new millennium. Doubtless there are short comings, emphases that one reader would like or another would find un-important. But it is a resource for future reading and exploration.

The value of the book is to be found in its double core assertion. Christian spirituality, the way of being Christian in the world, is dis-covered at the point where prayer and contemplation are informed by theological understanding and tradition, mediated through the living community and worship of the People of God, the Church. The spiritual life is, therefore, both individual and corporal, personal and shared, inward and social. This is, secondly, affirmed on the basis of recognising that at the heart of Christian faith is the person of Jesus Christ who is both the model to be emulated and the revelation of the God that informs the spiritual life. This points to a Trinitarian and in-carnational understanding of God that is particular and essential to Christian believing.

Revd. Professor Paul Ballard
Department of Religious and Theological Studies
Cardiff University

Preface and Acknowledgements

The popular interest in spirituality at present is well known. This reflects the current interest in self development and self identity in a secular and pluralist age. It finds expression in a variety of practices of spirituality as something that is fundamental to self understanding and self fulfilment. It is therefore true to say that spirituality has to do with something fundamental in the human condition.

This book is an introduction to the spiritual tradition in Christian theology, rather than an academic study of theology. But it cannot avoid asking the question, What is theology? and What is spirituality?, and How can we conceive of the relationship between them? It assumes that theology and spirituality are two sides of the same coin, and that both have to be set in the context of lived experience. This is a matter of the relationship of the self to other people, to the world and to God. It articulates the inner and outer world of human experience, and expounds what is involved in being human and developing human potential to the full.

By drawing upon the insights of the theologies and spiritualities from the age of the Church Fathers onward, we are able to see how Christian theologies and spirituality are different expressions of ideals and a process which seeks to identify the human quest for meaning and wholeness. The distinct but interdependent levels of understanding theology and spirituality raise our expectations that this is an area in which we can make progress towards perceiving more clearly the nature, meaning and destiny of human life. With this in view, we seek to draw upon the wealth and variety of Christian theology and its spiritual tradition so that, by listening to the voices of Christians among the desert recluses, ascetics, mystics, schoolmen, reformers, apologists and monastics, as well as visionaries, artists, poets, musicians and novelists, we see how they engaged the mind and soul as well as the heart and feeling in the quest for human wholeness.

The study also takes account of the various practices, especially of those such as prayer, meditation, worship and the eucharist, charity and virtue that express the heart of the relationship with the trinity of Christian belief. Such practices evoke feelings of awe and wonder and the mystery of life, the splendour of the universe and the power of silence, beauty, art and music for enriching the spirit and exploring in greater depth and meaning of existence.

It is hoped that the many accounts of the works and contributions of representative leaders of Christian thought and spirituality throughout the ages will give a flavour of the Christian tradition in theology and spirituality and stimulate further study of their works. It will be clear from the examples given that it is never possible to silence theological controversy completely, for what one tradition challenges another defends as a holy article of faith. Other writers might take a different route and make a different selection, but it is hoped that those chosen will captivate the interest and provide a wider horizon from which to view the practice of individual spirituality and the search for human solidarity.

I am indebted to Professor Paul Ballard and to Professor D. Byron Evans for their willingness to write forewords to this book. Their insights into the issue of theology and spirituality add a much appreciated dimension to the text.

I would like to thank Anthony Grahame, Editorial Director at Sussex Academic Press, for his perceptions and guidance in the preparation of this work, and also the assistance of Alun and Sallie Vaughan in the production of the manuscript. But the author alone is responsible for any errors that may remain.

The author and publisher wish to thank Phil Coomes at the BBC Stills Library; Perry Hurcombe at the BBC Picture Archives; Lesley Francis at the Bangor RE Resources Centre, University of Wales; Geoffrey O'Brien at Educational Resources; BBC Worldwide Ltd (formerly BBC Enterprises Ltd); BBC Educational Publications; and BBC Gwbodaeth Cymru/BBC Information Wales, for assistance in tracking down the artist of the Eucharist scene used in the cover design.

There is the inner man, the spiritual in the psyche.
Basilides

All that I have said is as nothing compared with what I feel within, the witnessed correspondence between God and the soul.
Catherine of Genoa

To be right, a person must do two things: either he must learn to have God in his work and hold just to him there, or he must give up his work altogether. Since, however, we cannot live without activities, we must learn to keep God in everything we do . . .
Meister Eckhart

Lord, you were within me and I outside. I sought you outside and in my ugliness I fell upon those lovely things that you have made. I tasted you and now I hunger and thirst for you.
Saint Augustine

1

Christian Theology and Spirituality

___

If we begin with the question, "What is theology?" or "What is spirituality?" and turn to a dictionary or other such authority for an answer, we shall not get very far. But if we ask what are the thoughts that we call theology and what are the experiences we call spirituality we might see more clearly what the answer should be. We should start, therefore, at the beginning – with our thoughts and experience. We have a pictorial way of thinking and our thoughts about theology and spirituality are about the making of images. Perhaps for many the most significant word in the title to this chapter is the conjunction "*and*". Theology and spirituality do not fit easily together nor is the link between them immediately obvious. We cannot label the connection neatly to suit our own requirements. This is so whether the image of theology is of the word of God (*theos*) at work in history and the image of spirituality is of the vitality or breath of life (*spiritus* = life breath), or whether we visualize theology as reflection on ultimate human questions and spirituality as relating to the spiritual domain of existence.[1]

The conjunction in the title assumes there is an inherent or an essential connection between theology and spirituality. Though on the surface they may appear totally dissimilar, once we begin to look into the heart of theology and spirituality we begin to uncover the affinities. We should therefore start at the beginning with ourselves, otherwise we dismiss a whole reading of the human condition. Beginning with ourselves we appreciate rather better the way in which the imagery of theology with its roots in experience, and the imagery of spirituality as normative to experience, is essential to seeing how theology and spirituality interfuse each other as light interfuses a burning candle.

In the light of this, on what grounds do we establish the connection between theology and spirituality? The question leads to a tangle with theology and spirituality, but the point at issue is the evidence that justifies the connection. Many people are suspicious of theological dogma or regard spirituality as a purely personal internal affair. Theology deals with what is believed and spirituality with personal perfection. But this is too facile and would keep theology distinct from spirituality. By designating theology and spirituality and the great corpus of activities associated with them as about the making of images, we have a way of making better and more modern sense of the relationship between them. But to speak in this way of the connection between theology and spirituality faces us with a whole phalanx of questions.

We believe that everyone is attuned to the impact of images, and appreciates rather better in this visually exposed age the ways in which images make sense. To speak of experience in theology and spirituality means speaking about the inner consciousness, and language is woefully inadequate for this purpose. This difficulty is greater when it is spiritual experience that is in view. The origin of such experience is never visible and cannot be quantified. But the reality is no less real for being invisible. Its substance embraces the whole self to the fullest possible degree. Theology and spirituality have to do with human wholeness. All life is experience and all experience is spiritual. There is in experience an "otherness" with which the self has to do but which does not originate with the self. Both theology and spirituality have a focus in the "other", and neither operates fully outside the experience of the "other", that is, God. Whatever constitutes the province of theology or the process of spirituality originates with God and finds its ultimate fulfilment in him.

Having said this, we ask whether the culture of our time is inducive to the development and advancement of Christian theology and spirituality. Does its influence stultify the role of theology and the process of spirituality or challenge it to greater expansiveness? Neither theology or spirituality operate in a vacuum. We have witnessed an undermining of collective self-confidence and sufficiency in the face of the development of a rampant individualism. In general terms this is due to the way modern life is construed and events are interpreted in what is called a postmodernist world. Human reason alone is powerless to define meaning or expound essential truth; there is no certain knowledge; truth is relative not absolute; meaning is found in segments or components of knowledge not in a central core of unified knowledge; good and evil are determined by personal inclination or choice not by an authoritative objective standard; morality is relative not absolute; truth is culturally conditioned by the dominant theories of science; the realities of religion are make believe. So we ask, where does this leave theology and spirituality? Neither functions in isolation from what has been called "the oblique and disparaging relativism" of postmodernism. Large areas of experience have been overshadowed by its pervasive influences.

Taken together Christian theology and its spiritual tradition offer incentives for fresh approaches to personal and social self-evaluation. They may take up a reactionary stance when confronting the personal and social ethos of the age or they may challenge the assumptions and outreach of postmodern thought and ideals with their own fundamental questions of meaning and purpose, especially with questions that bear upon the quality of life, the search for meaning and life's ultimate destiny. In these circumstances theology and spirituality seek to be heard and heeded. They coalesce in a common objective of promoting personal and collective progress to the ideal of human wholeness. In this connection spirituality processes what theology expounds needs to be done. The image of theology is one of action (*praxis*), that is, dynamic encounter with the fundamental phenomena of experience, and not just with cerebral, deductive, analytical, ecclesial investigation alone. This way of "doing" theology impinges on those values that lie at the heart of spirituality.

The data of theology is experience in the broadest sense; the task of theology is to make sense of this data; the method of theology is exploration, interpretation, evaluation and assimilation. The integrity of the data may not be questioned or justified, but rather investigated and expounded through the application of the necessary skills of "doing" theology or thinking theologically about the phenomena of experience. This will include "the critical explication of the 'sequelae' of individual religious beliefs and corollaries and interactions between religious beliefs in general".[2] Into this process Christianity "interjects" a divine–human encounter. The primary focus of Christian theology is Jesus Christ, and for this reason Christian theology and spirituality are in a dialectical relationship wherein Christian belief is conceived to relate to live authentic experience, rather than being the embodiment of a static phenomenon. Christian theology elucidates these beliefs through the exploration of Christian experience as a way of understanding Christianity.

The experience is also an encounter with Christ, and "doing" theology through encounter elucidates the nature, meaning and impact of Christian experience. The encounter takes many forms, including interpretation of the life, death and resurrection of Christ, the articulation of his significance and meaning in Christian history and for today. The outcome of such encounter cannot be predetermined – it may result in deeper knowledge and clearer insights or a state of "unknowing"; or in certainty or scepticism or in faith or doubt. But the encounter has to be "open" and allow for the outcome of "unknowing" or "doubt", as well as faith and commitment. "Doing" theology is not indoctrination. Doubt that is informed has a positive outcome and is a spur to further encounter. Christian theology through this existential encounter audaciously plots new ways of probing life's deepest questions. This way of "doing" theology as open existential encounter also gives a specific perspective and direction to spirituality.

There are therefore solid grounds for linking theology and spirituality. Basically they share common objectives. Different patterns of behaviour may decide the manner of approach, but in any case theology and spirituality operate at the highest level of collaboration in the pursuit of common goals. The defining moment in this collaboration is the conjoining of the theological mind and the spiritual heart in a single process whose goal is ultimate wholeness. But what more precisely is meant by theology and spirituality?

What is theology?

Can we extract from the term theology some further thoughts and nuances of what it means, especially in relation to spirituality? It is axiomatic that theology has a Godward dimension and is theistically orientated (theology = *theos* + *logos* = discourse, doctrine or word about God). Christian theology has its own way of looking at things and this includes a way of looking at God. Why God? Because he reaches out to the world and beckons people to himself. Nowhere outside Christianity is there greater diversity in theology, but at the heart of Christian theology is Jesus Christ who represents God to the world. Christian theology purports to create such images as will elucidate the nature of the person of Christ and the significance of his achievements. The images are rich and complex and through them an incredible network of ideas and insights are projected, but the validity of the images stands or falls according to the way they make sense of the unique life, work, death and resurrection of Christ. They focus on the key question, *What is Christian truth?* This is Christian theology's most crucial pursuit. It does not claim privileged knowledge of an answer but rather applies its skills in probing more deeply the *whole* truth. As we shall see, the question has been debated across the centuries. Theologians of the ages have vied with each other in their efforts to explicate and communicate Christian truth, and it is still warmly debated. Traditionalist and progressive approaches to the question continue to be made. In the early Christian centuries radical theologians claimed to bring fresh insights into the interpretation of the nature of Christ and the truth of Christianity, whilst more conservative theologians adhered to the exposition of traditional doctrines. The question is compounded today by the postmodernist relativizing of truth, that is, viewing truth as relative not absolute. Christian theology projects an image of truth that is constant, it combats error and answers doubt.

It does not set out to produce a monolithic system of truth, but it elucidates certain precepts that are at the heart of Christian truth. It takes account of the broad sweep of experience of Christian and secular truth in the world as it is, as to engage the relevance of Christian truth in the contemporary search for the meaning of reality and the ultimate goal of existence.

What is spirituality?

The focus of the answer, as was hinted earlier, is on the spiritual life as process. The root of the term spirituality, *spirare*, means "to breathe". In its Latin form it is used of "inbreathing", "inspiration", "to be alive" or "to be assimilated". In the biblical tradition breath is a synonym for the creative action of God, as at the creation God "breathed the breath of life and man became a living thing" (Genesis 2: 7). Spirituality, through its association with the animating life-giving breath, may be characterized as the spiritual energy that makes a person "full of life". It extends to the physical and non-physical components, that is, to the whole person and the totality of experience, physical, mental and spiritual. This is the biblical view of being "spirit-possessed'; the source of this "aliveness" is the breath (spirit) of God who also sustains its vitality. It is proper to use terms like "vitality" and "energy" to describe spirituality; they do not define it but create an image of its vitalizing and energizing force. The image symbolizes movement, motion, activity and progress; this is the opposite of deadness, dullness, passiveness and idleness. Spirituality then is process, activity and growth to the attainment of life's ultimate purpose, inspired by the energizing vitality of the breath or spirit of God.

Christian spirituality is Christianity's specification for attaining this ideal. Geoffrey Wainwright has offered this definition:

> Christian spirituality is an existence before God and amid the created world.[3]

We note especially the reference to "existence before God" and "amid the created world". Spirituality is practised before God but without being isolated from the created world. We shall observe frequently in the course of this work how the spiritual tradition in Christianity exemplifies this convergence in a variety of ways. Existence before God implies exposure to the reality of God who is at work in and beyond the visible world; existence before God involves response to his divine presence "amid the created world". Such existence also means that the spiritual life "is simply a life in which all we do comes from the centre, where we are anchored in God; a life soaked through . . . by a sense of His reality and claims, and self given to the great movement of His will".[4]

The centre of Christian spirituality is Jesus Christ. Christian spirituality is the spirituality of Christ, the founder of Christianity. The method and nurture of spirituality centres on the person and mission of Christ. His teaching is the bedrock of the Christian view of creation and of the nature, meaning, purpose and destiny of life. Existence before God is not static, but is progressive, it is movement to a destiny that Christ decreed.

So just as a traveller keeps an eye on the road, so Christian spirituality fixes its sight on the example, teaching and ideal of Christ. This engenders action of a particular kind geared to progress towards the ideal of the Kingdom of God.

Through this process the Christian experiences the transformation that spirituality engenders, that is, Christian spirituality through being Christ-centred promotes growth towards Christ-likeness. This relationship gives shape and pattern to such activities as to "lift the mind to God". The activities, to which we shall make further reference, are "stages on the way" to the accomplishment of the "eschatological vision" or the ultimate goal of Christian spirituality. In the process spirituality in all its diverse activities addresses external as well as internal issues and prepares the Christian for engagement with the wider world of secularism, as well as of religion.

The norms of Christian theology

St. Augustine stated that Christian theology is "reasoning or discourse about divinity". Christianity is monotheistic in its belief in one God and one God only. He is known through revelation and coordinates within himself three persons, Father, Son and Holy Spirit. The name Christians give to this coordination is Trinity; the Godhead is a Trinity of three persons. Jesus mentioned this in his teaching and the New Testament declares it as orthodox Christian belief. The Trinity is normative to Christian theology and spirituality. The revelation of God in Christ is revelation of the Trinity of Father, Son and Holy Spirit. The three persons are united in the single Godhead and have equal recognition. The inner life of the Trinity is an alternation between the activities of the three persons. The rich unity of the Godhead is functional, as Father, Son and Holy Spirit perform mutual functions within the Godhead. The functions consolidate the divine purpose and reveal this to the world. Everything unique to Christianity derives from and relates back to the nature and function of the Trinity. The ultimate attainment of Christian spirituality is immersion in the Trinity.

Elizabeth of the Trinity is one of the Christian spiritual guides who expressed with great passion and sentiment this sense of immersion in the Trinity, whilst at the same time experiencing the trinitarian God being involved in the human condition:

> O my God, Trinity, whom I adore, help me to forget myself entirely that I may be established in you as still and as peaceful as if my soul were already in eternity . . .
> O my beloved Christ, crucified by love, I wish to be a bride for your heart, I wish to cover you with glory, I wish to live now . . .
> O consuming fire, Spirit of love, "come upon me", and create in my soul a kind of incarnation of the Word: that I may be another humanity for him in which he can renew his whole mystery . . .
> O my three, my all, my beatitude, infinite solitude, immensity in which I lose myself, I surrender to you as your prey. Bury yourself in me that I may bury myself in you until I depart to contemplate in your light the abyss of your greatness.[5]

The rootedness of Christian spirituality in the Trinity is first realized "in terms of distinction between the 'persons' whereby we can know something of God". This was the view of Dionysius, a sixth-century writer and author of *Corpus Areopagiticum*, written in Greek on the theme of how God shares his life with the world.

Dionysius' thesis is that underlying the distinction between the persons of the Trinity, or contained within these, there is a synthesis or unity that is beyond ordinary comprehension. Therefore, he continued, the theology of the Trinity is a way of "knowing" because it seeks to affirm something about God. Yet, at the same time, it is a way of "unknowing" so that, paradoxically, the doctrine of the Trinity both reveals God and also means that God is beyond human knowing.[6] Warned of this paradox, we proceed to refer to the three "persons" of the Trinity in respect of the spiritual tradition in Christian theology, on the assumption that the norms of Christian theology are those that derive from the Christian revelation of God as Trinity.

God

Here the primary question is knowledge of God or of who God is. This is a question of identity: can we identify God? God cannot be reduced to any known human categories, for in the words of John of Damascus, "Inexpressible is the Deity, and incomprehensible." So then what kind of God is he? What analogies can be used of him? The Trinity identifies God in three persons, Father, Son and Holy Spirit; these three are persons as no other persons can be, but God is involved in the three, however mysterious this may be. The concept of God is inherently mysterious but is ultimately inseparable from the three persons of the Trinity. Christianity receives its knowledge of God through revelation. God who is "inexpressible" and "incomprehensible", or transcendent and omnipotent, can only be known if he himself makes himself known. The fact that God exists and what he is are ultimately connected, and revelation makes this known. Revelation is an act of divine exposure, an act of self-determination and divine affirmation. The origin of revelation is shrouded in mystery, but in Christian terms its purpose is redemptive. Hans Kung has postulated that revelation is an act of divine free will which is also an "ideological superstructure".[7] In such an "ideological superstructure" we may identify three phases of divine revelation, namely, in creation, human life and incarnation.

Creation   At the beginning God acted to make himself known through creation. His act of creation signified commitment to the world unencumbered by the restrictions that later theorists have placed upon it. The creation was freely undertaken by a self-motivating and self-sufficient creator who afterwards remained free to control and direct his creation. Why a perfect and absolute God created the world will for ever be a mystery, and we can only surmise what the answer is. Creation shares a special relationship with the creator. Christian theology sees God as intimately related to every aspect of existence in the natural world, and how the world is open to God and to his activity upon it. He continues to reveal himself in the creation; without him the world would be nothing, it would cease to be. Writing on this theme in the work of Dionysius, Rowan Williams says:

> God shares himself in creation because, just as we yearn for him, so he eternally "yearns" to give himself and to be loved. Dionysius strikingly picks up Ignatius' phrase, "my *eros* is crucified", and maintains that this divine eros, this longing, is fundamental to all we say of God. God comes out of his selfhood in a kind of "ecstasy" (*ekstasis*, literally, a "standing outside") when he creates; and his ecstasy is designed to call forth the ecstasy of human beings, responding to him in selfless love, belonging to him and not to ourselves. Thus in the created order there is a perpetual circle of divine and human love, *eros* and ecstasy.[8]

Creation is the visible sign of the outpouring of the life of God, the positive and affirmative act of divine revelation. By looking at the world it is possible to talk about God. The creation is caught up in the life of God as he gives himself to it. Here God is to be found, for every part of creation is sacred; "the place whereon you stand is holy ground", and all is "charged with the grandeur of God". But in the world evil is also encountered, so the Christian faces the ambivalence of loving the world as God loves it and rejecting the evil that denies this love. But this ambivalence is not just "out there" where there is evil that may be accepted or rejected, but there is an inner ambivalence where the inner and outer world interfuses. This is "the real world" which Thomas Merton described:

> The way to find the real world is not merely to measure what is outside us, but to discover our own inner good. For that is where the world is, first of all: in my deepest self . . . It is a living and self creating mystery of which I am myself a part, to which I am myself my own unique door.[9]

Talk of God as creator is not merely descriptive. On the contrary, it evokes "a living and self creating mystery". Furthermore, knowledge of the creator rebounds on human behaviour to authenticate the values and attitudes that accord with his will. The creator reveals his purpose of orientating conduct towards accomplishing his purpose. Knowledge of the creator evokes a numinous response in awe and worship and commitment to a God-like life-style. Christian creation theology embraces the entire creation and all that lives within it. In this respect creation theology and spirituality are inclusive of one another. This inclusivity is endorsed by the origin, nature and purpose of human life, as we must now show.

The image of God   Human life is created in the image of God. Here image signifies resemblance to the original, that is, to God. The resemblance is mirrored and nurtured through the cultivation of an intimate divine–human relationship which only human beings can experience. This sets human life apart from all other created life. Human beings have a unique existence before God, and this existence takes on a variety of forms. One is the freedom given to make choices. Choice that is freely made determines the quality and direction of life, for every choice made is between right and wrong or good and evil. No choice need be made without reference to the divine–human relationship.

The relationship which mirrors the image of God provides guidance in the deployment of human freedom. Choice that is made in the context of this relationship accords with the divine will and purpose. The choice made rebounds on life at every level, especially the quality of interpersonal relationships. Human life is made for community, "No-man is an island unto himself". Relationship with God is inclusive of relationship with fellow human beings.

The choice between good and evil enhances but never dilutes human dignity, for in relationship individuals discover their true identity. Any breakdown in human relationships rebounds on the image of God in human life. Relationship is not arbitrary, but is rather the sphere through which the image of God is nurtured as individuals progress to spiritual maturity.

Incarnation   The third aspect of the "ideological structure" of divine revelation sets the seal on the purpose of all the creator's work. The purpose of the creation of the world and human life is crowned with the act of revelation which Christians call the incarnation, that is, the advent of God in a human form to dwell within and among his creation. The advent of God the Son, the second person of the Trinity, inaugurated a new pivotal phase in the process of spirituality, so crucial as to be unsurpassable. In the words of Thomas Merton:

> Whatever I may have written, I think it can all be reduced in the end to this one root truth: That God calls human persons to union with himself and with one another in Christ.[10]

Christ

Christianity is the religion of Christ; in him God is revealed, thus reconciling the world to himself. Christ is the chief reference point of both
Christian theology and spirituality; he gives them shape, meaning and
direction. Christ is the focus of everything that bears the name
Christian, as Hans Kung has stated emphatically:

> the Christian believes not in the Bible, but in him it attests:
> the Christian believes not in tradition, but in him whom it transmits;
> the Christian believes not in the Church, but in him whom the church
> proclaims . . .
> What men can turn to as absolutely reliable for time and eternity are not
> the texts of the Bible, nor the Fathers of the Church, nor indeed an
> ecclesiastical mysterium, but it is God himself as he spoke for believers
> through Jesus Christ.[11]

Christian theology and spirituality are subsumed within the significance and impact of the life, death and resurrection of Jesus Christ.
Of his relationship with God we observe:

> Because the difference between Jesus and the Father is profound and
> evocative, it allows a reciprocity between them . . .
> The Son receives from the Father an origin, a raison d'être . . .
> He is nothing without the Father . . .
> At the same time the Father receives from the Son a recognition and an
> expression which he cannot give himself. He cannot be, without the Son
> also being in existence. Their extraordinary reciprocity ends up in a kind
> of identification: not an identity that would make it impossible to differ-
> entiate between the Son and the Father, but a profound community of
> condition, will and action.[12]

The reciprocity spoken of here means that Jesus was totally given to
God and God to him. Consequently Jesus is open to all people in virtue
of their being open to God the creator. Christians make their response
to God through him. The appropriate response is love as love is the
essence of Christ's manifestation of God. The incarnation was
conceived in love (God so loved the world that he sent his only begotten
Son); love is God's commitment to the world in a unique human life.
The historical Jesus confirmed and authenticated this commitment
through a life of total obedience, suffering, death and resurrection.

Incarnation is the Christian doctrine of God appearing to live on
earth the life of a recognizable human being. This human life was a
departure from every other known form of divine revelation. God
determined that in the human Jesus there should be laid open to the

world all the qualities of genuine humanity, along with that "special" quality that made Jesus unique. Jesus was ever ready to declare his consciousness of his unique relationship to God, "I and the Father are one." In word and deed he was sinless and had no need of forgiveness; he had uncanny knowledge of other human beings, and power to act and speak as no other person could; he had authority over other created beings and ability to predict the future. Yet he is a real human being who experienced deep human emotions of joy and sadness. Theology has from the beginning searched for an answer to the question of how to reconcile the purely human qualities of Jesus with the "special" qualities. The search still continues to this day. In the meantime we observe that the knowledge God has given through the incarnation is knowledge for perceiving his will and ways. This is continually the central point of reference in the process of spirituality.

The incarnation means that God committed himself to a human body (the Word was made flesh). But what kind of body? Christian theology has often been ambivalent in its answer, even contemptuous or hostile at times to the physical and material body. It has discriminated against the body as evil. Christians have felt ill at ease in yielding to the gratifications of the physical body and have been known to mortify the "sins of the flesh". Yet the incarnation portrays Jesus living within a human body with full knowledge of its nature and full experience of its instincts and emotions. He was a perfectly normal human being and incarnation affirms his real manhood. Yet Jesus was without sin in body as in spirit. What does this mean for the practice of Christian spirituality? Spirituality addresses the whole self, the physical and non-physical components. Spirituality is the lived experience of the whole self, which includes care for the nurture of the body. In subtle ways spirituality ministers to this wholeness. It does so in a conceptually coherent way that confirms confidence in the sacredness of the physical as well as the non-physical. In specific ways spirituality ministers to the purity and health of the body as integral to its ministry to the total human condition. This much is deduced from the incarnation. The body in itself is not evil.

Spirituality is ultimately concerned with redemption. Redemption is of the whole of life, and in any reformulation of redemption-theology it has to include the biological, psychological and sociological, along with the moral and spiritual aspects of experience as constituting an integral whole. The whole person bears the image of God, for the whole life is God's creation. The image that is mirrored in terms of divine–human relationship enriches, purifies and refines the body as well as the soul. Redemption of the body through the death and resurrection of Christ is a prime facet of Christian belief, and a focus of Christian theology and spirituality.

The Nicene Creed states, "For our sakes he was crucified." The crucifixion is attested by the New Testament as a redemptive offering and there is external evidence to testify to its occurrence. The astonishing words: crucified "for our sakes", have been the subject of much heart- searching amongst theologians. What does it mean that Jesus died for others? His death was not an accident, yet he did not try to escape from it; he did not will his death, but when it became inevitable he did not shun it; when the verdict on him was announced he submitted himself voluntarily to it. From the cross he uttered words that signified his complete submission to God. What is distinctive about the death of Christ according to Christians is that its redemptive purpose is "for them".

Christian theology has most frequently interpreted Christ's submission to death as an act of love. Love was the formative force in all that Jesus ever did and was so as he submitted himself to the death of the cross. Julian of Norwich portrayed the character of his love in lyrical words:

> At the same time as I saw the sight of the head bleeding, our good Lord showed a spiritual sight of his familiar love. I saw that he is to us everything which is good and comforting for our help. He is our clothing, who wraps and enfolds us for his love embraces us and shelters us, surrounds us for his love, which is so tender that he may never desert us.

Christians have interpreted this love "that embraces and shelters" and that "never deserts" as the dynamic of Christian salvation. The death of Christ "for our sake" means "for our salvation". We cannot here describe the various aspects of the Christian interpretation of salvation, except to say that theology explains it as redemption from the grip of evil and guilt. By submitting to death on the cross Christ accomplished this redemption. For this purpose he sacrificed his life, and through the agony of the crucifixion is met the cost of human redemption and hence of reconciliation with God. The depth of Christ's love in this submission is manifested in his utterances from the cross, especially his words, "It is finished," thus signifying that his work of reconciliation was completed.

The voluminous works of theologians of the ages who have expounded the meaning of the death of Christ "for our sakes" are a comprehensive commentary on the significance of the death of Christ as salvation for the world. As such, Christians "glory in the cross", they view this death as the redemption and hope of the world, they see it as the supreme fulfilment of a life dominated by love. The crucifixion was a public event open for the world to see, and the death evokes a response that no other death ever has. Christian spirituality responds to this by absorbing into its process the mingled flow of sorrow and love, guilt and forgiveness, alienation and reconciliation. These all coalesce in the process of spirituality which responds in reflection, meditation and devotion to the death on the cross.

Christian theology and spirituality inevitably give a central place to the belief that "Jesus is alive". But how does theology today understand and explain the resurrection of Jesus Christ? Apart from the resurrection there would be no Christianity or Church, but how to understand the resurrection is the hub of much controversy. The resurrection of Jesus Christ is not an aspect of Christianity but that which keeps it a living faith. The basic Christian claim is that "God raised Jesus from the dead". The declaration "Jesus is alive" affirms this belief. This declaration has been more thoroughly investigated and vigorously debated than any other statement, especially in recent times. It is unquestionably the most radical of all Christian beliefs, and few would doubt the fact that Christians have always trusted in the epoch-making claim that "Jesus is alive". But what is meant by this? The first Christians declared the resurrection to be the work of God – he raised up Jesus. This act inaugurated a new existence for his disciples. Only after he had given himself to the uttermost by dying on the cross, and only after God had raised him from the dead, did his followers come to understand that in him God had acted decisively to reconcile the world to himself. This then became the amazing message they proclaimed and spread. After being raised Christ took the initiative in making himself known to his disciples. His encounters with them in a garden, in the upper room, on a common road and beside a lake, convinced them that he was alive. He showed them he was free from the restriction of death and still available for them and for all people. From this they deduced he continued in the world ready to share his presence and be open to everyone. Encounter with the living Christ is the most transforming and life-affirming moment in the experience of Christians.

Then Christians, in the words of Thomas Merton, "most fully possess God . . . it is then they are filled with his infinite light . . . And at this inexplicable moment the deepest night becomes day and faith turns into understanding." The person who turns faith into understanding is not a dead figure belonging to the past but one who has to do with people in the present. This is the amazing but confident claim which Christian spirituality makes. Spirituality is elated through experience of the living presence of Christ continually revealing himself in the world and in human life. Christian theology expounds the resurrection as the act of God that brings Christ into an encounter with human life and establishes his presence within it.

One further point needs to be made about the person of Jesus Christ within the Trinity as the norm of Christian theology. Jesus provides tangible and perfect portrayal of love through his incarnation, crucifixion and resurrection. The essence of the being and nature of Christ is love and the unity of the persons of the Trinity is a unity of love. What unites the three persons of the Trinity is a relationship of perfect love. Love is a bond of union between Father, Son and Holy Spirit. Christian theology explicates this unity whilst Christian spirituality seeks to foster the love through its spiritual practices. The indissoluble union of perfect love that exists in the life of the Trinity provides a wide horizon for the practice of spirituality. This love is the mysterious heartbeat that throbs constantly throughout the process of Christian spirituality to maintain its impetus and stimulate progress to its ultimate goal. Love is the kernel of the relationship with God and other human beings in which spirituality lives and moves and has its being.

The Holy Spirit

The third person of the Trinity proceeds from the Father and the Son to make actual the awareness of the presence of God and to impart spiritual gifts. The Spirit is the immanence of God, who operates within the here and now as the *alter ego* of God the Father and God the Son. The work of the Spirit is variable but integral and expressive of the presence and purpose of God. The Spirit is the spiritual presence in which God operates most intimately in the human mind and heart. Geoffrey Wainwright characterizes the Spirit's activity as the confession of Jesus as Lord, an aid to prayer, the source of spiritual gifts, a transforming characteristic inspirational power, and the speaking in tongues.[13] This range of activities exemplifies the manner of the Spirit's operation within the processes of spirituality.

The Spirit that discloses the will and purpose of God also leads to participation in the life of God. The creative action of God the Spirit leads into all the truth and operates continuously to complete the work of redemption. The origin of the Spirit in God makes the action of the Spirit consistent with the will of God the Father and God the Son. The action is personal so that the Spirit informs about the self, and the nature, purpose and destiny of life. The Spirit reveals the secret of ultimate truth and the meaning of reality. The Spirit is a paradigm for the fundamental unity of the self and of all human beings. The work of the Spirit is not restricted by human whims or desires, or by time or space, for the "Spirit is of God", and God is beyond human manipulation. The Spirit operates where human beings cannot; the Spirit leads into the "beyond" that, on their own, humans cannot reach; the Spirit unravels truth that is otherwise hidden forever; the Spirit acts in unpredictable and mysterious ways but always for a redemptive purpose.

Christian spirituality is infused at every point with the Holy Spirit and only through the Spirit's aid can it progress to its rightful goal. The initiative of the action is the Spirit's prerogative, but individuals may invoke the aid or guidance of the Spirit. Each forward movement in the process of spirituality is a distinctive moment of creative newness in which the Spirit shares. This movement is a transformation of the mind and the proof of "what is the will of God, what is good and acceptable and perfect". The petitions in the prayer to the Holy Spirit in the *Dies Sacerdotalis* express the spiritual yearnings for those gifts that the Spirit alone can give:

> Come, O fire and flame of divine love, and burn away all our deadly wounds;
> may I be cleansed by thee . . .
> may I be enlightened by thee . . .
> may I be set on fire by thee . . .
> for to this end thou art sent from heaven, what else is thy will but to be kindled in us.

The action of the Spirit is within the self. It is all-embracing and covers all aspects of life and every facet of personal experience and spiritual growth. This involves beliefs, feelings, attitudes, relationships and all aspects of behaviour. The Spirit penetrates human life in depth and opens the way of entering into relationship with God.

This indwelling of the Spirit brings the self into a new relationship that is lived out in community with God as well as within the human community. The continual operation of the Spirit sustains the active nature of this community. Spirituality sustained by the Holy Spirit anticipates the fullness of life as an assurance not only of some future "eternal" life, but of a mystical sharing in the present of the life of the Trinity.

In conclusion to this section we may refer once more to the Trinity as a prime focus of Christian spirituality. It portrays an order within the

Godhead that provides a specific perspective on the intimate relationship spirituality engenders with the three persons of the Trinity. As this relationship deepens it also transforms the inner qualifying disposition of all human relationships. The inner motive and intention is perfected through relationship with the Trinity where eternal love is met with love. The whole rhythm and texture of life is brought before God and this informs and directs community relationships which are the hub of life. Much of what is valued most in life happens in community. From the moment of birth into a family, life is lived out in a neighbourhood, a nation, and such other social groupings as we share in. To the point of death, people are in community and to a lesser or greater degree all are dependent on it. Spirituality articulates the commitment necessary for wholesome community relationships. Equally it promotes knowledge of the whole self, for to be in relationship with the Trinity and to know the nature of the self as body, mind and spirit, are two sides of the same coin. The unity of the persons of the Trinity is a model of unity with the self and with others. The three persons of the Trinity are compatible with each other within the unity of the Godhead. Having said that, Christian spirituality is committed to a process that is trintarian in its promotion of unity within the self and amongst others. Christian spirituality is concerned with the cultivation of this unity in depth. Understanding what the unity means arises from the order and unity of the Trinity from which Christian spirituality derives its specific direction. This affirms that human beings are capable of entering into a relationship with the persons of the Trinity, and, furthermore, that this relationship gives to the self a unity that makes for personal wholeness. It is then lived out in a community of relationships. In brief, this is the soil out of which the spiritual life springs. Christian spirituality focuses on the Trinity as the kernel of truth and the place where personal unity is to be found and life lived in community in a spirit of reconciliation.

The process of spirituality

Spirituality is a process or movement. Like a river it rises inauspiciously from its source but soon gathers momentum as it progresses by assimilating new powers and resources of spiritual energy. Its flow, like the river, is sometimes swift and buoyant, and at other times more lethargic; it brings refreshment and fertility in its course, until eventually, like the river that flows into the ocean where its flow becomes richer and fuller, spirituality aims for its ideal. Christian spirituality is never stagnant but is constantly being refreshed and renewed by the vitalizing energies of the Spirit. These give it fresh impetus, just as meandering streams join to swell the river on its journey to the sea. As the process of spirituality advances it forges new paths of productivity until it advances to the point of being absorbed in the fuller and richer life of God. What activities, then, constitute the process of spirituality?

Prayer and spirituality

Prayer is the first indispensable aid to the practice of theology and spirituality. According to Evagrius of Pontus, "To be a theologian is to pray truly and to pray truly is to be a theologian."[14] The distinguished theologian Karl Barth vowed that theology can only be performed in an act of prayer.[15] Barth testified:

> Every act of theological work must have the character of an offering in which everything is placed before the living God. Because it has to be ever renewed, ever original, ever judged by God himself and by God alone, theology must be an act of prayer.

Prayer is the heartbeat of spirituality and its most characteristic practice. Prayer is addressed only to God out of a desire to draw closer to him and to know more of him. From the beginning God willed that prayer should be offered to him, and he made known his willingness to receive and answer prayer. Genuine prayer is fixation on God or the whole self being absorbed in the life of God. This may be termed the "I–Thou" relationship of prayer, whenever the relationship is maintained by the giving and receiving on the part of God and the giving and receiving on the part of the one who prays. In this mutual giving and receiving, on the part of the one who prays, there is thanksgiving, petition, intercession, as well as confession and doxology that one is met with forgiveness and blessing. The act of prayer cultivates an ethos wholly characteristic of intimacy in which there is dialogue, speaking and listening, desiring and willing, response and commitment. The ethos is akin to the experience of what Rudolph Otto called "the holy" (*numinous*), the awesome moment of communion with the "other" or the "transcendent", that absorbing moment of divine–human communication that for the one who prays is also a transforming moment.[16]

Along with prayer as personal communion with God, prayer also gives knowledge of the will of God and strength to fulfil it. Prayer is open to receiving the will of God for the world inasmuch as his will is performed within it. Prayer is not withdrawal from the life of the world, for to pray is to work to transform the world and to transform the world is to pray. Prayer opens the life to God in order to participate in the action of God's love for the world.

Karl Barth is said to have expressed this idea lucidly by remarking, "I take the Bible in one hand, the newspaper in the other, then read the paper in the light of the Word of God." Barth looked at the world through the Bible and prayer. Prayer moves the will to action, although it does not place God at anyone's disposal. Rather it finds an answer to Who is God? Through prayer God opens the mind to receive knowledge of himself which only he himself can give. The prayer of petition opens pathways along which God reveals knowledge of himself and of his will. This is true of communal prayer as well as personal prayer, for in the process of Christian spirituality communal prayer opens the gateway of opportunities for developing the life of wholesome community living.

Prayer as intercession brings others before God and into harmony with the divine will thus God is available to others as well as to oneself. Prayer as intercession expresses solidarity with others at the moment when it is offered. It may be spontaneous and express the instantaneous feeling for others at that time. It may not use many words, but can be effective nevertheless. The author of the *Cloud of Unknowing* asked:

Why does this short prayer of one syllable penetrate heaven?

And the answer is given.

Surely because it is prayed with the full spirit – that is in the height, depth, length and breadth of the spirit of the one who prays. In this height, for it is with all the might of his spirit, in the depth, for it is contained in all that the spirit knows; in the length, for should it always feel as it does now, then would it cry out as it now cries; in the breadth for it extends to all others what it wills for itself.[17]

It is a short step from the prayer of few words to the prayer of silence. Silent prayer is the most intense part of spirituality, that is unprogrammed and with no premeditated words. Silence is a wholly personal state, the vivid tranquillity that rises to God in wordless meditation, contemplation and reflection. Deep calls to deep in yearning that cannot be put into words. Silent prayer makes space for self examination, for making intimate confession of a naked soul before a naked God. Such silence is pregnant with the confidence of being heard and answered. Silent prayer is not hampered by words nor is it distracted by concern for any protocol or formality; silent prayer emerges from the inner sanctuary of the soul to feel the embrace of the divine spirit. Silent prayer, then, is the complete surrendering of the self to God, the entry through the gateway of grace into the ineffable presence. Silence is not aimless drifting but the wilful concentration of all the faculties in the act of prayer as internal dialogue with God.

It is difficult to state exactly how meditation differs from silence, but meditation is as purposeful a part of the spiritual process as is silence and spoken prayer. In the context of Christian prayer, meditation is a matter of bringing the mind to bear on God, who is the object of prayer, free from the restraints of conceptual thinking. Meditation, accordingly, sharpens and alerts the mind so that there arises therefrom an inner intense longing for complete concentration on intimacy with God. Through continuous and disciplined meditation is evoked a feeling of inner tranquillity that infuses the whole self until it is absorbed in God. In meditation there is recollection, that is, the spiritual act of recall of what God has accomplished and willed. Remembrance stimulates the desire to acquire qualities that will translate the recollection into deeds. Meditation then continues in a life immersed in action. It strengthens the bond of faith in union with God. Meditation also gives to life a certain balance between its physical and non-physical practices. It stimulates the unrealized vitality within and deepens the sense of human wholeness. Meditation aims at seeing all aspects of life from the perspective of the whole, including the mind, imagination, the soul and body.

In the practice of meditation Christians may take an object such as a crucifix, an icon, or a text from the Bible, as the focus of reflection. Single-minded and holistic reflection on the object conditions the mind to absorb its spiritual potency. This is tantamount to deepening awareness of God. Then through meditation on a crucifix Christians may attain profounder understanding of the death of Christ, may be drawn into the impact of his crucifixion and realize how through surveying a crucifix they are led to engage in quietistic meditation on the cross. This then leads to a realization of the significance of the death of Jesus and to an act of response. Then it may be seen that:

> The cross is the great Christian answer to the world as a problem. The cross is liberation. The cross is the only liberation from the servitude to the illusions which are packaged and sold as the world . . . the cross transforms the world . . . and once the cross has been accepted fully in our life then we can begin to make sense about this whole entity, the world.[18]

Contemplation in prayer is the offering of love to God, being completely absorbed and captivated in the process, being overwhelmed and lost "in wonder, love and praise". Contemplation is not tied to words, it has been described as a "wordless" approach to prayer. Thomas Merton has written of contemplation as awareness of reality and of that which is beyond:

> Contemplation is the highest expression of man's intellectual and spiritual life. It is that life itself, fully awake, fully active, fully aware that it is alive. It is spiritual wonder. It is spontaneous awe at the sacredness of life, of being. It is gratitude for life, for awareness and for being. It is a vivid realization of the fact that life and being in us proceed from an invisible, transcendent and infinitely abundant source. Contemplation is, above all, awareness of the reality of that source. It *knows* the source, obscurely, inexplicably, but with a certitude that goes both beyond reason and beyond simple faith. For contemplation is a kind of spiritual vision to which both reason and faith aspire, by their very nature, because without it they must always remain incomplete.

> Yet contemplation is not vision because it sees "without seeing" and knows "without knowing". It is a more profound depth of faith, a knowledge too deep to be grasped in images, in words or even in clear concepts. It can be suggested by words, by symbols, but in the very moment of trying to indicate what it knows the contemplative mind takes back what it has said, and denies what it has affirmed. For in contemplation we know by "unknowing". Or better, we know beyond all *knowing* or "unknowing".

> Poetry, music and art have something in common with the contemplative experience. But contemplation is beyond aesthetic intuition, beyond art, beyond poetry. Indeed, it is beyond philosophy, beyond speculative theology. It resumes, transcends and fulfils them all, and yet at the same time it seems, in a certain way, to supersede and to deny them all. Contemplation is always beyond our own knowledge, beyond our own light, beyond systems, beyond explanations, beyond discourse, beyond dialogue, beyond our own self. To enter into the realm of contemplation one must in a certain sense die: but this death is in fact the entrance into a higher life. It is a death for the sake of life, which leaves behind all that we can know or treasure as life, as thought, as experience, as joy, as being.[19]

Worship, liturgy and sacrament

Christian spirituality cultivates a life of communion with God through worship. Worship is a communal act of response to God and to none other. The necessity of worship as integral to the process of spirituality is expressed by the early Christian poet Caedman in these haunting lines:

> It is meet that we worship the Warden of heaven,
> The might of the Maker, His purpose in mind
> The Glory, Father's work when of all His wonder
> Eternal God made a beginning
> He earliest established for earth's children
> Heaven for a roof, the Holy Shaper;
> Then mankind's Warden created the world,
> Eternal Monarch, making for men
> Land to live on, Almighty Lord![20]

Caedmon's portrait of God as transcendent, Warden, Maker, Eternal, Holy Monarch and Almighty, encapsulates the "otherness" of God who alone is to be worshipped. Worship is response to this transcendent God; it is by its nature the acknowledgement of God for who he is. But as worship is offered God responds as love, joy, forgiveness and judgement. God meets the worshipper through worship and this conveys the "worth-ship" of worship. The worshipper experiences God as he is and shares the life of God, so far as this is possible. For the Christian, worship means being transported into the life of God through the actions performed. Prominent among these are celebration, praise, adoration and commitment. Caedman, in the above poem, expounds the necessity and value of worship, whilst Christianity teaches that worship is to be offered "in spirit" and "in truth".

The motive for worship is the desire to respond to the presence and action of God. In making the response, the whole person is involved in the movement of fixation on God. The "spirit" of worship is that of awe and wonder; Christian worship is resonant with joy, thanksgiving, and praise – through it the worshipper enters upon a "numinous" experience of being in the presence of God. Christianity does not conceive of worship as a convention but as the free response to God in a community of faith. No one is coerced to worship, but worship is nevertheless integral to the process of Christian spirituality.

Worship as an element of spirituality includes the performance of set rituals. These rituals acquire a special cultic or liturgical quality as they are employed in worship. The word liturgy can be used in a number of different ways, but especially as designating those components of communal worship that accord with its intention and promote its purpose. Praise and prayer, scripture and proclamation, sacrament and celebration are its most stable constituents.

The liturgy of the Word　　From earliest times Christian worship has had a focus in the liturgy of the Word, that is, in the Bible as Holy Scripture.

The Bible also provides Christian theology with its data and with a ground plan of its procedures. This collect expresses the basic principles in both theology and spirituality.

> Blessed Lord,
> Who caused all holy Scriptures
> To be written for our learning,
> help us to hear them,
> to read, mark, learn and inwardly digest them
> that through patience, and the comfort
> of your holy word
> we may embrace and for ever hold fast
> the hope of everlasting life
> which you have given us in our Saviour Jesus Christ.

Christian spirituality takes into its orbit the spiritual interpretation of Scripture. The Holy Spirit illumines the inner meaning of the Bible and directs its use in worship and private devotion. The content of the Bible was transcribed by human agents who were inspired by the Spirit, so the Spirit is the authoritative source of illumination on the truth and unity of the Bible. The core of its truth is the revelation of God in creation and human life that culminated in the incarnation, death and resurrection of Jesus Christ. The message of the revelation is transmitted in poetry and myth, story and symbol, parable and allegory, through which the Spirit interprets and expounds the meaning within and behind the literary forms. This elucidates the message as the word from God that he spoke through the characters, events and history of the Bible. The message was transmitted to real people in the actual situations of their lives, and it reveals God's dealings with individuals as well as his action in their history. It makes plain God's control of history and how through his intervention he directed the course of history to his own purpose. The Spirit sheds light on this purpose and shows how God ministered to people through his domination of their history. In various ways he ministered to their spiritual needs and opened to them the spiritual pathways that led them to knowledge of himself and to an understanding of his will. The action of the Spirit continues to illumine the message of God's revelation in the Bible, and to expound its relevance and significance for Christians today. The spiritual interpretation of the Bible creates an empathy between people today and the people of the Bible so that it is possible to identify with their experiences, and thereby discover the continuing impact of its message. This unfolds the secret of its authority and inspiration, it unlocks the key to its unity and truth, and in this way ministers to the process of spirituality. This is what Christianity means when it says that the Bible "speaks" to people today.

> Jesus not only spoke in the synagogue to Jews, but he is still speaking today, in His meeting among us. We are the Jerusalem over which Jesus is still weeping. We are the dead whom he awakens to life.[21]

Essentially the Bible is the Scripture of the Church. The community of the Church at worship is nurtured on the spiritual truth of the Bible. The liturgy of the Word dominates much of its corporate worship and serves as a focus of unity between all who take part in it. The spiritual mission of the Church also has a basis in the Bible. This mission is one of redemption and redemptive-revelation is a prime theme of theology. Christian spirituality also is redemptive-spirituality that feeds on the spiritual message of the Bible, as it "reads, marks, learns and inwardly digests the Holy Scriptures". Christian spirituality and worship are soaked in the Bible and in the spiritual message of the story it tells. The chief actor in the story is God who is centre stage from beginning to end, His action is promised to continue throughout all ages. The interaction between God and the people and events in the Bible continues through God's interaction with people today. He has for them the same redemptive purpose as in the time of the Bible. So the Bible is relevant to the promotion of contemporary spirituality, and the Spirit continues to lead into its truth. In whatever precise way we interpret the concept of the Bible as the Word of God, it still centres on divine action, and something spiritual that happens in history and in human affairs. At the same time it illumines the nature and content of human experience and destiny in relation to the divine intervention, that also shaped the experience of the people of the Bible.

Sacraments　The sacraments in Christianity have been the subject of theological interpretation from the time of the New Testament and their observance a source of spiritual nourishment. Today the observance of the sacraments is more prominent in some branches of Christianity than others, but the observance is always for the sake of achieving spiritual effects. The most widely accepted definition of a sacrament is probably that of Augustine of Hippo, namely, "a sacrament is an outward and visible sign of an inward and spiritual grace". The sacraments communicate sanctifying grace and this is equated with receiving divine blessing. Through the Christian sacraments the Christian is identified with Christ. The two central sacraments of Christianity which are most widely observed are the sacrament of baptism and the eucharist, although the Roman Catholic Church claims to observe seven sacraments.

Baptism   The rite of Christian baptism is traced to Christ and his commission to his disciples. Christian theology focuses on the meaning of baptism as participation in the life of Christ, and as a sign of the Kingdom of God. It is administered to believers, but in some churches to infants also. Theology has long wrestled with the question whether baptism is a divine or human initiative or whether baptism is a divine gift that evokes a human response. The question of unity between baptism of believers and infant baptism has proved contentious. Where infant baptism is administered the teaching of the Roman Catholic Church in the catechism of 1994 is broadly accepted:

> The sheer gratuitousness of the grace of salvation is particularly mani-
> fested in infant baptism . . . For all the baptized, children or adults, faith
> meant grace after baptism.

Christian theology has evolved many images as it expounds the meaning of baptism. One is incorporation, the baptized person is incorporated into the death and resurrection of Christ, that is, it is the old self's dying and being raised to a new life in Christ; initiation views baptism as entry into the new covenant which Christ initiated with God through his suffering, death and resurrection; baptism as gift represents it as an act of divine grace administered in the name of the Trinity; reception is the notion of baptism as acceptance into the family of God, that is, the Church; coupled with this is the idea of baptism as a condition of participating in the mission of the Church, sharing its faith and sacraments; baptism as renewal means entry upon a new life-style as a committed Christian who is henceforth identified with Christ and his gospel. Whilst all these images have been used in the exposition of the meaning and purpose of baptism there is agreement, whichever of the images is followed, that preparation for believers' baptism requires repentance and confession so that the spiritual purpose of forgiveness, sanctification and renewal might be achieved. The evidence that this spiritual purpose is fulfilled is the reception of the Holy Spirit to direct the flow of new life which the baptized experiences. The seal of the Spirit is essential as the assurance that the baptized is united with God. Baptism is a rite of unity that binds together all Christian believers, past and present, in an unbroken spiritual fellowship. Christian theology refers to this as "the communion of saints". The unity is the seal of the Holy Spirit whereby the baptized enters a life of mystical union with

God and with the Church of all ages. Henceforth the life of the baptized is bound by the life of God and the life of the Church. Supremely, therefore, baptism is the work of the Holy Spirit which initiates and confirms this unity. Hippolytus of Rome in his *Discourse on the Holy Theophany*, declared of baptism:

> He who comes down in faith to the laver of regeneration and renounces the devil and joins himself to Christ, who denies the enemy and makes the confession that Christ is God; who puts off the bondage and puts on the adoption – he comes up from the baptism brilliant as the sun, flashing forth the beams of righteousness, and which is indeed the chief thing, he returns a son of God and joint-heir with Christ.

Eucharist   The eucharist (communion or the breaking of bread) is Christianity's most characteristic act of worship. It was inaugurated by Jesus at the Last Supper and became the act by which the early church remembered him. Christian theology has treated the rite extensively, especially the questions, What is the eucharist? and How are its meaning and actions to be understood? The earliest theological discussion of the eucharist is the letters of St. Paul, although there are primitive expositions in the gospels. The first three gospels (Matthew, Mark and Luke) associate the last supper with the Jewish passover, but the Gospel of John follows a different tradition. In all four gospels the accounts are part of the passion narratives. This context is informative for the understanding of the eucharist, as has been said:

> The Eucharist is therefore a proclamation and a remembrance of what has taken place – or, rather, of what God has done – just like the Passover. What is to be emphasized is not the eucharistic elements themselves, but the sacrificial act they call to mind.[22]

The three terms used in this quotation are significant. The eucharist is proclamation not only in words but also in action. In the celebration, bread is broken and wine is drunk. This is action of a ritual kind. The breaking of bread is a symbolic act in the style of the symbolism employed by some Old Testament prophets (e.g. Jeremiah breaking the clay flask). The breaking of bread symbolizes the breaking of the body of Christ on the cross. Again, the eucharist is a remembrance. During the eucharist the communicants remember Jesus from the past, but also they remember his continuing presence. The remembrance of all that Jesus had done and continues to do through his death is the focus of the commemoration. The proclamation and the remembrance epitomize the significance of the sacrificial act of Jesus. Through this sacrifice the

Christian receives the gift of salvation. The eucharist recalls the past but it brings back the event it recalls as though it is actually present as an ever-living reality. This is sometimes referred to as "the real presence" of Christ.

In the course of the centuries Christian theology has dealt with the meaning and importance of the eucharist from many points of view. These have been the cause of sharp division within and between churches, and will be referred to as we examine the spiritual tradition. Christianity has evaluated the sacramental aspect of the eucharist and its celebratory nature very highly. In this connection theology has interpreted the eucharist as a sacrificial celebration of praise for the benefits of the work of Christ through his suffering, death and resurrection. At the same time theology has interpreted the eucharist as an offering of the whole community of believers in love for the sacrifice of Christ. The uniqueness of this act of offering is at the heart of the eucharist – a "memorial" of all that Christ accomplished. This is not merely an act of recollection or recalling the past but of making real the remembrance in the present moment of sharing the presence of Christ. Christ is present in the eucharist and the sacrament celebrates the continuing effect of all that he achieved through his incarnation, death and resurrection. The eucharist can only be justly celebrated and its meaning comprehended through faith.

> Word made flesh, by word he maketh
> Very bread his flesh to be;
> men in wine Christ's blood partaketh,
> and, if senses fail to see,
> faith alone the true heart waketh
> to behold the mystery.
>
> Therefore we before him bending,
> His great sacrament revere;
> types and shadows have their ending,
> for the newer rite is here;
> faith our outward sense befriending,
> makes the inward vision clear.
> (Thomas Aquinas)

Faith makes possible the reception of the Christian gift of salvation. In the eating of bread and the drinking of wine Christ grants communion with himself. Thus spirituality is deepened and faith revitalized. At the same time the eucharist assures the communicant of the forgiveness of sin. Closely connected with forgiveness is sanctification, for in the eucharist Christ accomplishes his purpose of equipping his people to live the life of his kingdom, and a life of service to all humankind. The sacrifice of Christ was made for all people; the bread and wine of the eucharist symbolize the share they all have in the giving of his life for the whole world. Christ unites his people as one with himself so that they may be made ready for serving the whole world. The eucharist, therefore, has an eschatological aspect, it presupposes what the world is to become through the work of Christ, that is, a universal communion of love and reconciliation. Those who share the bread and wine also share the travail that makes this reconciliation a reality; their reward is a foretaste of the final victory of the Kingdom of Christ.

Spirituality and holiness

The term holiness is used as a distinguishing mark of the Christian character. The biblical word for holy means to be different from or separated from all that is profane. It therefore stands for that which is sanctified or which shows itself to be holy. Christian theology develops character of this calibre that bears the marks of holiness. A whole branch of theological study is devoted to Christian piety, morality and ethics. The emphasis is on the distinctive features of the Christian character. These are described as the fruits of the Spirit. The virtues of love, joy, peace, humility, gentleness and compassion, are ones that all people of goodwill recognize as "good". So what, then, is distinctive about the Christian character? In brief, it is the added dimension of holiness.

Jesus directed attention to the inner motive as the determinative force of morality. *Why* the action is performed determines its goodness. The inner motive determines the distinctive quality of the action, it accounts for its holiness. Inner motivation is cultivated in relationship nurtured through the practices of spirituality. Action is then inspired by the Spirit and performs what Christ wills. Action is only good and pure if it is performed for the right motive. Thus holiness extends to all action and makes the whole character holy. It is the determinative factor of social as of personal behaviour.

The cultivation of this inner holiness is a focus of Christian spirituality. Holiness of motive is the drive of action in public and political life as well as in more domestic and private behaviour. Holiness as motive induces positive participation in public affairs and in national and international issues as well as in religion. It is outgoing in the way it challenges behaviour and structures that are unjust or that marginalize human beings in society or debilitate human dignity by denying human rights and access to the means of survival. Holiness motivates social inclusivity for all people and directs its action to this end. John Wesley declared that there is "no holiness but social holiness". This motive serves the whole person, not only the soul but the body, not only the spiritual wellbeing but the material wellbeing also.

Spirituality that professes to be concerned with the individual only and not concerned about social conditions lacks the motivation of holiness and is spiritually moribund. It denies the fundamental principle of Christian belief that every human being is created in the image of God for a life of relationship. Holiness of motive is a living part of the relationship with God which reaches out in specific ways in social and public service.

Spirituality and Church

Christian spirituality does not function cut off from Christian community. The Church is the community of Christians inaugurated by Christ when he called his first disciples "to be with him". The community was equipped and united by the Holy Spirit to be the visible presence of Christ in the world. Christian theology produces many images of the Church, especially that the Church is "the body of Christ". This conveys its corporate nature whilst at the same time enhancing the status and role of the individual member. Just as the body has many members, so the Church fulfils its mission through its individual members acting in unison. Spirituality is nurtured through the commitment and participation of the members in the worship and witness of the Church. The Spirit is at work within the community inspiring new depths of spirituality and creative responses to the purpose and unison of the Church. The action of the Spirit cannot be restricted to any particular formula, as its direction cannot be precisely predicted, but it ministers to the spirituality of the whole Church as well as to its individual members. The intimacy and ethos of the community in its worship and liturgy is generated by the Spirit to whom the Church is committed. The Spirit is active in conferring gifts, some receive a special *charisma* (gift) for particular service, or are gifted with spiritual authority to fulfil particular functions. Men and women are so endowed and diversities of functions are activated. Common to all who share in the community is the spiritual gift of witness and service according to the will of Christ. This witness is borne to the world as a focus of unity amongst all people. The witness is a sign of the presence of the Kingdom of God in the world and the hope of its consummation.

The Church is an eschatological community with a vision of being an all-inclusive community in which people of every nation will be part. Spirituality affirms the community for the fulfilling of its role in an effective and authentic way.

As we proceed from this point to traverse some Christian theological and spiritual pathways we shall encounter a vast variety of style and method of approach. Christian theology and its spiritual tradition have always been the subject of wide-ranging discussion and investigation. This is inevitable when the subject is theology, but to ask the question more personally as to what theology and spirituality could offer us today is to enter a minefield. The varieties of spirituality derive from the variety of human types as well as from the varieties of theologies. How to characterize the variety is difficult, especially in the prevailing cultural climate. A term often used in this context is that theology is in a state of "flux". Theology is no longer studied only as the history of ideas, and spirituality is believed not only to apply to the things of the spirit. Yet there is a point in practice where theology and spirituality meet. This raises a vast array of questions and the search is on for appropriate models of communication that will be intelligible and productive in the postmodernist age.

In earlier times the practice of spirituality often led people to withdraw from the world to live in hermitages or monasteries, but today there is a greater openness and exposure to the world and show of concern for it. Spirituality is more broadly conceived as being dynamic concern for living fully in the technological, cultured milieu of the age. Theology and spirituality are conceived from the perspective of functionalism, that is, regarding life as an entity where people search for inner satisfaction. Theology interjects into this search its own insights and lines of enquiry, it cannot act in dispassionate neutrality to the prevailing culture. To do so is neither possible nor advisable, Christian theology is charged with the task of propounding meaning and formulating those images necessary to promote "the profounder life of the spirit". This is inevitable, if we accept the view of John Hick that "As well as being intelligent animals we are also 'spiritual' beings," and are in tune with "the ultimate reality that underlies, interpenetrates and transcends the physical universe", or that we are "religious animals with an inbuilt tendency to experience the actual in terms of the supra-natural".[23]

2

After the Apostles

A confession of faith by Irenaeus of Lyons:

Here is the rule of our faith, the foundation of the building and that which gives steadfastness to our conduct:

God the Father, uncreated who is not contained, invisible, one God, the creator of the universe; that is the very first article of our faith.

And the second article is:

The Word of God, the Son of God, Christ Jesus our Lord, who appeared to the prophets after the manner of their prophecy and the state of the economies of the Father; by whom all things were made; who moreover at the end of time, to recapitulate all things, was made man among humankind, visible and palpable, to destroy death, bring forth life and achieve communion between God and man.

And as the third article:

The Holy Spirit by whom the prophets prophesied and the Fathers have learned the things of God, and the righteous have been guided in the way of righteousness and who, at the end of time, has been poured forth in a new way on our humanity to renew humankind over all the earth in the face of God.

This statement of faith by Bishop Irenaeus (130–200) introduces the style and intention of the Church or Apostolic Fathers. The Fathers were the successors of the first apostles who undertook the work of expanding, defending and consolidating Christian theology. As stated in Irenaeus' confession they expanded "the rule of faith" as the foundation of their conduct. The Fathers brought to the task intellectual rigour, spiritual commitment, tireless industry and enthusiasm. The age of the Church Fathers up to 451 is one of the best documented in the history of the Church. This was an era of immense theological

speculation to which the Fathers contributed by pioneering new structures and a methodology that gave shape to theological discussion.
They tackled major critical questions about Christ and redemption
in an era of intense intellectual restlessness and theological uncertainty.
Many answers given were tendentious and some left-wing theologians
propounded a new radicalism which more conservative theologians
vigorously contested. They were intent on preserving apostolic orthodoxy. Theological deviance threatened the Church with schism and this
had to be sternly resisted. At the same time the contemptuous attitude
of pagan philosophers to the claims of the Church to be the custodian
of ultimate truth had to be answered. The Church Fathers were
unyielding in the "advocacy of the truth", which they saw as equivalent
with "the teaching of the apostles".

The works of the Church Fathers preserve the line of continuity in
Christian theology from the first apostles. Clement of Rome (d. 110)
posed the question, "Have we not one God and one grace and one Spirit
of grace?" He then expounded apostolic doctrine unambiguously:

> The Apostles received the gospel from the Lord Jesus Christ . . .
> Christ is from God, the Apostles from Christ . . .
> they went out full of confidence in the Holy Spirit . . . [1]

Irenaeus developed this theme in his trinitarian confession. The sum of
the contribution of the Church Fathers (their *didache* = teaching
and *kerygma* = preaching) revolves around the Trinity of Father,
Son and Holy Spirit. Often their writings lack homogeneity and their
style and presentation varies, but their purpose was steadfast and
uncompromising. They were resolute in the defence and the exempli-
fication of the redemptive message and significance of Christianity. In
this respect they displayed impressive communication and debating
skills as they pioneered a theological system notable for its dogmatism,
its powers of interpretation, rational analysis, and philosophical
reasoning employed in the service of displaying the validity of Christian
truth and exhorting response in faith and conduct. Thus the Fathers
maintained the link between theology and spirituality.

The Fathers were obviously committed to the Christian religion as
the ultimate revelation of God's intervention in human life. Some of
them had been converted to Christianity from other religions, but they
all shared unequivocally the conviction that God had acted decisively
in Christ as redeemer. This action called for a response in faith and good
works. The Fathers articulated their own response, and at the same time
they generated appropriate patterns of spirituality, morality and the life

of devotion that served to evoke a similar response in others. In theology they speculated about the being and nature of God, the person and mission of Christ; in spirituality they aimed to cultivate the life of devotion and purity as a living testimony of the continuous presence of Christ through the work of the Holy Spirit. In this way they sought to make apostolic faith accessible and meaningful to the multi-religious and pluralist culture of their time, and to nurture the spirituality and moral virtues of informed and credible faith.

From Athens to Jerusalem

Tertullian of Carthage (160–220), a leading Christian apologist and scholar of independent outlook and sensitive spirit, was a keen advocate of dialogue between Christianity and contemporary culture. He posed the questions, "What indeed has Athens to do with Jerusalem?" "What concord is there between the Academy and the Church?" Rather than isolating itself against the acerbic challenges of a non-Christian culture the Church should enter confidently into creative dialogue with the world. If Christianity is to be seriously heeded and its truth made credible it must demonstrate its validity and appeal through engagement in informed, meaningful and robust dialogue with all who stood outside it. For the promotion and conduct of such dialogue the Church is equipped and sustained by the Holy Spirit. The Spirit is ever active and continues to illumine the essential meaning and purpose of God's revelation in Christ. As such dialogue proceeds, Tertullian declared, those who take part are given a "freedom of choice, affected by external events, mutable in its faculties, rational, dominant, capable of punishment, evolving in plurality, from one archetype". Freedom to choose, he maintained, is a divine gift, it allows choice to be made between right and wrong, truth and falsehood. This freedom rightly used promotes active goodness and leads to the discerning of Christian truth. Cyprian (d. 258), Bishop of Carthage, likewise strongly advocated the necessity of dialogue and the importance of demonstrating openly the relevance of Christianity to the current historical scene. Cyprian was a convert to Christianity who was irrevocably committed to the doctrines of the apostles. He urged greater emphasis on the practice of Christian moral teaching, and, as did Tertullian, he extolled the virtues and qualities of life which Christian faith generated. Cyprian believed that this fact needed to be proclaimed and demonstrated within the life of the contemporary world, as we gather from this excerpt from his writings:

All power for good is delivered from God, I say; for he is the source of our life and our strength; from him we gain vitality so that in our present position here we recognize beforehand the signs of things that are to come. Only let fear be the guardian of innocence, so that the Lord, who in his kindness has streamed into our minds with the inflowing of his heavenly mercy, may through righteous activity be retained as a guest of the soul that delights in him, lest the security we have received should produce heedlessness and the old enemy creep in unawares once more.[2]

Steps to truth

Lactantius in the fourth century, a distinguished teacher in the imperial courts, and an ardent opponent of Gnosticism, taught about "the many steps by which one mounts to the home of truth".[3] The first step is to accept the faith and teaching of the apostles. On this Irenaeus, Bishop of Lyons, the most ardent champion of Catholic orthodoxy, was insistent and uncompromising; Christ, he declared, was the full revelation of God, as the apostles taught, and he is the solid foundation of Christian truth.[4]

But steps denote advance and progress, in this case the progress and development of theological understanding and the activation of proper Christian practices.

Each new step is a step forward from the present to the fuller realization of the ideal of theological orthodoxy and spiritual illumination. In retrospect it is possible to trace the steps which the early church took on the route to the adoption of the Nicene Creed by the 318 Church theologians who constituted the first ecumenical council of the Church in 325.

Athanasius (296–373), Bishop of Alexandria, played a crucial part in the Council and contended that the creed then adopted incorporated orthodox Christian belief in its entirety. It had been formulated after prolonged controversy when every aspect of the Christian theological norms had been subjected to the most detailed scrutiny, alternative interpretations advanced and answered, and heresies combated. But in 325 the creed received the seal of conciliar authority. At last the Church had a formally agreed statement of faith.

However, Nicaea did not end the controversy surrounding the person and work of Christ; complete consensus was not then achieved, and the controversy rambled on. Hitherto there had not been a formal consensus among the Church Fathers or an agreed methodology for dealing with Christological issues, but after Nicaea the situation changed. On the one hand, the theological debate was henceforth conducted as a free and open forum; the Edict of Milan in 311 had freed the Church from the constant threat of imperial persecution, and theologians were now able to pursue their activities with freedom and openness. At the same time, the scope of the discussion of theological and moral questions was widened as others than Christians participated. History tells that the unsolved controversy eventually fragmented the Church, but there was a welcome agreement at Chalcedon in 451 that bore witness to the unity of faith and the criteria for assessing its life-style. The Church leaders affirmed their commitment to Christianity; they expounded its truth as the inexorable foundation of morals; they agreed directives to chart progress towards wholesome spirituality; they formulated points of contact between the "religious" and "secular" life. To this extent Chalcedon was a justification of the orthodox party, but without ensuring its universal acceptance by all Christians. It was the Council of Chalcedon that agreed a definition of the faith as "one Christ in two natures without confusion, without change, without division, without separation". The Chalcedon creed is the only creed regarded as authentic by the churches of east and west, although they do not agree about the statement that the Holy Spirit proceeds from the Father and the Son (the so-called *filioque clause*). It is the baptismal creed of the church of the east and the eucharistic creed of east and west.

The faith of Chalcedon

At the Council of Chalcedon, the Fathers, having solemnly reaffirmed the teaching of previous councils, in order to avoid controversies, added the following statements:

> Following, then, the holy Fathers, we all unanimously teach that our Lord Jesus Christ is to us one and the same Son, the self-same perfect in Godhead; the self-same perfect in manhood; truly God and truly man; the self-same of a rational soul and body; consubstantial with the Father according to the Godhead, the self-same consubstantial with us according to the manhood; like us in all things, sin apart; before the ages begotten of the Father as to the Godhead, but in the last days, the self-same, for us and for our salvation of Mary the Virgin Theotokos as to the manhood; one and the same Christ, Son, Lord, only-begotten; acknowledged in two natures unconfusedly, unchangeably, indivisibly, inseparably; the difference of the natures being in no way removed because of the union, but rather the property of each nature being preserved, and both concurring into one prosopon and one hypostasis; not as though he were parted or

divided into two prosopa, but one and the self-same Son and only-begotten God, Word, Lord, Jesus Christ; even as from the beginning the prophets have taught concerning him, and as the Lord Jesus Christ himself has taught us, and as the symbol of the Fathers has handed down to us.

The roots of morality

Returning to the question of the theological affirmations of the Church Fathers as a spur and stimulus of moral action, the words of Origen (185–254), one of the Fathers who was steeped in Greek philosophy, the most distinguished pupil of Clement of Alexandria (150–215) and the author of commentaries on a number of books of the Bible, merit attention as representative of the views of the Fathers as a whole. He wrote: "It is indeed distressing to find a man in error in respect of morality"; he then elaborated on this by expounding the inner spring of morality:

> To be pure in heart, I take it, means just this; to keep the heart clean from all false belief. But it must be understood that it is really impossible for a man's hands to be innocent unless his heart is pure; and, conversely, a man cannot be innocent in heart and pure from false beliefs if his hands be not innocent and pure from sin. Each entails the other, and innocent thought in the soul and irreproachable living are inseparable.[5]

Right living flows from right belief. Orthodox belief is the basis of Christian morality. Unorthodox belief darkens the mind, desecrates the character and impedes the work of salvation.

Origen and other Church Fathers insisted on the cultivation of an "alternative" life-style that would operate and articulate Christian values and patterns of behaviour. This "alternative" would regenerate the current depressed social order and fill the moral vacuum caused by a degenerate paganism.

As the Church Fathers laboured to interpret and commend Christian belief they also provided for the nurturing of spirituality and promoting a Christian life-style. Of paramount importance was cultivating Christian experience and a holistic spirituality. In this respect their theology was "applied" rather than "dogmatic". They taught an applied theology and a pragmatic spirituality inclusive of personal and social morality. The roots of such teaching spread like tentacles that penetrate into every facet of interpersonal relationships, such as marriage, family life, social relations, charitable works, citizenship, obedience to rulers,

in brief, whatever behaviour involved personal and individual participation and action. This emphasis is well expressed in *The Apology of
Aristides*, reputed to have been addressed by an Athenian philosopher
to the Emperor Hadrian (117–138), which states of Christians:

> They commit no adultery or fornication, they bear no false witness, they
> covet not other men's goods, they honour father and mother and love
> their neighbours, they judge righteously, and whatever things they would
> not have done to themselves they do not to another . . . If they see a
> stranger, they bring him under their roof, and rejoice over him as over a
> brother of their own, for they call not themselves brethren after the flesh,
> but after the spirit.[6]

Christian identity

The practice of this life-style marked out Christians from others whose
life-style was less regulated. Augustine of Hippo (354–430), an influential thinker and writer, conveyed this point in an illuminating way.
Christians, he declared, live in a world knowing that they are part of a
vast community whose life and worship is perpetually governed by
forces that cohere in God. God enables people through his grace to do
what is right. God bestows grace:

> not only in order that they may know, by manifestation of that grace,
> what should be done, but moreover in order that, by its enabling, they
> may do with love what they know.[7]

God confers his gift of grace on Christians through the infusion of his
Spirit. The Spirit is also the mediator of love that motivates action in
accordance with itself. Grace and love are the energizing source of
Christian conduct. Augustine deduced his belief from the character
of God and the salvific impact of the death and resurrection of Jesus
Christ. Augustine, a zealous champion of Catholic orthodoxy in
theology, held firmly belief in God as the sole creator and in his absolute
goodness as the source of human goodness. Christ entered the world as
God had foretold in order to manifest and transmit the grace of God in
a tangible form.

The grace of Christ elects those who are to receive the free gift of
salvation. This redeems them from the consequences of the mortal sin
of Adam.

Augustine's *Confessions* is one of the classical works of the patristic
age and still regarded as a spiritual gem. Augustine was converted to

Christianity from the religion of Mani, the Persian gnostic and ascetic, and baptized by Ambrose in Milan in 387. Thereafter he illumined the nature and outreach of Christian orthodoxy with his exceptional intellectual gifts and exegetical skills. His devotion to the Catholic Church was unerring and he served it as a powerful preacher and a contemplative philosopher of religion. He composed hundreds of sermons and wrote expositions of many books of the Bible. His theology was trinitarian; the Godhead consists of a unity in essence of relations rather than of persons. His views spread throughout the Church and he established himself as the foremost theologian and philosopher of his day.

> Truth has sprung up from the earth, and justice has come down from heaven.
>
> Awaken, O man; God has been made man for you. Awaken, you who sleep, rise from the dead and Christ will give you light. For you, I repeat, God has been made man. You would be dead for eternity had he not been born in time. You would never have been freed from sinful flesh had he not taken the likeness of sin.
>
> You would be the victim of misery without end had he not shown you his mercy. You would not have rediscovered life had he not shared in your death. You would have succumbed had he not come to your aid. You would have perished had he not come.
> Let us celebrate in joy the advent of our salvation and our redemption. Let us celebrate the festival in which, coming from the great day of eternity, a great eternal day introduces itself into our temporal day, short as it is. God has made us righteous by faith, so let us be at peace with God, because justice and peace have kissed each other. By our Lord Jesus Christ, for Truth has sprung up from the earth. It is he who opens up to us access to the world of grace in which we are established, and our pride is to have a share in the glory of God. Paul does not say to our glory but to the glory of God, because justice has not come forth from us but has come down from heaven. So let him who seeks his glory not in himself but in the Lord.
>
> *(Augustine, Sermon 185 for Christmas)*

In his seminal work *The City of God* Augustine expounded the role and status of the Christian Church in the world in a comprehensive way not previously attempted. He believed that theology must be related to actual situations and not pursued in a vacuum; its spiritual purpose is that of paving the way through the illumination of truth, grace and love for the universal recognition and acceptance of Christian faith as God's ultimate gift to the world. For this purpose he offered his evaluation of the nature of the Church and the role of the Christian in the world.

Augustine was inspired with a vision of the Christianization of the world. This had become more realizable after the conversion of Constantine and the Edict of Milan, and the fall of Rome and the inevitable demise of the Roman Empire.

Augustine posed the question of how Christians could live the life of faith with intellectual and spiritual integrity in a world of rapid changes. He aimed to offer Christians positive guidance and to explain the role of Christian action in the present world. Augustine was acutely sensitive to the impact of the practical revolution then taking place but he believed firmly that God was at work in the present situation. God's plan was for the redemption of the whole world but its present operation meant that no one who received his grace was doomed. It is the duty of the Christian to pursue the objectives of Christian living whatever changes take place. The Christian cannot ignore the impact of historical events but has to understand their revolutionary impact from a Christian perspective.

Turning to the relation between theology and spirituality in the works of Augustine we see how relevant is his personal experience in this context. His *Confessions* is an open book that lays bare the inner world of musings and the nature of his spiritual pilgrimage. It is said that "He looked beyond the aimless and bloody chaos of history to the world of eternal realities."[8] He explored and exposed this world of "eternal realities" with ruthless frankness and held nothing back in his account of his personal struggle between flesh and spirit. He fought against a multitude of temptations and a host of perplexities; he was haunted by multifarious pressures and strove daily against lusts and greediness, the pleasures of the flesh, the delights of the senses, vain desires and curiosity. All these disturbed his peace and spiritual equilibrium, as we gather from his penetrating analysis of temptation:

> Daily, O Lord, are we assailed by these temptations, unceasingly are we assailed. We are daily tried in the furnace of the human tongue. And in this matter also you command us to continence; grant what you command and command what you will. You know my heart has groaned to you about this and the tears my eyes have shed. For I cannot easily know how far I am clean from this disease, and I am in great fear of my secret sins – sins that your eyes see, though mine do not. For in those other kinds of temptations I have some power of examining myself, but in this almost none. For I can see how far I have advanced in power to control my mind in the matter of the pleasures of the flesh and curiosity for vain knowledge: I can see it when I am without these things, either because I choose to be or because they are not to be had. For this I can ask myself how much or how little it troubles me not to have them.[9]

As we read the following petitions in Augustine's *Confessions* we realize the importance he attached to experience, especially the experience of union with God.

> Let me know Thee who knowest me, let me know Thee even as I am known;
> It is with no doubtful knowledge, Lord, but with certainty that I love You.
> You have stricken my heart with my word and I have loved You.
> How then do I seek You, O Lord? For in seeking You, my God, it is happiness that I am seeking.
> I shall seek You that my word may live.
> For my body lives by my soul and my soul lives by You.
> What is the way to seek for happiness then? Because I have no happiness.
> Till I can say, and say nightly: "Enough it is there."

Augustine expounded his belief from this experiential reality which he wished others to share: "Come hither and harken," he pleaded, "and I will show what God has done for my soul." By laying bare his feelings and spiritual awareness Augustine gives access to his inward experience, he looks at himself not as through a glass darkly but under the arclight of the divine gaze. In his search for truth he portrays himself as a naked soul, and it is this intrinsic honesty that made him such an influential figure throughout the Church. He demonstrated the validity of truth received other than through the natural senses; truth arises from the experience within where the Holy Spirit is at work. In one of his *Sermons on Selected Lessons from the New Testament* he declared that:

> in every deed the Holy Spirit was with him in the washing of the outward man, to renew the inner man from day to day, and by the taste of spiritual rest is the affluence of the delights of God to soften down by the hope of future blessedness all present hardships.[10]

Augustine was deeply committed to the Church, "Our mother, prolific with offspring of her we are born, by her milk we are nourished, by her spirit we are made alive." The Church is the matrix of spirituality and the sustenance that nurtures true spirituality. This "high" view of the Church postulated Christ as the head and the sole author of the sacramental gifts mediated within the Church. The life of the Church is that of the community of grace; grace is received through participation in the sacraments. Only within the Church are the sacraments administered and their grace mediated. Observance of the sacraments is the certainty of being incorporated into the community of faith; through the sacraments love is engendered, and through devotion and prayer the participant deepens experience of the efficiency of Christ's redemptive work.

Those who participate in Christ's redemptive work also share in the unity and benefits that flow therefrom. Supreme amongst the gifts is the love that finds satisfaction and fulfilment in God. According to Augustine love is an elemental inner drive or desire that is directed upward to God; love that is directed to perishable things is false love, for love is of God who himself is love. This love God has been made accessible through Christ. Love that is directed to God unfolds the secret of genuine self-love. Love in action is the highest attainment of the human spirit, for nothing supersedes love. This is epitomized in Augustine's famous dictum, "Love – and do what you like". No one in his age expressed more beautiful or more appealing insights into the character and outreach of Christian love.

Love is the key that unlocks the comprehensive theology and spirituality of Augustine. He was a deep thinker who grappled with major spiritual questions in his search for "the pearl of great price", that is, for the ultimate knowledge of God and life. His influence continued well beyond his own age and had a considerable impact on the reformers of the sixteenth century. Martin Luther was indebted to Augustine for his exposition of the source and character of Christian salvation, especially to his teaching on grace. Augustine believed that divine love had rescued him from disillusion with his earlier beliefs, and that God had sought and received him out of love as a father. The secret heart of God's love was supremely manifested in the death and resurrection of Christ. Love of Christ paved the way to union with God and this made inner peace and bliss a present reality – "our hearts are restless until they find their rest in thee." Love and grace together gave shape and content to Augustine's theology and spirituality.

In a similar vein, even if less extensively, others of the Church Fathers described the vitality and richness of a genuine spirituality as the directing force of living a Christian life. They portrayed such experience as life-transforming and faith-affirming; coupled with right understanding it nurtured and sustained a holistic spirituality. In turn this became the key to harmonious relationship with God and assured growth in the spiritual life. The performance of the spiritual exercises is directed to this holistic end. Augustine's theological activities convinced him of the truth of the Christian faith, but not only in an intellectual sense, but as "My God and my life and my sacred Delight." This Delight brings with it an abundance of peace, according to Augustine, "peace, your gold; peace, your silver; peace, your property; peace, your life; peace, your God. Peace will fulfil your every desire."

Perspectives of Patristic theology and spirituality

Trinity

We noted how the orthodox Church Fathers wove their theology
around the Trinity of Father, Son and Holy Spirit. Bishop Irenaeus
expounded systematically the functions of the three persons of the
Trinity:

> The Spirit prepares man for the Son of God; the Son leads man to the
> Father; the Father gives man immortality . . . Thus God was revealed: for
> in all these ways God the Father is displayed. The Spirit works, the Son
> fulfils his ministry, the Father approves.[11]

Traces of the language and thought of Irenaeus appear in the works of
Tertullian of Carthage; Tertullian gave puritanical direction to the
Church in North Africa, as he reassessed the course of God's pro-
gressive revelation of himself:

> God is invisible, though he is seen; incomprehensible, though manifested
> by grace; inconceivable, though conceived by human senses. In this lies
> his reality, and his greatness.[12]

The God who is manifested to us is a Trinity of Father, Son and
Paraclete (Spirit), but according to Tertullian:

> the connection of Father and Son, of Son and Paraclete, makes three who
> cohere in a dependent series. And these three are one thing, not one
> person, in the same way as the saying "I and the Father are one thing"
> refers to unity of essential being, not to singularity of number.[13]

Tertullian therefore postulated the Son and the Spirit as separate
realities who each participated in the Godhead. He pointed to the unity
of a "concept" whilst at the same time preserving a distinction between
its members. He asserted, "For the Spirit is the substance of the Word,
and the Word is the activity of the Spirit, and the two are a unity."[14]

His contemporary, Clement of Alexandria, wrote about the exceedingly difficult task of discovering the original and supreme cause of all
that exists, and of the Father of the whole universe. God is indivisible
and infinite, without form and nameless. Though we ascribe names,
knowledge and truth, and the Holy Spirit, are inexplicable Wisdom. So
Clement cried, "O wonderful mystery! The Father of all things is
one; the Word of all things is one; the Holy Spirit is one and the same
everywhere."[15]

Origen, an original and radical thinker who lived a frugal life but worked hard in the service of the catechetical school of Alexandria and wrote extensively, also gave explicit concurrence to the importance of theology for right living. He described beautifully the work of God the creator in designing the universe and initiating the works of divine providence. Yet, declared Origen, no human mind can behold God as he is in himself, but the mind forms its concept of the creator from the beauty of his works and the loveliness of his creatures. So Origen stated:

> There is kinship between the human mind and God, for the mind is itself an image of God, and therefore can have some conception of the divine nature, especially the more it is purified and removed from matter.[16]

God is perfect goodness and confers on individuals the powers by which they are able to apprehend him as he really is and makes possible complete kinship with himself. He extends his providence to every rational being individually, yet his providence towards the whole of humankind is unaffected. Every individual who deviates from the Lord becomes more and more inclined to evil. Everyone knows the image of God and this makes possible complete consummation in God.

The individual made in the likeness of God is endowed with feelings and impulses that stimulate desire for goodness and progress to virtue. Were it not for the image of God and his aid, no one could achieve moral perfection.

Therefore it behoves the individual to show reverence to God, for by so doing Christ is at work, who

> began a weaving together of the divine and human nature in order that human nature, through fellowship with what is more divine, might become divine.

So the individual should

> take up the life which he (Christ) taught; the life which leads everyone who lives according to the precepts of Jesus to friendship with God and fellowship with him.[17]

In his portrayal of God, Origen combined metaphysical and philosophical attributes with moral and spiritual qualities. This combination illumines the purpose of God at creation which was that of conditioning human beings for kinship or fellowship with himself. This fellowship is the heart and product of Christian spirituality and nurtures a life of sanctification that reflects the ethical and spiritual character of God. To have fellowship with God is akin to knowing God, and in the light of this the Christian cultivates a particular life-style whose spirituality is an extension of the life of God. As Origen wrote:

> Thus the operation of the Father, which bestows existence on all, proves more splendid and impressive when each person advances and reaches higher stages of progress through participation in Christ as wisdom, and as knowledge and sanctification.[18]

Others of the Church Fathers developed the same line of thought. Tertullian wrote analytically of the reality and greatness of God, who is invisible, "though he is seen; incomprehensible, though manifested by grace; inconceivable though conceived by human senses".[19] He is the supreme being, unborn, uncreated, without beginning and end, but he did not wish to remain hidden for ever, but out of his goodness he created the first man and woman and shared with them his blessings, his indulgences, his providences, his laws and warnings. God endowed them with complete freedom of choice for good or ill, so that through the mystery of self each might cleave to good of their own accord. This ennobles the human condition, for how strange it is, asserted Tertullian, if human beings did not have control of their minds; therefore, for their own good they were equipped at creation with free will. Thus they are able to exhibit goodness as their own possession through the exercise of divine freedom as their personal endowment.

Clement of Alexandria, who became a Christian and eventually settled at Alexandria, and served as the associate and later as the successor of Pantaenus, the first head of the famous catechetical school, expounded the character of God as Father "of the whole universe".[20] God is indivisible and infinite, without dimension or limit. In his work entitled *Protrepticus* Clement wrote of the compassion of God and his yearning that every human being should be saved. This salvation is the work of Christ "who became man just that you may learn from a man how it may be that man should become God". Then he continued:

> You have heard, O men, the divine proclamation of grace . . .
> Through these the Lord saves, guiding man by fear and grace.[21]

And in *Stromateis* he wrote:

> The first inclination towards salvation is displayed to us as faith, then follows fear and hope and repentance: these advancing with the help of discipline and endurance, lead to love and knowledge.[22]

The Church Fathers treated the relationship between theology and practical living positively; surrounded as they were by a sea of paganism they felt it imperative to press home the positive virtues of a Christian life-style. Their creative approach is impressive as is also their un-flagging zeal, as evidenced by the extensive writings of Irenaeus, Tertullian, Clement of Alexandria, Origen, Augustine and Cyprian. They adhered closely to the apostolic tradition with its roots in divine revelation, but they also elaborated on this in order to make it more applicable to their own generation. In expounding and transmitting apostolic doctrine they also sought to promote sound spiritual practices. Christian orthodoxy involved spiritual guidance that had to be followed if progress was to be made in living the life of Christ. The method of "doing" theology which they pioneered was applicable to their own times, but it is remarkable how it is still the subject of discussion and evaluation.

Revelation in Christ

The Church Fathers gave the Church intellectual leadership as well as spiritual vision. Their aim was to enunciate an informed and intellectual vision of Christian truth. This centred on Christ, the second person of the Trinity, the incarnate Word who had existed eternally with God and was revealed to the world as his Son. In him the divine nature and wisdom was revealed in human form and this unique revelation needed to be explained and comprehended for its own sake. Also what Christ had accomplished through his life on earth, especially through his suffering, death and resurrection, needed to be interpreted and commended as the supreme act of redemption for the world. Thus the Fathers were impelled to devote their skills and energies to expounding the origin, nature, work and accomplishment of Jesus Christ, as the divine redeemer. This was the heart of their theology; the revelation in Christ revealed all that needed to be known of God and his ways:

> What man had any knowledge at all of the character of God, before Christ came? Or do you accept the empty nonsense talked by plausible philosophers, some of whom said that God was fire . . . others said he was water, others some other of the elements created by God; no man has seen him or recognised him; but God revealed himself . . . and made clear what he had prepared from the beginning . . . [23]

In expounding the uniqueness of Christ the Fathers started from the premiss that Christ was the incarnation of the Eternal Word; he had always existed with the Father, but he was made incarnate and became man; he took flesh and appeared on earth as the visible manifestation of

God, born of the Father's will. He established the divine truth in the world in a concrete way.

Of the divine origin of Christ the Fathers were convinced, and when it was questioned they were vigorous in its defence. They did not always claim to fully comprehend the mystery of his incarnation. Indeed, as Irenaeus asserted, "If any one asks us how the Son was 'produced' from the Father, we reply that no one understands that 'production' or 'generation' or 'calling' or 'revelation' or whatever term anyone applies to his begetting, which in truth is indescribable."[24] Nevertheless, the overall impression gained of the views of the Fathers is that the origin of Christ was with God, for "in the beginning was the Word . . . but when the Father willed . . . this indeed . . . the Word took earthly flesh", as Athanasius expressed it in his work *Against Arius*.[25]

Naturally the person and work of Christ were given major prominence by the Church Fathers. They seemed obsessed with explicating the correct interpretation of such matters as the precise relationship of Christ to the Father, and his genuine nature or person. The debate on these issues often aroused passions among theologians and the Fathers were determined and forthright in defending and propagating their own views. The orthodox among them like Irenaeus did not doubt that Christ was the Son of God, "the only begotten Word of God"; and he was amazed that others should doubt it. He declared this to be "a meaning which is a matter of common knowledge". Tertullian likewise spoke of Christ as the Son of God, albeit in a different mould. He asserted that God and Christ are two persons but conjoined; the Son is not other than the Father by separation "but by difference of function . . . for the Father and the Son are not identical but distinct in degree". Clement of Alexandria in his work *Protrepticus* wrote of Christ as the divine Word, "who is truly God most manifest, made equal to the Ruler of all; because he was his Son, the Word was with God". In essence, then, the Church Fathers identified Jesus as divine, thereby demonstrating that his character is the character of God; he actually expressed the nature of God, but in his incarnate form he displayed all the visible attributes of a human being. He expressed the full range of human emotions, joy and sorrow, he was hungry and tempted, he grew weary and tired. The Fathers present him as genuinely human, the human manifestation of God at work in human history. Justin Martyr (*c.*100–165) expressed the dual nature of Christ in his *Apologia*:

And the truth is that Jesus Christ alone has been begotten as the unique Son of God, being already his Word . . . By the will of God he became man, and gave us this teaching for the conversion and restoration of mankind.[26]

Tertullian attacked the gnostics who degraded the material world and human flesh as evil by composing a lengthy treatise on the nobility of flesh, which led him to assert of the reality of the human Jesus:

> For in all the form which was moulded in the clay, Christ was in his thoughts as the man who was to be; for the Word was to be made clay and flesh, just as that time earth was fashioned into man.[27]

Tertullian thought of Christ in his human character as being of the same substance as God. John Hick draws attention to the analogy used by Tertullian of the ray of light being of the same substance as the burning sun from which it comes. Hick quotes the words of Tertullian:

> Even when the ray is shot forth from the sun, it is still part of the parent mass; the sun will still be in the ray, because it is the ray of the sun – there is no division of substance, but merely an extension. Thus Christ is Spirit of Spirit, and God of God, as light is kindled of light.[28]

Athanasius was also most explicit in his assertion of the true humanity of Jesus. He wrote in his work *Against Arius*:

> Though he was God he had a body of his own, and using it as an instrument he had become man for our sakes. Thus it is that the properties of the flesh are said to be his, since he was in that flesh; hunger, thirst, pain, weariness and the like, to which the flesh is liable . . .[29]

The significance of the genuine humanity of Jesus, as the orthodox Church Fathers saw it, was that he thereby exhibited the qualities of God's grace and love. He demonstrated, as a human person, God's will and fulfilled this in his dealings with the people and the issues of his day. The human character of Jesus is in essence the extension of the character of God; in the human Jesus God made an entry into the life of the world as the human embodiment of his own will. This entry was for a definite purpose, as is conveyed by Irenaeus:

> At the same time he displayed God in visible form to men through his many acts of mediation, lest man should be utterly remote from God and so cease to be. For the glory of God is a living man; and the life of man is the vision of God. For if the manifestation of God in creation gives life to all who live on earth, much more does the revelation of the Father through the Word bestow life on those who see God.[30]

These words of Irenaeus explain the purpose of the incarnation as being "to bestow life on those who see God" (cf. the saying in St. John's Gospel on the purpose of the "good news", it is, "that Jesus is the Christ, the Son of God, and that believing you may have life in his name"). This leads us to refer briefly to the main aspect of the work of Christ, as portrayed by the Church Fathers. This was supremely redemptive, to make believers one with Christ as he himself was one with God (cf. St. John 17: 21). This is the burden of the saying of Irenaeus:

> Our Lord Jesus Christ, the word of God, of his boundless love, became what we are that he might make us what he himself is.[31]

Ignatius (35–107), Bishop of Antioch, and one of the early Christian authors, summarized the key aspects of the work of Jesus in respect of his mission of redemption: Christ, he said,

> was truly persecuted under Pontius Pilate, truly crucified and died while those in heaven, on earth, and under the earth beheld it; who was also truly raised from the dead, the Father having raised him, who in like manner will raise us also who believe in him . . . [32]

This focus on the rejection, suffering, crucifixion and resurrection of Jesus in the words of Ignatius is also the focus of the Church Fathers generally as they dilated on the work of Jesus Christ. His suffering was an act of atonement, for "he took upon him our sins . . . to show us that of ourselves it was impossible for us to enter the Kingdom of God" (*The Epistle to Diognetus*). Irenaeus taught about Christ, the Second Adam, through whom was wrought reconciliation with God, and who at the same time secured the forgiveness of sin – "As through a tree we were made debtors to God, as through a tree we receive the cancellation of our debt." Tertullian explained the death of Jesus as a ransom paid for the deliverance from evil. Christ was led as "a sheep to the slaughter" and "delivered up to the death of the cross", "all this that he might win us away from our sins". This act Tertullian portrayed as "an image of the sun made over the day of ransom, release effected in the underworld, and contact made in heaven". Therefore, the death of Jesus was essential to effect atonement for sin, forgiveness, reconciliation and the hope of heaven; the death of Jesus is the "whole essence and value of the Christian religion". At the crucifixion, however, Christ grappled with the serpent and enslaved the tyrant, death. Yet,

> though he was held captive by corruption, the Lord displayed him set at liberty by his outstretched arms. O wondrous mystery! The Lord was laid to rest and man was raised up.[33]

The resurrection of Christ

Belief that Christ had been resurrected and lives eternally coloured the teaching of the Church Fathers from beginning to end. Everything they wrote and declared about him was from the perspective of his resurrection. They did not always claim to understand fully the mysterious event of the resurrection, but its significance dominated their thought and percolated through their entire writings. Christ had been resurrected, after he had

> surrendered his body to death in the place of all men, and presented it to the Father . . . that by all dying in him the law of disintegration to which men were subject might be annulled . . . and that he might revive men from death by their appropriation of his body and by the grace of the resurrection.[34]

The Fathers testified that after his crucifixion Jesus appeared to his closest disciples to revitalize their faith and commission them to continue his mission for the whole world. The resurrection is the justification of God's call to faith in Christ and to a life of spiritual devotion to him. The continuing presence of Christ after his resurrection is the dynamic impetus for living the Christian life in close communion with God and obedience to the commission of Christ. Through the resurrection all who are mortal are clothed with immortality, "for disintegration in death no longer has scope".[35]

The immanent Spirit

Consciousness of the immanence and the continuing spiritual presence of Christ is the creation of the Holy Spirit, the third person of the Trinity. The theology of the Church Fathers in this context is definite and radical. The Spirit is the medium and sustainer of the inner awareness of the presence of Christ; the Spirit is the vehicle of the continuously unyielding revelation of God and how this authenticates his will for the Church and the individual Christian; the Spirit confers those peculiar gifts that empower moral and ethical action in conformity with the divine purpose. Apart from the Spirit's power such action is moribund. The persistent and emphatic attention which the Fathers gave to the nature and function of the Holy Spirit is testimony to their own reliance on the presence and experience of the Spirit for guidance and information. The Spirit is holy as its source is in God; evidence of the present manifestation of the Spirit is the reality of the union of the Christian with God and the performance of acts that express his holy will. The Spirit is the communicator and the medium of communication with Christ; this strengthens faith as "the ladder by which we ascend to God". This saying of Irenaeus affirms the union with God which the Spirit engenders, it asserts and also affirms that where the Spirit of God is, there is the Church. Without the Spirit none are "nourished and given life at their mother's breast; nor do they enjoy the sparkling fountain that issues from the body of Christ".[36] The Spirit is the gift of the Father; Father, Son and Holy Spirit, the three persons of the Trinity, coalesce in the witness which the Spirit bears. Tertullian used the word *paraclete* in describing the work of the Holy Spirit (*paraclete* = advocate, or one who pleads the cause of another), and elaborated on this:

> First, he will bear witness to Christ and our belief about him, together with the whole design of God the Creator, he will glorify him and remind us of him, and then when the Paraclete has thus been recognized in the matter of the primary rule of faith, he will reveal many things which relate to discipline.[37]

Origen asserted that the Holy Spirit resides within the law and the gospel and is for ever with God and Christ. The Spirit partakes of the nature of the Father and the Son. He provides the spiritual gifts of God as he participates in him; the grace of the Spirit is given to those who are not holy, by virtue of their participation in the work of the Spirit. As they receive the gift of the Spirit they are sanctified and endowed with the wisdom that progresses to the higher realm of purity and perfection. In brief, the experience of the Spirit engenders newness of life, to which Cyprian referred in his personal testimony:

> When I had drunk the Spirit from heaven, and the second birth had restored me so as to make me a new man, then straightway in a marvel-lous manner doubts began to be resolved, closed doors to open, dark places to grow light; what had before seemed difficult was now easy, what I thought impossible was now capable of accomplishment.[38]

In sum the Church Fathers perceived the experience of the Holy Spirit as the distinctive feature of Christian spirituality. The experience was the empirical proof of the continuing spiritual presence of Christ; it nurtured the gifts of the Spirit and directed their action; it induced the phenomena of Christian truth and affirmed its reality. Furthermore, the Spirit moulds and patterns the life of the Church, shapes its character and directs its activities. The Spirit creates union with God, otherwise all would be alienated and remote from him. In the words of Athanasius:

> We are united with the Godhead by participation in the Spirit; so that our being in the Father does not belong to us, but to the Spirit, which is in us and dwells in us.[39]

The indwelling Spirit is for the sake of human perfecting and the preparation for immortality; the grace of the Spirit induces newness of life and obedience; the Spirit is instructor, teacher and wisdom, and the dispenser of spiritual gifts now made available to all believers.

The Community of the Spirit

The central role which the Fathers assigned to the Holy Spirit is also the centre of gravity from which radiates their theology of the Church, the sacraments and the Christian ministry. The wealth of material they have bequeathed varies and sometimes this seems incongruous. Their assumptions and interpretations may indeed have disturbed the mind of the Church or seemed sometimes remote from its primary and more urgent concerns. Yet their commitment to the Church and concern for its unity and spirituality is always obvious and never in doubt. The task of coordinating their diverse theological views is complex, and any uniformity of doctrine of the Church is not easily obtained; but the contribution of the Church Fathers to the understanding of the nature and purpose of the Church and its central role in the mission of Christianity is indisputable. To promote the spiritual health of the Church for the sake of its unity, sacramental life and mission was the ideal to which all their labours were directed. The unity they coveted for the Church cohered in the eternal being of God and in Christ as redeemer; the perfection of this unity is the work of the Holy Spirit who for ever is present in the community of the Church and is the sustainer of all its manifestations. Tertullian summed up the provenance of the Holy Spirit in this informative way, "The provenance of the Holy Spirit is just this; the guidance of discipline . . . the reformation of the intellect, the advance towards better things." The discipline of the Church and the "advance towards better things" is achieved through the manifestation and action of the Holy Spirit. Irenaeus added his own insight into the effect of the Spirit in action in the Church; it is, he declared:

> for our perfecting. This is what the Apostle calls "a first instalment" which dwells in us and makes us even now spiritual, and thus our "mortality is swallowed up in immortality".[40]

These words reflect the apostolic view of the Spirit as the illumination of the transcendent vision that guides the Church and sheds light on the phenomena that govern its community and mission.

The vision of love

The vision of love which Irenaeus described is that of the love of God revealed in Christ. Love is the heart of God, as is made plain in the words and actions of Christ, it is also the heart of Christian spirituality as it is entirely absorbed by it. Love is the spirit of joy, that is, the joy and ecstasy of experiencing the divine presence in action. Clement of Alexandria asked, "What is the nature and extent of this love?", and in response he pointed to the way Christ laid down his life, namely, "The life that was worth the whole universe". Clement then asserted how God "requires in return that we should do the same for each other". In the individual person and the community of the Church love fosters the bond of unity that is the divine will of all believers. This love is the heart-throb of Christian spirituality.[41]

The model of prayer

To embark on the route of spiritual endeavour and perfection and sustain its impetus requires the constant practice and nurture of prayer. Origen characterized prayer as supplication and petition – supplication as request addressed to God and petition as asking for a boon not possessed at present. Supplication and petition are addressed to God as Father with thanksgiving; supplicatory prayer is only offered to God and not to any derivative being. To pray to the Son and not the Father "is most absurd", whilst "To pray to both would clearly imply the use of the plural in our requests."[42]

The Church Fathers did not treat prayer in an analytical, systematic or intellectually exhaustive manner, but they did traverse the pathway of prayer and describe the essential steps sensitively. They explained the various forms of prayer, they expanded on the spiritual benefits of prayer, they clarified why prayer is essential for the nurture of spirituality, and they elaborated on the inclusive nature of Christian prayer. Prayer is offered to a merciful and pitiful God, this assures that sins are forgiven; prayer offered in faith and sincerity activates a state of inner peace and serenity; prayer offered to God as King of the Ages intercedes for governors and rulers and all in authority; prayer with thanksgiving nourishes the life of the spirit; prayer offered in the name of Christ as mediator and interceder assures that those who pray communicate with God as sons and daughters of a heavenly Father.

The Fathers drew liberally on the classical imagery of Christian prayer and they insisted on the necessity of prayer as a continuous engagement with God. They expounded the various forms of prayer and how prayer is conducted in full awareness of the mediatorship of Christ. The Fathers decried prayer offered only as a formality without consciously seeking to communicate with God. Prayer as communication is all-embracing and expresses wholehearted love for God; it holds the whole universe and the solidarity of humankind in petition before him. God then reciprocates in love, so Origen urged:

> let us therefore address our supplications to the Father as God; let us make requests to him as Father; let us offer petitions to him as Lord; let us give thanks to him as God and Father and Lord; but being the Lord of those who are not utterly slaves. For the Father would rightly be considered also the Lord of the Son, the Lord of those who become sons through him.[43]

Empowering the Church

Holistic spirituality empowers the Church to be in truth the Church of the living God. The Fathers were committed to defending and teaching their doctrine of the Church as a divine creation. The Church is a divine creation, the vehicle of divine purpose, and therefore the custodian and expositor of apostolic doctrines. All who truly believe the Christian faith belong to the Church; they practise the liturgy, maintain its ministry, and promote its mission. Irenaeus expounded the origin, nature and role of the Church in a series of definite statements which declared that:

> The order of the Church was established from the earliest times . . .
> The Church is the distinctive stamp of the Body of Christ . . .
> The Church, is "the salt of the earth" . . .

And Tertullian declared:

> that the Church is properly and primarily the Spirit, in whom is the Trinity of one divinity, the Father, Son and Holy Spirit . . .
> The Spirit makes the assembly of the Church, which the Lord established in three persons . . .

According to Clement of Alexandria:

only in the true Church is the most accurate knowledge . . .
There is one Church, into which are enrolled those who are righteous . . .
The Church brings together, by the will of the one God through the one Lord those who were already appointed . . .
The pre-eminence of the Church depends on its absolute unity . . .

Origen expressed the absolute necessity of the Church in this way:

Outside this house, that is, outside the Church, no one is saved . . .
The Church as the bride of Christ is spoken of from the beginning of the human race . . .
The Church existed in all the saints from the beginning of time . . .

Cyprian added his contribution with the assertion that:

The Church is one, is flooded with the light of the Lord, and extends her rays over the globe
Whoever leaves the Church attains not of Christian rewards
Whoever rends and divides the Church cannot possess the clothing of Christ.

Spirituality and worship

These pointers to the estimate of the Church as a spiritual community created by God through Christ for the promotion of his witness to the world also point to the roots of spiritual growth within the fellowship of the Church. Growth in spirituality to maturity is nurtured and perfected in the Christian community. This fact, declared Justin Martyr, is what every man of sense will admit to be true. This growth is achieved through worship, and it is Christ who taught his Church this worship, according to Justin. So we ask with the author of the *Letter to Diognetus*, how then do Christians worship? The answers which the Fathers gave are also the recipe of spiritual growth within the Church. Justin martyr in his *Apology* provides this perspective on worship:

We worship the Creator, revealed by his Son.

We are not atheists, for we worship the Creator of the universe (while asserting, according to our instructions, that he needs no blood, nor libations, nor incense) with the word of prayer and thanksgiving . . . expressing our thanks to him in words, with solemn ceremonies and hymns, for our creation, for all the means of health, for the properties of things in their variety, and for the changing seasons: praying that through faith in him we may be born again in incorruption. Every man of sense will admit all this to be true of us. The master who taught us this worship, and who was born to this end, was crucified under Pontius Pilate, procurator of Judaea in the reign of Tiberius Caesar. We are sure that he is the Son of the true God, and hold him the second in order, with the Spirit of prophecy in the third place. I shall show that the honour which we pay is rational.

The Church Fathers traversed the varied contour of Christian worship but did not define it. They displayed acute understanding of the nature and purpose of worship and provided information on its many styles and provenance. Worship is a corporate act offered as response to God, it is accordingly a means of deepening unity and promoting fellowship within the Church. As response it also expresses the desire for union with God, the sole object of worship. Through this response and union the worshipper gains fuller knowledge of the inner self and rich experience of the spiritual realities that are the gifts of God. Worship may be offered in various ways, and, as we shall see, the Fathers dilated on these at length. The thread that connects the diverse dimensions of worship is also the self-surrender of the worshipper in willing response to its purpose.

The manner of the response is also the classical forms of Christian worship including, prayer, praise, celebration, teaching, preaching, sacraments, liturgy, meditation and contemplation. There is no place, as the Fathers saw it, for idle speculation or metaphysical musing in worship, but instruction in the Scriptures and in Christian doctrine and morality is integral to its spiritual purpose.

Spirituality and sacraments

There are two foci in the works of the Fathers relevant to their understanding of the sacraments as the vehicle of spirituality: namely, the union with God and the Church community effected through the observance of the sacraments, and the spiritual renewal that occurs through participation in the sacraments. This conviction is clearly expressed through the Fathers' treatment of the sacraments of baptism and the eucharist.

They received and welcomed both sacraments as from the apostles and they committed their observance to the Church as an external manifestation of inner faith and commitment. Both rites are vehicles of achieving deeper union with God and Christ and with the whole fellowship of the Church. The literal focus of these two sacraments is not severed from the other dimensions of worship. Every element of

worship contributed to the wholesome unity of its purpose, but the
efficacy of baptism and the eucharist consists pre-eminently in the
perfecting of a life lived more worthily as a witness to union with God
and movement towards spiritual perfection. We need to take a closer
look at these two major sacraments.

Baptism

The *Didache* or *The Teaching of the Apostles*, a work which emanates
from the early second century and reflects the earliest post-apostolic
Christian traditions, presents baptism as valid when it is performed "in
the name of the Father, and the Son and the Holy Ghost", a triune
formula used by Jesus when he commissioned his disciples to baptize
(Matthew 28: 19). Justin Martyr likewise stated that baptism is "in the
name of God the Father and Lord of all, and of our Saviour Jesus Christ
and of the Holy Spirit". The administration of baptism generally is in
the name of the triune God, and although there may be some shift of
emphasis this was the view of the Fathers as a whole. The style of
baptism is mentioned by a number of the Fathers – it was performed in
running water by immersion, but effusion was not unknown; Irenaeus
and Cyprian affirmed the role of the bishop as the administrator and its
administration in the presence of the congregation. But personal preparation for baptism and instruction in its purpose was a matter of
fundamental importance to the Church Fathers; in particular they refer
in their writings to the ways in which the person to be baptized must
prepare mentally and spiritually. Fasting was also a necessary pre-
requisite according to the *Didache*, and, according to Justin Martyr, the
baptized are "taught to pray and entreat God, fasting, for the forgiveness of their former sins". Fasting was accompanied by the confession
of faith, and a number of the Church Fathers stress also repentance as
a proper preparation for baptism.

Tertullian wrote of the need of the preceding repentance in the *De
Poenitentia*, with much emphasis on the genuineness of repentance,
which should shun deception. Tertullian also stated that the baptized
"have to exert ourselves in order to reach that point". Baptism was not
therefore administered rashly, but when administered truly the
baptized attains:

> the sacramental power of sanctification; for the Spirit straightaway comes
> down upon them from the heavens and is upon the waters sanctifying
> them by his own power; and being thus sanctified they are inbued at the
> same time with the power of sanctifying . . . [44]

Irenaeus made effective use of imagery in his account of the effectiveness and meaning of baptism; it is a step in the advance of progress towards the life of God. In his work *Against Heresies*, Irenaeus wrote:

> As dry flour cannot be united into a lumpy dough, or a loaf, but needs moisture; so we who are many cannot be made one in Christ Jesus without the water which comes from heaven. And as dry earth does not produce fruit unless it receives moisture; so we, who are at first as "a dry tree", would never have yielded the fruit of life without the "willing rain" from above. For our bodies have reached the unity which brings us to immortality, by means of the washing [baptism]; our souls receive it by means of [the gift of] the Spirit.[45]

The progress in spirituality through baptism, of which Irenaeus wrote, includes also the experience of regeneration. Justin Martyr asserted that the baptized are brought "to a place where there is water, where they are perfected". The baptized person was reborn in Christ; dedication to Christ was then complete; the baptized Christian identified with Christ completely. Christian baptism is therefore baptism in the Spirit; through baptism Christians become inexorably bound to the Church and endowed with the special gifts of the Holy Spirit. The Spirit raises up the baptized to God himself as he transmits his power, love and grace. The baptized is made one with Christ or constituted as a child of God. The baptized is also sanctified by grace and enters upon a whole new way of living. This is signified by the rising out of the water; the life of the baptized is now set on things above. It was the baptized who were sent by Christ into the world to preach his gospel (good news) and to bear witness to the Christ within. This mission was initiated and carried forward by the Holy Spirit; it is communicated in words but very specifically in a holy life-style befitting the baptized Christian.

The baptized person is exposed to an active life of godliness in the world and not locked into other worldly esoteric spirituality. Baptism conferred on the Christian a diversity of spiritual gifts essential to serve the common good of the whole world. Origen urged, "Let everyone of the faithful recall the words he used in renouncing the devil when he first came to the waters of baptism, when he took on him the first seeds (tokens) of faith and came to the saving fountain."

In other words, "when one is converted from sin, purification is granted . . . the gift of the Spirit is represented under oil; so that he who is converted from sin may not only achieve purification but also be filled with the Holy Spirit, whereby he may also receive his former robe and the ring, be reconciled completely to his Father and restored to the status of a son".[46] (The oil, chrism, provides intense awareness of the intervention of God, and of how God acts towards the baptized. Henceforth this direct action of God manifests itself through the medium of the Spirit actively directed to the life of the world.) Baptism in the name of the Father, Son and Holy Spirit is a metaphor as well as a formula for becoming a Christian, and initiates the baptized into living the life of Christ before the world as well as their entry into the privileges of the Church.

Eucharist

The validity of baptism as a rite of identity with Christ and the Church applies also to the eucharist. For this reason Ignatius urged Christians to be eager for more gatherings for eucharist, and it is why he urged them to take care to keep the eucharist. The eucharist is a rite of celebration which, according to the *Didache*, only the baptized should share in.

Bread and wine are shared by the communicants, according to God's will, in the belief, as Ignatius expressed it, that "there is one flesh of our Lord Jesus Christ and one cup to unite us by his blood". According to the *Didache*, thanksgiving was given over the cup of wine and over the broken bread. Then there were the prayers for the Church, similar to that in the *Didache* itself:

> As this broken bread was scattered upon the mountains and was gathered together and became one, so let thy Church be gathered together from the ends of the earth into thy Kingdom: for thine is the glory and the power through Jesus Christ for ever and ever.[47]

The Fathers developed a mystical explanation of the eucharist, especially of the real presence of Christ. In the age of Justin Martyr the bread and wine of the eucharist were seen to be transformed into the flesh and blood of Jesus:

> This food is called Eucharist [thanksgiving] with us, and only those are allowed to partake who believe in the truth of our teaching and have received the washing for the remission of sins and for regeneration; and who live in accordance with the directions of Christ. We do not receive these gifts as ordinary food or ordinary drink. But as Jesus Christ our Saviour was made flesh through the word of God, and took flesh and blood for our salvation; in the same way the food over which thanksgiving has been offered through the word of prayer which we have from him – the food by which our blood and flesh are nourished through its transformation – is, we are taught, the flesh and blood of Jesus who was made flesh.[48]

Irenaeus explained the cup of wine as the new oblation of the New Testament (Covenant) and a pure oblation offered by the Church to the Creator as the "communion and unity of flesh and spirit". The offering was a sacrifice, as indeed are all Christian actions sacrificial. Tertullian likewise viewed the eucharist as a sacrifice and wrote of it also as a sacrament. Origen provided a spiritual interpretation of the bread and wine of the eucharist, believing that communicants acted faithfully on the words of Jesus, "Unless you eat my flesh, and drink my blood, you have no life in yourselves. For my flesh is really food, and my blood is really drink." So Origen considered the eucharist to be a rite of spiritual nourishment, the bread is the word which nourishes the soul, and the wine is the word which "so wonderfully refreshes and inebriates". The covenant of God is set out in the "blood of the passion of Christ", although it is only of the cup it is said, "This is the cup of the New Testament." Whilst this is a great mystery the communicant experiences how the memorial meal "effects an immense propitiation". In fact, it is the only memorial "which makes God propitious to men".

The different manner of the interpretation of the eucharist in no way obscures the common conviction of the Church Fathers of the necessity of observing and sharing in the sacrament. The experience of the eucharist was paramount for the nurture of the life of faith and for growth to spiritual maturity. Christ had inaugurated the sacrament and participation in it was an act of obedience and union with God achieved through the passion of Christ. Although the language is different, the Church Fathers all expounded the eucharist as a rite of unification and a re-enactment of the means of Christian salvation. It re-enacts the redemptive work of Christ and expresses through the symbols of bread and wine the love and passion of Christ.

Participation in the sacrament is an act of submission to the redemptive will of God. W. H. C. Frend in his seminal work *The Rise of Christianity* writes of how the institution of the eucharist was commemorated in the words of St. Paul in 1 Corinthians 11, and the offering of the loaf and the cup made in thankful remembrance. Then followed the invocation of the Holy Spirit (*epiclesis*):

> And we beseech thee, that Thou send Thy Holy Spirit upon this offering of the holy church. Unite it, and grant to all the saints who partake of it to their fulfilling with the Holy Spirit to their strengthening of faith in truth, that we may praise and glorify Thee, through Thy Servant, Jesus Christ, whom to Thee be glory and honour to the Father and the Son and the Holy Spirit in Thy Holy Church now and for ever.[49]

This conception of the eucharist as sacrifice, the means of unity, the source of strength in faith, and the glorification of the Father, Son and Holy Spirit, accords well with the thought of the Church Fathers as a whole.

The Christian life

In an illuminating passage in his work *Against Heresies* Irenaeus wrote of how God endowed every human being with knowledge of good and evil. Goodness consists of obedience to God and the observance of his commands. God has shown his kindness so as to enable people to distinguish between good and evil and make the right choice:

> For just as the tongue by means of taste gains experience of sweet and bitter, and the eye by vision distinguishes black and white, and the ear through hearing learns to distinguish sounds; so the mind experiences good and evil, and by accepting the discipline of the good becomes more determined in preserving the good by obedience to God.[50]

All the Church Fathers aimed to relate the Christian life of obedience to God, to the observance of the liturgy and sacraments. This is the will of God and the teaching of Christ. The Fathers pointed to Christ as the surest guide to right behaviour and the pattern for the cultivation of Christian character. Christians do not differ from others in their natural endowments and they live in the same world as others. Yet they are not of the world but are, in the words of Ignatius, proofs of God's presence within it. Christians have the holy teaching of Jesus fixed in their hearts and should obey it. This is the leavening of Christian example in goodness that transforms the face of the world. To this end, having observed that the Christians are subject to the same natural order as others, Justin Martyr stated, "Lest you should think that we are just making a case, here are a few of Christ's teachings," and then in his *Apology* he quoted large sections of the Sermon on the Mount as a guide to living the Christian life. Justin and other Church Fathers placed much stress on the necessity of love and reverence between people, readiness to obey God's commands willingly, exulting in good works, overcoming malice and evil, and acting as the Spirit determines. According to the *Didache* Christians should follow the rule of hospitality and give assistance to the traveller, but also be wary of those who "traffic upon Christ". They should assist all who are in want, help the poor to bear spiritual fruit, warn of the spiritual danger of preoccupation with material wealth, but use their wealth in acts of mercy and alms-giving. God is perfect goodness and in him there is no moral contradiction, for, according to Irenaeus, his moral goodness, mercy, patience etc. are perfect. In a life of obedience to him the believer also is endowed with these qualities of moral rectitude. The Church Fathers were insistent in their teaching and preaching that living a Christian life is the most effective indication of Christian faith and its eternal significance. What better way was there, they asked, of indicating the relevance of the teaching that had been handed down by the apostles than practising its precepts? Thus Clement of Rome spoke of the Christian way of life as "walking after the ordinances of God". Clement also posed a series of questions that merited an answer:

> For who that had sojourned among you did not approve your most virtuous and steadfast faith?
> Who did not admire your sober and forbearing piety in Christ?
> Who did not publish abroad your magnificent disposition of hospitality?[51]

One of the most insistent advocates of the relation of worship and praxis was Justin, who in a powerful passage wrote:

> After these things we always remind each other of them; and those of us who have means assist all who are in want, and we visit each other continually; and for all that we receive we bless the maker of all things through his Son Jesus Christ and through the Holy Spirit. And on the day which is called the Sun's Day there is an assembly of all who live in the towns or the country; and the memoirs of the Apostles or the writings of the prophets are read, as much as time permits. When the reader has finished the president gives a discourse, admonishing us and exhorting us to imitate these excellent examples. Then we all rise together and offer prayers: and, as I said above, on the conclusion of our prayer, bread is brought, and wine and water; and the president similarly offers up prayers and thanksgivings to the best of his power, and the people assent with *Amen*. Then follows the distribution of the Eucharistic gifts and the partaking of them by all; and they are sent to the absent by the hands of the deacons. The well-to-do who wish to give, give of their own free choice and each decides the amount of his contribution. This collection is deposited with the president, who gives aid to the orphans and widows and all who are in want through sickness or any other cause; he is also the protector of those in prison, of strangers from abroad, in fact, of all in need of assistance.
>
> We hold our common assembly on the Sun's Day because it is the first day, on which God put to flight darkness and chaos and made the world; and on the same day Jesus Christ our Saviour rose from the dead; for they crucified him on the day before Saturn's Day, and on the Sun's Day,

which follows Saturn's Day, he appeared to his Apostles and disciples and taught them these things, which we have handed on to you for your consideration.

The Christian life cannot be lived in isolation; it can only be lived fully in community with others. None should neglect the assembling of themselves together in the community of the Church; in this community Christian character matures and develops fully. In Christian community God, self and others harmoniously participate; creative human intercourse through community makes for social cohesion. Tertullian viewed social cohesion as the gift of God and the consequence of healthy community relations, and so he urged:

> We remember our debt of gratitude to our Lord God the Creator, and do not spurn any of the fruits of his works . . . [52]

Clement of Rome likewise expressed how the way of union with Christ, self and neighbour, issues in a cohesive community experience:

> Let our whole body be preserved in Christ Jesus, and let each man be subject to his neighbour, as he has his place assigned by his spiritual gift.[53]

What is striking about the contribution of the Church Fathers to the study of Christian theology and its spiritual tradition is their pragmatic approach and emphasis on the relationship between theological illumination and pragmatic spirituality. As they expounded the rudiments of apostolic faith they also sought to cultivate the spiritual practices that give meaning and significance to belief and theological understanding. In the idiom of the Church Fathers spirituality is enmeshed in the faith of the apostles and the Spirit who, according to Origen, has inspired every saint, prophet and apostle. The model of spirituality is the life of Christ, who, said the Fathers, they clearly set forth, using as materials, both the Scriptures that prophesied about him and the accurate traditions received. Their theology is not ephemeral or their teaching theoretical, what makes their works fascinating, if in places puzzling, is their insistence on the need for correct and orthodox understanding of the effective presentation and application of Christian truth. Their works are not all equally attractive, and some speak only for themselves and to their own times; nevertheless, they constitute a valid principle in all theological discourse, namely, that of keeping an eye on the ultimate significance for faith and spirituality of all theological activity. It may be said of the Church Fathers that they were obsessed with the substance and outcome of their thinking, that they never lost sight of the unity that lies at the heart of experience and the universe. The mainspring of their spirituality has to be reconciled to this. The Fathers all contributed to the vision of Origen:

> When all rational beings have been restored then the nature of this body of ours will be changed into the glory of the spiritual body.

3

Eastern Christendom

Following the first Christian Pentecost, Christianity spread to many cities of the Roman Empire and established Gentile churches. Divisions developed between them on matters of faith and belief which gradually reflected divisions between east and west within the empire. This led eventually to schism within the Church, and the Church in the east developed its own distinctive tradition in theology, spirituality and churchmanship.

In the year 1054 Pope Leo IX issued an order excommunicating the Greek patriarch and his followers from the Church of Rome. At last the schism between the churches of the east and west was formalized. The pope's envoy, Cardinal Humbert, who had drafted the order, placed the document on the altar of the cathedral church of St. Sophia. The order was not rescinded until 1965 when Pope Paul VI and Patriarch Athanagorus of the Greek Orthodox Church authorized the withdrawal.

The schism was the culmination of controversy and tension between east and west that had smouldered ever since Constantine embarked on his policy of imperial consolidation. After his victory over Licinius, the emperor of the east, in 323, Constantine established Byzantium, on the frontier between Asia and Europe, as his capital. Here Christ was enthroned as the *Pantocrator*, Lord of the universe, and Constantine, "the remaker of the world", his viceroy. Constantine was determined to save the empire from moral and political disintegration; he installed the Patriarch of Constantinople (the new name for Byzantium and the modern Istanbul) as spiritual head of the Church and himself as its defender. With such accord between Church and state the advent of the Kingdom of God seemed imminent. Eusebius of Caesarea (260–340), the father of church history and admirer of Constantine, described him as an icon of the Kingdom of Heaven, "carved in the image of the heavenly Kingdom, gazing upwards, he steers and guides humans on earth according to the pattern of his prototype (God)". Constantine chose the double-headed eagle which faced east and west, and backward and forward in time, as the emblem of his city. He built many new churches, and the magnificent cathedral church of St. Sophia became the focus of Christian spirituality. Constantinople became the hub of Christianity and Christianity the most potent force in Constantine's empire. Its civilization absorbed the spirit of classicism, the Greek language flourished, and the arts were well patronized. The imperial policies and ambitions augured well for the Church until the emperor's authority and spiritual autonomy began to be challenged.

The way of the desert

Rowan Williams has shown that this rift manifested itself far away from Constantine's seat of authority. The peasants of Egypt and Syria made the first move; they felt themselves marginalized socially and geographically, and whereas the emperor and his followers "might be an icon of the court of heaven, but for the peasant they could not be other than a remote despotism responsible for ever more ruinous taxation".[1] They rejected the allure of the imperial "culture-religion" and instead answered the call of God to a monastic existence as "a highly responsible and effective protest and opposition to the world, and not least to a worldly Church, a new and specific way of combating it".[2] The peasants who withdrew to the desert were following the footsteps of those Christians who in earlier times had withdrawn from a secularized church and its wealth and power politics, or who had escaped to the desert in times of persecution. The example of St. Paul the hermit who escaped to the desert in order to avoid the persecution of Decius in 251 set in motion a tradition that developed into the very highly influential monasticism of the Eastern Orthodox Church.

But the precursor of the Christian monastic movement is Antony of Egypt (250–355). Antony, a young Egyptian farmer, the son of wealthy parents from Heracleopolis, entered upon the solitary monastic life in obedience to Scripture, following the example of Jesus and John the Baptist in retreating to the wilderness in the search for spiritual re-generation through a time of solitary refinement. The spark that triggered Antony's decision to embark on the life of a hermit was the saying of Jesus, "If you will be perfect, go, sell all that thou hast and give to the poor, and come, follow me." Antony lived a life of spiritual

introspection and deliberate austerity. He was subjected to visions and
was often tempted by the devil to abandon the monastic life, but he
firmly resisted every temptation. He gained many disciples who were
attracted to him on account of his holiness and austerity, and he coordinated these into monastic communities along the Nile valley.
Antony became the superior and spiritual father of these monastic
communities, and he encouraged their members to engage in social and
charitable work amongst the poor and the exploited. He did not withdraw completely from worldly activity or from the theological debates
of his time. He had little truck with secularism but he was committed
to the welfare of his communities and to people in need. He sided with
Athanasius and his teaching about Christ as the Word of the Father,
Christ alone he believed was worthy to suffer for the sake of others in
order that they might be reconciled to God. Athanasius is reported to
have written a life of Antony, and it has been said that Antony's
teaching was "marked by keen psychological insight and the mechanics
of temptation and self control, and by a firm attachment to the dignity
and potential of human nature, in its bodily as well as its spiritual
aspects".[3] The fact that by the fourth century monasticism was an established order in its own right is due in no small measure to the pioneering
spirit of Antony. To this the ascetic ideals of Clement of Alexandria and
Origen also made a notable contribution.

A monastic church

The Byzantine church became essentially a monastic church and
monasticism the core and vehicle of its spirituality. The community of
the monastery became the cell of the Church. The pioneers of this
movement appeared early in the history of Christianity, and some of
the Church Fathers also played a key role. Eastern spiritual theology is
much indebted to the monks whose theology and spirituality were
fashioned in the monastery. The monks lived a life of spiritual discipline
according to set rules but without isolating themselves completely from
secular society. They engaged in charitable and merciful works, but also
worked to support themselves so as not to be a burden on society. They
followed the command of Christ in living a life of voluntary poverty
and regarded the monastic fellowship as the ideal Christian community
in the world. Ideally the monastery was "a spirit filled world". The
nurture of spirituality as a priority in the Eastern Orthodox tradition
has never been overshadowed by theological speculation. Spirituality is

conceived as embracing the whole of life and all activities in conscious response to God. The life of the monastery is organized around a carefully regulated time-plan of worship, prayer, meditation and observance of the sacraments. Thus the monks devoted themselves wholly to living the life of the spirit; their religious observances were seen as steps along an inner spiritual pilgrimage whose end is perfect union with God.

The monks lived in a state of spiritual elation and expectation, and whatever worldliness they may have renounced was for the sake of cultivating deeper dedication to the spiritual quest. The monastery, then, is the crucible of Eastern Orthodox spirituality; it projects a holistic view of spirituality as all-embracing. Historically this has received precedence over theological and philosophical disputations; the hope of union with God is ever the ideal. Christian living must find a place for silence and prayer, contemplation, personal reflection and listening to God's voice of calm, as its first priority.

Monasticism spread throughout the East and developed in a number of characteristic and distinctive practices. The ideal of personal salvation was actively pursued and whatever might impede this was denounced as heretical. Members of monastic communities were honoured for their commitment and devotion to God, and for their ability to interpret the divine will. Monks took upon themselves to be the custodians and champions of Orthodox Christian faith and professed their complete commitment to the rules and styles of the monastic life. They maintained contact with the civilian authorities and were loyal to the state, but they shunned the allurement of wealth and worldliness, and were ready to combat social ills.

In the early period Antony had many imitators and monasticism spread, especially among the Coptics. A certain Amoan established a monastic settlement at Wadi Natrun that grew to five thousand, all of whom remained under the authority of the bishop. The members fulfilled their vocation in a life of obedience, asceticism and austerity as a means of acquiring holiness and union with God. Pachomius (290–346) established a strict monastic order at Tabennisi in Egypt on the east of the Nile by acting, so he believed, on the command of God: "Stay here and build a monastery and many will come to you in order to become monks."[4] The leader of the monastery also gave information to novices and oversaw their regular association for prayer and practical work. The members plied their own trade but they all took their authority from the superior (abhot) of the monastery. Discipline was strict: the members ate one meal daily, they wore a brown habit with a hood, a sleeveless tunic, a mantle of goat skin and a girdle. The eucharist was observed twice weekly and on Easter, and on Founders Day (13 August) there was a general assembly at Tabennisi. When Pachomius died there were nine monasteries and two nunneries.[5] An ancient writer said of these communities, "Their chief concern is the love which they show to one and towards such as by chance reach that spot."

As monasticism developed in the east it catered for women's vocation as well as men's.[6] It did not develop uniformly throughout the Eastern church and individualist characteristics appeared along with the common emphasis on the life of holiness. Monasticism was not averse to reform but it has adhered tenaciously in its particular approach to religion and the cultivation of the Christian character. Its theology, however, has remained strictly trinitarian, and this is everywhere combined with deep piety and intense spiritual concentration. The trinitarian theology is consistent with the decree of the Council of Chalcedon, which, under the direction of two church leaders from Constantinople, agreed a statement of faith to the effect that Christ is perfect God and man, equal with God in his Godhead and with human kind in his manhood.

Between his two natures there is neither separation or confusion, both natures are combined to form one person. The east accepted the Chalcedonian formula as formative, and this has always been the bedrock of Orthodox and monastic theology. It is the baptismal and the eucharistic creed of the Eastern Orthodox Church to this day.

Eastern monasticism even to this day includes the three characteristic forms of the early movement, namely, asceticism, monastic communities and eremetic groups (loosely-knit groups, small in number, living together under the guidance of an elder). But there are no monastic "orders" as such in the Eastern Church.

The Cappadocian Fathers

In this context the contribution of the Cappadocian Fathers, Basil the Great, Gregory of Nazianus and Gregory of Nyssa, merit special mention. They pioneered an interpretation of the doctrine of the Trinity which was affirmed by the Council of Constantinople in 381 and eventually endorsed by the Council of Chalcedon. The Cappadocians regaled the exposition of trinitarian theology with intellectual vigour and combined piety which led the way to it becoming the cornerstone of Eastern Orthodoxy. Basil the Great (330–379) was a devotee of the teaching of Origen, especially of his philosophy. Origen displayed notable pastoral and social gifts and Basil too took an active part in social life. He was a friend of Basil, Bishop of Ancyra, and in a letter he expressed his respect for the monastic life:

> I admired their (monks') continence of living and their endurance in toil. I was amazed at their persistency in prayer . . . They showed in every deed, in what it is to have one's sojourn for a while in this life and have one's citizenship and home in heaven. I prayed that I might imitate them.[7]

Basil lived a life of quiet contemplation whilst aiming to achieve *enkrateia*, "the mastery of whatever is within".

The monasteries which Basil founded in Asia Minor were compact communities of thirty or forty members under a superior overseer. The monks held property in common and wore a similar habit, but they avoided excesses of fasting and asceticism. Prayer was conducted regularly throughout the day and night, and the eucharist was celebrated four times a week. Life in the monastery provided the opportunity to imitate Christ and of overcoming evil.[8] But this did not mean severing all connection with the life of the world:

> The solitary life has one aim, the service of the needs of the individual. But this is plainly in conflict with the law of love. The Lord for the greatness of His love was not content with teaching the word only, but that accurately and clearly he might give us a pattern of humility in the perfection of love, He girded Himself and washed the feet of His disciples in person. Whose then wilt thou wash? Whom wilt thou care for . . . How will that good and pleasant thing, the dwelling of brethren together . . . be accomplished by dwelling solitarily?

The monks served the wider community, especially hospitals, schools and orphanages. They had set times for study, especially for study of the Bible. They engaged in theological debate, and Basil expressed his view of the relationship of the Father and Son within the Godhead in a letter he wrote in 361:

> If I may speak my own opinion, I accept the phrase "like in substance" provided the qualification "invariably" is added to it, on the grounds that it comes to the same thing as "identity of substance".[9]

Basil made a decisive contribution to the debate about the nature of the Trinity by declaring that the Father, Son and Holy Spirit were united in perfect equality. This doctrine subsequently came to be applied to baptism and other sacramental rites of the Eastern Church. He must be designated one of the precursors of Eastern Orthodoxy, and of him, and the other two Cappadocian Fathers, it has been said, "they were also important for the development of a Christianized culture and philosophy in this period of rapid adjustment to being the 'established' religion of the Empire, and the range of their writings, orations, exegetical treatises, letters etc., reflect this".[10]

In another respect also Basil made a notable contribution to the developing theology of the time. He propounded a doctrine of God as one who is unknowable and incomprehensible, which, as we are yet to see, became an established view within the Orthodox Church. Basil wrote, "We know our God from His energies but we do not claim that we can draw near to this essence. His energies come down to us, but his essence remains unapproachable."

The three Cappadocian Fathers used very similar language to convey their doctrines. Gregory of Nazianus (330–389), son of the Bishop of Nazianus, and Gregory of Nyssa (335–394), Basil's younger brother, like Basil claimed the theological mantle of Athanasius, who had advocated the Apostles' Creed at the Council of Nicaea and defended its doctrine in a series of treatises and sermons. Gregory of Nazianus presided at the Council of Constantinople after the sudden death of Miletus and allowed people from across the social divide to be involved in theological discussion. Gregory was an austere character who despised worldly ways and ostentation in dress and life-style, and in a sermon he declared ironically, "I was not aware we ought to rival consuls, governors and famous generals – or that our stomachs ought to hunger for the bread of the poor, and expend their necessities on luxuries, belching forth over the altars."[11] Gregory was also devoted to the classical tradition in literature, but in theology he was a firm defender of the decrees of the Council of Nicaea.

Gregory of Nyssa engaged enthusiastically in the theological controversies of his age. He too imbibed some of the ideas of Origen and was a firm supporter of the Nicene formula. He developed mystical tendencies under the influence of certain aspects of the mystical thought of Philo and these coloured his contemplative experience.[12] Mysticism is an ellusive term that is not easily defined, but here it is used of the inner experience of being transported into a wholly spiritual communion with the transcendent and eternal God. Gregory came also under the influence of Plotinus (205–269), a neo-Platonist, who taught the predominance of the spiritual and its transcendence over matter and time.

The operation of the Holy Spirit, Gregory maintained, confers on the individual the capacity to rise above the limitations and imperfections of the visible material world to enjoy a state of communion with the perfect and transcendent God. From this mystical experience there dawns the consciousness of the unity at the heart of all that exists. It embraces the souls of all who live and who have passed into the non-visible world. Gregory viewed the shrines of the martyrs as places where pilgrims are surrounded by "the cloud of heavenly witnesses", and of the prayers of the pilgrims he said, "they address to the martyr their prayers of intercession as though they were present". The communion of saints embraces the living and the departed. The departed saints abide with God and bring blessing to the living as they commune with him. The mystical union with God and the saints is the core of Eastern Christian spirituality and the perennial source of spiritual renewal and vitality.

Holy Tradition

The Eastern Orthodox Church has abided from the beginning by the authority of the ecumenical church councils. They are an integral part of the Holy Tradition that the Church regards as incontrovertible and the summation of its doctrine, polity and government.

It is not easy to quantify everything the Holy Tradition contains or the range of matters it embraces. Its absolute comprehensiveness is conveyed accurately in the definition, the "Tradition is the life of the Holy Spirit" (Vladimir Lossky).[13] The Spirit pervades every aspect of the life of the Church; no aspect of the rich and varied life of the Eastern Orthodox Church exists whose sources are not in the Holy Tradition. So the Orthodox pray daily:

> Oh heavenly King, Oh Comforter, the Spirit of truth, everywhere present and filling all things, the treasury of blessings and giver of life, come and abide in us. Cleanse us from all impurity, and of your goodness save our souls.

The Tradition includes Scripture on account of its divine authority. Scripture is therefore binding upon every member, and every convert to the orthodox faith vows:

> I will and understand Holy Scripture in accordance with the interpretation which was and is held by the Holy Orthodox Catholic Church of the East, our Mother.

The uncorrupted teaching of Christ delivered to the apostles and transmitted to the Church from age to age is also part of the Holy Tradition.

Christ is the effulgence of divine glory perfect in every way, therefore

> Behind the veil of Christ's flesh, Christians behold the Triune God.

Belief in the Triune God is included within the Holy Tradition, as is also the Church's liturgy and sacraments, church government, the priesthood, the teaching of the Church Fathers, and every approved doctrine and practice of the Church.

But the Holy Tradition is not simply an accumulation of matters of past history nor is it regarded simply in a perfunctory way or recited in parrot-like fashion. The Holy Tradition is a vital creative force that permeates every authentic aspect of the Eastern Orthodox Church. Timothy Ware (Bishop Kallistos of Diakleia) quotes the saying of Georges Flovovsky about the Holy Tradition as a living reality.

> Tradition is the witness of the Spirit; the Spirit is unceasing revelation and preaching of good things . . . To accept and understand the Tradition we must live within the Church . . .
> Tradition is not only a protective conservative principle; it is primarily the principle of growth and regeneration.[14]

The Church of the Holy Tradition would not be an inappropriate shorthand description of the Eastern Orthodox Church. The Council of Chalcedon confirmed the four principal sees of the Church as Constantinople, Alexandria, Antioch and Jerusalem. The Patriarch of Constantinople was accorded the position of seniority as the first among equals. All who are in communion with the Church believe they also enter the universal and eternal realm of God.

The word "orthodox" means "correct", and the Orthodox Church has been entrusted with the "correct" faith to keep and practise under the guidance of the Holy Spirit. The term "eastern" refers to the Christian world when it was commensurate with that we today know as eastern Europe. The unity that cemented the Church of the east began to disintegrate as doctrinal discord erupted in the post-Chalcedon era. Division developed between Nestorian and Monophysite factions.

Nestorius (d. 451), a monk and controversial theologian, disputed that Christ was born of a woman and that Mary was the mother of God (*theotokos*). He saw in this view a confusion of Christ's divinity and humanity. Mary should be called *Christotokos* (she who received Christ) as she is the bearer of his humanity but not of his divinity. Nestorius questioned the decree of the Council of Ephesus (431) that Mary bore a person (Christ) as an indivisible divine–human being. For this Nestorius was condemned and accused of propounding an unwholesome interpretation of the person of Christ. It separated the person of Jesus into two and compromised the Christian message of salvation as the work of a divine redeemer. He said of Christ, "The essential characteristics in the nature of the divinity and in the humanity are from all eternity distinguished." In Christ there are two distinct natures, one human and one divine, as against the teaching of the Church that Christ was a divine person who became incarnate.

The Nestorians settled in the Middle East and withdrew from the Constantinople (Byzantine) Church and formed a separate communion which rejected the doctrine of *theotokos* and became known as the Church of the East.[15] It gained strength in eastern Syria, in Mesopotamia and Babylonia. The Orthodox, however, believed the Virgin Mary to be all pure and as reigning in heaven in close fellowship with her Son, Christ. Hymns and prayers are addressed to her. She bore the perfect divine–human being.

The Monophysites gave precedence to the divine not the human nature of Christ, but without denying altogether his genuine humanity. After he appeared in the world Christ bore only the single nature of God.

To their opponents it seemed that the Monophysites wanted to destroy the reality of the human Jesus. This may not be the case, but Monophysites certainly described Christ as a being of one nature. Nevertheless, they rejected the Chalcedonian formula. Eastern Orthodoxy was thrown into a state of crisis. The confusion that resulted aided the success of Islam in the seventh century.[16]

The Monophysites, unlike the Nestorians, remained as a dissident movement within the Byzantium Church. But they existed as non-Chalcedonian churches, and eventually formed the Coptic Ortho-dox Church. The Monophysite churches were the Syrian Orthodox Church, the Ethiopian Orthodox Church, the Syrian "Jacobite" Church, and the Orthodox Church of Armenia. The Monophysites in Syria suffered persecution and monks were forced to flee to the desert for safety. Justinian (483–565), the eastern emperor, in spite of his Chalcedonian sympathies, brought the persecution of Monophysites to an end. Justinian sought to accommodate the Monophysites and the Nestorians without offending Rome. The Monophysites included Christians of radical and conservative views who all contributed to the spread of Christianity. The Church as a whole, however, did not achieve the unity it coveted.

By the end of the sixth century the Patriarch of Constantinople was installed as the ecumenical patriarch. The Greek word "ecumenical" means "the management of the house", but it came to be used in the sense of "universal", as is generally the case today. In effect, this gave the Patriarch of Constantinople prominence over the other three ancient patriarchates. At the time, the other churches did not have the jurisdiction of either a patriarch or a bishop.

They were known as *autocephalous* churches. Reference has already been made to the four ancient sees, but the geographical spread of the *autocephalous* churches in Russia, Serbia, Rumania, Bulgaria, Georgia, Cyprus, Greece, Poland, and Albania became quite extensive. There is today a substantial number of Orthodox churches in western Europe and America, and these too are held together by a single organization and adherence to the Holy Tradition.[17] There is, therefore, a clear pattern of relationship between all branches of the Orthodox Church. They use their own native language and history and, in general, reflect the culture of the countries in which they operate. But the strong link is the common commitment to the Holy Tradition so that we can confidently speak of the "commonality" of Eastern Orthodox theology and spirituality. The Eastern Orthodox Church traces its origins to Christ and the apostles. The Apostle Paul, for example, established the Church in Greece (The Book of Acts 16–18), and he wrote letters to churches in the Greek cities of Corinth, Philippi, and Thessalonika. Peter is reported to have founded the Church of Antioch, and other churches were founded by the apostles in Jerusalem, Alexandria and Cyprus. The Orthodox churches of these places have survived from apostolic times, and as a result of missionary expansion the Church has spread to Russia and the other countries listed above. The Church is apostolic in respect of its doctrine and teaching; it is catholic or universal in its conception of Orthodox faith; it is orthodox in its adherence to the unchanged teaching of Christ; it is holy in its operation through the Holy Spirit; it is loyal to the formulae of the Council of Nicaea and to the other ecumenical councils; it is united through living the life of the early Church; it is authoritative through the observance of the Holy Tradition.

Teaching

Orthodox Church teaching has been transmitted in a number of ways, for example, through the enactments of the ecumenical councils and authoritative patriarchal pronouncements, the works of the Church Fathers, interpretations and expositions of the faith in sermons and treatises, the liturgy of worship, the Bible and the Holy Gospel, instruction and study in the home and Sunday School, and common law.[18] The forms and manner of transmitting the teaching vary but the centrepoint of belief – God, Jesus Christ and the Holy Spirit – has remained constant and unchanged. To a brief description of these terms of Orthodox Church theology we now turn.

God

The Orthodox Church is unyielding in its teaching that the essence of God is beyond the reaches of human understanding: neither words or image are wholly adequate to convey his essence; he transcends all that language and logic can comprehend. God is unseen, unperceived, and beyond imagination . . .

> That there is a God is clear; but what he is by essence and nature, this is altogether beyond our comprehension and knowledge.[19]

Belief in transcendence does not preclude intense yearning for communion with God. Nor does it quench the desire to search out the deep things of God. The means of cultivating communion with God are paramount in Orthodox spirituality. The premiss "that there is a God" or "that God exists" is not questioned; if God did not exist there would be no way of accounting for the spiritual yearning for communion with him; the experience of communion with God is the inner confirmation that "God is", and is also a foretaste of the essence of who God is. Orthodox theology of God holds together two seemingly contrasting ideas, namely, that God is unknowable and that communion with him is a spiritual reality. The Orthodox Church distinguishes the essence of God from the energies of God. God reveals himself uniquely to the world through his energies.[20] His energies are manifested as grace and light; these are not abstract qualities but living manifestations of his presence and power; through the action of the divine energies the way is prepared for the human being to commune with God. Grace and light belong together, and through them God communicates directly his gracious favour and his power. The experience of divine grace and light equals the consciousness of spiritual renewal. This experience also nurtures in the believer the character that mirrors the essence of God. The Greek word *theosis*, which appears frequently in works on Eastern Orthodoxy, conveys this fact. Its basic meaning is "deification", the underlying assumption being that as Christians share communion with God in a deeply meaningful and absorbing way they become perfectly one with God, that is, they achieve "deification". The Christian character then acquires the attributes of the divine character, the very essence of God himself.

The impact of the experience of the divine energies is demonstrated in obedience and commitment to the divine will. The ensuing "deification" generates a life of perfect subjection to the will and order of God. The energies are the self-motivated action of God in grace and redemption; they empower response on the part of the Orthodox Christian in a life of all-embracing spirituality in the Church and in the world. The response is all-consuming, it is neither bound by time or restricted to place or situation. The self-motivated revelation of divine energies culminates in the revelation of Jesus Christ, whose life and work signify that God "is not cut off from the world which He has made; God is personal, that is to say trinitarian; our God is an incarnate God".[21] The union between God and humanity is perfected through Christ; the results of this union are made incarnate in the subsequent life-style of the Christian.

The Orthodox Christian who experiences this union with God is freed henceforth from seeking vainly for what "is beyond human comprehension and knowledge", or speculating about the inner divine essence. Through the experience the believer is embraced by God and participates in the divine action. The energies of God are transmitted through the incarnation, crucifixion, resurrection and glorification of Christ, and their meaning and purpose discerned through the operation of the Holy Spirit. This function of the Holy Spirit is a present reality, and it also empowers the individual for living the life of the Spirit. The mystery of this operation is beyond pure intellect to comprehend yet it extends to every aspect of the Church's Holy Tradition. It is the heartbeat of the Church's liturgy, and the efficacy, efficiency and blessing of the sacraments. Through the experience divine and human spirituality cohere in harmony. The initiative of the all-consuming experience is with God through the transmission of his grace and light; the individual who receives the revelation responds in love and commitment. The response is to the Trinity – Father, Son and Holy Spirit – three persons of one essence (*homoousius*). Such response is realized through the communion of the Church and is carried into the life of the world.

Jesus Christ

The historical Jesus is the ultimate visible manifestation of the divine *energeia*. His incarnation is the supreme act of God's commitment to the world in love and redemption. A favourite image of this gracious event is that of God cradling the human person in the embrace of love. St. Maximus the Confessor (580–662), a hermit and a speculative theologian, gave pride of place in his extensive writings (he wrote around twenty major works) to the nature and impact of the incarnation of Jesus. Jesus entered the world, he said, as a complete person in whom the divine and human natures were perfectly combined. In a paper written in 1959, the Coptic theologian Abba Gregorios put the Coptic case:

> We people of the east are most fearful of using philosophical terms to define divine meanings. The non-Chalcedonian Orthodox Churches believe in the deity of the Christ as well as in his humanity. But the Christ is to us One Nature. This may seem contradictory. Whatever the rational contradictions may be our Church does not see any contradiction in her profession concerning the Nature of the Christ.
> There is always a mystical and spiritual solution that dissolves and overcomes all contradictions. Because of this mystical experience we do not always ask why and how.

Through his incarnation the Christ event became a supreme love-event, the perfect expression of the divine energy and grace made visible in a real person. Love, as the most perfect virtue, permeated the character, words and deeds of Jesus; this love is also the bond that binds the perfect (God) and the imperfect humanity in harmonious unity. The love act is perfected in the incarnation as a permanent reality; it never changes its character or diminishes its appeal. Through the liturgy of the Church this immortal love is extolled as the noblest of virtues and the motif of Christian redemption. Experience of this redemptive love makes for new life for the believer and makes the Church a new creation. The experience consummates human beings into the being of God (cf. the concept of deification) and visualizes the world as a new creation.

Orthodox theology does not distinguish the love of the incarnation from the work of redemption. Maximus the Confessor described how evil entered the world and how love acted to redeem it. When the human spirit rebelled against God it rejected the dominion of reason and went in search of pleasure. It thereby fell victim to ignorance, and needed to be liberated from its stranglehold. Ignorance needed to be overcome and replaced by reason and rebellion by virtue. In order to effect this transformation Jesus Christ acted in grace and light, empowering through grace the life of holiness and through light, reason and virtue.

According to Maximus, Christ's will and his works are one and inseparable, in the same way that the two natures of Christ are one and indivisible. Maximus developed a Christocentric theology which brought together faith and action, understanding and spirituality. He viewed life as a whole and did not differentiate between the spiritual and the secular. He taught that only a perfect God could redeem an imperfect world; only God could effect the perfect harmony of all that exists. Christian redemption means deliverance from evil, disunity and death, and this is achieved through the incarnation, death and resurrection of Jesus Christ. Redemption is the perfection of the love activated in the incarnation of Christ to restore humankind to harmony with God and a life of holiness.

Redemption is at the heart of orthodox theology. Christ is redeemer, and he not only redeems from sin but he also redeems the sinner for God. Sin abounds in the world and the human spirit yearns for liberation from its debilitating evil. This deliverance is accomplished by Christ the redeemer; the experience of Christian redemption through Christ also promotes the "deification" of the redeemed, a belief that is grounded in Scripture: "By which he has granted us his precious and very great promises, that through these you may escape from the corruption that is in the world because of passion, and become partakers of the divine nature" (2 Peter 1: 4).

Through redemption the redeemed embarks on a new life of union with Christ and of fellowship with the Holy Spirit. The old life is abandoned for the new life of holiness and "oneness" with God. The new life is also one of alliance with God's will for the world. The new life is lived in anticipation of the ultimate fulfilment of the divine purpose for the whole creation, not only as conceived of in past history or as expected in the future but as a present reality.

Holy Spirit

In the eighteenth century a prominent Russian monk and religious teacher, Seraphim of Sarov (1759–1833), spent many years as a hermit and then felt called to devote himself to counselling and offering spiritual guidance to those who needed it. This work he believed was inspired by the Holy Spirit, the source of all true spiritual guidance. Seraphim inspired one of his "spiritual children", Nicolas Motovilov, to investigate for himself how anyone could be sure of "being in the Spirit of God". He received his answer from Seraphim and then he wrote:

Then Father Seraphim took me very firmly by the shoulders and said: "My son, we are both at this moment in the Spirit of God. Why don't you look at me?"

"I cannot look, Father," I replied, "because your eyes are flashing like lightning. Your face has become brighter than the sun, and it hurts my eyes to look at you."

"Don't be afraid," he said. "At this very moment you yourself have become as bright as I am. You yourself are now in the fullness of the Spirit of God; otherwise you would not be able to see me as you do."

Then bending his head towards me, he whispered softly in my ear: "Thank the Lord God for His infinite goodness towards us ... But why, my son, do you not look me in the eyes? Just look, and don't be afraid; the Lord is with us."

After these words I glanced at his face, and there came over me an even greater reverent awe. Imagine in the centre of the sun, in the dazzling light of its midday rays, the face of a man talking to you. You see the movement of his lips and the changing expression of his eyes, you hear his voice, you feel someone holding your shoulders; yet you do not see his hands, you do not even see yourself or his body, but only a blinding light spreading far around for several yards and lighting up with its brilliance the snow-blanket which covers the forest glade and the snow-flakes which continue to fall unceasingly ...

"What do you feel?" Father Seraphim asked me.

"An immeasurable well-being," I said.

"But what sort of well-being? How exactly do you feel well?"

"I feel such a calm," I answered, "such peace in my soul that no words can express it."[22]

From this passage, Timothy Ware deduces how the conversation expresses the essential work of the Holy Spirit in sanctification, deification and union with God. In Christian theology sanctification literally means "to make" or "to be holy". It is the process of freeing a person from sin and eradicating its consequences through the action of the Holy Spirit. In Eastern Orthodox teaching sanctification means simply a course of moral development or the sublimation of unholy desires, but also the transfiguration of the whole person, soul and body. The whole person is filled with the Holy Spirit and enters into the light and grace of God himself. In other words, sanctification is akin to "deification" (*theosis*).

The ecumenical council, as we saw, is the seat of authority in the Eastern Orthodox Church. The decrees of the bishops agreed in council become authoritative for the whole church. The Holy Spirit guides into the whole truth, so that the decrees of the council, conceived under the guidance of the Holy Spirit, are deemed to be correct (orthodox) in all respects. The norms of Christian theology – God, Christ and the Holy

Spirit, three persons in perfect union – are also the sinews that bind together all facets of the varied life of the Church. Herein lies the source of its spiritual unity. The model, preservation and continuation of the unity is the interpersonal relationships of the persons of the Trinity, God, Christ and the Holy Spirit. The unity is the trinitarian gift which has been transmitted from apostolic time through episcopacy and priesthood and the diverse content of the Holy Tradition. The Eastern Orthodox Church is hierarchical in its government; the hierarchy is responsible for providing spiritual leadership and ensuring the unity of the Church's life, but lay members also have a full share in this unity.

Patterns of spirituality

This unity, at the heart of the Orthodox Church, is reflected visually and architecturally in the design and shape of the sanctuary, although this may vary from place to place. Among the common features of the eastern churches is the dome that covers the central space of the sanctuary. Looking up at the dome lifts the mind to God as the dome symbolizes the union of heaven and earth.

Across the width of the sanctuary is the *ikonostasis*, its most prominent piece of furnishing. This magnificent screen is covered with icons and pictures. In the centre of the *ikonostasis* is the holy door, and on either side are two smaller doors that are used during the liturgy. Behind the *ikonostasis* is the *hieron* (altar) or Holy Table where the eucharist is celebrated. Behind this is the seat of the patriarch or bishop, although he may also have a seat in the centre of the nave. Surmounting the *hieron* is a large cross with a painted figure of Christ, and on the altar there are many candles, along with the book of the gospels, and a hand cross used by the priest when he blesses the people. The centre of the sanctuary is the nave (*naos*) where there is a prominent icon, and the walls and pillars are also covered with icons.

An icon is literally a "picture writing". It might be a painting of the Virgin Mary or one of the saints, or of an angel, or it may be a visual representation of Christ. It is like a language; to understand it the icon has to be "read", and its images have to be interpreted in their literal and symbolic meaning. The icon is a two- or three-dimensional representation of a person or object. The image only points to one particular meaning and communicates this meaning directly to the worshipper. There are portrait icons of saints and icons which portray religious scenes or which express the meaning of Christian beliefs and practices.

They convey the inner meaning and significance of the vision shown. A controversy developed over the use of icons in 726 but this was resolved by the second Council of Nicaea in 787, which decreed that it was theologically acceptable to portray Christ and the saints in visual forms. The conflict did not end there but continued until 843 when the Empress Theodora decreed in favour of icons. On the first Sunday in Lent 843 the Patriarch Methodius (815–885) celebrated the festival of the icons. Ever since, this has been commemorated in the Church as the Feast of Orthodoxy or the Triumph of Orthodoxy.

Icons are venerated in worship in the belief that God may be worshipped through images in paint and wood as well as through words. In churches in the Byzantine tradition incense is offered to icons and candles are lit before them, they are carried in procession and are used during liturgical prayer. Thus the icon has a spiritual and theological significance; it has sacramental value as it brings the worshipper face to face with the vision portrayed, that is, with Christ or one of the saints. By virtue of this the worshipper stands on "holy ground" and is sanctified and receives grace transmitted through contact with the icon. Throughout the Eastern Orthodox Church the icon is a focus of veneration and devotion. Eastern Orthodox spirituality is maintained through the devotion and vision which the icon imparts of the eternal spiritual world. Traditionally there have been no seats or chairs in these churches, although there might be benches along the walls. But this varies. The shape of the orthodox church is designed to express the deep unfathomable sense of mystery and of the sacred; entering the sanctuary the worshipper is transported into an atmosphere of "heaven on earth".

The liturgy

Clergy and laity share fully in the liturgy of the Church. Liturgy in this context signifies the manifold aspects of the Church at worship. The whole spiritual life of the Church is gathered around the beauty of the liturgy. The main gathering for worship is on the Lord's day (Sunday), but there are other services of worship, especially with the monks singing the offices every day.

The liturgy of the Eastern Orthodox Church is noted for its beauty and richness, its fixed hymns and litanies, and its joyfulness. The liturgy embraces heaven and earth so that the worshippers are elevated in spirit to the heavenly places. The worship of the Orthodox Church is fully communal and is drenched in a spirit of joy that is expressive of the wonder, triumph and glory of the resurrection of Jesus Christ. The spirit of Orthodox worship is the joyful reality of the presence of Christ resurrected and alive. All the worshippers take part in the whole of the worship and expect to give themselves wholly to it. They share in the movements of the liturgy, namely, vision (viewing the icons and the priestly symbolic vestments), scent (the smell of incense), hearing (listening to the Holy Gospel and music), taste (sharing the holy communion), touch (kissing the icons, lighting candles, anointing with oil). Each movement affirms the divine presence of the resurrected Christ, as the priest declares, "Christ is with us." After sharing the kiss of peace the priest's assistant responds "He is with us and will be with us." The rite of the eucharist is the central part of the worship; this is the divine liturgy. The eucharist is a focus of unity between the worshippers and between heaven and earth; it is expressive of the love that unites the life on earth with the life of heaven, "just as it unites individuals in their earthly life".[23] The Eastern Orthodox Church believes that the bread and wine of the eucharist are transformed into the body and blood of Christ. The true body and blood of Christ are received as the means of communion with God.

As the liturgy begins, the priest and the deacon perform the "office of preparation" privately, then the congregation share in a service of hymns, prayers and readings from Scripture, and then the eucharist itself. The Book of the Gospel is carried in procession through the congregation, and the bread and wine are carried to the altar through the Holy Door of the *ikonostasis*. At the moment of consecration of the bread and wine the *epiclesis* of the Holy Spirit is said:

> Send down your Holy Spirit upon us and upon these gifts here set forth,
> And make this bread the Precious Body of Your Christ,
> And what is in this cup, the Precious Blood of Your Christ,
> Changing them by Your Holy Spirit. Amen, Amen, Amen.

This is from the liturgy of St. John Chrysostom (347–407), a famous preacher known for his love of the Scriptures. Two forms of liturgy are used in Orthodox churches, that of St. Chrysostom and that of St. Basil. The one is used for most of the year and the other in Lent or on the eve of festivals. The liturgy is always sung and never said, and this is by a choir or can be without accompaniment. Few hymns have survived from early times but the vesper in use in the time of Basil is still used, and John Keble's translation is available in English:

> Hail gladdening light, of his pure glory poured

> Who is the Immortal Father, heavenly blessed,
> Holiest of Holies, Jesus Christ Our Lord.

At the moment of consecration the bread and wine become really the body and blood of Christ, but the manner of this change is a great mystery. It can never be fully comprehended. At the eucharist it is Christ himself who is offered, the bread and wine are taken up into Christ's body and blood. It is Christ also who performs the act of offering; he is the *offered* and the *offering*. But the offering is made to the Trinity, that is, to Christ together with the Father and the Spirit. The offering is made on behalf of the living and the dead.[24] The Eastern Orthodox Church has a profound sense of the communion of saints and a deep sense of relationship with the departed and the saints of past ages. Symeon (949–1022), the New Theologian, wrote of the saints as forming a golden chain:

> The Holy Trinity, pervading everyone from first to last, from head to foot, binds them all together . . . The saints in each generation joined to those who have gone before, are filled like them with light, become a golden chain, in which each saint is a separate link . . . So in one God they form a single chain which cannot quickly be broken.

Symeon insisted on the primacy of experience which is as a fountain of light springing up within the heart or which is the glow of the uncreated and eternal light of God himself. Through the direct conscious experience the individual knows what it means to be "in heaven". The commemoration of the eucharist brings back the event it recalls and makes it a living reality.

Baptism

The first sacrament in time is baptism, although in the Eastern Orthodox Church this is closely linked with the eucharist and the other sacraments. The theology of baptism does not differ in intention from that of the eucharist, it ministers to the initiation and the deepening of the unity of the baptized with God and the community of the Church. The performance of the rite, however, has certain distinct features, as can be seen from the Byzantium rite. Baptism is by immersion three times. The formula used is highly personalized, it reads "The servant of God A. is baptized in the Name of the Father, Amen, and of the Son, Amen, and of the Holy Spirit, Amen." The person to be baptized may wear a baptismal dress, and once baptized is permitted to share in the full privileges of the Church. Infants are confirmed by being immersed in the water of the font. This is followed by *chrismation*, anointing with oil, as a rite of confirmation, and the words, "The seal of the gift of the Holy Spirit" are spoken. Immersion signifies the symbolic entry of the baptized into the waters and then being raised out of them as a "new" person. The descent signifies the cleansing from sin and the rising "putting on Christ" as the sign of new life with him. In the Orthodox Church only an ordained person is permitted to administer baptism. Immediately afterwards the child who is confirmed and anointed is then admitted to the eucharist.

Baptism is an essential rite of the sacramental life of the Eastern Church. It marks the entry of the baptized into membership of the Church and the acceptance of forgiveness and spiritual renewal. The rite is integral to the belief pattern of the Orthodox, it has deep religious meaning and spiritual power. It is associated with the death of Christ who died and was raised, it symbolizes being buried to sin and raised to newness of life. The Spirit activates this raising to new life, and the expression "in Christ" is used to signify how it incorporates the believer in Christ in a very real way; this being so, baptism is only undertaken once. The Christian is then made one with Christ (cf. deification).

And being raised to new life the person is sanctified by grace to become a member of the Church, the body of Christ. The baptized also receives the *"charisms"* (gifts) of the Spirit that serve to invigorate the spiritual vitality and the life of the Church. The gifts of the Spirit are a living sign of the sacramental life to which the baptized is committed.

Confession

The Eastern Orthodox Church observes seven sacraments; in addition to the dominical sacraments of baptism, chrismation and eucharist, they observe the sacraments of repentance, ordination, marriage and anointing the sick. Repentance or confession is made normally four times a year, but this may vary, and, as in the case of the Greek and Russian Orthodox churches, confession is required before communion, but again the practice varies. This means that the reception of the eucharist cannot be more frequent than the number of confessions made. Children of seven years of age must go to confession before receiving communion, and it is only the priest who hears confession.

Normally the person kneels before the priest or stands before the *iconostasis*, prayers are said, the priest asks questions, and at the end he pronounces absolution. This amounts to a "second baptism" and the beginning of a sin-forgiven life. As God alone can forgive sins the priest only acts the part of a witness, "bearing testimony before Him (the Lord Jesus Christ) of all the things which you have to say to me". In the Greek Orthodox Church the prayer of absolution is:

> Whatever you have said to my humble person, and whatever you have failed to say, whether through ignorance or forgetfulness, whatever it may be, may God forgive you in this world and the next . . . Have no further anxiety; go in peace.

Ordination

The sacrament of ordination relates to the threefold ministry of the Church, namely, bishop, priest and deacon. Ordination takes place in the presence of the congregation during the liturgy. Each candidate is ordained individually and, before this, receives instruction from a spiritual guide. The congregation signify approval of the ordination when they cry *axios* (= worthy). The ordination then proceeds. The priest conducts the ceremony by the laying on of hands, but in the case of the consecration of a bishop, two or three bishops are expected to officiate. Some ordained priests are celibate and live a monastic existence, whilst others are married. They are known respectively as "black" or "white" priests

After ordination marriage is disallowed. A bishop is usually appointed by the synod of each *autocephalous* church or in some instances, in Russia for example, a bishop is appointed by the clergy and laity of the diocese. The deacon holds a much respected office in the Church whose function is to share in the celebration of the liturgy. The deacon usually takes part in singing the litanies and identifying himself with the congregation. Up until the eleventh century an order of women deacons was recognized, but it has not been revived since then.

Marriage

Marriage in the Eastern Orthodox Church is also known as the sacrament of "crowning". Concurrence in the divine institution of marriage means that the Church accepts it as a sacrament and administers and blesses the marriage union. In the marriage ceremony the bride and groom repeat the words, "The servant of God A. is crowned unto the handmaid of God B. In the name of the Father and of the Son and of the Holy Spirit." Marriage is then pronounced to be a *charisma* (gift) of the Holy Spirit. The marriage ceremony includes the receiving and blessing of rings, as a token of the couple's willing consent to the union. Then follows the ceremony of coronation, when crowns are placed on the heads of the couple as a mark of special grace and a symbol of joy. A cup of wine is given to the bride and bridegroom in memory of the wedding in Cana of Galilee (The Gospel of John 2), and is shared between them as a symbol of their new life together. Marriage is regarded as a life-long commitment, although divorce may be obtained from a bishop's office; but when a person marries for the second time the joyful elements of the ceremony are omitted. Common Law allows only a second or third marriage but no more.[25] Only if the Church has granted the divorce is remarriage in church permitted. Sexual intercourse outside marriage is frowned upon and homosexuality is disallowed.

Opinion is divided over the use of contraception, some more liberal theologians give approval of its responsible use. Abortion is condemned outright.

Holy Unction

The last of the seven sacraments is anointing the sick, or Holy Unction. This sacrament is based on the custom mentioned in the New Testament, Epistle of James 5: 14–15. The sacrament holds together, as one, the forgiveness of sins and the healing of the sick. We observe once more the characteristic emphasis of Eastern Orthodox Christianity on the indivisibility of body and soul, the material and the spiritual. The anointing is for the healing of the *whole* person. The anointings, there are usually seven, are made on the brow, nostrils, cheeks, lips, breast, and on both sides of the hands. Each anointing is accompanied with the prayer, "Heal thy servant A . . . from the ills of body and soul." There is no magic in the act of anointing and there are times when the sick do not recover, in which case the anointing serves as a preparation for death. The words of Sergius Bulgakov express succinctly this view, "This sacrament has two faces: one turns towards healing, the other towards the liberation from illness by death."[26]

Spiritual guides

A characteristic feature of Eastern Orthodoxy is the service and status of the spiritual guide or the elder. This is a person of known spiritual attributes and wisdom who is able to offer guidance or advice to others.

The guide may be a priest or monk, a man or woman of special gifts, or a person without special position or unordained. They believe themselves to be called by the Holy Spirit to be spiritual mentors to others and to offer them guidance along the road of their spiritual pilgrimage. They serve as spiritual counsellors or educators and are ready to be consulted on all spiritual matters. Such persons are highly respected on account of their *charisma* and spiritual maturity. Such a person in Greece is known as *gerôn* and in Russia as *starets*. They are mainly persons of a mystical disposition and their theology reflects this. They are dedicated to the principle of *hesychasm*, that is, the nurturing and achieving of perfect union with God.[27] The spiritual guide is heir to a tradition that can be traced back to the time of Antony and the Desert Fathers. The ascetic Nilus in the fifth century said of the method of the spiritual guides:

> But what if someone, not from any choice of his own, is obliged to accept one or two disciples, and so become the spiritual director of others as well? First, let him examine himself carefully, to see whether he can teach him through his actions rather than his words, setting his own life before him . . . He should also realize that he ought to work as hard for his disciples' salvation as he does for his own; for, having once accepted responsibility for them, he will be accountable to God for them as well as himself.
>
> That is why the saints tried to leave behind disciples whose holiness was no less than their own, and to change these disciples from their original condition to a better state.

The word ascetic (*askesis*) means exercise undertaken for a particular purpose, what today might be called training, but it is significant that Nilus should have urged the "trainers" to examine themselves as to their fitness to be an example to others and to work as hard for their salvation as for their own. The ideal aim of the guide is "to change these disciples from their original condition for a better state". The value to anyone of having such a guide is set out in the work called *Unseen Warfare*:

> A man who follows their guidance and verifies all his actions, both inner and outer, by the good judgement of his teachers – priests in the case of laymen, experienced *startzi* in monasteries – cannot be approached by the enemy.[28]

In the early centuries the Church produced many eminent spiritual leaders, including Cyril of Alexandria (d. 444), Severus of Antioch

(d. 538), Paul of Somosata (3rd century), John Chrysostom (347–407), Theodore of Mopsuestia (380–428).[29] Many writings from these early centuries are only known to us in fragments and we can only here refer to a selected few of the notable spiritual guides. Among these is John of Damascus (675–749) whose guidance in the use of icons in the Church's liturgy was notably effective. John was devoted to the use of icons in devotion and he wrote of their efficacy:

> "What the written word is to those who know letters", he taught, "the icon is to the unlettered; what speech is to the ear, the icon is to the eye."

He wrote a work called *On the Orthodox Faith* and compiled an anthology of doctrinal statements relating to the incarnation of Jesus Christ and the Trinity. He has been described as one of the first of the schoolmen,[30] but he rebuked those iconoclasts whose religion was only steeped in intellectualism. He taught the sanctity of matter as the creation of God and the inherent spirituality of the material world as God's gift. Therefore he maintained material objects and human skills can be used for the glory of God; God created a material world and every material object (e.g. an icon) is a divinely created act. John of Damascus also made a stand against certain claims made by Muslims once they began to spread the Islamic faith after the death of the prophet Muhammad (570–632).

John opposed their claim to have descended from Abraham and was highly critical of the Muslim use of the Bible, both the Old and New Testaments. He tended to dismiss Muhammad as a false prophet and Islam as a pseudo-faith. He dismissed the Muslim claim of descent from Abraham and called them "the bastard descendants of the slave girl Hagar". In his theology John of Damascus assumed the mantle of the orthodoxy of eastern Christianity. His prime work is called *The Fountain of Knowledge,* which offers a systematic theology of the Church of the east in a clear and logical way. He taught that God is infinite and incomprehensible, and therefore cannot be compared with anything that exists because he is beyond existence.

He adhered closely to the notion of Holy Tradition, that has been previously described. He insisted that the Tradition should be received as transmitted and not altered: "We do not change the everlasting boundaries which our fathers have set, but we keep the Tradition just as we have received it." This included the death of Christ as a sacrifice to God, and the eucharist as the body and blood of Christ transformed by the Holy Spirit. His words on the use of material objects used apply-particularly to the elements of bread and wine in the eucharist:

My salvation was brought to me by material means, and I venerate the word of the blessed cross, not as though it were God, but as being full of the work and of the grace of God. The hill Calvary, the tomb, the stone, the very source of the Resurrection – all are material; the ink and the prayers of the Gospels, the table from which we take of our salvation and all its furniture, the very body and blood of our Lord – are all material. You must either forbid all respect to these images consecrated to the name of Christ and to his friends, the saints, as being overshadowed by the force of the Holy Spirit . . .

John of Damascus is the author of two Easter hymns that are still sung in English translation:

> Come, ye faithful, raise the strain
> Of triumphant gladness . . . .
>   (English Hymnal 131)

and

> The day of resurrection,
> Earth fell it all abroad . . .
>   (English Hymnal 137)

Reference to the mystical theology of John of Damascus should also take note of the wider appeal of mysticism after the seventh ecumenical council in 787. A prominent theologian of this tendency is Symeon the New Theologian who, as we have indicated, wrote sensitively of his mystical experiences and of the consuming fire of divine love that he felt burnt within him. This awareness of the uncreated light he described as similar to the experience of the disciples of Jesus on the Mount of Transfiguration when his garments became glistening in the celestial light (The Gospel of Mark 9). Symeon described this light as spiritual and eternal, the very light of God himself, the flame of joy, grace and peace. This he expressed in his poetry as light that filled his whole being yet without annihilating his own personhood:

O power of the divine fire, O strange energy,
you who dwell, Christ my God, in light wholly unapproachable,
How in your essence totally divine do you mingle yourself with grass?[31]

This mystical experience led Symeon to view the true Church as other than an institutional organization, yet he did not deny that the Holy Spirit operated throughout the Church as a whole. His whole life was Spirit-controlled, and this consciousness dominated his ecclesiology and his cosmology. Every Christian has the capacity to share consciously in the experience of the all-pervading Spirit:

> Do not say, it is impossible to receive the Holy Spirit;
> Do not say, It is possible to be saved without him;
> Do not say that you can possess him without knowing it.[32]

The Spirit is the factor that unites the saints of the past and present in an unseverable bond of union. This he described as "forming a golden chain".[33]

In this brief examination of the contribution of spiritual guides within the Eastern Orthodox Church, whose aim was to help others to a better state, we should include the missionary labours of Cyril (826–69) and Methodius (815–85), known as the pioneers of the Slav mission. Cyril (previously known as Constantine), a monk and teacher of philosophy, and Methodius, a provincial governor, both natives of Thessalonika, were sent by the Byzantine emperor Michael II on a mission to the Slav people. They were both conversant with the Slav language but hitherto the attempt to compose a Slav alphabet had proved abortive. Cyril and Methodius were commissioned to translate the Christian gospels into Slavonic. This was achieved, and in addition they made a translation of "the whole ecclesiastical office, matins, the vows, vespers, compline and the mass". This translation opened up a new world of theology and spirituality for the Slav people, and eventually their language became the third international language of Europe. It spread rapidly, but Methodius fell victim to persecution, which led him to make a complete break with Rome and convert to the Greek Orthodox Church. In theology Methodius followed the original Chalcedonian formula. The attempt to found a national Slav Church in Moravia did not succeed; even so, the work of Cyril and Methodius spread to Bulgaria, Serbia and Russia. They prepared the way for the Christian faith to be heard and understood in the language of the people and this proved to be a powerful weapon in the cultivation of a wholesome spirituality as well as the spread of Christianity.[34]

The reference to Methodius' identity with the Greek Orthodox Church opens the way to considering other examples of spiritual guides and the patterns of spiritual nurture employed in the Greek Orthodox Church. As the name suggests, the Greek Church has been distinguished from the beginning from the Latin Church of the west in language and culture. Its approach to Christianity has from the commencement been theological, but without ever losing its vision of the all-inclusiveness of the faith. Its liturgy is notably rich and elaborate, with iconography and colourful ritual at its centre. The characteristic trends of Eastern Orthodox monasticism, asceticism and mysticism are also representative of Greek Orthodoxy throughout.

By adhering to the most ancient traditions of Christianity, as expressed by the apostles, the Greek Church Fathers, canonical law, liturgy and spirituality, the Greek Church claims to stand in continuous succession from the days of the apostles. It has also maintained close association with Greek culture throughout the centuries and is still active in national affairs.

Since 961 when St. Athanasius of Althon settled on Mount Athos on a small peninsula in north-east Greece, high above the Aegean Sea, the monastic centre on this spot has grown to be one of the most outstanding and influential centres of monasticism in the east. It has a distinct international flavour, for there are nineteen monastic institutions on the mount. They exist as a monastic republic governed by monks. The oldest is the Simonopetra Monastery founded in the fourteenth century, four centuries after Athanasius settled there. The monasteries have many priceless relics and a large library; among the most precious possessions are fragments reported to be of the cross of Jesus, a cloth dropped by the Virgin Mary at Calvary, and parts of the crown of thorns worn by Jesus. Here monks spend their lives in communion with God, but women are not allowed to visit Mount Athos. Meals are simple and the monks are sworn to chastity, obedience and poverty. They spend much time in private meditation and communal prayer. The method of prayer used is *hesychasm*, equivalent in meaning to the word quietism, or the prayer of the heart. They work and support themselves but their life is very simple and austere. There are strict observances of the Christian festivals. Timothy Ware has conveyed the criterion for discerning the influence of the monastic settlement on Mount Athos as the quality of the spiritual life, high standards within the monasteries, continuing vitality of the spirituality, the nurturing of saints, asceticism and prayer; the current resurgence of the monasticism of Mount Athos he attributes in part to the personal guidance of a spiritual father.[35]

The nurture and enrichment of spirituality through colourful festivals and celebrations is a feature of the Greek Orthodox Church, in the way that the celebration of key events in the liturgical calendar is common to churches everywhere. In the Greek Orthodox tradition the festivals celebrate the central events of the Christian faith, the incarnation, death and resurrection of Christ, and focus on their inner meaning and message. The forms of celebration vary but there runs through every celebration a thread of joyful participation in the existential experience of entering the rhythm of the Church's year. There is some local diversity in the celebration, but the joy and spiritual elation, the purpose and expectation are constant, whether the celebration is Epiphany, Good Friday or Easter, three main festivals; the preparation invokes the action of the Holy Spirit whose presence constitutes and consecrates the celebration. Every religious celebration is a time of reliving the events celebrated, that is, heightening the awareness of the eternal merits of those supreme moments in history of God's intervention for the sake of human redemption. The celebration enhances experience of the continuing flow of the divine energies and the drawing power of the Holy Spirit to whatever is of eternal significance. Every festival is a community occasion, the sharing of joy, remembrance, hope and vision. The celebration imparts a vision of the truth the festival enshrines; the appearance of Christ at the Epiphany, the message of the crucifixion of Jesus on Good Friday, the hope beyond the here and now at Easter. Such celebration shapes the life of the Church and for the Christian it is a time of reliving the events, absorbing their significance, deepening memories of God's intervention, realizing the origins and call of faith. All festivals are celebrated consciously in the presence of God, and are times for renewing commitment and spiritual devotion.

The liturgical calendar begins on 1 September and includes fixed and variable festivals. To take one example, Easter, the earliest Christian festival to be celebrated in the Orthodox Church, continues to follow the Nicene rule that it should be celebrated after the Jewish Passover.[36] One of the older customs in the celebration of Easter includes a procession to honour the dead and celebrate the resurrection of Christ, carrying icons from the main Orthodox church to the cemetery where prayers are said over each grave; the icons are then carried to small private chapels in the fields where further prayers are offered. The Easter festival is joyful and emotional, and special preparations are made for the celebration. After grieving for the departed on Good Friday, the solemn mood changes on the Saturday night. All the lights in the church are put out to symbolize the darkness of the world. At midnight the priest steps from the Royal Door bearing a huge lighted candle, and chants, "Come forth and receive light from the unwaning light and glorify Christ who has risen from the dead." Members of the church then move towards the priest's candle to light a candle of their own, and then they carry the "holy" light to their own homes. The sermon preached by Leo the Great (Pope Leo I, who was Pope from 440 until his death in 461) expounded the key beliefs of the Church on the resurrection of Christ. These were common to the whole church of the time and are still today the fundamental truths of the resurrection believed amongst all the main churches. Leo's sermon, delivered on Holy Saturday in the vigil of Easter, was on the theme "Partakers in Christ's resurrection life", and it centres around these salient points:

> We must all be partakers of Christ's resurrection life . . . the life of believers contains in itself the mystery of Easter . . . we must die therefore to the devil and live to God . . . God did not leave His soul in hell . . . The Saviour's resurrection did not long keep His soul in Hades, nor His flesh in the tomb . . . Christ's manifestation after the Resurrection showed that His person was essentially the same as before . . . Being saved by hope we must not fulfil the lusts of the flesh . . . our godly resolutions must continue all the year around, not be confined to Easter only . . . These thoughts, dearly beloved, must be kept in mind not only for the Easter festival, but also for the sanctification of the whole of life . . . [37]

In the twentieth century in the Greek Orthodox Church a pioneering movement called *Zoe* (life) has breathed new vitality into its spirituality, missionary, educational and social work. *Zoe* is a non-monastic movement, a brotherhood of theologians who have undertaken vows to renew the spiritual life of their church. The members must be unmarried and hold property in common, as was the case in the communal movement of the first apostles (The Book of Acts 2). The vows are not life binding, but members undertake missionary work throughout Greece under the supervision of the bishops. They are engaged in preaching, teaching and training as spiritual guides, and hearing confessions. They associate with other organizations who share their wish to see the spiritual renewal of the Greek Orthodox Church and the Greek nation. Whilst the Brotherhood is supervised and used by bishops it is not directly under hierarchic control but rather is governed by its own officers. However, priests as well as laymen are members of the movement. A special emphasis is placed on the spiritual training of children and youth. *Zoe* also actively promotes study of the Bible.

In recent years the Zoe movement has lost much of its impetus, but its vision is still shared by many earnest members of the Greek Church who are committed to its ideals.

The Greek Orthodox Church lays claim to its own roll of honour of saints and spiritual guides some of whom are among the most eminent exponents of this tradition. One who merits mention is Kosmas Aitolos (1714–74), a priest and monk, a popular preacher and educator. He entered the monastery on Mount Athos where he was prepared for the priesthood and ordained. He was called to undertake an itinerary mission of preaching which proved to be popular and productive. He spoke the language of the people and gained respect as an effective communicator, and a reputation for his sanctity. He travelled to remote villages and collected many followers. He disregarded material wealth and possessions, concentrating instead on a life of selfless service. The core of his preaching was love and justice, and equality between all people. He believed passionately that the laity should be educated and was responsible for funding many elementary and secondary schools for the education of children. He became known as the "teacher of the nation". He succeeded in effecting changes in the moral behaviour of the nation and is said to have raised its moral and ethical standards.[38]

Others of the saints and spiritual guides of the Greek Orthodox Church who merit a brief mention include the Abbot of the monastery of Dionysiou, Father Gabriel (1886–1983); and Archimandrite Sophrony (1896–1993) who edited the poetic theological meditations of St. Silouan of the Russian monastery of St. Panteleimon; Father Joseph (d. 1959) who gathered together a group of disciples dedicated to "mental" and "inner" prayer, which signified particularly the Jesus prayer; St. Nektarios (1846–1920), founder of the monastery of the Holy Trinity on Aegina where he served as chaplain and became known for his humility and life of great poverty; and St. Nicholas Planas (1851–1932) who empathized very much with the poor and was greatly loved and devoted to all-night vigil services. All these contributed in one way or another to the culture of spirituality and the monastic ethos of the Church. Each in his own way demonstrated exemplary devotion and faithfulness in the pursuit of the spiritual quest which served to invigorate the life of the Church.

There are now in the Russian Orthodox Church patriarchs of Moscow and of all Russia. This is today numerically the largest of the Orthodox churches. The first centre of the Russian Church was Kiev and then Moscow. The founding of the Russian Orthodox Church was the indirect consequence of the Slav mission referred to above. The Patriarch Photius sent a mission to Russia in the mid-ninth century, but Christianity only took firm root in the country in 988 with the baptism of Vladimir (956–1015), the prince and ruler of Kiev. At first the Russian Church was under the jurisdiction of Constantinople, but it gained its independence in 1448 and in 1589 it became a patriarchate. Following the advent of Christianity to Russia the tone of society generally underwent a change. A new spirit of tolerance, compassion and humility spread, and a willingness to witness openly to the new faith. In this, monasteries played a part as the radial points of the new spiritual and social ethos.

After the Turks possessed Constantinople in 1453 the leadership of the Eastern Orthodox Church passed to Russia, and the Tsar of Russia was said by the monk Philotheus in 1510 to be "on earth the sole Emperor of the Christians, the leader of the Apostolic Church which stands . . . in the blessed city of Moscow". In the early seventeenth century the Church experienced a spiritual revival, the deepening of devotion to the ordinances of the Church, and improvement in the moral tone of the clergy and laity. But also during the seventeenth century the intrusive policy of the Patriarch Nikon created disputes between the conservative and progressive factions in the Church. The patriarch himself had political ambitions. These were not realized, but they brought about the subordination of the Church to the state, and in 1721 Peter the Great replaced the patriarchate by the Holy Synod or Spiritual College, with himself as the Supreme Judge. This remained the situation for the following two centuries. Still the Church played a part as a reforming catalyst in the state as well as the custodian of tradition. It also produced some notable spiritual leaders. Russia regained her patriarchate in 1917, but the following years were exceedingly stressful for the Church. A decree of the communists in 1918 deprived the Church of its freedom to propagate its faith, yet some church leaders sought an accommodation with the communist regime. After the upheaval, the communist stranglehold was lifted in the 1980s and in 1988 the Church celebrated the first millennium of the Russian Orthodox Church and the conversion of Prince Vladimir to Christianity. A recent estimate of the position of the Church in Russia today concludes:

> In the USSR itself the national church has made an accommodation with the state, by which it effectively forfeits any political role in order to preserve as far as possible intact its devotional life and its institutional existence . . . churches are looked to as providing the inspiration for a more open society.[39]

That the Russian Orthodox Church survived the traumatic years of oppression and anti-religious propaganda is in no small part due to its deep reservoir of spirituality and its patriotic stance. Certain theological developments may be recorded, one example of which is the Solovetsk Document, a memorandum by the bishops in 1927 which in part defined their view of the Church and its function. Here are some selected excerpts:

The Church recognizes the existence of the spiritual principle . . . believes in the living God, Creator of the world, Guider of its life and fate . . . The Church sees the aim of a man's life in the heavenly calling of the spirit . . . The Church believes in the steadfast principles of morality, justice and law . . . The Church instils the feeling of that humility which elevates man's soul . . . Our Lord Jesus Christ has ordered us to give unto Caesar what belongs to Caesar . . . He left no commandments to His followers to seek to alter the forms of government or to guide its activity . . . [40]

Here we can only refer to a few representatives of the spiritual guides and saints of the Russian Orthodox Church who have made significant contributions to its spirituality. One of the most notable is St. Seraphim of Sarov who we met earlier in connection with his emphasis on the work of the Holy Spirit.

He entered the monastery of Sarov and lived there for sixteen years. Afterwards he withdrew to live in the forest as a recluse and later in a cell in the monastery. He equipped himself for the office of eldership so as to be able to help everyone who came seeking guidance and advice, especially the sick and people needing succour. Such was his skill that hundreds came seeking his guidance, and in the history of Russian Orthodoxy he is still venerated as a saint who faithfully adhered to the tradition of the early monks and acted faithfully upon it. Under his influence the monasteries increased greatly. He expounded the core of Russian Orthodox spirituality as a life of contemplation and mystical devotion, and espoused the concept of *sobornost* (catholicity) in dealing with all who came to him for counselling.

Another Russian Orthodox monastic saint is Joseph of Volokalamsk (1439–1515), an abbot of the monastery of Borovsk. He was dedicated to the monastic life and toured Russian monasteries in search of the most congenial models of monastic community life. Eventually in 1479 he established a new monastery at Volokalamsk. His theology was trinitarian and he took up the cudgels against the Judaizers who opposed this. His opposition went to extremes and he urged the state to eliminate all heretics. He wrote a work called *The Enlightener* which is anti-heretical in tone. Not even if they repented should heretics be spared. Joseph helped to shape Russian monastic discipline so as to ensure it practised strict piety and sobriety and performed the liturgy regularly. Members of the monastery were committed to living a life of poverty, but they were also expected to serve the community at large, especially in times of sickness, distress or famine. The monastery Joseph founded maintained an orphanage for fifty children. He believed monasteries should own land and practise Christian philanthropy, he led a party known as the Possessors, but he was critical of those who lived only an extreme ascetic life.[41]

Tikhon of Zadonsk (1724–83) is a notable Russian Orthodox bishop and saint. He was raised in poverty but entered a monastery and was ordained to the priesthood in 1758. He became Bishop of Novgorod and finally settled at Zadonsk. He was canonized in 1860. Tikhon was disenchanted with the ecclesiastical and political life in Russia, so he devoted himself to a life of continual prayer and reading the Bible, especially the gospels, psalms and prophets. He studied the works of the Church Fathers and the earlier saints of the Orthodox Church, especially St. John Chrysostom, whom we met earlier in connection with the Orthodox liturgy. Tikhon wrote *A Spiritual Treasure Collected from the World* and *On True Christianity*. The former work reflected his interest in western literature. He was devoted to pastoral care and to the regular observance of the sacraments and liturgy of the Church. Tikhon only celebrated the sacraments and liturgy in his rank as bishop at the festivals of Christmas and Easter. He mixed easily with the poor, peasants and beggars, and he himself lived a simple and modest life. He was a man of melancholy spirit who lamented the unspiritual state of the Church and the world. He spent much time interceding with God for the Church and praying for mercy and forgiveness. As well as reading western literature Tikhon used western pictures which portrayed the person of Christ as aids to devotion. His teaching made an impact especially upon intellectuals, including the novelist Dostoevsky.[42]

Tikhon (1865–1925), Patriarch and Metropolitan of Moscow, projected a vision of the Orthodox churches of the different nations of the east forming a single church, initially centred on the Russian Orthodox Church, but then moving towards a state of each being *autocephalous*. At one stage in his patriarchate he stood firmly against Christians who collaborated with the communists after the 1917 revolution, but he also denounced persecution of the Church as the work of Satan. In a pastoral letter of January 1918 he wrote of those who persecuted the Church: "By authority given us by God, we forbid you to approach the holiness of Christ, we excommunicate you if you still bear the name of Christian, and in accordance with your birth belong to the Orthodox Church. We exhort you all true believers in the Christian Orthodox Church not to enter into communication with such outcasts of the human race." He called loyal members of the Church "true sons of the Church" and "beloved children of the

Church", and in instructions issued to the Church Tikhon and the synod urged Christians to exert extraordinary care and unusual efforts in carrying on the requisite spiritual work, to guard and protect the Holy Church, to defend all the sacred things, to maintain educational and charitable work, and to report to the Church authorities any interference with the work of priests or members of the Church.[43] Tikhon's appeal was not heeded and some Christians formed themselves into the "Living Church" in opposition to the Orthodox Church's appeal to traditional canonical authority. Tikhon saw this as a threat, but he himself compromised with the state after the dreadful famine of 1921. Tikhon was arrested and a Supreme Church Administration (*sobor*) was established that declared that all attempts to use the Church for temporal political schemes must cease, for "the Church belongs to God and must serve Him only". At the second *sobor* in 1923 the Patriarch Tikhon was defrocked, but the case against him was suddenly dropped, and he lived out the rest of his life in the seclusion of the Donskoi monastery. In the context of the present study of the spiritual tradition the importance of his contribution is his view of the Church as the "One Catholic Apostolic Church", and that "all attempts coming from my side to embroil the Church in the political struggle should be rejected and condemned".

The highly contentious issue of church–state relationship has engaged Christians from New Testament times. In the volatile political conditions of Russia after the 1917 revolution it created immense problems for the Russian Church. Tikhon dithered and eventually compromised, Sergius (1867–1944), Metropolitan of Novgorod, initially argued, as had Tikhon, for complete separation of Church and state, but eventually he developed a leaning towards the compromising "Living Church", and made concessions to the state. Sergius urged the clergy to pledge their allegiance to the state, and in 1927 he wrote, "We wish to be Orthodox and at the same time to recognize the Soviet Union as our civil fatherland. Every blow against the Union . . . we regard as a blow against us." We may ask whether this is still the position of Eastern Orthodoxy.

The unyielding determination of the Eastern Orthodox Church to abide by and uphold the Holy Tradition is the ground of its stability and unity. In all matters of faith and spirituality it derives strength, guidance and enlightenment from the apostolic tradition to which it is inexorably committed. Yet its spirituality is not incestuous but is a window through which the Church looks out upon the world and sees the need for moral and spiritual renewal in every department of life.

The world of theology and spirituality is changing rapidly, and a Church, although bound to its tradition, cannot be oblivious to the new fresh questions of the new age in religion, morality, politics and national affairs. It remains to be seen how far the Eastern Orthodox Church can translate its traditional beliefs and ideologies into creative action in the shaping of the east, on the assumption that "The future is not something to be sought or hoped for, but something to be created."

4

Christianity in the West

The gradual disintegration and collapse of the Roman Empire posited a period of unprecedented historical and political upheaval in western Europe. Invading tribes engaged in internecine strife out of which eventuality there was born the European nations as we know them today. Many crucial developments produced all kinds of repercussion on the cultural, social and religious life of Europe between the fifth and fifteenth centuries. Europe did not enjoy the benefits of one homogeneous culture from north to south, and Christian theology and spirituality passed through periods of ebb and flow. The circumstances changed as did attitudes towards religion; there was orientation away from corporate identity with Christian faith as well as adherence to traditional beliefs and practices. To define this fluctuation in terms of exact periodization is hazardous, but in general terms we are able to chart the course of growth and transition in theology and spirituality from the "dark ages" to the end of the Middle Ages as we concentrate on some major developments.

In the earlier centuries the fate of the Roman Empire dominated the historical scene. This was followed by some reformative and constructive developments that strengthened the hold of the Church on European life and thought and consolidated its hierarchical position. From the eleventh century new patterns of devotion, the rise of the nation state, the emergence and development of scholasticism, and the strength of the papacy, provide evidence of innovations and pointers that mark off the medieval from the modern age. In general terms it can be said that throughout the Middle Ages Christianity in the west underwent many transformations in styles, forms, corporate and individualist attitudes and aspirations. With the invading "barbarians", who brought the Roman Empire to its knees, and settled as natives, the geographical and demographic landscape changed. In nascent cultural centres the

Christian presence was established but was not manifested uniformly in every place. There were times when the Church provided the mainstay of social and cultural stability; it projected a cohesive image of itself in organization and government, liturgy and ritual, theology and spirituality. By the eleventh century Europe was formally Christian and the Church the architect, custodian and transmitter of its civilized values; from the Church there emanated the ideas and ideals that created and shaped Europe's social, political and national institutions. Christian theology and spirituality crystallized with the pope of Rome as the focus of its authority and unity. The centralization of the spiritual–temporal authority of the papacy proved a powerful stabilizing influence; the voice of the Church was heard as the voice of God. In doctrine the pope stood in a line of succession that originated with the first Christian apostles and the decrees of the Council of Chalcedon; in spirituality and in ritual the Church abided by the baptismal and eucharist rites of the early church; the clergy stood in the tradition of apostolic succession; the laity were expected to maintain and conform to this tradition; the pope was the vicar of Christ on earth. When he spoke on matters of faith and doctrine *ex cathedra*, as well as on matters of human welfare and spirituality, his words were received as authoritative. The papacy was located in Rome, "the greatest of cities", but its influence penetrated to every part of western Christendom. The papacy received the ultimate accolade of its spiritual and institutional authority in the edict of the Council of Rheims (1049), which decreed that the pope alone was the primate and apostolic of the universal Church.

However, towards the end of the Middle Ages the papacy began to be openly criticized on account of the Church's teaching, its faithfulness to apostolic doctrine, its administration and interpretation of the sacraments, and its method of government and of financing its work. In order to gain a perspective on the changes throughout the medieval period we need to keep an eye on the context. Change and advance is not only the product of a particular time but also development from earlier progress. In illustration of this there are some key activities in theology and spirituality that merit special attention; especially, papacy, monasticism, mysticism, scholasticism and the arts.

Papacy, authority, theology and spirituality

The word pope (*papa* = father) was used by those Christians who stood in a filial relationship to a bishop. They felt a spiritual affinity with him as their "father in God". As the Church became more powerful in Rome, the capital of the empire, so the Bishop of Rome came to be looked upon as the leading authority in matters relating to the doctrine, practices and administration of Church affairs. Throughout the Middle Ages the popes established their claims and primacy with consistent determination, and some of them achieved fame as notable reformers, spiritual leaders and ecclesiastical administrators. These were men of vision and leadership who made an impact on the shape and role of the Church in promoting the Christianization of the west. Many of them though were vulnerable to the values, influences and patronage of worldly wealth and secular authority. Hence the ebb and flow to which we referred earlier. The present purpose is to refer to some of the most significant of the medieval popes who made a positive and progressive contribution to the development of the spiritual tradition in Christian theology.

Gregory the Great

The first of the notable popes of this period is Gregory the Great (540–604). He assumed the papacy at a time when the nominally Christianized west was immersed in what has been called "a sea of darkness". The Church was like a fortress under siege, for when Gregory became pope in 590 the Arian Lombard invaders were causing great havoc in Italy. Gregory was made prefect of the city of Rome in 573, but a year later he felt called to the "religious life". He then became a monk and devoted his energies to founding monasteries. He was the first monk to be elevated as pope, even though he did not covet such a position. He still continued to practise his monastic ideals but he also displayed unusual political and diplomatic skills. This became evident as he dealt with the Lombards who had encroached on the estates of Italy.

Gregory's theology was Christ-centred and he was drawn particularly to the efficacy of the sacrifice of Jesus Christ on the cross. The sacrificial death of Jesus was the single hope of redemption; only the experience of redemption could bring about reconciliation to God. Gregory's teaching was basically evangelical in tone, as might be expected from someone so fervently devoted to the spread of the Christian message. During the 590s the controversy between the Monophysites and the Chalcedonians (see chapter 3) flared again. The Chalcedonians, knowing Gregory's theological inclination, sought his active support.

However, Gregory diplomatically refused to become embroiled in theological controversy with Christians in the east. Instead, he devoted his energies to the concerns for which he is best remembered. One of these was his deep interest in the pastoral mission and ministry of a bishop. He wrote a work called *Liber Regulae Pastoralis* in which he set out practical directions for exercising pastoral care: these display his concern for the practical, human and spiritual welfare of those in his care. Among his other writings is a commentary on the Book of Job, which also exudes his passion for the care of souls. The commentary describes the biblical patriarch Job in the throes of perplexity and anguish in the face of excessive suffering. This was Job's dark night of the soul, which Gregory compared to the "sea of darkness" through which the Church was passing. The Church was under attack and there were forces at work that would have destroyed it. Was this the sign of the vengeance of divine displeasure and anger? Only through the redemptive sacrifice of Christ on the cross was there hope of deliverance. Gregory taught a basic evangelical faith which pointed to the fundamental essentials of Christian belief welded to charitable practices. In this "sea of darkness" the Church could not afford other than to hold fast and concentrate on the first principles of Christian faith and action.

The survival of the Church and Christianity was a major concern of Gregory. This, he contended, depended on expansion of its message to those places where it had not hitherto penetrated. Gregory was the instigator of the Christian mission to France and England in 596. He commissioned Augustine, a member of an episcopal household, along with forty monks from Rome, to undertake a mission to the French and English, but before Augustine set out on this mission, Gregory characteristically displayed his pastoral care by sending Augustine a letter of encouragement, in which he wrote, "Do not let the hardships of the journey or the evil tongues of men stop you. Although I cannot labour beside you, yet because I long to do so I shall enter into the joy of your reward." Augustine landed in England in 597 and converted King Ethelbert to the Christian faith. But the depth of Gregory's zeal for winning others to the faith is also known from his instructions to a priest named Candidus to make provision for the spiritual welfare of pagan boys, especially for those who were sick. He instructed Candidus to house these boys in a monastery where they would be sheltered and cared for, taught the way of salvation and baptized into the faith. At that time slavery was part of the social structure, and Gregory instructed Candidus further by directing him to buy English slaves so that they could be brought up in monasteries with the prospects of them becoming believers in Christianity.

Naturally, Gregory's spirituality, missionary zeal and pastoral care were embodied in the Church. In this connection his contribution to the reform of the Church's liturgy, and especially its liturgical music, is noteworthy. Music, psalmody and hymnology had been a feature of Christian worship from New Testament times. St. Paul had encouraged Christians to "speak to one another in psalms, hymns and songs; sing and make music in your heart to the Lord" (Ephesians 5: 19). The tradition continued and developed. The younger Pliny, governor of Bithynia, reported to the Emperor Trajan in 112 on how Christians met together before daylight and sang by turns "a hymn to Christ as a God". Clement of Alexandria also informs about the use of music in church worship, but emphasized that it should be appropriate and austere.

As time went by, the antiphonal singing of hymns was introduced, and so also was the chanting of psalms. St. Augustine is particularly informative about this, for he wrote in his *Confessions*:

> Yet when I remember the tears I shed, moved by the songs of the Church in the early days of my new faith ... when they are sung with a clear voice and proper modulation I recognize once more the usefulness of this practice.

Augustine approved the use of music in church, but he was aware of the danger of paying more attention to the music than to the holy words that "kindle more religiously and fervently to a flame of piety". Nevertheless, he observed of the music "that all the varying emotions of my spirit have modes proper to them in voice and song, whereby, by secret affinity, they are made more alive".

Obviously the Church's tradition in music goes back to the earliest times, but, as can be seen from these references to Clement and Augustine, it was not without controversy. The question of how far the Church should make use of the productions of human ingenuity in its worship was one that seemed to cause some friction. Only a few examples of the earliest Christian hymns survive, but by the age of Gregory the Great, chanting seems to have become accepted. Gregory's contribution is thought to lie in this, but it is not certain that what became known as the Gregorian chant originated with Gregory himself. This is a kind of plainsong that became used widely in church worship.

Gregory drew unstintingly upon his undoubted gifts as a reformer and administrator and made a lasting impact on the papacy. His greatest passion was to see Christianity blossom and flourish. To this end he

worked to help Christians to a better understanding of the implications
of living the Christian life in the contemporary world; he expounded
the patterns of Christian morality and advocated that Christians should
act accordingly. In order to ensure that Christians should live the
Christian life to the full he used his episcopal position to develop a
congenial Christian community on the assumption that here alone
could Christian living be perfected. The clergy had a key role in creating
such a community. They could exercise their spiritual authority to
direct and foster spiritual nurture and keep the ideal of spiritual wholeness ever in view. For this purpose Gregory enlisted the services of holy
men and monks, ascetics and wandering preachers, evangelists and
miracle workers. He specified the contribution these men could make
in his *Dialogues*, and impressed upon them how crucial their role was
in winning a nation state to Christian ways.[1] He thus laid the foundations for the spread and purest practice of Christianity, and this made
an enduring impact, even though his successors did not always build on
the foundations. His biographer said of him that he never rested, but
rather that:

> he was always engaged in providing for the interests of his people, in
> writing some composition worthy of the Church, or in searching out the
> secrets of heaven.

Gregory contributed handsomely to the religious and spiritual life of
his age. He became involved in a number of controversies concerning
the monastic life and the army. He was a gifted statesman who acted as
a peacemaker between the Lombards and the king. In theology Gregory
taught a doctrine of heaven and hell and the ultimate fate of the human
soul. Between heaven and hell there is an intermediate stage and no soul
was abandoned to hell for ever. He encouraged this teaching in his
Dialogues:

> Clearly everyone will be brought to the Judge in his exact state at death,
> but there must be a purging fire before judgement because some little
> faults may remain to be purged . . . this can only be for minor faults, such
> as idle chatter, too hearty laughter, mistakes in the care of property . . .
> or errors due to ignorance in trivial matters . . .

He attributed his teaching to the doctrine of the Apostle Paul who had
taught that Christ is the doctrine's foundation. When Paul said that
salvation was achieved by passing through fire he was speaking of
mortal sins which cannot be destroyed by fire. Therefore, declared
Gregory:

we must remember that no one will be purged in the world to come, even of the slightest faults, unless he has deserved it through the good deeds done in this life.[2]

Gregory's spirituality is displayed in his classical *Pastoral Care* which expounds how the spiritual care of others should be exercised. It adhered closely to Scriptural teaching:

the spring of pastoral care is love;
love of God and neighbours is its heart;
helpfulness, moderation, discretion, discerning speech are its essential guidelines;
sympathy for all people in their trouble is its core;
love of God and people of high and low estate is its unity;
loving kindness, preoccupation with the need of neighbour is its landmark;
imitation of the path of Christ in teaching and sound doctrine is its pattern.[3]

In addition to Gregory's contribution to the liturgical worship of the Church, we should also take note of his sacramentary of prayer. In this he added to the sacramentaries of two earlier popes, Leo the Great (d. 461) and Galasius (d. 496). A number of the collects of Gregory are known from Cranmer's *First Book of Common Prayer* (1549). This example exemplifies Gregory's exaltation of love as the supreme Christian virtue:

God, who hast prepared for them that love thee such good things as pass men's understanding, pour into our hearts such love towards thee, that we, loving thee above all things, may obtain thy promises, which exceed all that we can desire; through Jesus Christ our Lord.[4]

Gregory is also the author of hymns, two of which are still included in English hymnology,

Father, we praise thee, now the day is over . . .

and

O, Christ, our King, Creator, Lord . . .

It has been necessary to dwell at length on the stature and work of Gregory the Great as the outstanding pope of the early Middle Ages. No successor to the papacy of his calibre and influence emerged until the eleventh century. Theology, too, during these centuries was denuded of any radical fresh developments that would have reinvigorated the theological scene and contributed substantially to the furtherance of understanding and interpreting Christian doctrines and their provenance. With the few exceptions of Alcuin of York (735–804), a Carolingian scholar, and Theodulf of Orleans (750–821), who took part in the revival of learning in monastic schools, directed by theological objectives, theology passed through a dormant period until the eleventh century. Then there re-emerged a revived interest in the study and interpretation of Christian doctrine, and new methods of "doing" theology were produced. A number of eminent scholars contributed to the development but for the present we shall focus on the contribution of the holders of the papal office.

Acting on the principle of their contribution to the development of theology and spirituality, there are few other popes who stand out and merit special mention. This does not assume that no other pope contributed to the development and enhancement of the institution of the papacy or exercised a civilized influence in the fulfilment of their vocation. Many of these did in their own way work harmoniously for the good of the Church and the spread of Christian faith. But in so far as we are attempting to assess significant contributions to theological thought and spirituality selection is inevitable, it is expedient to refer to two of the later popes who pursued the highest aims and rank as men of rare genius and godliness.

Gregory VII (Hildebrand)

Pope Gregory VII is assumed to be the founder of the greatness of the medieval papacy. He held this office from 1073 to 1085 and is one of the most distinguished papal reformers, who has many accomplishments to his credit. Charlemagne, the Holy Roman Emperor (741–814), a man of exceptional personality who held in high esteem the responsibility of his exalted office, strove to maintain the orthodoxy of the Christian faith and to ensure the good order of the Church. He was lord over all things to his age, preserver of order, patron of learning, and devotee of the pope as the chief prelate of his realm. After the death of Charlemagne the empire crumbled into decay, but in Germany the Holy Roman Empire was revived in the latter half of the tenth century.

The papacy, however, had fallen into disrepute, until the advent of Hildebrand (Gregory VII), a young scholar from Italy, who devoted himself to a life of reform. He applied himself to reforming the Church with unyielding single-mindedness and firmness of will, and brought to the task one of the sharpest intellects of his day. His view of the papacy

was absolute and uncompromising; he was determined to free it from
the control of the emperor on the belief that, "The Pope can be judged
by no one." Gregory insisted that the Church on earth should be under
the sole control of the pope as the vice-regent of God. Bishops should
be appointed by the pope and not the emperor, and, as the Church was
founded by Christ, only the spiritual elite had the right of government
and control. Gregory pursued his demands with vigour, challenging the
secular authorities "in the name of the Lord of Hosts". His objective
was spiritual, but his claims brought him into conflict with the temporal
rulers. However, Gregory followed faithfully his vision of the religious
and secular authorities working together in unison and collaboration to
achieve God's purposes.

At the same time he denounced the interference and intrusion of
secular authorities and standards into the affairs of the Church. Indeed,
he condemned as the work of Satan the activities of secular bodies who
neglected the instruction of the Scriptures, and he was highly critical of
any clergy who gave them encouragement. No one up to this time had
laid such universal claim to the moral and spiritual authority of the
papacy. In point of fact, Gregory claimed that the pope, as the successor
of the Apostle Peter, to whom Christ had assigned special authority on
earth, had authority over the secular powers:

> It is your good pleasure that the Christian people, who have been
> committed to you, should especially obey me because you have given me
> your authority.

These claims to universal sovereignty may have seemed to succeed and
the much publicized sight of the German emperor kneeling in the snow
before Pope Gregory VII may seem to epitomize the triumph of
the papacy over the secular authority. Yet it is very unlikely that the
emperor committed himself so completely to the papal sovereignty, as
later history was soon to show.

The sovereignty of the papacy is inexorably linked with the notion
of spiritual authority, with Church discipline and with orthodoxy in
faith and doctrine. Herein lies one of the central tensions of
Christianity, the demarcation of authority between Church and state.
The dream of Gregory VII of papal sovereignty was not wholly
utopian, for he discerned in Christian faith a focus that provided a
centrepoint of unity between the spiritual and secular authorities. The
Church is a faith community, but it also is an organic unity under a
central control and authority. Why should the Church not infuse the
state with its unitary authority? In a sense, the vision of Pope Gregory

seemed to be the ideal way for the Church to exercise its spiritual authority and its ethical policy in correcting the imperfections and abuses of the state and thereby bringing about a consensus of harmony between Church and state. History, however, shows how impossible this ideal is of being realized.

One other factor of Gregory's role as pope merits mention. By the time of his reign the Islamic faith had made inroads into the west as well as eastern Europe. Islam was born during the lifetime of Muhammad and in the following century Islamic mosques were established in Constantinople, the main centre of the Byzantine Church. In the west Pope Gregory VII had dealings with the Muslims on a theological issue, namely, the belief in one God (Islam like Christianity being a mono-theistic faith), and the common roots of the two religions in the faith of Abraham, "the father of the people". Gregory is reputed to have written to the Islamic ruler Al-Nasir that, "we believe in and confess one God, admittedly in a different way". On the surface this may signify a spirit of tolerance and reconciliation between the religions, yet, on the other hand, we are told that Gregory, when speaking to a Christian audience, would refer to Muslims as pagans. Even so, Gregory worked for the conversion of Muslims to Christianity. This was one of the objectives of the military Order of Santiago which Gregory founded. This fits in well with Gregory's theory of a papal world government, but it is here presented as an example of Gregory's spiritual vision of papal primacy that he believed came from Christ himself; he visualized a world theocracy at whose heart is the Roman Church and its papacy, which is above error or division.

Boniface

The successors of Pope Gregory VII during the two following centuries included some worthy Church leaders. Innocent III (1198–1216) undertook to compile and enforce a responsible marriage law and to combat heresy. He proved to be a powerful pope, who insisted that "We are the successors of the Prince of the Apostles, but we are not his vicar, nor the vicar of any man or apostle, but the vicar of Jesus Christ himself." But here we shall elaborate briefly on the papacy of Boniface (1294–1303).

Boniface issued two papal bulls, *Ausculta Fili* (1301) addressed to the King of France, and *Unam Sanctum* (1302), both of which associated and defended the spiritual and temporal authority of the papacy. The rift within the relationship between Church and state was widening and the secular rulers were drifting away from the authority of the Church and its jurisdiction over secular life. The belief the secular rulers propagated was that God had conferred authority equally on the Church and state. God had bequeathed to temporal rulers jurisdiction over the Church in their own territory. This clearly went against the teaching of the Church and the ideals of Gregory VII, as described previously. In effect it meant bringing under state control such ecclesiastical matters as patronage, the nomination of bishops and the deployment of clergy, which the Church believed to be in its control. As the Church became more and more pressurized by these notions, the issue of involvement by the civil government in the affairs of the Church and vice versa became crucial. Boniface made a firm stand on this issue that involved him in a bitter struggle with King Philip IV of France.

Boniface became involved in controversy on another issue also. The preaching order of the friars and their overt activities raised angry protests from clergy who believed their territory was being invaded and their authority being undermined. In 1298 Boniface issued a papal bull (*Super Cathedrum*) on the teaching and activities of the friars. The friars were preaching the advent of a truly and wholly spiritual church that would supersede the present institutional church.

Its advent would signal the end of the present temporal order. Such a church would practise literally and fully the virtues and privations of poverty and humility that would bring it more perfectly into tune with the teaching and example of Jesus Christ. The effect of this would be that the Church as presently organized and structured would be transformed; it would relinquish its considerable wealth and property, would abandon its hierarchic structure, and abnegate its position of prestige in society. The Church reacted to this preaching with vigour; whatever sympathy there might have been with the spiritual aspirations of the friars, their teaching, if carried to its logical conclusion, would spell catastrophe for the Church. It would revolutionize the entire structure and organization of the Church, the institution of the papacy, the ministry of the clergy, the government and administration of Church policy. Boniface made a strong defence of the primacy and authority of the papacy in the face of this preaching. Later, in 1323 Pope John XXII made an outright denunciation of the views of the friars. In response to this the friars forged an alliance with the pope's political opponents.

During his papacy Pope Boniface fostered a number of reforms that became common practice. One was the veneration of saints, another the spiritual value of pilgrimage to sacred shrines. Boniface appointed the year 1300 as a year of jubilee or holy year of pilgrimage to Rome. Rome would then be the centre of celebration and commemoration, from which the Church would gain from the many pilgrims who would throng the city. In return the pilgrims hoped to gain the promised plenary indulgence for their devotion and visit to the sacred shrines.

As we observed earlier, by the end of the medieval period the papacy was in a state of decline. Yet in earlier times the institution of the papacy was inherently strong even though its influence was diverse. The papacy was a universal phenomenon in the west; it gave central direction to Christianity, its practice and power was felt in every nation state; it dominated large areas of social and personal behaviour; it maintained a link between religion and secular life. By the time of Boniface the papacy had procured for itself an almost all-embracing sovereignty; it was prepared, in practice, to enter into alliance with the temporal rulers and share the benefits that might accrue from this. Yet evaluation of the papacy during the Middle Ages does not universally reveal significant fresh theological movements emanating from or initiated by the popes themselves; there are few innovative or outstanding theologians among them. At the same time it has to be said that their adherence to orthodox belief and moral principles helped to sustain the authority of the Church through times of transition. They also tackled some of the major issues that arose from the special mission of the Church as a divine community in the world, and aimed, in the style of Gregory the Great, to promote the highest calibre of Christian life. In this lies the strength of their contribution to the moulding of a genuine Christian spirituality during the Middle Ages.

Monasticism in the West

The attempt to categorize the theology and spiritual tradition of the Middle Ages is bound to encounter the dynamic forms and vitality of the monastic orders. Monasticism flourished throughout the period and ideally was the matrix of the nurture and practice of a durable Christian spiritual life. The monastery was the custodian of orthodox Christian belief and piety, a sacramental community dedicated to the practice of Christian idealism in a life of devotion, education and philanthropy. Monks and nuns who answered the call to the monastic life embraced a discipline that absorbed the whole of their lives – physical, mental, moral and spiritual. Life in the monastery was conditioned by the submission of its members to obedience and the works of love, humility, self-rejecting service and charity. In brief, the commitment was to living a life of "spiritual wholeness". Discipline was strict, rules were rigid and comprehensive, and every detail of physical, ethical, intellectual and spiritual life was purposefully regulated, so the life of the monastery was seen as the incarnate life of the Body of Christ (the Church) on earth. The community of the monastery was a mirror of the union between Christ and the Church.

Even so, there is ebb and flow in the history of monasticism during the Middle Ages. Monasticism did not consistently adhere to the high ideals of the religious life to the ultimate. By the end of the Middle Ages there were signs that the "institutionalism" of the monastery and its maintenance was more prominent and absorbing than its "charismatic" function; many monasteries had accumulated substantial wealth and lands, and their inmates, including abbots, lived profligate. The pioneering religious spirit of the earlier monastic reformers had waned and the monastery was no longer the spiritual focus of enlightened faith, sound doctrine, self-denying service and spirituality it was intended to be. Of course there were exceptions, and it is only possible to make a fair and balanced judgement about this great movement, which co-existed in unison with the Church, after detailed evaluation of the evidence. Our purpose here is to indicate the contribution of monasticism to the progress of Christian theology and its spiritual tradition, and to describe the role of some leading devotees and reformers who contributed to this. It is pertinent to observe at this point how certain traditions of eastern monasticism (cf. chapter 3) also characterize monasticism in the west, especially the stress on the charismatic life, discipline, sacramentalism, confession, penance, and liturgy. But, as will become clear, monasticism in the west developed in such a way as to embrace every kind of religious nurture and a wide spectrum of religious and social activities.

Gregory of Tours and Benedict of Nursia

Monasticism was established in the west at an early age. John Cassian (360–435), a Scythian, is worthy of mention as the founder of two monasteries in the region of Marseilles in France. Men and women were catered for separately in these. Cassian had previously visited a number of monasteries in the east in order to discover for himself how they functioned and especially how he could promote in the west their educational services. He was a scholar and an ascetic with a desire to promote the intellectual purpose of the monastery. A man of great culture, he believed that the long years of theological debate needed to be replaced with sustained concentration on the intellectual perspectives and creditability of Christian belief.

Cassian, therefore, deliberately avoided in his own theology the extremes of Pelagius' doctrine of human free will as sovereign, and he also steered away from the emphatic stress in Augustine's doctrine of free grace and determinism. He conveyed his own reflections on the monastic life in two works entitled *Institutions* and *Conferences*. In the spiritual tradition of the west Cassian is remembered for his concept and promotion of the importance of spiritual growth towards Christ. He wrote:

> the life of growth towards Christ as saviour and servant is possible only in the context of humanly directed charity and compassion in the corporate life of humility and patience.[5]

We observe here, in this quotation, how Cassian couples together three elements in the life of spiritual growth towards Christ, the awareness of Christ as saviour and servant, the practice of charity and compassion, and the corporate observance of humility and patience. These conditions became vital characteristics of the nature and action of Christian spirituality at its best wherever monasticism flourished.

This brief insight into the contribution of John Cassian provides a backcloth to the very different role of Gregory of Tours (540–94), a bishop and historian. We observed earlier how Gregory the Great was reluctant to enter the theological controversy between the Monophysites and the Chalcedonians, whereas Gregory of Tours showed no such reluctance. Nor did he adopt John Cassian's line that theological disputation should give way to other intellectual pursuits. Gregory of Tours saw the continuing debate about the Holy Trinity as a thorn in the flesh of the Church. The King Chilperic had written a treatise on the Trinity in which he contended that God the Father is the same as God the Son, and God the Son the same as God the Father, and the Holy Spirit the same as the Father and the Son. In his treatise Chilperic also advocated that God should not be called a person lest this should make him like other persons. Gregory of Tours felt obliged to answer these contentions. First, he refuted the argument of Chilperic by declaring that only the Son had been made incarnate. And secondly, this fact meant that the Son could not be the same as the Father. The incarnation of the Son differentiated him from God the Father.

Gregory also took up an opposing stance against what he saw as "corrupting Arianism", that is, the denial of the pre-existence of Christ as God; he hailed the conversion of the Franks as an act of deliverance from the heresy of Arianism. Gregory, furthermore, showed great veneration for the Christian martyrs who, he declared, were to be revered as "the snow white number of the elect". He was drawn also to the veneration of relics in the belief that they embodied special powers, and, in particular, they should be honoured as an extension of the martyrs. In an age when pilgrimage to sacred sites was gradually becoming the norm of piety and spiritual observance, Gregory urged that the pilgrim:

> should he wish to bring back a relic from the tomb . . . pray confidently and, if his faith is sufficient, the cloth, once removed from the tomb, will be found to be so full of divine grace that it will be much heavier than before. Then he knows that his prayers have been granted.[6]

It is clear that Gregory was devoted to the memory of the past greatness of Christianity and this vision penetrates throughout his thought. It contrasted with the present state of spirituality, about which Gregory expressed dismay, as though it was overshadowed by a cloud of darkness. Nevertheless, he laboured energetically to present the Christian faith to everyone who was ready to listen. He advocated that those who were converted should be absorbed by the spirit and practice of their new faith. Nothing, he believed, especially not wealth or position, should take precedence over this.

Benedict of Nursia (480–547) is the outstanding monastic reformer of the early Middle Ages, who also represents in his own life and teaching the monastic ideal at its best. The motto he adopted for the order he founded, *Ora et Labore* (prayer and work), expresses succinctly his ideal. In founding an order of monks, the Benedictines, he departed from the tradition of the east where, although there were monasteries, there were no monastic orders. His description of a monk became a classic in its own right; a monk he claimed is:

> one who is putting aside his own will so as to go to war under Christ the Lord, the real King, picking up the keen and glittering weapons of obedience.

He also compiled *The Rule for Monks*, which achieved the status of a classic of its kind. It is a work of rare genius even if "what is significant is that Benedict wisely took what he thought was good from existing rules and practices, evaluated the material in the light of his own experience and blended the elements to form a balanced, positive and flexible synthesis . . . it combined sound spiritual teaching with pastoral details covering most aspects of community life".[7] The system of monastic community life he developed was under the authority of the abbot, but it also allowed the monks to share in discussion and to offer advice. Benedict defined the fundamental spiritual values of his "rule" as humility, obedience and prayer. The "rule" was written in vulgar Latin so that it could be understood by everyone; it is simple and broad but accessible and adaptable as well.

Benedict's "rule" became the standard for western monasticism. It was not altogether original, as we indicated above. It was indebted to the earlier rules of St. Basil and St. Caesarius of Arles (470–542). But Benedict's "rule" was established on the principle of a monastery as "a school of the service of the Lord". Benedict mitigated the extreme forms of asceticism in order to concentrate more on the cultivation of self-control, self-conquest and obedience to the liturgy, and doing "whatever work is useful". He viewed life as a pilgrimage progressing through many stages and forms of service, of overcoming temptations galore as it advances and attains the ultimate goal of finding God. The "rule" was the *regula* (order) for living the life of the gospel. It aimed to transpose the radical principles of the gospel into daily life, covering work and all its activities. It was practical not theoretical, its operational centre was God, within and around whom the whole life was centred.

The opening part of Benedict's "rule" encapsulates its tone and purpose:

> Listen, my son, to your master's precepts, and incline the ear of your young heart. Receive willingly and carry out effectively your loving father's advice, but by the labour of obedience you may return to Him from whom you had departed by the sloth of disobedience.

Each monastery was autonomous and the monks vowed to remain in one place. They were allowed sufficient food, clothing and rest, but they were to fulfil their holy vocation in benefiting others. This work could be intellectual as well as manual, and monasteries developed into centres of education and learning. But the life of prayer was at the heart of monasticism, private prayer, meditation and silence, but especially liturgical prayer in the celebration of the mass. Possessions were held in common, whilst service to others in works of mercy and compassion was obligatory. Service to those who needed it was to be given selflessly, undertaken as the outreach of devotion and virtue, and so acting as Christ to everyone. Guests were to be received as Christ himself. Benedict did not found the monastery in order to form a special service to the Church, nor were the monks clergy:

but simple people, Italian peasants and rustic Goths. They needed to learn letters for their duty of devotional reading (nothing is said of learned study) and for the daily offices, "the work of God" (*opus dei*) which Benedict regarded as central to the life of the community.[8]

The rule of Benedict did not immediately replace the individual "rules" of other monasteries. Augustine laid down his own rules for the monastery in Canterbury and the Augustian Order spread to Germany and elsewhere. In Whitby also, the monastery founded by Bishop Wilfred mingled Roman and Celtic traditions. At Cluny, Abbot Hugh of Semur laid foundations of his own for the monastery that he founded. But Benedict's "rule" became predominant. In time its appeal spread and became widely accepted. It has been acclaimed for its common sense, its humanity, its devotion to the weak and the sick, and its combination of prayer and meditation with practical work. Today the Benedictine Order is widespread throughout the world and there are confederations of Benedictine Sisters as well. For a period the Rule of Benedict formed a bond between the autonomous abbeys, but early in the ninth century there was a move in the direction of greater uniformity, and the relaxation of Benedictine discipline tended to the formation of new separate orders with greater emphasis on austerity and collectivism. In this respect the popes and councils of the Middle Ages influenced the centralization. Following the Protestant Reformation the Benedictine Order suffered oblivion, but in the early nineteenth century it saw a remarkable revival in Europe and America.

Celtic monasticism

We noted earlier Gregory the Great's commissioning of Augustine to undertake a mission to England, and we need to make brief reference to the introduction and activities of Christianity in the northern region of Europe. Notable in this connection is Columba of Iona (550–615), who came here from Ireland about the year 563. He was accepted as a committed Christian, and under him Iona became a leading centre of Christianity in Scotland. Here a monastery was founded and led by an abbot who was an ordained priest. Columba exercised jurisdiction over the whole province, and displayed immense skill as a statesman, missionary, scholar and poet. A life of Columba was written by Adamnan who told how he took the name of Columba or Dove when he became a monk, which in its full form is Columcille or Church-dove. His holiness contrasted with the unholy lives of many people around him and with the neglect of holiness by many professing Christians. Columba is reported to have performed a remarkable miracle on the shores of Loch Ness where one of his companions was terrorized by a savage water beast with a gaping mouth, but Columba, so his biographer told:

> raised his holy hand and drew the saving sign of the cross in the empty air, and then invoking the name of God, he commanded the savage beast and said, "You will go no further. Do not touch the man, turn beast speedily."

> The beast did as the saint commanded and the pagan barbarians who were there at the time, impelled by the magnitude of this miracle they themselves had seen, magnified the God of the Christians.[9]

We cannot know the shape of the cross which Columba is supposed to have drawn but the traditional form of the Celtic cross has a circle connecting the arms and the stem and is to this day a notable symbol of Celtic spirituality.

Many legends are associated with Columba, but for the present purpose it is sufficient to stress his personal spirituality and zeal for the spread of Christian faith. From the monastery of Iona missionaries were despatched to convert the Picts and to preach the faith to other Anglo-Saxon kingdoms. In contrast to some other monastic houses, under Columba, Iona became a place from where monks were sent to convert others. Bede told how Columba came to preach the word of God to the provinces of the Northern Picts, and Adamnan tells of Columba's journey to King Brude, in the present territory of Inverness, and how when the saint came to the king's fortress he "traced on them the sign of the cross, knocked, laid his hands upon the doors and they flew open of their own accord, and in he went with his company". It was Columba's spirituality that gained entrance to the fortress of King Brude. Those who were converted, Columba baptized in springs of water. We are told, "The Saint went up. He raised his holy hand and called upon the name of Christ. Then he washes hands and feet, and with his companions drinks of the water he has blessed."

One result of the missionary outreach of Columba of Iona was the coming of Christianity to Lindisfarne or Holy Island in the north-east of England. The Venerable Bede (673–735), a monk of Jarrow, the greatest scholar of his age and distinguished author of *Ecclesiastical History of the English Nation*, tells how King Oswald asked for a bishop to be sent to confer the blessings of the Christian religion on the English. Aidan, a monk of Iona, was despatched and he settled in

Lindisfarne in 634. He was a holy and zealous Christian, known for his humility and moderation. Here he preached the Christian message with great effectiveness and baptized many who believed. The sacraments were administered and many churches were built throughout Oswald's kingdom. Aidan also trained young men in the Christian faith, some of whom later became prominent in the Church, including Chad and Wilfred. Eventually, after the Synod of Whitby (665), which settled the date of Easter, the Church of Northumbria became fully integrated with the Church of the west. The monastery of Lindisfarne assumed prominence as a centre of spirituality and of missionary activity. Its influence spread not only in England but also into the continent. Aidan of Lindisfarne was committed to Christianity as a missionary faith but it had to be propagated for the sake of its own survival. It thrived and flourished only as it fulfilled the commission of Christ to preach the gospel to all people. Lindisfarne developed its own typical spiritual tradition. Aidan travelled on foot, asked those he met to think of Christian baptism, then he would confirm them, encourage them by example to charity and good works, to read the Bible, learn the psalms. A monk of Lindisfarne was assured of respect as a man of God, and listened to intently.

Another name that merits mention is Patrick of Ireland (b. 389) who told how, at the age of sixteen, he was carried from Britain to Ireland with members of his family and many thousands of prisoners of war. Patrick was already a Christian, the son of a deacon and the grandson of a priest, and for a time he was an inmate of the monastery of Lerins. He was a shepherd by calling, but was very dependent on prayer for his spiritual sustenance; he declared that he prayed constantly, offering many hundreds of prayers daily and many more at night. Patrick believed that prayer had saved his life in the days when he was the slave of heathen masters. His departure to Ireland was the result of the vision of a man called Victoricus who appeared with a letter which began, "The voice of the Irish".

He also heard in a dream a voice speaking to him of Christ who had laid down his life for him. Patrick awoke rejoicing. He was now certain of his vocation, and was ordained as a deacon, and then in 432 was consecrated a missionary by Bishop Germanus of Auxerre. Patrick steeped himself in knowledge of the Bible and made extensive quotations from its text in his *Confession*. He also composed explanations of the text for the benefit of simple people. For instance, he interpreted the account of the crucifixion of Jesus in Matthew 27: 45ff:

... darkness until the ninth hour. And about the ninth hour, Jesus cried with a loud voice ... And some said, This man called Elijah ...

This cry Patrick explained is the rising of the sun; in the gospel the darkness descended before Christ had uttered his last words; once he had spoken for the last time the darkness was over. Patrick then made this meaning applicable to his own experience. In the day of trouble – in the dark night of the soul – the whole of life is in darkness; the Spirit of Christ is called out for the sake of transforming the darkness into light.

Patrick's mission to Ireland, "where they never had the knowledge of God", was fruitful, and those who were converted he urged to fear God and to hold their faith as a gift from God. By 540 there were many monks in Ireland and these established trading contacts with the Loire Valley. Irish Christianity developed a social aspect, and monasticism a mobile element. He introduced the system of diocesan bishops into Ireland. Patrick died in 461 and many legends survive about him, but probably his most notable legacy to Christian spirituality is the prayer:

> I arise today
> through God's strength to pilot me:
> God's might to uphold me,
> God's wisdom to guide me,
> God's eye to look before me,
> God's ear to hear me,
> God's word to speak to me,
> God's hand to guard me,
> God's way to lie before me,
> God's shield to protect me,
> God's host to secure me,
> against snares of devils,
> against temptations of vices,
> against inclinations of nature,
> against everyone who shall wish me ill,
> far and near,
> alone and in a crowd.

At Whitby a monastery was founded by a Northumbrian princess named Hilda in 659. She had already become a nun in 647 and had been made abbess of Hartlepool by Aidan. Bede referred to her as the successor of Heiu, "the first woman in Northumbria to take vows and the habit of a nun, consecrated by Bishop Aidan".

Hilda was the grand-niece of King Edwin. She ruled the monastery (men's and women's) at Whitby. The monastery at Whitby was highly influential and, according to Bede, it produced five bishops. One of the talented monks of Whitby was Caedmon, who had a remarkable gift for composing religious and devotional verses based mainly on the Scriptures. These verses expressed the themes of Christian faith in a simple and accessible form and won many to the faith on account of their spiritual depth and appeal. In his verses Caedmon expounded the biblical themes of creation, the origin of life, the story of the exodus, the incarnation, passion, death and resurrection of Christ, and the coming of the Holy Spirit. Many learnt the rudiments of the faith through memorizing the verses of Caedmon. Here is an example of a verse on the praise of God:

> Praise now the Keeper of the heavenly Kingdom,
> The power and purpose of our Creator,
> The acts of the Author of glory. The eternal God,
> Maker of marvels, almighty Preserver,
> First raised the sky as a roof for the races of men,
> And then spread the earth beneath them.

Also in this period we note how Boniface (680–754), a scholarly monk from Crediton in Devon, secured the support of the pope for a mission to Germany. Boniface has been called the Apostle of Germany. He did not make a complete break with the English, but he is remembered, amongst much else, for his view of how the Church and the state need each other. He sought to enlist the aid of the state in the service of the Church. An English recruit to his mission, named Willibald, wrote a life of Boniface. Boniface also enlisted the help of women in his mission. He acknowledged the kindness, comfort and practical help they gave him, and requested them, "So now I pray you to add to what you have begun by transcribing for me in gold the Epistles of my Lord St. Peter the Apostle, to gain honour and reverence for the Holy Scriptures when they are preached before the eyes of the heathen."

Boniface was a strict moralist, as became evident in his address to the King of Mercia. In this Boniface praised the king's alms-giving to the poor, the way he prohibited theft, purgery and plunder, defended widows, and kept the peace. At the same time he pointed out the king's misdeeds, especially his unlawful behaviour, lust and adultery. This behaviour Boniface comdemned as shameful in the sight of God, and reprehensible in the eyes of his subjects. He also remonstrated with the king for his treatment of monasteries and nuns; this he regarded as violation of the bride of Christ. He pleaded that kindness should be shown to his disciples in the future and to all foreigners. He declared that none of these should forfeit the law of Christ. Boniface himself was devoted to the papacy, as he made clear when he set out on his German mission. His missionary methods are reputed to have been sometimes dramatic but otherwise straightforward, but he was notably successful in his mission of evangelism.

As well as his missionary accomplishments, Boniface set his mind on reform of the slack state of the Frankish Church, which had developed a worldly and materialist tone. Boniface impressed upon the king of the Franks the urgent need for reform, and after his pleading a number of reforming councils were held between 742 and 747. The councils formulated a number of measures aimed at reform but how far these were put into practice is uncertain. The character of Boniface is reflected in his letters, and it has been said of him:

> Notwithstanding his devotion to the papacy, he was an embryonic English Protestant. He had a strong sense of responsibility to his vocation of preaching and loved to compare himself to Saint Paul. He was very aware of his duty to his conscience.[10]

In the west, in Wales, the age of the Celtic saints from the fifth to the seventh century was one of fervent and varied religious activity. The monks settled in enclosures (*llan*) which developed into centres of Christian communal activity, education and missionary work.

The names of some of these saints, such as St. David, St. Cybi and St. Deiniol, are commemorated in places and churches to this day. It seems that monasticism reached Wales from Egypt, where, as we have seen, hermits lived a secluded life of prayer and fasting. These are two characteristics also of the Celtic saints of Wales and the inspiration of their missionary labours. The Celtic Church developed its own form of ritual, especially of baptism, and its own date for Easter, which differed from that of the Church of Rome. Many of the earliest Celtic saints were wandering ascetics who travelled by sea as well as on foot. They established monasteries wherever they settled, and the remains are found in many parts to this day. These were often just cells sufficient to provide shelter and basic amenities, but with time they developed into community centres. One feature of this development was the observance of special occasions in the Christian calendar, for instance, Lent. During Lent the monks might withdraw to some quiet island off the coast for a period of meditation and spiritual devotion and refreshment. These "holy" places of retreat also became places of pilgrimage, and the saints maintained that three pilgrimages to a holy place, for example, St. David's, was equal to a pilgrimage to Rome.

The Cistercian Order

The application of the rule of Benedict is significantly represented in the Cistercian Order of the eleventh century. The monastery founded by St. Robert of Molesme (1024–1110) at Citeaux became one of the leading monasteries of the twelfth century. By the middle of the century there were well over three hundred abbeys of the Cistercian Order. Whilst they stood in the tradition of the Benedictines the Cistercians added their own rule for the governance of sister houses, called the "Charter of Charity". Still they kept to the principle of some form of central government. In contrast to the Benedictine Order, which accepted boys for training to be monks, the Cistercians recruited young men who had rejected the values and life-style of contemporary society. The Cistercian Order was strict in the regulation of its devotional life; one requirement was the practice of silence in a community devoted mainly to prayer and the performance of the liturgy.

But it has been said that the Cistercians interpreted their return to the rule of Benedict in economic terms, and that in a time of population growth and an expanding society the Cistercians became "the agricultural apostles of Europe's internal colonialization". "Most of them were aristocrats, the younger sons of magnates. They saw themselves as a small, pure elite. Their discipline was ferocious. They developed a great driving force, became outstanding managers, and so prospered enormously."[11]

The Cistercians rejected all adornment, such as jewelled crosses and ornaments and hill towers; their life-style was simple and their diet vegetarian, and they made no provision for recreation. As time passed they relaxed some of these stricter practices, especially as they amassed wealth from sheep farming. The Cistercians are believed to have had a part in the creation of the feast of *Corpus Christi*, the feast of the Eucharist (Blessed Sacrament) ordered by Pope Urban IV in 1264, and celebrated today on the first Thursday or Sunday after the feast of the Holy Trinity. This popular feast paid respect to the body of Christ transubstantiated in the host, in the same way as respect was paid to the bodies of the deceased.

It is thought by some that Thomas Aquinas composed the liturgy for this feast. It was observed by offering special indulgences and the performance of miracle or mystery plays.

Bernard of Clairvaux

The most famous member of the Cistercian Order, often regarded as its second founder, is Bernard of Clairvaux (1090–1153), theologian and preacher, author of a treatise *On Consideration*, in which he complained about certain practices of the papacy, and champion of the pastoral ministry of the Church. Bernard has been described as an extraordinary man of genius and one of the most powerful men in Europe.[12] He is known as a pope-maker. He was a capable administrator, he worked to win recruits for the second crusade in 1146, and was made a doctor of the Roman Catholic Church in 1153. By nature he was conservative and anti-worldly; he viewed the monastery as a spiritual centre, a foretaste of the life of heaven.

In his teaching Bernard was committed to the ideal of Christendom united under the governance of a strong papacy, as well as "to the eschatological pressure of the gospel which he knew to be the real source of his identity and his call".[13] He wrote a treatise *On Loving God* which explains the relationship between the self and God as degrees of God's love. The four stages are loving self, loving neighbour and God, loving God for God's sake, and love of the soul for God's sake.[14] The concept of Christian love dominated his thought. Love for its own sake is possible through what God has done, self-love loses itself in the love of God until its will becomes one with the will of God. This fusion may be experienced on earth but is eternal after death. How it is achieved is a mystery. The union of the self with God is like the mixing of water in wine and heating iron in the fire. Bernard described the intimacy of this love relationship as "summertime", summertime in love:

> The summertime has come with Him who, set free from icy death to live in the spring season of new life, tells us, "Behold I make all things new".[15]

Through the image of summertime Bernard conveyed the sweetness of response to the love of God and how it blossoms in dignity, knowledge, virtue, gratitude, and the recognition of God's gifts to humankind. These gifts are supremely manifested in Christ and the personal awareness of his care. Only then can love of self for self's sake liberate the individual to love of the neighbour as oneself.

> This is the fulfilling of the commandment to love God with a whole heart and soul, when the needs of the flesh cease to press and body and soul are in perfect harmony.[16]

Bernard did, however, conceive of the divine and human love as being on different planes. The one was not confused with the other. The union between them is not a union of substance but of wills. This differs from the union of God and Christ, which is an eternal union of will. No person can confront God as being on the same human level, yet Christ meets and loves eternally.

This meeting expresses the fullness of the humility of love which Christ showed and conceived as he identified himself with those who were in need of compassion and succour. This humility shown by Christ is essential for the Christian, "there is no danger however much you may humble yourself, that you will regard yourself as much less than you really are – that is to say, than truth holds you to be". The stress which Bernard placed on meeting Christ face to face arises from his emphasis on the significance of the humanity of Jesus. He referred frequently to the gospel portrait of Jesus not merely as an example of spirituality but as the incarnation of the divine action of love. The effect of this loving action is to change the human heart. Devotion to the humanity of Jesus is one of the gifts of the Holy Spirit. The love which Christ radiated is spiritual love, it bears the characteristics of the fullness of the Spirit. So meeting Christ is to be enlightened by the Spirit and never to be drawn away from him by any false spirit. This is the message of a sermon on the Song of Songs delivered by Bernard:

> Let Christ who is the power of God, strengthen you so that you are not overcome by any enemies. Let Christian love strengthen your desire to do good: let Christ's wisdom rule you and direct your life and let steadfastness make you persevere in this. Your Christian love must not be lukewarm, timid or indiscreet. This is what is laid down in the Law, when God says, "Love the Lord your God with all your heart and with all your soul and with all your strength" (Deuteronomy 6: 5).

The above sermon is a helpful illustration of Bernard's gift as an expositor of Scripture. He developed a spiritual approach to the Bible. Throughout his expositions there is a deep sense of union with God and spiritual intimacy with Jesus. The intimacy between the soul and Jesus is one of grace; it is the source of confidence and deep passion. Jesus is described as bride as well as bridegroom of the human soul. Love creates a seeking and a longing for this relationship and for the good of the one who is loved.

Waldensian deviance

During the early part of the twelfth century the Church passed through a period of unrest and had to combat the rise of heresy and attacks on the devotion paid to images such as the crucifix, or the orthodoxy of infant baptism, and on the standard and conduct of the priesthood. It was necessary for the Church to respond quickly and firmly. One form this response took was popular preaching as a way of keeping active the nature and practices of orthodox faith and spirituality. About 1174, Peter Waldo, a wealthy merchant of Lyons in France, and an orthodox Christian believer, broke with the pope and he and his followers formed the Waldensian movement, which separated from the Church and spread rapidly. Most of the Waldensians were poor people but they were strictly orthodox in their beliefs. They based their preaching on the Bible and took literally the injunction to live a life of poverty. Their defence of orthodoxy was uncompromising and they maintained that their poverty and holding all things in common followed the tradition of the first apostles.

The Waldensians were excommunicated in 1182, and in 1209 Pope Innocent III ordered a crusade against them. In the late Middle Ages the Waldensians founded communities in Italy and Germany, but by today they survive only in southern Italy. We know of the early Waldensians only through the writings of their opponents, but we gather how they were disenchanted with a rich and unspiritual church and opted for a life of following the apostles, "possessing nothing . . . naked following the naked Christ". They became known as the poor in spirit, following the beatitude of Jesus, "Blessed are the poor in spirit". Yet such was their humility that they said they were also poor in the Holy Spirit. They rejected contemptuously the indulgences granted by the Church, they abandoned saying prayers for the dead and belief in purgatory. They forbade judging others as prohibited by God but they had power to hear confessions even though they were not ordained. They were, however, ostracized as heretics.

The Friars

During the early years of the thirteenth century some decisive steps were taken to address the ills that had befallen the Church in the previous century. In 1215 the Lateran Council aimed to reconstruct the pastoral ministry of the Church and to develop the understanding of the faith of its members and promote their spirituality. Pope Innocent III, who was pontiff from 1198–1216, took the initiative in this and lent support to the promotion of the pastoral work of the Church. He instituted a deepening awareness of the importance of confession and self-examination before the mass, the provision of counselling services and teaching of the faith, as well as an improvement in the training of clergy for their duties. Innocent also encouraged and supported the ministry of the friars, particularly Dominic (1170–1221) and Francis of Assisi (1181–1226). Innocent looked upon them as the spearhead of reform that would inaugurate a new life of spirituality into the Church.

Dominic was a powerful and influential preacher who was wholly committed to preaching as a medium of Christian communication. He created a small community of preachers in Toulouse where he aimed personally to live out to the uttermost the principles of the Christian life in obedience and holiness. He directed his preaching in the main to the poor and people who were marginalized by society. His constant prayer was that he "might have a true love of souls and ability to help others". He embraced a life of poverty and shunned material possessions. His preaching was mostly in the open air, but of those who worshipped in a church building, which was sparse, he said:

> These people gave us need to temporal things but with fervent desire and impetuous energy labour every day to withdraw perishing souls from the vanities of the world and lead them with them . . . They live after the model of the early Church . . . [17]

Dominic founded his preaching order to combat Albigensian heresy, that is, dualism or antagonism between matter and spirit and light and darkness. Innocent III launched a crusade against the heretics which led to a long and bitter struggle. Dominic seems to have approved the crusade, but only on the proviso that heretics who converted after leaving his and the friars' preaching should not be rejected.

The order of "preaching friars" spread rapidly to many parts of Europe and as it took root it also exercised a ministry of teaching the faith. It was influential in Paris where the important convent of St. Jacques was established.

An order of women was also founded, and in 1221 the Dominicans reached England. They entered the country bare-footed and in dire poverty. They soon settled and built a number of simple meeting houses from where they wandered around the country preaching. They wore a black habit and claimed to have forsaken the things of the world in order to follow Christ. The resident clergy viewed their mission with great suspicion, but the Dominicans attracted some leading mystic luminaries to their ranks, including Meister Eckhart, Johannes Tauler, and Henry Suso. The Dominican Order thrived through its reforming spirit and its modernism and intellectual integrity. Its members sought passionately the salvation of souls other than their own.

Francis of Assisi is arguably the most charismatic and fascinating figure of his age. The Christian values of love and humility were so perfectly blended in his character that he seemed annexed to the character of Christ himself. His life and work testify to his unsullied vision of the universal presence of Christ in all things. His theology was steeped in the transcendent nature of God whose spirit indwells every part of creation and "all creatures great and small". He loved all living things. The whole creation in every part is bonded to God, so Francis confessed in one of his *Canticles*:

> for the element of air which he has appointed for you, and giveth you the streams and the fountains for your drink, the mountains and valleys are your refuge . . . and because you do not know how to spin or sow, God clothed you and your children, therefore your creator loveth you much.

All that lives and moves is radiant with the supernatural presence that induces intense feelings of rapture and delights in the divine providence. This rapture exemplifies the joyous presence of Christ, and ever since Francis took his monastic vows he felt he was girding himself to Christ. It is said of him that "his life was to be nothing less than 'an imitation of Christ', conscious, literal, and uncompromising".[18] He described his vocation as being "a gay adventure, for Christ". He immersed himself completely in his vocation and was so absorbed in his awareness of Christ that he believed that Christ spoke directly to him.

Francis's order of "little friars" included laymen; he demanded from them all obedience to the pope and bishops. The friars were recruited mainly from the poorer classes and by the beginning of the fourteenth century there were nearly a thousand, and five hundred Franciscan houses. Francis's greatest passion was to follow in the steps of those who Christ sent out to preach the gospel. He commanded them, "Everywhere on your road preach and say, 'The Kingdom of God is at hand'." He willed his order to be identified by its preaching, prayer, joy, simplicity, poverty and charity, such as characterized the work of Christ himself. Francis believed he was charged with a special commission to rebuild the wholesome life of the Church, that was in danger of crumbling; this was only possible if he imbibed the divine spirit and was intoxicated with the divine love. The focus of this love was the suffering and death of Jesus. The thought of this sacrificial love moved him to tears as he dwelt on his own sin. This conscious sense of spiritual need moved Francis to bind himself to Christ in a life of discipline, prayer, unselfishness, simplicity, poverty and begging.

One of his companions said that Francis willed and preached to them that they should desire to be founded on holy humility, imitating pure simplicity, holy prayer, and on holy poverty, on which the saints and friars did build. And this, he used to say, was the only way to one's own salvation and the edification of others, since Christ, to whose imitation we are called, showed and taught us this alone by word and example alike.[19]

A second order for women, the Poor Clares, enjoyed the same ideals as the Franciscans. Clare of Assisi and the sisters of her order remained in the monastery without wandering from place to place as did Francis and the Franciscans. The sisters lived a life of contemplation and followed the example of Jesus by living in poverty. The order now became known as the "Brothers and Sisters of Penance". Some members of the Franciscan Order distinguished themselves as poets, some of whose work is familiar in English and sung today. *Dies Irae* (day of wrath, day of mourning) and *Stabat Mater* ("By the Cross her stature keeping, stood the Virgin Mother weeping") are the compositions of Franciscans, probably Thomas de Celano (1200–55). Francis himself was devoted to the papacy and wrote a "rule" in ten parts for his Order, and this was accepted by the pope. The Franciscan Order flourished and spread and inaugurated missions as far afield as India and China. Francis himself travelled the country giving counselling to people in trouble and exercising a pastoral ministry. He was usually received with joy and would preach to the people. His preaching was centred on the love of God and God's love for all creatures. In one of his *Canticles* Francis addressed "My little sisters", spoke of how God feeds the birds and provides them with fountains of water and so many other benefits, and said that they must "beware of the sin of ingratitude, and study always to give praises unto God". The praise of God is the theme of one of the greatest Christian hymns, known as the *Canticle of the Sun*, in which Francis praised the Most High, Omnipotent, Good Lord for all his works – sun, moon, star, wind, air, breezes, cloud, weather, water, fire, earth, food, grass and flowers. These he addressed as mother, brother and sister. His prayer for peace is still used regularly to this day:

> Lord, make me an instrument of thy peace. Where there is hatred let me now love; where there is injury, pardon; where there is doubt, faith; where there is despair, hope; where there is darkness, light; where there is sadness, joy.

The Dominican and Franciscan Orders (or the Mendicant Orders) provided the Church with an upsurge of spiritual vitality. They supplied a deep reservoir of spirituality to clergy and laity.

They responded more positively and enthusiastically to the spiritual needs of their age than the older monastic orders of the time. The friars kindled a bright flame of evangelical fervour that the monastery had lost, and they also contributed substantially to the fabric of western civilization and to the scholastic revolution that was overtaking the Church. In this context the name of St. Bonaventura (1217–74), a scholastic theologian, merits mention. He became minister general of the Franciscan Order and employed his great learning in its service.

Bonaventura was one of the Franciscans who helped to replace the monastery with the university as a centre of western culture. He and others of the same ilk established the university as a centre of philosophy and theology. Many leading scholars of the thirteenth and fourteenth centuries were friars. Bonaventura was learned in the classics and wrote extensively, whilst at the same time integrating his writings with the teaching and thought of Francis. He wrote works on *Evangelical Perfection, On The Mystery of the Trinity*, and *The Journey of the Mind to God*, among others. His theology was cohesive and all-embracing; it owed much to Francis of Assisi, and is entirely Christ centred. The incarnation of Christ is the basis of his doctrine and he adhered firmly to the orthodox explanation of the Trinity. Human reason of itself can neither deny nor affirm the existence of God, but God's closeness to the human spirit is indisputable. Only deficiency in human reason can deny the existence of God; God is love, and love transcends reason; the goal of love is knowledge of God. Christ is the centre of reality and his incarnation made this centre historically visible. Christ is also the centre of the Trinity; he mediated the divine nature to perfection, through his incarnation he became the centre of the universe. Like his theology, Bonaventura's spirituality is akin to that of Francis of Assisi: its centrepoint is Christ, the mediator of grace and the mentor of the soul. Love is the summit of the soul and through his incarnate life Christ mediated values that are indispensable if life is to be transformed and conform to Christ's pattern of grace. Through his resurrection Christ exercises a ministry of purgation, illumination and perfection. The perfection of the soul issues in ecstatic loving union with God, the primacy of God's love is the spring of union between the human and divine beings; the human soul is enjoined in a spiritual pilgrimage whose goal is spiritual union with God. This pilgrimage is integral with the spiritual pilgrimage of the Church towards the realization of the era of the Holy Spirit, the new age of contemplation, spirituality and peace, in brief, the dawn of the day (*eschaton*) of Christ.[20]

Bonaventura was a man of prayer who kept long vigils. He exercised strict control over his body and physical passions. He imposed discipline over his brother monks but also displayed tolerance and compassion and a real desire for the salvation of his neighbours. He urged his fellow monks to preach this message, to found priories and to live a frugal life by relinquishing all material wealth. Bonaventura befriended the poor and pagans and people of other faiths. He observed the law of silence and agonized long in prayer to God for the sins of others. He also spent much time in studying the Scriptures of the Old and New Testaments.[21]

Mysticism and the love of God

No overview of the spiritual tradition of the Middle Ages can overlook the flowering of mysticism and mystical theology. The fourteenth century was the classical age of mysticism. As the word implies, there is a certain "mysteriousness" here that beggars definition. The most spiritually sensitive souls, whom we call mystics, enjoyed communion with God in a very special degree; they shared an ecstatic vision that others only saw vaguely; they experienced an immediate, intense and rapturous relationship with God; they were participants in the divine presence to the extent of achieving self-identity with God. The core of this identity was love, but this involved experiencing the whole range of human emotions, including passing through "the dark night of the soul", the despair of spiritual nihilism or angst along with flights of ecstatic joy. This was the struggle to have Christ born in the soul and to be filled with his love and enjoy him for ever. Mysticism is the experience of the soul immersed in love to God and consummated by love. In illustration of this spiritual tradition we may refer to two notable mystics from this period.

Meister Eckhart

Eckhart (1260–1327) belonged to the Dominican Order and entered the priory at Erfurt where it is believed he may have received his education in the arts. As was the custom of the time he moved to other centres of learning, including Cologne and Paris. Eventually he was appointed as prior of Erfurt and later vicar general of the province of Bohemia. From the time of his appointment to these ecclesiastical offices Eckhart undertook teaching of the faith and providing for the spiritual nourishment of his fellow monks. He composed a *Commentary on the Lord's*

Prayer and Talks of Instruction for this purpose, but most of his work survives in sermons. He exercised a compassionate pastoral ministry but he also took an active part in theological debate. In 1310 he was elevated to the Dominican chair of theology in Paris, but from here he moved to Strasbourg, and in 1324 to Cologne. He gained a reputation as an eminent teacher and a speculative theologian.

Relationships between the Dominicans and Franciscans were not harmonious, and the Franciscan Archbishop of Cologne made accusations of heresy against Eckhart. Eckhart was defended by his immediate subordinate, Nicholas of Strasbourg. The accusations against Eckhart were drawn from his writings, but Eckhart contested them on the assumption that heresy is a matter of the will. On this assumption none of his teaching could be "heretical". The propositions of Eckhart were considered by a papal commission who divided them into three groups — those which were questionable, those which showed error, and those which were consistent with orthodox belief. These were included in a papal bull by Pope John XXII in 1329, and condemned.

Eckhart has been described as a theological mystic and a mystical theologian, that is, his teaching is in essence a system of thought that comes to terms with personal mystical life-experience. He was guided to this personal life-experience of mystical union with God through every point of his theological speculative system. The experience is indefinable, elusive and challenging. It scales the contemplative heights and at heart is dynamic not static.[22] This experience is possible because God has implanted something of himself (of his essence) within the human being: this gives it the capacity to reach the heart of the Godhead by transcending the natural world and penetrate to profounder levels of reality.[23] He taught that what is real in all things is divine. There is a spark of this divine reality in everyone.

In the history of theology Eckhart stands in the tradition of Thomas Aquinas, to whom we shall refer later, especially in respect of his theological methodology. This method is that of describing phenomena in the form of an image, as "the active intellect pouring images into the womb of the passive intellect until the latter becomes pregnant, 'conceives' the object as intelligible".[24] For example, in prayer "the active intellect is superseded and the agency of God himself is the inseminating force – [the] intellect's response is, then, a simple, completely focused act: the mind is refined to a point of concentration".[25]

Among other elements of Eckhart's teaching that are relevant to our purpose are his view of the soul as like God in its perfect unity, as the image of God's solitude: when the soul is pure of all else God comes in without any hesitation or delay; the soul is the heart of pure being which reflects God, and so "is" God; in grace the soul takes on the shape of that which it contemplates, yet God never shows himself in his purity to finite persons in this life; Christian growth is a constantly deepening attention to the pure, a readiness to let go of self-directed thoughts; all external devotions are adjuncts of this. The true following of Christ is the following of the whole Christ, the divine Word and the human Jesus. The Trinity is God, not Godhead; as Trinity God acts, as Godhead he is at rest; as in eternity the Godhead blossoms into Trinity, so in the soul it flowers into the birth of the eternal Word. The Word is in the Father as the intellectual image of his divine essence. Father and Son wrestle to beget the Spirit. The soul meeting God unites with his trinitarian movement of being one with the naked Godhead of which the Trinity is the self-revelation. This union is achieved by laying aside all selfish desires until it finds God in every experience and activity; this God-like life is accessible now as it relies on renunciation and meaning-ful experiences in prayer. This leads to the heart of God's silence.[26]

All these ideas flow as streams to swell the ocean of perfect spiritual fulfilment. The contribution of Meister Eckhart to our appreciation of the Christian spiritual tradition is consistent with the mainstream teaching of the Catholic Church. This is another way of saying that his importance:

> is chiefly in his insistence that union with God is a reality affecting the whole of experience, not merely its religious moments. The foundation on which all else rests is the displacement of the self's longing for dominion and satisfaction; when this occurs, in or out of prayer or reli-gious practice, the self enters into God's life and "works God's works". What matters is not "ecstasy" in the common sense of abnormal spiritual experience but the ecstasy of understanding, the transition of subject into object, the setting aside of self in order to let the observed and understood reality act without impediment. The self when made naked and poor is free to go forward to God and be welcomed into God.[27]

Julian of Norwich

Julian of Norwich (1353–1416) has been called the leading woman visionary of her age. She was subject to many "showings" that are the core of her mysticism. We know of these visions through her work *Revelations of Divine Love*, which is one of the classic works on Christian spirituality. The visions were an answer to prayer when Julian was at the point of death. Through them she received a message that she should share in the sufferings of Christ at his crucifixion. She was deeply committed to prayer and this experience led her to adopt a solitary life of interior devotion to God, lived in a cell attached to the church of St. Julian in Norwich. The name of the church is the only name by which she is known.

Julian's writings are rich in knowledge of the Gospel of John, the letters of St. Paul and the works of Augustine. She made no claim to formal learning yet she displayed considerable skill as a theologian and is well known for her exposition of Jesus as our Mother, "who carries us within himself in love".

> Jesus is the true mother of our nature, for he made us. He is our Mother, too, by grace, because he took our created nature upon himself. All the lovely deeds and tender services that beloved motherhood implies are appropriate to the second person. In him the godly will is always safe and sound, both in nature and grace, because of his own fundamental goodness.

Jesus as our Mother epitomizes his relation to humankind as well as his love. From this axis point Julian explored the mysteries of God's relationship with human beings and her own inner sense of intimacy with him. This led her to expound her view of how God deals with human sin and effects human redemption. She tackled some of the intractable theological problems of the ages, such as how God permits sin in a world created by him who is wholly good. God saw that the world he made is good, from whence then comes the sin that is all too obvious? Julian's expositions are not just speculative or analytical, but they are woven around the "showings" of her visionary experiences. She found enlightenment on the questions through pondering the inner meaning of these "showings". For instance, in a vision of a servant who had fallen into a pit whilst on his master's business, she had a "showing" of Adam's fall into sin; the master's pity for his servant is a "showing" of Christ's descent in a compassionate human act to save people. The existence of sin made necessary the act of God in the incarnation of Christ; the all-consuming purpose of the incarnation was to manifest the love that is the heart of God. The divine love is extended to rescue and forgive; love, declared Julian, is the key that unlocks the meaning of the incarnation; incarnation is the revelation of love; love is the purpose of the incarnation.[28]

Two other aspects of the theology and spirituality of Julian deserve notice. She proclaimed firmly belief in the ultimate redemption of the whole world. God so loved the world he made that the final outcome of his creation must be its complete consummation into his love. The perfect redemption of the whole world is consistent with the purpose of creation. Complementary to this is Julian's confident hope, that she conveyed in a daringly simplistic saying, "All shall be well, all manner of things shall be well."

This is not optimism divorced from the harsh realities of life in the fourteenth century in Norwich. War, plague and famine blighted life around her. Her belief was grounded in the invincible love that had brought the world into being and that was destined to be victorious over all else. Her hope was engendered by the reality of love and how in its own mysterious way love will act to bring about the transformation of all that is.

As the mystical tradition in Christian spirituality blossomed so we encounter some of the great personalities of late medieval Christianity, such as Johannes Tauler (?1361), a Dominican preacher of Strasbourg, Blessed Henry Suso (?1366), who believed that "God did gladden the heart of the sufferer in return for all his sufferings with inward peace of heart", John Ruysbroeck (1294–1381), who was influenced by Eckhart, and Gèrhard Groot (1340–84), a noted scholar and preacher from the Netherlands. The writings of the mystics, some of which are anonymous, are rated as the classics of Christian spirituality, works like *The Cloud of Unknowing, Revelations of Divine Love, Seale of Perfection*, among many others. Their theme is the mystic union of the soul with God in a life of contemplation; the inner awareness of the presence of God within is all pervasive, it constitutes "a spiritual marriage" of complete natural reciprocity in love.

Mystical theology expounds the nature and meaning of this mystical experience. Its operational force is divine grace, which acts as a transforming agent to create perfect union or the dynamic affinity of love between God and the human soul. At the heart of the love there is a yearning for unity within and between the whole creation and the divine creator. Mystical theology explicates the nature and action of this divine yearning; the exercise of spirituality is the experience of its unifying potential.

Scholars, theology and spirituality

From the eleventh century onward the west witnessed a notable upsurge in intellectual pursuits and a sharpening of the human mind. New centres of learning sprang up which were Christian or Church based; they operated under Church law with theology as central to their learning and teaching. Many of the most respectable intellects of the day contributed seminally to the new development by employing a methodology of philosophical concepts and technical language coordinated into a system of learning that became known as scholasticism. In these influential medieval centres of learning the works of the Church Fathers, and especially of St. Augustine, were a core element in the study through providing complete and intricate training of the intellect and the skills of theological disputation, analysis and argument. A new generation of theologians arose who contributed to this expanding educational provision through pioneering new expositions and education of the nature and essence of Christian truth. Scholasticism may, therefore, be seen as a bridge between the late medieval and post-reformation world of European culture and religion. The schoolmen as they engaged in an expanding programme of theology also stimulated and nourished a spirituality of deeper insights and activity. They aimed to present Christian truth in a logical form. We can only here refer to a few representative contributions to this productive tradition.

Anselm

Anselm (1033–1109), a native of Italy who became Archbishop of Canterbury, was an outstanding intellect and original theologian. Anselm has been called the father of the schoolmen. He was committed to the papacy and championed its authority, was active in reform and rooting out of the church nepotism, simony, and establishing the rule of clerical celibacy. He called for complete commitment on the part of the clergy to their clerical duties and the dedication and nurture of spirituality of all Christians. His personal piety and sense of dependence on divine providence is expressed in his work *Cur Deus Homo* written about 1097, in which he stated:

> What a man has, not from himself but from God, he ought to regard as not as much his own as God's. For no one has from himself the truth that he teaches, or a righteous will, but from God.

In philosophy and systematic theology Anselm is well known for his argument for the existence of God. Christians who believe in God should be able to give reasons or explanations for their belief. Anselm was the first to state clearly the ontological argument for God. Simply stated the argument is that the existence of God is self-evident; from the very notion of God it is evident that God exists; we could not conceive of God unless God exists; existence is inseparable from the notion of

God, therefore God must exist. In the *Proslogion* Anselm wrote:

> We believe that you are something than which nothing greater can be
> thought. Therefore, if that than which nothing greater can be thought
> exists in the understanding alone, then the very being than which nothing
> greater can be thought is one than which a greater can be thought. But
> this is certainly impossible. Hence, there is no doubt that there exists
> something than which nothing greater can be thought, and both in the
> understanding and in reality.

Starting from the premiss of the existence of God, Anselm developed
an *a priori* argument based on the idea of God rather than an *a posteriori* argument based on the works of God. God, he maintained, is the
greatest being humans can conceive; of God there is no greater. Those
who reject the idea of God's existence altogether must admit that he
exists in the mind of the believer. Yet being greater than any other being,
how can God exist only in the mind? In reply Anselm argued on the
assumption that if God only exists in the mind it is possible to think of
something greater, namely, the same being (God) existing outside the
mind, that is, existing in reality. So Anselm arrived at his conclusion that
God exists both in the mind and in reality. This conclusion could be
proved by formal arguments. He asserted that faith and understanding
belong together, understanding without faith is impossible and vice
versa.

Anselm also expounded a doctrine of the atonement as satisfaction
to God's justice. He began by referring to and exhibiting the human
situation which called for a divine atonement, God made provision for
this in the work of Christ and his death. It was the passion and cross of
Christ that made atonement possible. Atonement is something done by
Christ and accepted by God in expiation of human sin. For this work
of atonement Christ was ordained by God, for declared Anselm:

> Christ therefore came not to do his own will, but the Father's because the
> righteous will which he had was not from his human but from his divine
> nature.

Anselm is also the author of *Prayers and Meditations*, a collection of
prayers written to help others pray. Many of his prayers focus on love
as their theme, and this dominated Anselm's intercessions for his
friends, as in this example,

> Blessed Lord, who hast commanded us to love one another, grant us grace
> that, having received Thine undeserved bounty, we may love everyone in
> Thee and for Thee. We implore Thy clemency for all, but especially for

the friends whom Thy love has given to us. Love Thou them, O Thou
Fountain of love, and make them to love Thee with all their heart, that
they may will, and speak, and do those things only which are pleasing to
Thee. Amen.

Peter Abelard

Peter Abelard (1079–1142) was gifted with an acute religious mind and
was a teacher and theologian of outstanding brilliance. He is remembered as a monk, a teacher and a lover. He, like Anselm, contributed to
the development of educational institutions that became the precursor
of the university as we know it today. The educational system was
rigorous and in theology it emphasized the importance of pure thought
and involved students in disputations with masters. Knowledge of
Scripture and its systematic exposition was basic.

Abelard's great work *Sic et Non* (Yes and No) is a rational exposition of the Christian religion written with the aim of promoting and
strengthening faith. It set side by side texts from the Scriptures and the
works of the Church Fathers which superficially seemed to contradict
each other. The intention was to show how they could be reconciled.
Abelard asserted that "by doubting we come to questioning, and by
questioning we come to the truth". Thus he promoted his student's
ability to analyze texts critically and to develop skills of interpretation
and synthesis. Among the themes of *Sic et Non* are how to study, but
more attuned to his theology are the themes of the atonement, that is,
how Christ through his sufferings and death rendered adequate and
superabundant atonement to God for the sins of human kind, and the
authority of the Church. Abelard did not reject the works of the Church
Fathers or the creeds but believed that they should be subject to philosophical and critical evaluation. He taught that the human race had
inherited punishment and not faith from Adam, and that good and evil
were in the will rather than in the performance. He rejected the idea of
a ransom being paid to the devil and viewed the death of Christ as the
supreme expression of divine love. Through this act of love God
awakens love in people so that a bond of union is thereby sealed
between them.

As well as his distinction as a theologian (he has been called "the first
of the modernists"), Abelard displayed passionate devotion to Héloïse
in one of the great romances of history. Abelard became a monk and
Heloise a nun, and he conveyed his love in hymns which he wrote for
use in Héloïse's nunnery at Nagent-sur-Seine. Their theme centred

around the love of Christ in his death which awakens a response in love, or how "love answers love's appeal". Many of his hymns have been translated, such as this one by John Mason Neale, which also conveys Abelard's doctrine of the Trinity:

> Low before Him with our praise we fall,
> of whom and in whom, and through whom are all;
> of whom, the Father; and through whom, the Son;
> In whom, the Spirit, with these ever one.

Abelard also composed a series of nocturnes for Good Friday, of which this example is the third:

> Good Friday: *The Third Nocturne*
>
> Alone to sacrifice thou goest, Lord,
> Giving thyself to death whom thou hast slain,
> For us the wretched folk is any word,
> Who know that for our sins this is thy pain?
>
> So may our hearts have pity on thee, Lord,
> That they may sharers of thy glory be;
> Heavy with weeping may the three days pass,
> To win the laughter of thine Easter day.

Thomas Aquinas

Thomas Aquinas (1225–74), a Dominican monk, was one of the most formidable theologians of his age. His writings are still widely respected and treasured by the Roman Catholic Church and are still the subject of discussion and interpretation by Neo-Thomists. Aquinas was a pupil of the Dominican friar Albertus Magnus, and is known as the distinguished author of the highly influential *Summa Theologica*. He used the deductive method in his theological writings along with the categories of reason and revelation. It is impossible to simplify the basic themes of this monumental work in a brief space, but only possible to provide pointers to his seminal thinking and his spirituality. The all-embracing term by which his teaching is studied today is Thomism, but this is variously interpreted and applied. It expounds a theory of knowledge and an argument for the existence of God that employ cosmological categories. These take account of reason and revelation. The Bible is a channel of revelation. Proof for the existence of God is inherent in the motion that brought the universe into being at the beginning.

This belief is an item of revelation, but revealed theology can only be understood through the power of reason to defend and systemize it.

This being the case, the universe is seen to be a work of design and from this fact it is proper to infer the existence of a designer, "For these things which do not have knowledge do not tend to an end except under the direction of someone who knows and understands; the arrow, for example, is shot by the archer. There is, however, an intelligent personal being by whom everything in nature is ordered to its end, and this we call God." Yet God does not belong to any class.

This being the case it is evident that God is the cause and power of every operation; he gave being to things when they first began and accounts for their operation – "God alone can move the will, as an agent, without doing violence to it." He works in us the power of willing in a way that makes us will this or that. This willing persists until it achieves its object, but God alone can move the will, and "It is God who awakes in us the wish and to accomplish, according to his good will."

The willing persists until it achieves its object in so far as it is perfect, and a thing is perfect "in so far as it is actual". All things aim at their own perfection. In so far as being exists so does something good, and, in reality, goodness and being are one and the same. Reality, however, points to what is beyond, namely to God. Essential to the under-standing of the underlying theme at this point is the call for reconciliation between the natural and supernatural order. Natural order can be studied by reason but the supernatural order is known through grace. Natural reason can postulate the relationship but it is only perfected through faith. Faith and reason therefore belong together; to distinguish between natural reason and revealed faith is "frivolous" (Aquinas' term); to assent to faith that is not justified by reason is untenable; faith is no excuse for disposing of reason, on the contrary, faith is the assent of reason. Accordingly knowledge of God is accessible to natural reason. The general features of the external world provide "a knowledge of God which is easier and more certain than our knowledge of the things of the world".

Turning to Aquinas's spirituality and ethics we see how his natural-istic view of the unity of creation leads to the discovery of natural moral laws. A world that is governed by divine providence and reason postu-lates moral imperatives. The eternal law of God regulates and subjects all things to divine providence, but natural reason leads to obedience and a share in the eternal law, so that:

> It is as much as to say that the light of natural reason, by which we discern what is good and what evil – is nothing but an imprint of the Divine Light upon us. Hence it is clear that the law of nature is nothing but the partici-pation by a rational creature in the eternal law.

The eternal law is prescriptive of God's direction to human beings as to the way they should order their lives and the beliefs they should foster. Such an approach makes true what it asserts in terms of belief and behaviour. The fact that God governs means that his being and his doing are one and the same, his is never passive but is pure action, and "his movement of understanding and love is therefore primarily towards himself".[29] Through his action God imparts his providence and grace and ensures the knowledge of God through the divine impact on human life. This culminates in the experience of union with God which Aquinas described in terms of affection and deep feeling. This experience embraces his concept of meditation, contemplation and prayer. These are activities of the highest order for human beings, they expose them to direct communication with God and a boon of inestimable value. Rowan Williams, however, has shown how contemplation, although its destiny is glory and purification, involves a struggle, reminiscent of the struggle of Jacob with the angel at Bethel; nevertheless, Aquinas has given the first thorough philosophical exposition of the experience of confrontation with God in contemplative prayer.[30] Through the experience of contemplative prayer the human being achieves "wholeness"; in so far as understanding does not occur without mental imagery, the image of prayer as divine grace transmitting itself into the finite soul (so that the soul comes to know and love the divine through one act of response) is the supreme end of a life of contemplation.

Aquinas's spiritual perception may be gleaned from this letter written to a certain John who was dear to him in Christ; the letter reveals Aquinas as a deeply religious and prayerful man:

> since it is wiser to reach the more difficult things by way of the less difficult things. This, then, is my advice and information. I charge you to be slow to speak and slow to frequent places where men talk. Embrace cleanness of conscience. Be constant in prayer. Live to dwell in your call if you would penetrate into the call of your Beloved. Be courteous to everyone. Do not look too deeply into the deeds of others . . . Do not in any way wish to pry into the words and deeds of worldly people . . . By these steps you will bring forth useful branches and fruits in the vineyard of the Lord of Sabaoth while life is in you.[31]

We also get a glimpse of Aquinas's sense of spiritual commitment and reliance on God in one of his prayers that have survived:

> Grant me, I beseech Thee, Almighty and Most Merciful God, fervently to desire, wisely to search out, and perfectly to fulfil, all that is well pleasing unto Thee. Order Thou my worldly condition to the glory of

Thy name; and, of all that Thou requirest me to do, grant me the knowledge, the desire, and the ability, that I may so fulfil it as I ought.

Theology, the arts and spirituality

Earlier in this chapter we referred to the ways in which Christianity
dominated much of the west during the medieval period. It is extremely
hazardous to make generalized statements, but life for much of the time
was dominated by religion, the Church was the centre of community,
and the demarcation between sacred and secular, although often hazy,
was not an issue. This applies broadly to the cultural life of Europe as
we progress towards the end of the Middle Ages.

Christian ideas, adaptations and representations deposited a culture
through which artists and others expressed their creative talents and
spiritual visions and aspirations. Of course, it goes without saying that
there are many heterogeneous styles in every branch of the arts, but the
question we now pursue is how far literature and the arts were used as
the media of expressing theological truths and spirituality. This is a
medium different from structured argument, philosophical analysis,
and theological disputation, rational expositions or liturgical practice.
To assess how far this is so we may refer briefly to:

Poetry and drama

In the poetry and drama of the late Middle Ages there are examples of
how Christians used this as a vehicle for expressing and presenting their
own distinctive faith, perceptions and theological and spiritual
purposes. Poetry and drama had been used by the Church from the
beginning as media of communicating Christian truths and ideals, and
in the late medieval period many churchmen found in poetry a production or medium for conveying sacred and spiritual truths. Many
examples survive of devotional poetry on a range of religious themes,
poetry on a monastic theme, and poetry that portrays and interprets the
Christian story and its message. One example is a thirteenth-century
poem on the theme of death and sin. The poet treats the desire to escape
from both, but declares that death is the single inescapable certainty, for
"There's none so strong or tough or keen, / that he can dodge death's
wither clench," and then the poem continues:

> Go by Solomon the Wise,
> O Man, and prosperously do;

> Follow his teaching and advice,
> Then you never shall undo,
> Whatever ending comes to you . . .
> Consider, Man, how you should go,
> And study in what plight you're thrown . . .
> Alas! By death you're dragged below,
> Just when you thought to stay on throne! . . .
> By world and wealth you're led astray,
> They are your enemies, I know . . .
> Therefore, Man, let pleasure go,
> And earn your bliss another day.[32]

A further example of the present theme is the passion play, a dramatic rendering of Christ's passion as part of the ritual of the Church. These plays began as liturgical drama performed at Christmas, Easter, and other Christian festivals to illustrate the birth, death and resurrection of Christ. The earliest examples are from the tenth century, but passion or miracle plays became popular performances in the market places of many towns in the following years. As well as being religious drama of a primitive kind these productions are an erstwhile representation of the community life and spirit of the town or village where they were performed. The plays may have lasted for up to seven days and many told a Bible story and its message.

The advent of the players would be announced by the town crier and the performance was given in public. They are also called morality plays on account of the moral message they transmitted. Many miracle plays have survived and we may refer, by way of illustration, to the religious theme and message of one that seems to have been popular, namely, *God's Promises*, a play whose author was born in Suffolk in 1495. *God's Promises* is a tragedy composed around the theme of the promises of God to all people in all ages, from the fall of Adam to the incarnation of Christ. The subjects of the seven acts of the play are: Adam the first man; Noah the just; faithful Abraham; Moses Sanctus; Pious King David; the Prophet Isaiah; John the Baptist. There is also a prologue and epilogue. Elements of theology and spirituality are interwoven throughout, as these lines from the epilogue illustrate:

> The matters are such as we have uttered here,
> As ought not to slide from your memorial;
> For they have opened with comfortable gear,
> As to the health of this kind universal,
> Graces of the Lord and promises liberal,
> Which he gives to man for every age,
> To knit him to Christ, and so clear him of bondage . . .

Where now is free will, which the hypocrites comment?
Whereby they report they may at their own pleasure
Do good of themselves, though grace and faith be absent,
And have good intents their madness with to measure,
The will of the flesh is proved here small treasure,
And so is man's will, for the grace of God doth all,
More of this matter conclude hereafter we shall.[33]

This is one of many examples of how through drama pious and devoted Christians applied their skills to the interpretation and support of the Christian religion. They did much to make accessible and meaningful the text of the Bible, the teaching of Christian morals and a single vision of life inspired by Christian faith. These plays also combined thought about the relevance of religion in this world created by God and the destiny of life in the world beyond.

Art and architecture

The Dutch artist Van Gogh (1858–90) said of works of art –

to try to understand the real significance of what the great artists, the serious masters, tell us in their masterpieces, that leads to God.

Art is spiritual in the sense that it conveys visually the artist's concept and insight into meaning and reality. A work of art is a medium of communication between the artist and the spectator; it may be the vehicle of communicating a wide range of thought and emotion indicative of the personal experience or perception of the artist. Through the visual experience of viewing the work of art the spectator may be enlightened and informed and enabled to appropriate the meaning or message that the artist conveys in a representational or literal form. The spectator is then able to identify with the artist and respond to the meaning it conveys. The artist may depict visually a story or an event and thereby literally inform or educate, at the same time he or she may induce a spiritual response of awe and wonder, or maybe one of negativism or revulsion. In any case the response is individualistic and personal. In the case of religious art the artist portrays the subject with the purpose of expressing its inner meaning or message so as to induce the response which, in the words of Van Gogh, "leads to God".

The renaissance of classical learning in the latter years of the Middle Ages produced a most riveting change in the intellectual and cultural climate of the west. Such was its impact that it deposited a radical change in the outlook on the nature, meaning and purpose of human life in the present and the future. It brought about a spiritual transformation to which some of the great Renaissance artists made a lasting contribution. Many Renaissance artists of great eminence directed their creative artistic gifts to producing works of art on religious themes that also expressed their own religious beliefs and spiritual insights. The subject might be a religious idea, truth or concept, or a religious scene or story, but within the visual production there is inner meaning that the artist intended to communicate. Many such works depict the major themes and events in the Bible, such as creation and exodus, scenes from the gospels, the birth of Jesus, his works, suffering, death, resurrection, and the descent and operation of the Holy Spirit. The visual picture brings the spectator eye to eye with the artist's message or it instils a search for the inner meaning or maybe arouses expectation of truth perceived.

This will become apparent if we visualize the famous painting by the fifteenth-century artist Piero della Francesca (1420–92) called *Nativity*. The artist depicts a group of people, including a baby and the Virgin Mary, all together in a field. Along with these there is an ass and ox, and in the lower left of the picture there are goldfinches and a magpie perched on a roof. The centrepiece and the emotional focus of the picture is the baby with his mother kneeling in adoration. She is clothed in blue, the symbol of her royal status as the queen of heaven; the intimacy of mother and child expresses movingly the bond of affection between them. The goldfinches and the magpie are symbolic of the passion of Christ and the agony of his crucifixion.

Francesca's *Nativity* is a work of art that portrays a gospel theme and at the same time conveys the artist's feelings of awe and wonder, his personal perception of Christian truth and meaning and his own response. The richness and variety of the symbolism induce in the spectator feelings of wonder and a sense of the numinous, that is, it evokes a response to the birth and death of Jesus. In this picture we see how the artist Francesca has portrayed a biblical scene with characters who are highly individualized so that they communicate personal thoughts and feelings. The child is worthy of their adoration; the symbolism expresses the compelling passion of love. The discerning spectator is bound to interact positively or otherwise with the characters portrayed.

It is impossible to define art precisely or definitively, but it is possible to assume a point of view or express individual perceptions. All art is highly personalized. All works of art differ to some extent in their qualities; no single quality is common to all art. But the purpose of religious art, if it may be so expressed, is to convey a message and induce a response, to enhance religious experience and spiritual empathy.

In essence this is what is meant by "the spirituality of art", the nurture of spiritual perception through viewing the art with proper intensity and intention. This turns the mind to God. To achieve this end artists used different media, colour, light, perspective, movement, vision, and symbolism, with the purpose of achieving effect, of stirring emotion, inducing thought, stimulating imagination, promoting empathy, evoking positive response.

Many works of religious art from the period of the Renaissance depict the story of Jesus and his mission of salvation. By portraying visually events that actually happened, especially the numerous pictures of the crucifixion, and by wide and effective use of symbolism, many works depict central theological themes and divine attributes, or maybe, notions of vice and virtue, goodness and evil. They also portray variously and generously characters from the gospels or from Christian history in order to depict their participation, reaction and spiritual wonder. By encountering these characters the spectator is made aware of their role and their significance. The narrative content is their vehicle for informing and communicating attitudes and reactions. This adds a further spiritual dimension of enlightenment and stimulating further spiritual growth. In this context the words of Gregory the Great in his *Commentary on the Song of Songs* are applicable to religious art as a whole:

> The sacred scriptures are made up of words and meanings just as pictures are of colours and meanings, but no one should be so stupid as to absorb the colours of a painting and ignore the meanings which have been expressed with colours.

Is there a spirituality of architecture? With daring generalization we may say that architecture has embellished the Christian Church for the glory of God. With the advent of Gothic architecture there evolved a complicated philosophical and conceptual style that in the mid-twelfth century inaugurated features different from those of earlier times. In 1288, for example, the first stained glass window with a figurative design was installed in Siena Cathedral. Figure sculptures and painted murals began to be designed and installed. These represented or identified a scriptural story or an incident from Christian history. Many stained glass windows depicted the Last Supper, the crucifixion and resurrection, or other scenes from the Old and the New Testament. These were designed to make it easier for people to learn and digest the biblical narratives, and Christian architects paid attention to the structural shapes and decoration that would achieve this purpose.

In its style, church architecture provided visual aids to its religious purpose and was then a medium of communication. It was designed for the glory of God and to serve the purpose of the worshipper. The architecture combined a subtlety of design with spiritual interpretations of a biblical theme for the purpose of performing a religious and spiritual function. The external style and the internal furnishings performed a spiritual function of directing the mind to the object of worship, and beauty, form and design were used to achieve this purpose. The architecture of religion created a sense of awe, wonder and splendour; it blended with the splendour of the universe and the sovereignty of God. It also performed a didactic function, it taught the faith through picturesque designs, and stimulated a sense of devotion that turns the mind to God.

By making extensive use of symbols, for example the cross and altar, the architecture created a sense of the numinous and of awe and an awareness of the inner meaning and significance of the symbol. The aim of the Christian architect was to build to the glory of God, to portray in a visible form the reality that exists beyond the actual and tangible. It had the capacity to stir the emotions and create a sense of the mystery of the greatness and majesty of God. The worshipper was brought face to face with the transcendent through encountering the tower or the spire that pointed the thought to God. The font, the altar, the nave, the lectern, and other architectural features, were intended to perform a spiritual function of directing the attention to God who is beyond as well as within.

This brief survey of aspects of theology and spirituality in western Europe during the medieval period has referred only to some leading personalities and mainstream Christian movements that give us a "feel" of this crucial period. It was an age of considerable fluctuation in the fortunes of the Church, but at the same time it is illumined by a succession of notable spiritual "luminaries" who pioneered new creative and progressive developments. Such pioneers were more fascinated with the essence of faith and spirituality than with the structure of religious organization. They displayed a refreshing willingness to traverse territory hitherto untravelled; in this way they widened the horizons of religious understanding and practice.

Towards the end of the period there emerged a broader intellectual interest in theological and spiritual matters; whilst still remaining loyal to the centralized church with its hierarchical sturdiness, its uniform liturgy, and its common language, a number of individual scholars were intent on demonstrating the intellectual credibility of Christian truth and paved the way to a new liberalism. Their enthusiasm led them to enquire more closely into the nature, practices, structures and government of the Catholic Church, and in so doing they began inadvertently to bridge the divide between the Middle Ages and modern European history.

5

The Age of Reform

Catalysts of reform

Christendom in the west was on the verge of its greatest crisis. Ponderously the Middle Ages meandered towards the dawn of a new age. The groundswell of reform that had uneasily gathered momentum in the medieval Church now seemed irresistible. Nominally Europe was still a Christian society; ostensibly its citizens were loyal to the Church, but there were ominous signs of disintegration in its hitherto seemingly solid and impregnable structure. Zealous churchmen of vision and conviction were sowing seeds of reform, intentionally or imperceptibly, and these were coming to fruition. The clamour for reform mounted and action could not for ever be delayed. The Church as an institution is always in need of reform, and it could not now withstand the pressure; the established hierarchic edifice that had stood like an impregnable fortress could not resist the invasion of its freehold. The effervescence of medieval Christendom was under threat from more than one quarter. The primal Christian vision of harmony and cohesion was tarnished, and a power struggle between Church and state was inflamed by revolutionary spirits on both sides. The disaffection with the clergy, and their lack of spiritual guidance, was outwardly exposed, and certain of the traditional doctrines and practices of the Church were being subjected to stringent scrutiny by ardent churchmen of deep spirituality and intellectual power.

The new learning

The invention of the printing press by William Caxton (1422–92) inaugurated a new era in the circulation of the written word. The printed word became a catalyst of reform in a number of ways. The wider circulation of radical thinking conditioned many minds in favour of reform. Thus a spiritual climate was created conducive to the reception of new ideas and ideals, and the will to see these put into operation. It brought a fresh vitality to the quest for knowledge and truth. When Desiderius Erasmus (1466–1536) produced his works, *Praise of Folly* and *Instruction of a Christian Soldier*, the ground had already been prepared for the reception of new and buoyant messages. Erasmus exposed the trivialities and formalities of religion and its practices in stunningly sarcastic terms that pierced the soul of the age like a poisonous dagger. Erasmus had joined the Augustinian Order at the age of eighteen, but he became disenchanted with its formalism and rigid routine and stinted practices. He spent years seeking to release himself from its legalistic stranglehold. He expressed powerfully his opposition to the oppressive rules and restrictive life-style of the religious orders of his day and advocated their dissolution. He broke with the Augustinian Order in 1499 and eventually came to settle in Oxford.

In Oxford Erasmus met John Colet (1466–1519), dean of St. Paul's, a distinguished preacher and notable exponent of Scripture. Erasmus and Colet were kindred spirits, and Erasmus was soon engaged in writing books on the reform of religion and on the Christian life. He made a close study of the works of the Church Fathers and wrote also about Church and state. He was greatly interested in education, and his most durable achievement is his edition of the New Testament in Greek. This proved to be a watershed in the process and the mounting clamour for reform.

This version of the New Testament had a wide circulation and opened many minds to the treasures of the Scriptures. It promoted the message of the New Testament as a focus of basic understanding of Christian truth and doctrine. Erasmus contended that all believers should have access to the truth of Christianity without the necessity of an intermediary; the truth of the Bible should be directly accessible to everyone. This would promote deeper spirituality and enrich the devotional life. Reliance on external religious practices would disappear, and formalities such as pilgrimages to shrines, masses for the dead, and indulgences would be made obsolete. Such externally imposed customs were an encumbrance to genuine spiritual religion, as Erasmus stated scathingly:

> Perhaps thou believest that all thy sins are washed away with a little paper, a sealed parchment, with the gift of a little money, or some wax image, with a little pilgrimage. Thou art utterly deceived.

Wholesome spirituality is promoted through prayer and personal devotion. This yields direct knowledge of God and does not require the intervention of an intermediary. Nor is proficiency in dogmatic theology or metaphysical speculation necessary for enjoying communion with the Holy Trinity. Nor is ability to distinguish between the Father, Son and Holy Spirit, the three persons of the Trinity, the condition of acquiring moral virtues and building character on Christian foundations for, declared Erasmus:

> You will not be damned if you do not know whether Spirit proceeded from the Father and the Son had one or two beginnings, but you will not escape damnation if you do not cultivate the fruits of the Spirit: love, joy, peace, kindness, goodness, long suffering, mercy, faith, modesty, continence and charity.

A spirituality expressive of inner peace and harmony is closest to the example and teaching of Christ. The cultivation and practice of such spirituality is the surest way of enlightenment and transformation in the life of the Church. Moral action is an imperative and is effective wherever individuals are free to use their own resources in working out their own salvation. Moral action exudes the maximum of Christian virtues, but only the minimum of speculative theology. Humanism, as applied to the teaching of Erasmus, and other devotees of the new learning who will be mentioned below, does not mean turning away from the divine and the supernatural. Erasmus did not advocate a break with the Catholic Church, or the turning away from the ways of God. Rather he aimed to use his intellectual and human skills in the service of truth and its advocacy. This meant entry into a wider world of exploration than that currently provided by the world of traditional sacramental and hierarchic religion. It means engagement with the wealth and variable legacy of classical learning, philosophy, and literature. Encapsulating sacred and secular learning in a common endeavour would promote a single vision of wholeness. The one need not be subordinate to the other nor need they be opposed to one another. The employment of human skills, i.e. the search for truth, leads to personal identity with truth, and its apprehension gives dignity and status to the individual.

It is the prerogative of human beings to use their personal skills and gifts to the maximum, and this, according to Erasmus, is consistent with Christian teaching about the intrinsic dignity and worth of human life. The aim of so doing Erasmus asserted unequivocally:

> All studies, philosophy, rhetoric, are followed for this one object, that we may know Christ and honour him.

Erasmus maintained that the humanism he espoused and practised was consistent with the humanity of Jesus, and was in fact the means of paying him honour.

The momentum of Christian humanism in the late medieval period stimulated the intellectual rigour of a group of distinguished scholars and made its impact felt in many European countries. In England, John Colet, a foremost educationalist, founded the famous St. Paul's grammar school and pioneered the new learning. Colet made a public protest against mechanical Christianity; he refused to venerate relics and spurned the external paraphernalia of religion. He spent years studying the epistles of St. Paul and expounding their theological message for contemporary Christianity. He hoped thereby to promote better informed personal spirituality.

In Italy Lorenzo Valla (1406–57) devoted his intellectual gifts to interpreting the fundamentals of Christian belief and developing a humanist theology. He was secretary to Pope Nicholas V and a keen student of the original Greek and Hebrew texts of the Bible. Before his time the Bible had only been heard in Church in the Latin version of St. Jerome (342–420). Now Valla developed expository principles that made the teaching of the Bible more accessible and understood. His expositions were well received and the new status given to the Bible in faith and life kindled and spread the spirit of reform. Valla disapproved of the wealth and sovereignty of the papacy and the restrictions and extremity of monastic views. His was a liberal spirit critical of the institution of monasticism and much else in the Church and theology of his day. He even questioned whether the Apostles' Creed was the work of the apostles.

In Germany, the cause of the new learning was advancd by Johann Reuchlin (1455–1522) who is known for his devotion to the Hebrew language and Jewish literature. Reuchlin produced the first Hebrew–Christian grammar in 1506 and made other valuable contributions to biblical scholarship. In a modest way Reuchlin may be regarded as the founder of the discipline we now call biblical criticism. His biblical studies, especially his critical examination of the Vulgate version of the Old Testament, brought him into conflict with scholastics and humanists. The conflict concerned the use of Hebrew, the language of the Jews who had crucified Christ. His detractors said that Jews should be condemned by all faithful Christians, and those who studied their language should be denounced as heretics. Reuchlin published an enquiry in 1505 as to why the Jews had been so long in tribulation, and concluded that this was on account of the way they had rejected Christ and blasphemed his name. Yet Reuchlin exhorted his fellow Christians to seek to win Jews to the Christian faith by showing them love and then instructing them in the true meaning of Christianity.

Erasmus, Colet, Valla and Reuchlin, vanguards of the new learning, as a consequence of their intellectual activities and moral insights, opened the way for others to promote a more radical reform of the Church in root and branch. Inevitably, some of their ideas were contradicted and some of their assumptions opposed. They all displayed a common devotion to the Bible, which they were equipped to study in its original languages of Hebrew and Greek, and this facilitated the approach of the major Protestant reformers of the sixteenth century to the role of the Bible as the centrepoint of their reforms.

Hitherto the use and exposition of the Bible had been restricted by the intransigence of the clergy and by the adherence of the Church to the Latin Bible of Jerome (the Vulgate), which it regarded as sacrosanct. The new openness which Erasmus and others brought to the study of Scripture gave positive impetus and direction to the later reform movement. The broadening intellectual and spiritual horizon has to be judged from within the historical and cultural situation of the end of the medieval period. Other than those here we have mentioned must be credited with a share in the creation of this more open liberal climate. William Tyndale (1474–1536), an Oxford graduate, translated the Bible into English. He believed that God had called him to translate the Bible for the benefit of the uneducated people of England, so that "a boy who drives the plough" might know the Scriptures. Everything necessary for salvation, he asserted, is to be found in the Bible. The key that unlocks this truth is "evangelism", that is, that which "signifieth good, mercy, glad and joyful tidings, that maketh a man's heart glad, and maketh him sing, dance and leap for joy".[1]

The Bible was destined to be a key factor in the theology and spirituality of the Protestant Reformation. By referring to the pioneers of the new learning we can see how the way was prepared for this major upheaval that changed the face of the Christian Church. The Protestant Reformation was not a sudden instantaneous event, rather it was the eruption of the momentum that had been gathering pace over many years. With its erupting we may say, in daringly general terms, that the contribution of Erasmus, Colet, Valla, Reuchlin, Tyndale and others, was integral to the Reformation. They pioneered "the rediscovery of the Bible" through their translations and expositions, and their open access to the Bible proved to be a transforming factor in the achievements of the Protestant reformers. Still, in general terms, we may say that the labours of Erasmus and the others were inspired by their common conviction that the Bible is the undisputed foundation and essential resource for understanding Christianity and its importance. The Bible had therefore to be made accessible to people in their own language if its wealth was to be experienced and its message understood and applied. Tyndale aimed to ensure that the Bible was seen to be "the people's book", and that it should be for churchmen the heartbeat and sustenance of their Christian faith. These biblicists interpreted the Bible as a model of divine revelation and redemptive knowledge on which the faith of the Church must rest; it was the "canon" or "measuring rod" of Christian belief and ethics. When Martin Luther set about exposing the roots of Christian salvation, and expounding the shape, life and culture of the early church, he knew that the seeds of reform had already been sown by the late medieval devotees of the Bible.

Devotio Moderna

Another influential contribution to the emergent process of reform towards the end of the Middle Ages was the production of devotional literature, that is, works whose focus was on deepening the personal experience of spirituality and the nurture of personal knowledge of God. During the fourteenth and fifteenth centuries there was a quickening of interest in spirituality and the cultivation of personal devotion. A number of devotional works testify to this development. One is the *Cloud of Unknowing*, a late medieval writing considered to be one of the classics of English mysticism. The author has been variously described as "a cloistered monk" or "a rural parish priest". In part the theology of the *Cloud* echoes that of Thomas Aquinas, although its focus on grace as a conscious divine gift makes communion with God a reality. The "unknown cloud" is a description of the negative way of ascent to God and the cry of the soul for the possession of God himself, for what God is by grace. To this cry God responds in mercy and compassion, and then the spirituality of the *Cloud* exposes love as a "sharp dart of longing". This dart of longing pierces the "cloud of unknowing" that exists between the soul and God. As the dart of longing pierces the soul the soul is freed from the intellectual and speculative misgivings that impede the movement to perfect union with God. As the *cloud of unknowing* is penetrated the soul is elated to a state of spiritual visibility and alertness and purged of all material and worldly acquisitions. The soul enters a state of mystical absorption with the divine and the ineffable union with God that is perfect joy and harmony. The mind is then fixed on God, it discerns the meaning it seeks, it is fixed on love and the secret of union with God, it finds the secret of real contemplation and right action, for then

> you will go about your daily rounds, eating and drinking, sleeping and waking, going and coming, speaking and listening, lying down and rising up, standing and kneeling, running and riding, working and resting. In the midst of it all, you will be offering to God continually each day the most precious gift you can make.[2]

The theology of the *Cloud* conceives of God as the creator and redeemer who by grace calls upon people to love him. The fitting response to his grace and love is to listen to him. Through listening God declares his great kindness and goodness and worth. The soul that penetrates this *cloud of unknowing* continues to listen to God. The longing to hear what God says is planted in the soul by God himself and can only be satisfied in union with him.[3] For this purpose the author says:

> your whole life now must be one of longing if you are to achieve perfection. And this longing must be in the depths of your will, put there by God, with your consent.[4]

This longing for God and single-minded concentration on him finds at first only darkness, *a cloud of unknowing*, but then the soul perceives in its longing for God the object of its love. The *cloud* may observe or obstruct but the search has to be continued until the goal of union is attained. Even though the *cloud of unknowing* encircles the soul it must not abandon the search. The soul even then continues to be aware of God's presence although it may not comprehend God fully. God assures that his presence is felt through his actions of grace and love.

The *cloud*, therefore, can mercifully be the place of contemplating and meeting God. The *cloud* "indicates our intimation of the presence of God within the 'divine darkness'". This "intimation of the presence of God" is linked with another image, namely of "a cloud of forgetting" under which everything is hidden. The soul must be rid of dependence on any other creatures so as to be free to ascend to God, and "to think about him as he is and praise him for himslf". All knowledge and feeling must be subsumed under the "cloud of forgetting". This then issues in pure devotion, self-discipline and perfect contemplation. It generates a spirit of humility and love and straightforward acts of mercy and charity. It perfects the contemplative experience that is the essence of spiritual vision; it emphasizes how God, who is the goal of contemplation, plants that desire for himself in the soul and then becomes the means of satisfying it. On the culture of contemplation the *Cloud of Unknowing* states:

> If you ask me how you should begin contemplation, I would pray for Almighty God to teach you himself by his immense grace and kindness. Indeed, it is important that you know that I cannot teach you. This is not surprising: this is the work of God. He will bring it about in which ever way he pleases, irrespective of its merits. Without God's grace neither saint nor angel could ever begin to think of desiring the life of contemplation.
>
> The nature of contemplation is such that when it comes, the soul can practise it and know that it is doing so. It is impossible to have it otherwise. The capacity for contemplation and the act itself are one and the same thing. Only the person who feels able to contemplate, can, in fact do so, nobody else. Without the prior working of God the soul is dead, and unable to desire or covet it.

From the same circle as the *Cloud of Unknowing*, whose anonymous author, by reacting against the religious formation of the time, dwelt instead on the notion of Christian spirituality as introspective wisdom, came the works of the group known as *Devotio Moderna* (Modern Devotion). It is associated in the Netherlands with the Brethren of the Common Life, but Erasmus, Luther and the Catholic reformers shared its emphasis on personal piety and enlightened spirituality. Members of the group sought to promote genuine spirituality that had hitherto been stifled by the accretions of intellectual persuits and the formalism of hierarchical religion. In its place the group advocated greater stress on the Christian ideals of simplicity, self-denial, prayer and charitable works. A leading part in this was taken by Gèrhard Groot whose powerful sermons evoked a remarkable response. The message Groot and his disciples in the *Devotio Moderna* taught was mainly

> a call to conversion, meditation, imitation of the life and death of Christ, death to the world, charity and humility.[5]

They took the call to conversion and holiness seriously and those who responded were expected thereafter to live a life of poverty and engage actively in social and philanthropic works. The *Devotio Moderna* gave the Bible a central place in their devotions and practices, but its members recoiled from elaborate ritual in worship, even from polyphonic singing. They were expected to make the body of Christ as evident in the life of the world as it is in the secluded life of the cloister. The members never took formal vows although an Augustinian congregation of the Brethren of the Common Life was established at

Windesheim. Their overriding aim was to make the "imitation of Christ" their ideal for personal and public living.

Another spiritual classic of the late medieval period is *The Imitation of Christ* by Thomas à Kempis (1386–1471). The author, from Kemper near Cologne, was immersed in the spirituality and ideals of the *Devotio Moderna* and dedicated to a life of prayer and devotion. The primary theme of *The Imitation of Christ* is spiritual and moral renewal through meditation on the substance of the Christian gospel and imitation of the character and behaviour of its founder. It expounds the norms of Christian piety and devotional practices by reference to the Christian gospel and the spiritual masters of the Church. It expresses the author's yearning for a recovery of the love of prayer and the zeal for virture that were conspicuous in the early church. Then spiritual discipline was practised along with obedience and reverence, in contrast to the current decline in spiritual fervour and lukewarmness. The renewal of spirituality alone can lead to union with God and to living a virtuous life. To love and serve God is the first and highest form of piety. Thomas à Kempis asked:

> If you knew the whole Bible by heart, and all that philosophers have said, what would it be for you without the love of God and grace?

He therefore appealed for a return to God and the nurture of the life of the soul; let Christ come and make his dwelling in the soul as the outward things of "this miserable world" are relinquished. Christ's dwelling within consummates the joy of the Kingdom of God and the peace of the Holy Spirit. The soul is then freed from uncontrolled desires and the heart is made pure and its spiritual vision becomes perfectly luminous. The soul is now free to seek the will of God and the good of neighbour, temptation is resisted and no longer is the soul "battered by all kinds of temptation like a ship with no steersman, driven to and fro by the waves". The way to resist temptation is to be alert to its danger, "because it is easier to defeat the enemy if we do not allow him to set foot inside the door of the mind but meet him on the step as he knocks".[6]

The Imitation of Christ is a call to meditation on all aspects of the life of devotion. It is essentially a handbook of spirituality written for members of the community of the monastery of St. Agnietenberg where Thomas à Kempis was sub-prior. Its attitude towards the speculative theology of the schoolmen and the sacramentalism of the Church is tangential, but throughout the four divisions (books) of the *Imitation* the common theme is the imitation of Christ as the prime admonition for living a life of true spirituality. This is the doctrine of truth which the author intended to convey:

> From one Word are all things, and all things utter one word, and this is the Beginning, which also speaketh unto us.
> No man without that Word understandeth or judgeth rightly.
> He to whom all things are one, he who reduceth all things to one, and seeth all things in one, may enjoy a quiet mind, and remain at peace in God.
> O God, who art the truth, make me one with thee in everlasting love.

There is particular emphasis in *The Imitation of Christ* on spiritual introspection. Thomas à Kempis remained within the Catholic Church but appealed little to its doctrine of salvation through works. The stress is on the direct access of the soul to God rather than through the medium of external observance or the performance of good works. This is part of the appeal for a reform of the fundamental essentials and practices of Christian spirituality. Such practice is open to everyone and not just the learned. Spirituality means the cultivation of personal concentration on the life of God. Such concentration does not rule out the necessity for good works, but rather it sees good works as the outreach of love for God; "for God weigheth more with how much love a man worketh, than how much he doeth. He doeth much that loveth much. He doeth much that doeth a thing well. He doeth well that serveth the common weal than his own will."

In one respect the theme of *The Imitation of Christ* received prominence in the late medieval period on account of the preoccupation with death. Conditions were such that the incident of death had a macabre influence on society. The soul, it was felt, lived in the shadow of death, but this was no reason for abandoning good works. On the contrary, counselled Thomas à Kempis:

> Do with thy might what thou doest, labour faithfully in my vineyard; I will be thy reward.
> Write, read, mourn, keep silence, pray, suffer crosses manfully; life everlasting is worthy of all these, yea, and of greater combats.
> Peace shall come in the day which is known unto the Lord, and it shall be neither night nor day, such as is ever, but everlasting light, infinite brightness, steadfast peace, and secure rest . . .
> thine shall be no more anxious thoughts, but blessed joy, sweet and lovely company.

The writer does not ignore the day of judgement that awaits all people (another recurring theme in late medieval thought) but stressed God's mercy and the Christian hope that shares the glory of Jesus Christ:

for after winter follows summer, after night the day returneth, and after a tempest a great calm.

Whoever lives life in imitation of Christ is bound to share the sufferings of Christ. Thomas à Kempis developed a deep attachment to the sufferings of Christ, especially to his crucifixion. Christ took upon himself the sorrows of others out of love and the desire for their salvation; from the moment of birth until his death on the cross Christ was never free from suffering. But the crucifixion is the supreme act of love in suffering for others and their salvation:

> In the cross is salvation, in the cross is life, in the cross is protection against our enemies, in the cross is infusion of heavenly sweetness, in the cross is strength of mind, in the cross is joy of spirit, in the cross is the height of virtue, in the cross is the perfection of sanctity.
> There is no salvation of the soul, nor hope of everlasting life, but in the cross.

The cultivation of the presence of Christ is another recurrent theme of the *Imitation*. This includes experience of the real presence of Christ in the eucharist. Participation in the eucharist is the means of fostering personal relationship with God and deepening spirituality. The eucharist is a noble gift and a precious consolation, and the prayer of the participant is:

> Grant, O Lord God, my Saviour, that by frequenting the celebration of thy mysteries the zeal of my devotion may grow and increase.

The Imitation is regarded as the flower of mysticism, it speaks to the heart of the love that seeks God through a life of self-renunciation and meditation. As such it has to be viewed as one of the most significant contributions to the kindling of the spirit of religious reform that pervaded the closing years of medieval Europe.

The impact of these individuals and movements mentioned here is best measured in the way they infiltrated their ideas and hopes into the prevailing climate of change and unease and not in any direct result we are able to quantify. If the aim was to reform the Catholic Church from within then this did not happen. Reform when it came was a revolutionary break with the Church. The reforming councils of Pisa (1409), Constance (1414–18) and Basle (1431–49) did not achieve the goal of internal reform. The Reformation when it happened split the Church and pointed European civilization in a number of different directions.

The Luther affair

The event that triggered the Protestant Reformation was the act of Martin Luther (1483–1546) when he posted his ninety-five theses on the door of the Cathedral Church of Wittenburg in October 1517. So we note at this point how:

> The reformation began in Germany in the 1520s, with the "Luther affair", the controversy precipitated by Martin Luther's attack on indulgences and the indulgence trade in October 1517. The subsequent furore spilled over from being a disagreement among theologians and churchmen into the wider public sphere, quickly drawing into its wake questions of politics, social grievance, popular religious discontent, constitutional and legal issues from the level of the empire down to the smallest communities. It quickly spread beyond the borders of Germany, first into German speaking territories such as Switzerland and Austria, into lands such as the Low Countries, then across more substantial linguistic borders into England, Scandinavia, France, Italy and into Eastern Europe.[7]

This statement demonstrates the threefold impact of the Reformation on religion, society and nations. Its impact was not uniform everywhere and it is proper to bear in mind the rich variety of phenomena, religious, political and economic, that the Reformation embraced. For our purposes "the Luther affair" is that which bears upon the development of Christian theology and its spiritual tradition. Luther was educated in law and medicine as well as in theology, a fact that has some bearing on his method of "doing" theology. However, he answered the call to the monastic life and in 1505 he entered the Augustinian convent at Erfurt as a novice.

His monastic vocation seemed irreversible, "I never thought to come out of the convent, I was clean dead to the world, until God deemed fit to call me out, and Tetzel compelled me." What precisely led Luther to quit the convent is difficult to specify, but we can surmise how he must have spent time in intense reflection and deep meditation on his spiritual condition. In the convent he was encouraged to study the Bible, but this created in him a deep spiritual restlessness. He was deeply troubled by his sin and felt he was destined for eternal damnation. He was helped through this period by John Staupitz, a "spiritual director", and gradually felt he was being drawn away from the legalistic restrictions of ecclesiastical piety and the observance of religious formalities as a means of attaining inner peace. He confessed:

> If ever a monk could have got to heaven by mockery I might have done

so, I wore out my body with watching, fasting, prayer and other works.
I was a criminal self-torturer and self-destroyer.

The just shall live by faith

Luther was ordained to the priesthood in 1507 and made a pilgrimage
to Rome. As he ascended the twenty-two steps of the Sanatus Salle
(the staircase of the judgement hall of Pilate) and prayed, the words,
"the just shall live by faith" came into his mind. This saying became a
keynote of his theology. The more he dwelt upon these words the
more dissatisfied he became with the Church's doctrine that repentance consisted of contrition, confession and satisfaction. The notion
that the temporal consequences of sin could only be avoided by the
performance of good works and discipline became abhorrent to him.
Likewise the teaching of the Church about the treasury of good works
filled by the merits of Christ and the saints lost its appeal.

Luther rejected the payment of an indulgence as the means of
achieving merit and forgiveness. In the same vein he denounced the
external ritual and observances of the Church, pilgrimage and pecu-
niary offerings, in place of the development of inner spirituality and
the life of personal devotion.

Luther's thought moved away from the general framework of
Catholic theology. He gradually developed his own personal theology
and undertook a radical rethinking of the origins and motif of
Christianity. His theology is crystallized in the saying "justification
by faith", a doctrine he derived directly from the New Testament, but
as well from the writings of St. Augustine, to which Luther was also
devoted. Fundamentally the religion of Luther centred on God *and*
the New Testament. From this he deduced that there is a bridge that
brings together God and human beings, namely, faith. In his commentary on Paul's letter to the Romans Luther wrote:

> Faith is a living unshakeable confidence in God's grace; it is so certain,
> that someone should die a thousand times for it. This kind of trust in
> and knowledge of God's grace makes a person joyful, confident, and
> happy with regard to God and all creatures. This is what the Holy Spirit
> does by faith.

Faith is reposed in Christ alone and is the possession of each individual
believer, who is thereby assured of the certainty of salvation. Salvation
is an act of grace which mysteriously works in love and mercy to rescue
sinners from the law with its emphasis on sinfulness and unworthiness
in the sight of God.

This rescue is effected by the work of Christ; the sinner is justified in God's sight through faith in Christ who made atonement for sin. Thus salvation is assured by faith alone. The source of salvation is the unique work of Christ undertaken for the benefit of reconciling human beings to God. Personal salvation is achieved through faith. As a natural consequence of salvation the Christian lives a life of union with God and of good works. The Christian, through union with Christ, is empowered to serve him as partners in a spiritual marriage. The Christian lives in Christ by faith and so is as Christ to others. In his work *Treatise on Christian Liberty* Luther declared:

> Therefore, if we recognise the great and precious things which are given us . . . we also ought freely to help our neighbour through our body and its works, and each one should become as it were a Christ to the other that we may be Christ to one another and Christ may be the same in all, that is, that we may be truly Christians.[8]

The authority of scripture

In 1552 Luther published a German version of the New Testament. The translation was a landmark in the development of the German language and literature, but, more importantly, it made the message of the Bible accessible to ordinary people in a language they could understand. Luther made every effort to ensure that this was the case; he chose the words of his translation with attention to their meaning and connotation, so that everyone could have access to the truth they conveyed.

He said of his objective, "I tried to make Moses so German that no one could ever suspect that he was a Jew." His purpose was to communicate the extant meaning and authority of the New Testament for the cultivation and practice of authentic Christian faith. He willed it to be an educational and theological tool, the means of educating Christians in the truth of Christianity and its fundamental doctrines. The Bible is the revealed source of authority for the Church and it needs to be made real to each new generation as the Holy Spirit makes this manifest. The Church is under the judgement of Scripture; through Scripture the revelation of God and his purpose is made known; the essence of Christian belief is distilled in Scripture and through the action of the Holy Spirit the Christian is enabled to appropriate this. Knowledge and understanding of the Bible, mediated through the Holy Spirit, nurtures the life of faith and loyalty to Christ; it is the basis of orthodox belief and reveals the will of God. God speaks directly to the Church through the Bible, but only as the Spirit illumines its meaning.

The Spirit enables its message to be heard and empowers the Christian to abide by this. It is the spirit and not the letter of the Scripture that imparts its meaning and power. Whereas the Catholic Church determined doctrine for its members, Luther judged the Church and its doctrine by its loyalty to the content and message of Scripture.

Priesthood and sacraments

Luther had no intention of withdrawing from the Catholic Church but he was excommunicated in 1520. The authors of the Augsburg Confession (1530) hoped for reconciliation between the Catholic Church and Lutheranism, and that matters of difference "may be settled and be brought back to one perfect truth and Christian concord that for the future one pure and true religion may be embraced and nurtured by us, that as we all serve and do battle under one Christ, so we may be able also to live in unity and concord in the new Christian Church". This hope proved abortive, and Lutheran churches were established outside the hierarchical structure of the Catholic Church. One distinctive mark of the Lutheran churches, apart from the belief in justification by faith and the supreme authority of Scripture, was the priesthood of all believers. By this is meant, not that all members of the Church are ordained priests, but that every church member has a vocation to live the Christian life. The call of the priest is no more sacred than the call of the lay person to witness to Christ in the Church and to serve him in the daily life of the world. Every believer is called by Christ to be a minister to others in his name. The priesthood of all believers implies that the vocation of every believer is from God himself to participate in the ordinances and mission of his Church. Such privilege is the corollary of the right of every believer to direct access to God. On this Luther was adamant: "Every shoemaker can be a priest to God, and stick to his own last while he does it." In the *Treatise on Christian Liberty* Luther wrote, "Surely we are named after Christ . . . that is, because we believe in him and are Christs one to another and do to our neighbours as Christ does to us."

Of the seven sacraments of the Catholic Church Luther retained the two that had a distinct scriptural basis, namely, baptism and the eucharist. Both of these are closely linked with the Bible and enacted as the saving action of God directed to personal redemption. Baptism is the sacrament of entry into membership of the Church and symbolizes the reception of the forgiveness from sin and/or being raised or renewed to living a new life in Christ. The symbolism of baptism is that of human redemption and transformation. The eucharist is the sacrament of the ordinace of the eternal love of God expressed decisively in the crucifixion and resurrection of Christ. Through the regular observance of the eucharist the communicant is brought into relationship with Christ. Luther propounded a high view of the eucharist as the vehicle of experiencing the presence of Christ and entering into union with him. By the "real presence" of Christ in the eucharist he meant that within the bread and wine the body and blood of Christ were really present. He took the words of Jesus at the Last Supper, "this is my body", "this is my blood", to be literally true, but he also stressed the necessity of faith on the part of communicants. Only "the believing heart" is able to experience and appropriate the grace of the eucharist.

Worship and liturgy

Lutheranism pioneered a new spiritual tradition in worship centred on liturgy, preaching and hymnology. The Lutheran Church was basically congregational, but its order and liturgy differed from those of the Catholic Church. Some traditional practices, however, were retained, especially auricular confession, the wearing of vestments, certain symbols such as lamps, statues and stained glass. Preaching was given a pre-eminent role and the sermon defined as a sacrament of the proclamation of divine redemption. It was Bible-based and it expounded and proclaimed God's revelation through Scripture. Thus the spiritual and moral rules of Christian faith were communicated and their practice advocated. Preaching and spirituality were bonded together in the creation of a united church in line with the apostolic church of the New Testament. So much is this the case that Luther declared it to be the duty of every Christian government to ensure that the word of God was preached to its subjects and that it "be delivered pure to the people".

Church music and hymns were given prominence in the congregational liturgy of the Lutheran Church. Hymns became a powerful adjunct in spreading the message of reform among the German people. Luther himself composed hymns of considerable religious and psychological power, and he also adapted the music of medieval songs into new tunes for use in congregational worship. Religious music and hymnology received greater prominence in worship than hitherto. Luther built upon the tradition of the Latin hymn of earlier times, and one of his greatest is the hymn *Ein' feste Burg*, which has been called "the Marseillaise of the Reformation"; this opens with the lines:

> A safe stronghold our God is still,
> a trusty shield and weapon;
> he'll keep us clear from all the ill
> that hath us now o'er taken.

This hymn was inspired by Psalm 46 and very likely was written at the time of the Diet of Speyer. It has been described as "The greatest hymn of the greatest man in the greatest period of German history."[9] Luther had a distinct purpose in mind when composing his hymns. He wrote to his friend Spalatin:

> It is my plan to make vernacular songs for the people – we seek everywhere for poets: I desire that new-fangled and courtly expressions may be avoided, and that the words may all be exceedingly simple and common, such as plain folk may understand, yet withal pure and skilfully handled.[10]

Luther discovered a spiritual void that he intended his liturgical reforms and compositions to fill. He wished to provide the ordinary people with the spiritual nourishment they needed to develop their Christian spirituality to the full. To this end he aimed to pioneer fresh ways of presenting and interpreting God's revelation in Christ by asserting the freedom and responsibility of individuals for their own salvation. In this way he kindled a flame of religious enthusiasm, especially by the powerful appeal of his doctrine "by faith alone". The spiritual freedom he enunciated for the Christian, "Who is a free lord of all, and subject to none", struck a responsive chord. This pragmatic spirituality, with its focus on individual freedom, grace and personal experience of Christ through faith, disposed people of all walks of life to attach themselves to this new vitality in religion and its practices. They saw that Luther had reduced Christianity to its original minimum, which was the gospel of Christ's grace to be received through faith, a process of living experience and perfect spiritual trust. They felt relieved of the absolute necessity of conformity to hierarchic procedures and enactments.

Brothers of the Reformation

A confession of faith by the Brothers of the Reformation.

> I believe that God has created me and all other creatures. He has given me my body with its members and my spirit with its faculties, and he keeps them in being. Each day he gives me abundant food, clothing, a home and all things necessary to support this life. He protects me from all dangers, preserves me and delivers me from all evil; all this without my being worthy of it, through his sheer goodness and fatherly mercy. This is what I firmly believe.

I believe that Jesus Christ, true God and true man, is my Lord. He has redeemed me, lost and condemned though I am, by delivering me from sin, from death and the power of the Evil One, not at the price of gold and silver, but by his suffering and by his innocent death, so that I may belong to him for ever and live a new life like him who, risen from the dead, lives and reigns eternally.
This is what I firmly believe.

I believe that the Holy Spirit calls me by the gospel, illuminates me by his gifts and sanctifies me; that he keeps me in the unity of the true faith, in the Church which he brings together day by day. He, too, it is who fully forgives me my sins, as he does those of all believers. It is he who on the last day will raise me with all the dead and give me life eternal in Jesus Christ.
This is what I firmly believe.

Confession of faith of the Reformed Church of France based on Martin Luther

The crown rights of conscience

Although Huldreich Zwingli (1484–1531), a Swiss reformer of liberal tendencies, was influenced by Luther, he developed his own distinctive theology. This is not surprising as Zwingli did not feel committed to the past traditions of the Church as did some other reformers. He preached a more radical doctrine than Luther. Zwingli's reform movement was centred on Zurich where he propounded and propagated a doctrine of the immanence and universality of God. The immanence of God became the leading theme of Zwingli's spirituality as he stressed the importance of spiritual experience. He drew a sharp distinction between "inward" and "outward" devotion, and asserted the inner life of devotion to be the distinguishing mark of true Christian discipleship. Thus he cast aside the external observances and customs of religion, which he believed savoured of worldliness; he removed images from churches, abolished the Catholic mass and all ritual ceremonial; he forbade the use of organs in worship and fasting during Lent; he disapproved of monastic vows and he set in motion the radical reform of monastic orders, dissolved monasteries and dispersed their wealth for the education of the poor.

Throughout this time he acted as the people's priest in the Great Minster of Zurich and here he laid the foundations of Swiss protestantism. He was a gifted preacher with a genuine passion for religious reform. He drew his inspiration from the Bible, and held firmly the belief that the Christian should follow the dictates of conscience in matters of faith and doctrine, and reject the beliefs and practices that are not specifically prescribed by Scripture. His religious beliefs were distinctively subjective. He exercised the power of reason in expounding religious truth and became known as a clear-sighted theologian who stood for the universal rights and freedom of conscience. The Christian must follow the Scriptures as the rule of faith and religious observance and only act on what they prescribe. Zwingli applied this principle also to his reform of worship and the Church system.

He disapproved of the Catholic Church's teaching of the priestly mediation of grace through the eucharist, and declared that in no way could the bread and wine be the vehicles of spiritual redemption. The sacrament was only an outward observance. Whereas Luther, as we saw, believed in the "real presence" in the bread and wine, Zwingli, on the other hand, held that the body and blood of Christ were absent.

The eucharist is a memorial feast, the bread and wine are memorial signs of the sacrifice of Christ; through the eucharist the communicant receives spiritual nourishment and the assurance of God's grace in forgiveness. "At Zurich the Lord's Supper was divested of its medieval ceremonial and given a purely commemorative interpretation. The unleaven bread and wine were placed in the centre of the nave rather than on the altar at the east end of the church. The ministers, wearing their everyday garb, facing the congregation, carried the bread on a large wooden trencher for distribution to the people."[11]

Zwingli's spirituality found its application also in social reform. Spirituality was the motivation of social as well as ecclesiastical reform. Zwingli had strong humanist leanings and broad horizons and an all-inclusive concept of Christianity. He cherished political as well as religious ideas, and hoped to secure an alignment of Protestant states throughout Europe; he cared about changing the political and social context of life as well as reforming religion. His reform was thorough, yet it was carried through quietly but with determination. There were certain conditions in Zurich that worked in favour of Zwingli and reform and these contributed to the swift progress of the changes which he pioneered. He valued greatly the art of expository preaching and the work of the local pastor, and he wrote extensively in the defence of his own reforming beliefs. He expounded the major Reformation doctrines of covenant, grace and election, and whilst his main centre of influence was Zurich his work extended to other parts of Switzerland, including the international centre of Geneva. Geneva then became the focus of further reform, as we shall now see.

Covenant and election

John Calvin (1509–64) was a convert to Protestantism, and ranks with Luther and Zwingli as a luminary of the "magisterial" Reformation. He was a Frenchman, the son of a lawyer, but he is most closely associated with Geneva where his main work was done. He is credited with many comprehensive achievements, particularly as a theologian, educationist, biblical commentator, church organizer and reformer. His theology revolved around Christ as the sole object of faith and Lord of the Church. God had entered into a covenant of irresistible grace which is his gift of justification to all those who are chosen by him. This is the basis of Calvin's doctrine of predestination and spirituality; God's covenant assured the union of the believer with Christ, and this assurance enables life to be lived in confidence without the anxiety of pending judgement. God has already made the choice; God has asserted his absoluteness and sovereign power to act in his own way. This is clearly the doctrine of Scripture by which everyone should abide:

> If men were taught only by nature they would hold to nothing certain or solid or clear cut, but would be so tied to confused principles as to worship an unknown God . . . Now, in order that true religion may shine upon us, we ought to hold that it must take its beginning from heavenly doctrine and that no-one can even get the slightest taste of right and sound doctrine unless he be a pupil of Scripture.[12]

In accordance with this doctrine of divine sovereignty everything works according to God's plan, and this is directed towards salvation. The testimony of Scripture affirms it and the Holy Spirit authenticates it. It is the prerogative of God to select whom he chooses. God is absolutely supreme and he ordains and determines all that is. God holds the destiny of every person for good or evil in his hand. No one can rescue the self or any other from the abyss of evil alone, but God in mercy has effected deliverance through the death of Christ, "who bore in the soul the torture of condemned and ruined men".

The work of Christ is, therefore, permanent for human redemption. Christ is divine and he resides within the Trinity of Father, Son and Holy Spirit; each person of the Trinity is wholly divine, yet God himself is one. In Christ divinity and humanity are united, Christ is God *and* man, and in his incarnate role he made atonement for human sin by submitting himself to death on the cross:

> Scripture teaches that (man) was estranged from God through sin, is an heir of wrath, subject to the curse of eternal death, excluded from all hope

of salvation, beyond every blessing of God, the slave of Satan, captive under the yoke of sin, destined finally for a dreadful destruction and already involved in it; and at this point Christ interceded as his advocate, took upon himself and suffered the punishment that, from God's righteous judgement, threatened all sinners; that he purged with his blood those evils . . . that by his expiation he made satisfaction and sacrifice duly to God the Father . . . This is our acquittal . . . Not only (was) Christ's body given as the price of our redemption, but he paid a greater and more excellent price by suffering in his soul the terrible torments of a condemned and forsaken man.[13]

Through the sacrifice of Christ, God bestows grace on whom he will, and so affirms the act of redemption as a supreme act of divine love. Sins are remitted through the death of Christ and God receives into his favour those who are so redeemed. The outcome is a life justified by God and enabled to be lived in righteousness before him and the world. Being justified the redeemed enjoy communion with Christ and with the Church: "Whoever finds himself in Jesus Christ and a member of his body by faith, he is assured of his salvation." From the acceptance of this doctrine Calvin urged the first step in complete dedication to God be taken:

Let this therefore be the first step, that a man depart from himself in order that he may apply the whole force of his ability in the service of the Lord . . . for it ought to occur to us how much honour God bestows upon us in thus furnishing us with the badge of his soldiery . . . Each individual has his own kind of living assigned to him by the Lord as a sort of sentry post so that he may not heedlessly wander about throughout life . . . [14]

Calvin's overall doctrine of the Church is a model of comprehensive theological understanding and statesmanship, blending a view of the true invisible church with a visible church as consisting of those who are the children of God through grace and sanctified by the Holy Spirit. He wrote, "the Church includes not only the saints at present living on earth, but all the elect from the beginning of the world".[15] This fellowship, united with the elect from the beginning of the world, profess and worship God and Christ. They observe the sacraments which, in Calvin's understanding, are "an outward sign by which the Lord seals on our consciences the promises of his good will towards us . . . and properly fulfil their office only when the Spirit, that inward teacher, comes to them, by whose power alone hearts are penetrated". However, salvation does not depend on the observance of the sacraments, and in the eucharist it is by the Holy Spirit that the body and blood of Christ are communicated. Thus it is through the power of the Holy Spirit that Christ feeds his people with his body and blood. So it is that the body and blood of Christ are exhibited in the sacrament. This may be described as a spiritual doctrine of the "real presence" of Christ in the eucharist.

Calvin's statesmanship is displayed most impressively in his organization of an ecclesiastical consistory of pastors and elders, and in the constitution he designed for the Church. The consistory was made up of pastors and elders who were persons of good conduct and endowed with spiritual wisdom. They were chosen by the civil authority and were expected to observe a code of orderly discipline. This would ensure an honourable relationship between Church and state. In this respect education was given an essential role. Calvin pioneered a progressive system of education by establishing schools and an academy under the auspices of the Church that resulted in Geneva becoming a leading centre of learning. Calvin himself contributed handsomely to the cause of sacred learning; he was an accomplished interpreter of Scripture who used his ability to expound its inner meaning in a balanced and reverent way. He systematized the doctrines of the Protestant Reformation and structured its ecclesiastical discipline, and those whom he trained and influenced became the harbingers of the spread of his doctrines to Germany, the Netherlands, France, Scotland, Hungary and Poland. Calvin is credited with having a real if unofficial oversight over large numbers of churches whose thought was moulded powerfully by his doctrines and ideals. He was the leading reformer of his age and the first who may justly be called international.

The fellowship of the holy

The spiritual tradition in Christian theology received a fresh impetus from the radical reformers of the sixteenth century. They were intent on a more thorough-going Protestantism than Martin Luther had envisaged. They demanded complete independence between Church and state, absolute freedom of conscience in all religious matters, the right of independent gatherings for worship, and authority to determine belief and order within the Church under the sole guidance of the Holy Spirit. The Bible was the inspired Word of God, and this called for a more radical reform and a more embracing spirituality than had been achieved hitherto. The radical reformers covenanted together to form exclusive communities of kindred spirits and aspirations. They were the true believers led and nurtured by the Holy Spirit, who were not bound by any external authorities or formulae. They awaited the return of Christ as he had promised to come to establish a "new heaven and a new earth". In the meantime they abided by his promise and fulfilled their mission in the power of the Holy Spirit. The Anabaptists were prominent amongst the radical reformers and they too relied heavily on the guidance of the Holy Spirit and personal commitment to Christ. They restricted baptism to believers only, who at their baptism made a public confession of their spiritual faith. The Anabaptists had a substantial following in the Netherlands and Switzerland, but they were persecuted for their seemingly extreme beliefs.[16] They endured persecution stoically believing that they were destined to suffer as did the early Christians for the sake of Christ. Thereby they gave proof of their unconditional commitment. In complete submission to Christ and absolute subservience to his will they discarded all external objects that might direct them from this; screens and images, frescoes and pictures were removed from churches; the pulpit with the open Bible was made the central feature of the church building; festivals and saints' days were abandoned, and Sunday was kept as a holy day for worship; Bible reading, prayers, preaching and hymn singing for the nourishment of the spiritual life became the regular diet of Sunday worship.

Thomas Müntzer (1490–1525) was an ardent supporter of this radical movement. He was attracted to the apocalyptic doctrine of the return of Christ, which he described as "harvest time" when there would be an ingathering of souls into God's Kingdom:

> Harvest time is here, so God himself has hired me for his harvest. I have sharpened my scythe, for my thoughts are most strongly fixed on the truth, and my lips, hands, skin, hair, soul, body, life curse the unbelievers.[17]

In preparation for this spiritual harvest Müntzer practised a strict puritanism and a spiritualizing of all Christian rites and ordinances. He called for absolute reliance on the promise of the Holy Spirit, complete abandonment to divine guidance and commitment to the spiritual renewal of society. He cared little for institutional structures, and so presented a challenge to all formalized interpretation of Christian truth. However, the Radical Reformation lacked cohesion, but it was said of Müntzer that he did "the work of a Zealot who had brought Jerusalem down in ruins. Indeed, he signed his letters with a sword of Gideon and the phrase, "Thomas Müntzer the Hammer."[18] Furthermore, Müntzer behaved like a biblical warrior priest whose motto was, "Let not the sword of the saint get cold." He adopted a red cross and a naked sword as a heraldic emblem. He was not averse to war in a just cause. Violence, he claimed, could be justified as "a sort of peremptory apocalypse before the true one when . . . human institutions would wither away and the parousia would mark the beginning of eternal and perfect government".[19]

What Müntzer and the radical reformers demonstrate is that there were divisions within the reform movement as well as opposition from without. In the wake of this there sprang up a number of sects and parties which often broke into controversy among themselves. The most prominent of them traced their lineage to the new spiritual awakening, and some were intent on carrying to their ultimate the doctrines and principles they imbibed. Others tended to mitigate the more extreme rigour of radicalism. The reform movement splintered into separate groupings which then cultivated their own styles of spiritual activities, so that however unorthodox they might now seem they demonstrate the variety within the spiritual tradition of Christianity.

Spiritual vision and recovery

The Catholic Church did not underestimate the impact of a movement that induced so many out of its communion. It reacted in a number of ways, especially by making a vigorous defence of its traditional doctrine, a call for a more enlightened intellectualism, and a fresh emphasis on piety and moral purity. In Spain, Cardinal Ximenes (1436–1517), Archbishop of Toledo, set about reforming the Spanish Church, first by reforming the Franciscan Order and then by instigating the publication of the Polyglot Bible. In Rome, reform centred on the founding of the Oratory of Divine Love by churchmen who combined devotion and the new learning with a life of fervent faith, prayer and meditation. At the same time Pope Adrian VI, pope from 1522 to 1523, a man of deep religious piety, carried through reform of the papal court and its discipline of the clergy. Other reform movements were mounted especially by the Society of Jesus, which had the greatest impact. The founding of this Society was destined to influence the Catholic Church in a number of ways and this reverberated throughout Christendom. Ignatius Loyola (1491–1556), who founded the Society, was a Spanish soldier of humble birth. He devoted himself to the study of the life of

Christ and the Church Fathers, and resolved to become a soldier of Jesus Christ. He combined within himself the insights of clear spiritual vision and religious zeal with astute worldliness and practical ability. In 1534 he founded, with a few associates, the Society of Jesus, and was elected the superior general, and so Ignatius spent the rest of his life leading its work from its headquarters in Rome. The Society made a vow of obedience to the pope, but its members also took vows of poverty, chastity and obedience. They also vowed obedience to the general of the Society. The system of discipline adopted was expounded in *The Spiritual Exercises* (1548), a powerful work of Christian spirituality which also incorporates the quintessence of Catholic moral philosophy. The Jesuits, as the members of the Order became known, took as their motto "for the greater glory of God"; they became zealous missionaries bent on spreading the Catholic faith world-wide. The power wielded by the Order was enormous, and its influence spread far beyond the continent of Europe. *The Spiritual Exercises* prescribed specific instructions that gave precise direction to the lives of their members, who were to spend time in retreat under the guidance of a spiritual director, spend many hours in prayer and silence and observe mass regularly. The strict discipline was intended to induce clear spiritual vision and confirm and deepen the resolve to follow the way of Christ at all costs.

Surrender of life to divine guidance and the service of others was made a priority; members of the Order were expected to live a missionary life-style and follow a strict path of spiritual and moral obligation. They strove also to equip themselves to be the servants of Christ in every possible way, of whom Ignatius said:

> Now if you just reflect, that these desires of serving Christ as Lord are not from you but from him, and when you say boldly that he has given them to you, you publish his praise and glorify him, not yourself ... Do not merely venture to say that you are desirous of serving the Lord, when you ought to proclaim and confess boldly that you are his servant, and that you would sooner die than desert his service.[20]

The Spiritual Exercises was structured as a kind of military manual for the Christian as a commissioned member of Christ's army who was expected to campaign in the world as the soldier of Christ. The Jesuit was not bound by worldly ties but was to serve Christ in the world and be ready to go anywhere in his service. The Jesuits constituted a modified monastic order disciplined to propagate the doctrines and ideals of the Catholic Church. They engaged in teaching and in service to the poor, observing the principle of strict obedience, of which it has been said:

> the assurance we have is that in obeying we can commit no fault . . . you are certain you commit no fault as long as you obey, because God will not ask you if you have duly performed what orders you have received, and if you can give a clear account in that respect you are absolved entirely . . . God wipes it out of your account and charges it to the superior.[21]

The Jesuits undertook a wide variety of tasks, but were particularly active in teaching, constructing catechisms, administering the sacraments, fostering spirituality, and seeking to win converts to the Catholic Church.

Spiritual pilgrimage and the flame of love

The spiritual pilgrimage of the soul on the way to union with perfect transcendent love was given passionate and ecstatic expression by two intensely entranced mystics of the sixteenth century. Teresa of Avila (1515–82), or Mother Teresa of Jesus as her contemporaries called her, travelled the secret way of the mystics in her search for perfect peace and union with God, the way she believed that led her from desert to oasis, from sensual death to spiritual resurrection, and from worldly abandonment to a life of spiritual holiness. Teresa belonged to the Carmelite Order and practised faithfully its strict discipline. She engaged in the reform of the Order and founded many new houses of nuns. She lived a life of poverty, so much so that the reform movement came to be known as "Shoeless". She endured many trials, including severe illness, which profoundly influenced and tested her spirituality. She described the experience of suffering as a spear penetrating her soul, but this she confessed was her vision of Christ to whom she was totally devoted. Her spiritual pilgrimage led her through the perils of the dark to the dawn and light of mystical union with God. Each step in the progress of this journey was marked by prayer, meditation and contemplation.

Teresa of Avila was a pragmatic mystic. As her spiritual journey led her through the abyss of darkness she emptied her soul of self-seeking and striving in order to submerge herself in love of God and practical service to others for his sake. Her *Life* and her *Interior Castle* (two of her writings) both tell of the activities of a practical mystic and a practitioner of holiness. She wrote about the abandonment of self:

> It is a great grace of God to practise self-examination . . . believe me, by
> God's help, we shall advance more by contemplating the Divinity than
> by keeping our eyes fixed on ourselves.

And she expounded the meaning of love for others in the *Interior Castle*
in this way:

> We cannot know whether we love God, although there may be strong
> reasons for thinking so, but there can be no doubt about whether we love
> our neighbour or no. Be assured that in proportion you advance in
> fraternal charity, you are increasing in your love of God, for His Majesty
> bears so tender an affliction for us, that I cannot doubt He will repay our
> love for others by augmenting, in a thousand different ways, that which
> we bear for him.

Whereas Teresa was sustained and guided by her mystical experience,
she also felt drawn to that vision of wholeness that holds together the
mystical and the practical. In this she felt at one with Christ, as is
expressed in her saying, "To give our Lord a perfect hospitality, Mary
and Martha must combine." It is not irrelevant in this context to refer
to Teresa's aim of securing, "the integrity of a pattern of corporate
contemplative life for men and women, a pattern visibly detached from
many of the conventions of contemporary monasticism".[22] This pattern
of the contemplative life is formed within where God dwells, therefore
Teresa urged in *The Way of Perfection*: "Remember how important it
is for you to have understood this truth – that the Lord is within us and
that we should be there with him."

John of the Cross (1542–91) was a contemporary of Teresa of Avila
and he was also a member of the Carmelite Order. He experienced
many dramatic upheavals in his life, notably on account of his work for
the reform of his Order. He was imprisoned by his opponents, and it
was during his imprisonment that he began to compose the poetry for
which he is rightly famous. When he escaped from prison in Toledo he
brought with him his book of poetry, *Spiritual Canticle*, which is a
masterpiece of spiritual theology, passion and conflict. His theology has
to be understood against the background of his suffering and the
struggle of a soul on its poignant journey in search of peace and union
with God. On the one hand, his verses express the failure of any image
or metaphor adequately to describe God. Nevertheless, through the
mental anguish and the dark night of the soul in its relentless search,
grace breaks through and love becomes real:

> . . . One dark night,
> fired with love's urgent longings
> – Ah, the sheer grace! –
> I went out unseen,
> My house being now all stilled . . .
>
> O guiding night!
> O night more lovely than the dawn!
> O night that had united
> The lover with his beloved,
> Transforming the beloved in her Lover.[23]

These verses mirror the experience of their author, they reflect the inner characteristics of the soul's vision of the dawn that breaks through the night of darkness, poignancy and frustration. They express the experience of lostness through which the soul passes on the journey of abandoning and forgetting self until it arrives at the condition of "Laying my face on my Beloved." This is a journey "towards fulfilment not emptiness, towards beauty and life, not annihilation. The night – to use a favourite image – grows darker before it can grow lighter."[24] The light is the purging of the soul, the reality of purification, the dissolution of the self and the expurgation of sin, the experience described by John of the Cross saying "This life I live is vital strength"; it dawns "When the soul is least thinking of it. God is wont to give it these Divine touches by causing it certain recollections of Himself."

When God gives the soul these "Divine touches" and "certain recollections of Himself" then he nurtures and caresses the soul "like a loving mother who warms her child with the heat of her bosom, nurses it with good milk and tender food, and carries and caresses it in her arms". At the same time John of the Cross, unlike Teresa, did not relish the public scene;[25] rather he asserted how "The grace of God acts just as a loving mother by re-engendering in the soul new enthusiasm and fervour in the service of God." The performance of this service is the action of love:

> He who acts out of the pure love of God, not only does he not perform his action, to be seen by men, but does not do them even that God might know them. Such an one, if he thought it possible that his good works might escape the eye of God, would still perform them with the same joy, and in the same pureness of love.

The model for anyone "who acts out the pure love of God" is Christ, who is "the Way", the norm of the "inner life", and who is "most totally active for the world's salvation". Therefore, "If God is to work in us as he wills, we must become Christlike."[26] To become Christlike sums up the coordinating theme of Christian spirituality and the quest for inner peace and illumination. Christian spirituality is being at the heart of Christlikeness in belief and action. St. John of the Cross insisted that this transcends cerebral truth, for it is never possible to find satisfaction "In what you understand about God, but in what you do not understand about him." The Christian never stops with loving and delighting in the understanding and comprehension of God but perseveres to love and delight in "what is neither understandable or perceptible of him". The approach to God becomes closer and consequently the spiritual illumination and action more Christlike. To live in the fellowship of Christ's sufferings, without being morbid or oblivious to the agony of the cross, is the experience of the pilgrim on the journey to the goal of illumination, spiritual maturity, inner harmony, good works, and the joys of the Christian life.

English spirituality

The spiritual reforms of the sixteenth century in Europe had their counterpart in England, but here they developed certain distinctive characteristics. The reforms of Henry VIII (1491–1547), and the religious settlement under Elizabeth (1533–1603), had decisive consequences for the history of religion in England.

The reforms may be described briefly as having passed through three phases, namely: Henry's conflict with the pope and the assumption of religious supremacy, the manipulation of the Church by the King, and the suppression of the monasteries and its aftermath.

As happened on the continent, the seeds of reform were planted in earlier centuries although they did not bear fruit immediately. The able preacher and theologian John Wycliffe (1329–84) was one of the catalysts of the reform movement in England. Wycliffe translated the Bible into the vernacular, and then preached that it was more beneficial to know the Scriptures than to attend the mass. Wycliffe sought to create a spiritual culture that was biblically centred, but he met fearsome opposition. The circulation of the Bible in the vernacular was forbidden at the time, but this did not deter Wycliffe and his band of faithful preachers. Knowledge of the Bible spread, and quickened the conscience of lay people to their spiritual needs. The Bible in English was not totally suppressed and Wycliffe and the Lollards made great effort to ensure that its contents were known. In doing so they roused considerable anti-clerical feelings as they denounced some of the basic teachings and practices of the Catholic Church, notably, transubstantiation, monasticism, worship of saints, pilgrimage and other common late medieval customs. They also criticized the Church's hierarchy, the papacy, its wealth and corruption. The principal followers of Wycliffe's movement were drawn from the poorer classes and included women, but their life was difficult and they were persecuted as heretics.

John Colet was one of the seminal thinkers who sowed the seeds of reform. As mentioned earlier he was dean of St. Paul's, a leading educator and a powerful preacher. He denounced the worldly ways of the clergy and their profligate life-style but his powerful and scholarly preaching from the pulpit of St. Paul's did not go unheeded.

A number of other factors contributed to the emergent spirit of reform in England, including the growth of the spirit of nationalism and the call for more freedom and self-expression in religion. Coupled with this was a new sense of national assertiveness and self-sufficiency, and antipathy to foreigners. Another factor was the growing dislike for the papacy and discontent with the vast economic wealth of the Church.

Religious houses also came under attack for their affluence and worldly life-style. In the late medieval age, England underwent far-reaching social and economic changes that accentuated the divide between rich and poor. The Renaissance, although late in coming to England, stimulated intellectual activities and encouraged interest in the new learning in the study of religion and the Bible. The reformers generally shared great devotion to the Bible and its authority as is seen from Article XXXVIII of the Thirty-nine Articles of the Church of England, which stated:

> We give not to our princes the ministering either of God's Word or of the sacraments; but the very prerogative which we see to have been given always that they should rule all estates and degrees committed to their charge by God, whether they are Ecclesiastical or Temporal.

Steps in reform

One name figures prominently in the English reform movement of the sixteenth century, namely, Thomas Cranmer (1489–1556), who was made Archbishop of Canterbury against the wishes of Catherine of Aragon. Cranmer was responsible for the theological and liturgical changes that became an integral feature of the reform movement in England. His doctrines bear evidence of the influence of the continental reformers, but the concepts and language he used were typically English. Cranmer was the main compiler of the epoch-making *Book of*

Common Prayer, under whose authority the clergy of the Church of England minister to this day. Every clergy, man or woman, ordained today to the priesthood of the Church of England is expected to declare:

> I assent to the Thirty-Nine Articles of Religion and the Book of Common Prayer . . . and in Public Prayer and Administration of the Sacraments I will use the form in the said Book prescribed and none other, except so far as shall be ordered by lawful authority.

The Prayer Book contains the complete compendium of services for morning and evening prayer, holy communion, baptism, confirmation, marriage and burial. The Prayer Book also contains elements of Lutheran and eastern liturgies. The first Prayer Book was completed in 1549 and a Second Prayer Book in 1552. In the second the title mass was dropped and the communion service was reconstructed as a commemorative rite. According to this the presence of Christ is believed to reside not only in the heart of the communicant but also in the bread and wine. So the reading of the ordinance is "The body (or blood) of our Lord Jesus Christ preserve thy body and soul unto everlasting life."

The Book of Common Prayer received a unique status in the liturgy of the Church of England in the time of the Reformation. It has kept the Church united ever since in its form of worship, and it has been said that "The Book of Common Prayer is a rule of life. It is meant to describe, shape and support, the Anglican way of being Christian."[27] In this respect it has also helped to shape the liturgical language of Christian prayer, as in this example:

> O Lord, who hast taught us that all our doings without charity are nothing worth, send Thy Holy Spirit and pour into our hearts that most excellent gift of charity, the very bond of peace and of all virtues . . .

As well as providing a uniform service book of worship in English prose, Cranmer also contributed to the cause of reform a *Book of Homilies*, intended as a book of instruction in the Christian faith which clergy were to read to their congregations. Cranmer also drafted the Forty-two Articles, later reduced to the Thirty-nine Articles of the Church of England.

Defender of the faith

The title was given to Henry VIII in respect of his involvement in the reform of the Church in England. Two aspects of this are noteworthy in this context, namely, the dissolution of the monasteries, and Henry's accession as Supreme Head of the Church of England. Economically the vast wealth of the religious houses was a temptation to people of high position who wished to improve their own financial status. It was under Henry that the dissolution of the monasteries began, and the king's need of money contributed to their demise. The royal treasury needed replenishing as the employees of the royal household increased. Seizing the wealth of the religious houses gave Henry and the nobles the relief from financial stringency they so much needed. This happened as the consequence of the appointment of Thomas Cromwell (1486–1540) as vicar-general in 1535, and was why he made his crucial systematic visitation of the monasteries. Dissolution not reform of the monasteries was his aim, the only way of dealing with the disreputable conditions into which many of them had lapsed. The monasteries had lost their credibility as oases of spirituality and abandoned the monastic ideal to a large extent. Their members had become more worldly in outlook and action, and the number of those who took monastic vows had declined. The minority who clung to the old ideals, and who struggled to practise them, had become exhausted or embarrassed by the degenerate state of the monasteries and were not averse to their urgent reform. Whether they were prepared to contemplate their dissolution is another matter. However, Henry presented his bill to parliament for their suppression in March 1536, and this produced a lightning effect. Within four years the dissolution of the monasteries was virtually accomplished; England was officially a monasticism-free nation.

This event was a further step in the complex process that sought to rid England of all Catholic dispensations and papal authority. The Statute in Restraint of Appeals of 1533 declared the Church of England capable of exercising control over its own affairs without papal interference. But the crunch came when the pope excommunicated Henry in the matter of his marriage to Anne Boleyn. Henry ignored the pope's decree, and in November 1534 parliament enacted the supremacy of the king as head of the Church. The royal supremacy over and against the authority of the pope was legally established, though the king retained the title of Defender of the Faith, given him by Pope Leo X in 1521.

How deeply the reform movement had penetrated the heart and mind of England by the end of Henry's reign is an open question. What is certain is that it was given expression and implementation in many and varied ways.

In some respects the foundations of a completely transformed church had been laid; the influence and interference of the pope of

Rome had been circumscribed; the liturgy had been revised to meet the needs of a reformed Church; the Bible was made a more open and accessible book, the vestiges of the medieval Church such as images, pilgrimages, and indulgences were done away with; the power of the monasteries had been suppressed; the theology of the mass had been revised. Whilst this is the case, and the Church of England was established by king and parliament as the Church of the English nation, it did not absolutely and completely suppress the vestiges of Catholicism, or indeed, completely eliminate the minority of recusants and separatists.[28] Even to this day the Church of England is referred to as catholic and reformed.

In conclusion to this chapter on reform in the sixteenth century we may observe how it divided the Church in the west. Reform was inevitable, but when it came it sharpened in the most extreme way the perennial question of how to reconcile the immutable origins of Christianity, as enshrined in an authoritative hierarchic Church, with the expanding reach of the modern mind and the reality of life in an evolving universe. Reform claimed the initiative and authority of the divine Spirit at work through the human spirit, liberating it to engage in its own spiritual quest, illuminating it with new insights into eternal truth, and transforming it by its positive and creative action. The reform of religion in the sixteenth century bore the three marks of divine–human spiritualization, it liberated many Christians from the hierarchic control of the Church, it illumined the understanding of Christian faith and belief, and it transformed the liturgy and practices of the Church.

Spiritual reform is the gift of the divine Spirit, it makes realizable the highest human potential in conceiving, fulfilling and accomplishing the divine will. In the sixteenth century, reform entailed renewal and revival, as well as severance, all within the prevailing religious and non-religious culture, and in answer to the inner promptings of the Spirit. The reformers, without exception, demonstrated how the response and commitment of the Spirit gave them justification for action, and coherence to their common cause, however diverse their presumptions, or however different their methods and achievements were.

6

From Reformation to Romanticism

Of the influences affecting Christian theology and its spiritual tradition, none has been more confrontational than the so-called "age of reason". At the beginning of the seventeenth century Christianity was still a dominant force in the life and culture of Europe. But the hopes and expectations of the Protestant reformers had not been realized, and this created a situation of unease and aroused prejudice, cynicism and suspicion among ordinary people. The zeal and enthusiasm of the reformers had succumbed to a coldness and formalism and a reversion to the laconic spirit and stringent methods of the medieval schoolmen, referred to in chapter 4. Discontent and indifference gripped the human spirit as people's yearnings for social reform were thwarted and peasants continued to be beholden to oppressive overlords. The sense of disillusionment reacted on the ecclesiastical hierarchy as well as on the civic rulers. Poverty and plague, war and famine, added to the troubles of the time. A wave of secularization began to sweep across the continent.

We cannot pinpoint precisely when the forces which edged Europe step by step to the dawn of the modern age first began to fragment the fragile unity, but during the seventeenth century they gathered momentum in a whirlwind of radical transition that revolutionized the intellectual and cultural scene. New ideas about religion and philosophy were openly propagated that a century earlier would have been impossible. Yet this transformation, which extolled the power of rationalism and individuality, did not mortally paralyze the Christian religion, for we gather that:

> Christianity was itself evolving in ethos and doctrine, finding new emphasis, new inspirations, appealing in new ways to new classes of people, even as the world changed around it – and, indeed, contributing to and focusing on that change. European life was being secularized;

religion was becoming personalized, individualized; the two things went together, and were interdependent.[1]

Consolidation and fragmentation

How did Christian theology and spirituality fare in this time when "European life was being secularized" and "religion was becoming personalized and individualized"? The Catholic Church had generated a spirit of reform "from within", and through the Counter Reformation had aimed to reaffirm the purity of its doctrines and the orthodoxy of its practices. The two most potent factors in this renewal were the Council of Trent and the work of the Jesuits. The Council in 1545 had reacted strongly to the protests of the Protestant reformers in an attempt to stem the tide of Protestantism, but more positively it took practical steps to restore the dominance of Catholicism. It defined the orthodoxy of its doctrines as continuation from primitive Christianity, it consolidated the Church's creed and reiterated its universal authority. The Council reaffirmed the validity of the seven sacraments, and most significantly asserted its strict adherence to the doctrine of transubstantiation, that is, that in the eucharist the bread and wine are transubstantiated into the body and blood of Christ. The Council also outlawed clerical pluralism, enforced the celibacy of the clergy, legislated on the universality of the papacy, and also defined the process by which believers are made ready for the afterlife in heaven with God. In the remoulding of the Catholic Church and the fulfilment of its mission the Jesuits played a central role, as we indicated earlier.

Puritanism

Protestantism, on the other hand, was beset by fragmentation in theology and spirituality. In theology Luther and Calvin deviated in certain minutiae of doctrine, in their attitude to religion and in the style of worship. Lutherans advocated a greater freedom for the individual in matters of faith and its interpretation, whereas Calvinists were more inclined to central control. The former laid greater emphasis on the subjective element in theology whilst the latter stressed absolute submission to the controlling mind of God. It was inevitable that there should be reaction to this division. The ferment of new ideas propagated by emergent groups within Protestantism led to division and fragmentation. Theological disputes, which at the time seemed irreconcilable, caused considerable disruption. Separatist groups began to crystallize not only on the basis that their theological views differed from those of other Christians, but because they held more egalitarian views of the nature of the Church and of church government. When King Henry severed his relations with Rome in 1534 the immediate consequence was a reformation of the Church in England. But there were many Christians who, whilst they were not enamoured with the centralized power of the papacy, were disenchanted also with the new royal domination of the Church. During the early years of the reign of Elizabeth I many churchmen began to voice their convictions more openly. The Elizabethan Settlement of 1570 was disliked by the more individualist Christians and in consequence "puritanism" emerged and enlivened the religious scene with a strict extremism and many shades of opinion. Puritans felt they could not achieve their purposes from within the Church of England, so they withdrew. The main plank in Puritanism was its theology of the Holy Spirit. Puritans claimed to be wholly dependent on the Holy Spirit to shed light on God's will and purpose, especially on his word in the Bible. The Puritans believed that God's mind was made known through Scripture and they sought the testimony of the Spirit to illumine this. The interpretation of Scripture through the illumination of the Spirit opened up new vistas of understanding and also gave clearer insight and recognition of the power of the Holy Spirit.[2]

The Puritans were an amorphous group who posed a challenge to the very existence of the established Church of England. It is difficult to define their boundaries but their religion was devout and their resoluteness uncompromising. They displayed great enthusiasm for their cause and were zealous and unyielding in pursuing their goals, and for this they were frequently accused of being ostentatious in their religious practices and self-righteous in their personal and public demeanour. Robert Browne (1550–1633), a native of Norwich and a graduate of Corpus Christi, Cambridge, was a leader of the Puritans and the author of a *Treatise of Reformation without Tarrying for Anie*. In this he taught a congregational view of the Church as a gathered community of believers. In this community Christ was present through the Holy Spirit. No external authority was therefore necessary to constitute the Church; the Church was free from state control and priestly domination. Browne rejected the Elizabethan Settlement and the English Prayer Book. The Spirit alone was guide. Browne was persecuted for his beliefs, and eventually imprisoned.

The Puritans practised a strict morality and formed a distinct group who believed they were the elect. They wore a distinctive form of dress and they spoke a language that made them the butt of the withering humour of Shakespeare and other contemporary dramatists. They shunned pleasure and equated gloom with piety and excessive ardour with sin. They rejected the use of images and statues and all the external paraphernalia of worship; their faith was belligerent but they believed their faith and worship to be based on reformed theology. Some of the notable spiritual authors of the age were Puritans, including Richard Baxter (1615–91), John Milton (1608–74) and John Bunyan (1628–88).

Richard Baxter

Baxter was a distinguished scholar and an effective preacher. He wrote two books which are acknowledged as classics and amongst the most influential productions of the seventeenth century, namely, *The Reformed Pastor* and *The Saints Everlasting Rest*. He was outspoken in his criticism of political leaders, especially of their moral lapses. He proclaimed fervently the divine origin of Christianity and produced a solid body of evidence to substantiate this. In theology he may be termed a "bridge builder", that is, he sought to avoid assuming extreme positions and wished to reconcile conflicting viewpoints. He expounded systematically those spiritual qualities which Christians should cultivate and radiate as the distinctive characteristics of living a Christian life. One of Baxter's outstanding achievements was a complete reformed liturgy, which was a form of petition to the authorities that each minister should decide whether he wished to employ the *Book of Common Prayer* as it stood or the proposed revised version. He believed the individual should choose the most profitable way, knowing he is free to do what he wills. God alone, he declared, has absolute right, and no one should try to impose this on another except God.

John Milton

John Milton was born in London. A man of strong Protestant leanings, he stood by allegiance to conscience and integrity of intellect, and showed a great passion for human liberty. Milton was a distinguished poet and man of letters with a great love of music. His poems include *L'Allegro* and *Il Penseroso*, but his best-known work is *Paradise Lost*. Milton created many memorable images in his poetry and used his gift

of imagination to illumine eternal truth, nowhere more effectively than
in his poem *On His Blindness*, which so serenely expresses his commitment to God, his Maker, who is self-sufficient within himself:

> God doth not need
> Either man's work or his own gifts; who best
> Bear his mild yoke, they serve him best. His state
> Is Kingly: thousands at his bidding speed,
> And post oe'r land and ocean without rest;
> They also serve who only stand and wait.

John Bunyan

John Bunyan is undoubtedly one of the most formidable spiritual giants
of the seventeenth century. His great allegorical classic *The Pilgrim's
Progress* is one of the monumental achievements of the human spirit.
This allegory describes the journey of the Christian pilgrim through the
world to the celestial city. Its primary themes are the Church and the
City of God. The imagery of the journey is steeped in Scriptural images
and thought forms, and is a timely reminder that the Authorized (King
James) Bible had been completed in 1611. Bunyan was a skilled communicator of biblical teaching with a consuming passion for nurturing
the spiritual life on its truth. *The Pilgrim's Progress* is cast in the format
of a dream which depicts life as a pilgrimage of many variable memorable exciting experiences and encounters.

   Throughout his pilgrimage the persistent question that lurked in the
mind of the pilgrim was the perennial human question, What shall I do?
A personal decision had to be made. As he journeyed the pilgrim dwelt
on the conditions of his spiritual progress, especially, prayer, reading,
reflection and solitude. The burden of sin weighed heavily on his mind,
and he agonized over the question, "Whither must I fly?" Help came
from a sympathetic Evangelist:

> He said Evangelist, pointing with his finger over a wide Field, Do you
> see yonder shining light? He said, I think I do. Then said Evangelist, Keep
> that light in your eye.[3]

The pilgrim did not journey alone, for he had the support of Evangelist,
Hopeful and Great Heart, but he also met Pliable, Worldly Wiseman
and Despair, characters who represented the vicissitudes of the
pilgrim's journey through the world. Faith did not come easy to
Bunyan, and the characters that the pilgrim met on the journey to the
celestial city mirror the diverse experiences of hope and despair,

helpfulness and hindrance, guidance and temptation that characterize everyone's journey. Nevertheless the pilgrim's eyes were set on the celestial city and release from the wilderness of the world. Although he was faced with many impediments on route, including doubt and despair, "grace abounded", as conveyed in the words of the Interpreter:

> I have showed thee this picture first, because the Man whose picture this is, is the only Man, whom the Lord of the Place whither thou art going, hath Authorized, to be thy Guide.[4]

The Christian pilgrimage is a variable journey and for this, Christian needs the equipment and protection of the whole armour of God in order to make progress. The spiritual equipment is provided not for self-improvement or self-aggrandizement but that the Christian might journey confidently and serve God and others on the way. The pilgrim's task is that of service in the world where the pilgrim's life is spent; the Christian pilgrim must take up the cross and follow Christ, as he himself commanded. Christ supplies the needful grace and faith, as faith bids the pilgrim:

> Come on then, and let us go together, and let us spend our time in discovering of things that are profitable.[5]

The pilgrimage takes the pilgrim through the hubbub of the world's vanity fair, the trade and traffic, where the false values and immorality are a temptation to engage in wrong priorities and cling to benefits that will not last. But the pilgrim has the duty to resist these temptations and discouragements and persevere in witnessing to the truth. Persecution is unavoidable, but the destination is certain, for the pilgrim is assured of entry "into a certain Country". This country is alive with the sound of birds singing and with flowers blooming under the light of the sun that shines by night and day.[6] Bunyan's vivid picture of the heavenly country eliminated mortality as a thing of the past; in heaven all affliction and evil is ended, all temporal things are swallowed up into eternity. In this eternal country all things are immortal. This is the destination of the pilgrim and the certainty of salvation.

The Quakers

The Quakers, or the Society of Friends, emerged as an extreme form of Puritanism during the seventeenth century. Their founder, George Fox (1624–91), a native of Leicestershire, in his youth had many remarkable religious experiences through which he heard the call of God commissioning him:

> Thou seest how young people go together into vanity and old people into the earth; thou must forsake all, both young and old, and keep out of all, and be a stranger unto all.

Fox accepted this as his call to his life's work and from then on he knew himself to be in continual and direct personal communication with Christ. Christ "opened to him" what he should do and what he should refrain from doing. Fox's spirituality was rooted in the inner operation and power of the Spirit, which continued to shed light on God's will, as it had from the beginning. God continues to reveal himself to the human spirit, to address each person directly, and he alone speaks immediately to the human condition:

> There is one, even Christ Jesus, that can speak of thy condition.

Through the action of the Spirit the Christian has experience of the living Christ or the Christ within; the Spirit sets the pattern for all the Christian should do and is available to all who seek "inner light". The "inner light" is God known within. The Spirit is light and a life-transforming power. True knowledge of God is mediated by the Spirit. Christ is the supreme revelation of God and his death a supreme act of love.

> Now the hand God opened to me by his invisible power, that everyman was enlightened by the divine light of Christ and I saw it shine through all; and they that believed in it came out of condemnation to the light of life; and became children of it.

George Fox founded a society in 1666 which became known as the Society of Friends. This was conceived as a league of individuals, as it is to each single person that God speaks directly. The Society has no set creed or structures, no priesthood or hierarchic ministry, and does not administer sacraments. It is untrammelled by external rules or liturgy or churchy organization. The Society is open to men and women, there is complete equality, for it is possible to find God in everyone, and all and every life is sacramental.

The Quakers (as they became known) believed the Scriptures to have been given by divine light, but they set the authority of the inner light above the authority of Scripture. George Fox declared that the touchstone for judging the Quaker is "the Holy Spirit, by which the holy men of God gave forth the Scriptures". The Bible is referred to as "a secondary rule" or "a declaration of the fountain but not the fountain itself".

The spirituality of the Society of Friends is characterized by total reliance on divine guidance through the inner light of the Spirit. God is in everyone and the reality of God forms part of everyone. The search for guidance and the recognition of reality are identical. Much emphasis is placed on silence. Where the Spirit of God unites in a gathered meeting there is "a living silence". Out of this silence an individual may be moved to speak or read from the Bible or some other book or to give "testimony". An important aspect of the spirituality of the Quakers is philanthropy and social service. This consists of providing practical help to relieve distress and suffering outside the official channels of government. They consider this to be part of their "testimony" to the inner light.

Quakers are pacifists who believe it is possible to govern without armies. They consider that there is no end that can be attained that justifies war. George Fox preached a message of truth and love. He rejected violence completely, even when he was persecuted and imprisoned. The Friends have a "conscientious objection" to bearing arms. It is contrary to the Christian spirit; people who are confronted by the anger and violence of war must be shown a peaceful spirit that will shame them out of it. The aim of the Society of Friends is active peace-making and not merely seeking freedom from war. But every Friend has to follow the guidance of the "inner light", and discover personally what God wills to be done. There is no strict policy or party line or credal directive. The early Friends refused to take part in war and were, as Fox said, "peace-makers" and not "peace-breakers", because they believed that war was contrary to the Spirit of Christ. They asserted:

> the Spirit of Christ by which we are guided is not changeable so as once to command us from a thing as evil, and again to move unto it, and we certainly know, and testify to the world, that the Spirit of Christ which leads into all truth, will never move us to fight and war against any man with outward weapons, neither for the Kingdom of Christ, nor for the kingdoms of the world.

These words come from a declaration from "the harmless and innocent people of God" called Quakers, given to Charles II on 21 January 1661 and printed and sold up and down the streets.

Dissent

Other splinter groups fragmented the Christian Church and formed separate churches, developing their own styles of worship. Some believed the Church of England was too popish, others wished to give greater prominence to the Bible, others disapproved of the use of vestments, and others regarded a state church as an abhorrence.

These groups were known as "dissenters" and "nonconformists", and acquired different names, such as Independents or Congregationalists, who took up a particular view of the Church and of church government in the belief that Christ rules in his Church and hence in every local congregation. Another group were known as Baptists on account of their insistence on believers' baptism only, and their refusal to baptize infants. The Presbyterians are another dissenting group, who laid much emphasis on discipline and orthodoxy and the right of lay elders to take part in the government of the Church. There is a spiritual kinship between these three "denominations", this is particularly so in the matter of belief which is rooted in the doctrine:

> There is One Living and True God, who is revealed to us as Father, Son and Holy Spirit; Him alone we worship and adore.

In rejecting the Church of England the three denominations declared:

> We believe that the Catholic or Universal Church is the whole company of the redeemed in heaven and on earth, and we recognize as belonging to this holy fellowship all who are united to God through faith in Jesus Christ.[7]

The emergence of these groups, whilst exposing spiritual ideals that were meant to elevate the soul, sowed the seeds of dissension. Division and fragmentation were bound to cause tension as each group contended for greater authority and more liberty to govern and organize their life and to interpret their beliefs. Some gave primacy to conscience and the right of direct personal communion with God through the Spirit without the aid of any other intermediary, whereas other groups organized their life around a more central and rigid authority. A theology of the heart and of the intellect drove them in different directions. At the same time the issue of faith versus reason and the impact of the cultural milieu accentuated differences rather than promoting harmony.

Theology and rationalism

Theology continued to be taught in the universities albeit in an esoteric way. Theological dogma was subjected to analysis and rational exposition without attention to the living issues of faith and morality. The analytical methods of science were applied to theological questions and Christian truth was evaluated according to the tenets of rationalism. The new philosophy of rationalism was in the ascendancy and this was assimilated into the Christian world view. Enthusiasm was curbed and the method of "doing" theology lacked the regenerative spirit of zest and vitality. At the same time scientific enquiry was extended to questions of meaning and purpose that were once thought to be the prerogative of theology. Rationalism protruded into the realm of ultimate questions with a confidence that threatened the integrity of the methods and aims of theology.

The impact of rationalism was cataclysmic. Religious beliefs, hitherto taken for granted, were treated with scepticism, indifference or agnosticism. Traditional beliefs about God were not immune from the analytical processes of rationality or objective evaluation. Reason was enthroned as the sovereign arbiter of truth and this so bolstered the self-confidence of rationalism that religion was driven more and more onto the sidelines. God was not dismissed but he was relegated to a position outside the universe; he may have been conceived as its first cause but was not relied on as its controlling force. The upshot was to declare God an absentee deity rather than an imminent presence who gave direction, meaning and purpose to creation. Miracles were treated with scepticism or discarded; belief in the supernatural was circumscribed; divine revelation was not a condition for acquiring knowledge of God; reason, not blind faith, was the open sesame to truth; rational proof, not spiritual insight, was the ground of ultimate certainty.

Biblical criticism

One example of the chilling influence of the age of reason is the treatment of the Bible. During the seventeenth century a new and critical way of viewing the Bible became evident, and a new method of explaining its composition, interpreting its content, estimating its nature and authority began to be formulated. This was the origin of the modern discipline of "biblical criticism", as the new approach became known. In brief, the methods of historical and scientific enquiry were applied to the study of the Bible. This approach raised many challenging questions about the status of the Bible as the word of God, about its inspiration, authority and the traditional view of the Bible as divine revelation. One of the pioneers of this critical approach was the French physician Astruc (1684–1766) who questioned the unity of the

Pentateuch (the first five books of the Bible), which tradition had attributed to Moses. Astruc claimed that these books contained materials earlier than the time of Moses and were a composite set of writings containing data drawn from a number of different sources and from different ages. From then on a number of scholars in different parts of Europe began to apply their wits in studying analytically and scientifically the composition, history, literature, authority, religion and theology of the Bible. Some of their conclusions and assertions initially created a sense of incredulity but they also spread alarm and doubt about the veracity of the Bible as the authoritative foundation of faith. The findings of the critics were thought to undermine the integrity of the Bible as the Word of God. To study it in the same way as studying any other ancient literature was to denude it of its special aura, and the preoccupation with the human factor in the making of the Bible overshadowed the divine. On what assumption could the Bible be believed as the self-manifesting Word of God? The controversy which then began has still not been resolved.

Deism

A further radical influence on the development of Christian theology and spirituality was that of the deists – rationalists who propounded a theory of natural rather than revealed religion. They adhered to belief in God as the creator of an ordered universe but contended that God had allowed the world to function according to its own natural laws. God is to be apprehended by reason and not by revelation. God is the source of moral truth but has no part in the pursuit of truth. The founder of English deism, John Toland (1670–1722), the author of *Christianity Most Mysterious*, expounded reason as the irrefutable means of comprehending all that exists. Reason, not revelation, is the final authority and revealed knowledge must be tested by reason; reason is the ground of certainty and the guarantee of truth. Toland maintained that Christian truth is feasible for there is nothing in Christianity that is contrary to reason. Not all deists were as temperate as Toland, but all who subscribed to this philosophy relied on freedom of thought and the supreme evidence of reason. This freedom was a mark of natural justice arising from the belief that everything essential to faith and morality must be freely pursued and accord with natural reason. The deists maintained that truth is implanted in the mind by God and can only be conceived through the exercise of reason. They asserted the existence of God but questioned the view of Christianity as a revealed religion. It can be said of the deists that they prepared the ground for a rational scientific approach to Christian truth.

We see from these remarks how the earlier reference to individuality and personalization became a driving force in the enthronement of the primacy of reason in matters relating to religion. This movement characterized the study and controversies of religion throughout Europe in the seventeenth century. It developed in the wake of the secularization that in history is known as the Enlightenment. Many distinguished philosophers, astrologers and rationalists are identified with this movement, including Johannes Kepler (1571–1630), Francis Bacon (1561–1626), Isaac Newton (1642–1727), René Descartes (1596–1650), John Locke (1632–1704), Immanuel Kant (1724–1804), Voltaire (1694–1778) and Jean-Jacques Rousseau (1712–78). This galaxy of eminent leaders of thought exuded a spirit of confidence in progress and the advancement of world domination. The age of superstition and clerical control gave way to the new age of intellectual freedom. Its spirit can be summed up in the dictum of Descartes, "I think, therefore I am." The meaning of existence and related questions could be resolved by the application of reason. The doctrines of Christianity were made subject to refined scrutiny, and the philosopher Locke presented a basic form of Christianity couched mainly in ethical terms. Many traditional religious observances were dispensed with, and the dominance of clerical control and ecclesiastical rule was discarded. This accentuated a division between theology and spirituality. The advance in education opened up new opportunities for many people, and, as we shall see, the churches also took advantage of the new facility for producing catechisms and a spate of religious literature directed to the education of their members in the faith.

Catholic and Protestant churches produced works to guide their members in the spiritual life, especially in the practice of prayer and Christian morality. In part this was Christianity's response to the pressures of the age. The fact is that Christianity was itself "evolving in ethos and doctrine". Whilst the rationalists produced proofs for the existence of God, such as Kant's ontological, teleological and cosmological proofs, churchmen such as Count Zinzendorf (1700–60) exemplified the heart of Christianity as revealed love. Churchmen also resisted the tendency of rationalism to reduce religion to a system of moral laws which left little room for the exercise of an other worldly spirituality. They saw that Christianity needed to develop fresh interpretations of its beliefs and new styles in theology commensurate with its own spirit. The impact of the age of Enlightenment could not have been more searching, and echoes of this are felt to this day. The balance between secularity and spirituality, the dichotomy between individual free will and determinism, the relation between science and religion, and the transcendence and immanence of God, are live issues even today. Theology continues to grapple with the consequences of the intellectualism of the Enlightenment and its rational concept of truth. There are rumblings of suspicion still heard about the relation of theology and spirituality. Dogmatic theology is often suspect, and experiential truth thought to be unreliable. Even so, in the age of Enlightenment, in theory if not in actuality, the nurture of spirituality was more openly and universally available than when confined to the elite, cloistered within some monastic institution. Furthermore, spirituality assumed a more all-embracing dimension. Zinzendorf subscribed to this by engaging in a wholesome cultivation of "inner religion" and personal relationship with Christ as the Saviour of the whole world. He taught the universality of love as the heart of religion and theology:

> As soon as truth becomes a system one does not possess (love).

Accordingly God is only known through his Son Jesus Christ, and the Son can only be known through love. The love of Christ precedes any love that can be shown to him; the core of Christian belief is love for Christ. The sufferings of Christ express the depth of divine love, and death is a joyful incident, a "going home".[8]

Free will and determinism

However, there was no let up in the theological controversies that had disturbed the ranks of continuing Lutheranism and Calvinism. One such controversy centred on the thought of Jacobus Arminius (1560–1609) in Holland where the spirit of tolerance prevailed over the more rigid structures of the Calvinist doctrine of predestination. Arminius, a much respected preacher and pastor, argued the question whether God decreed election and then permitted the fall of man as a means of carrying out the decree. Or did God foresee the fall of man and then decree the predestination of some for salvation? On this issue Arminius came to the conclusion that the individual was gifted with freedom and therefore must reject the Calvinist doctrine of unconditional predestination. Arminius insisted that genuine human free will is incompatible with belief in absolute divine sovereignty. So he rejected the doctrine of election and taught that Christ had died for all people, as is consistently testified within the teaching of the Bible. Arminius' views were rejected by the Synod of Dort (1618–19), but there are still adherents of this liberal theology in the modern church.

In this connection it is appropriate also that we refer to the lingering influence of Socinus (1525–62), the Latin name for the Italian Sozini, known initially for his evangelical opinions, but who later also voiced his objection to the doctrine of divine predestination. Socinianism, as it became known, spread and developed after the death of Socinus through the works of his distinguished nephew Fausto (1539–1604) and made a considerable impact in Poland. Here the Socinians produced a Racovian Catechism (so named after the city of Rakov), which set out the basis of truth as centred in the Scriptures. Divine truth is relayed and supernaturally tested in the Bible, and authentic guidance is offered here on the path to eternal life. Socinus believed that there are no distinctions within the Godhead; God's will is a unity and his relation to human beings is as one God. The doctrine of the Trinity is rejected on the grounds that there can be no conflict between the justice of God the Father and the grace and benevolence of Christ the Son. This belief is consistent with human reason and must be accepted, as nothing that is contrary to reason is valid. Every person is free to choose the right and follow it. The doctrine of the death of Christ as a satisfaction made to God for sin is rejected. Christ was a human being who lived a life of compassion and of exemplary obedience to God; the supreme significance of his life is the way he manifests God's purpose and forgiveness of sin. For this life of exemplary commitment to the will of God, Christ was rewarded with resurrection and so is able still to hear prayer.

Along with Arminius and Socinus from this period we include the theologian and publicist Hugo Grotius (1583–1645). Grotius was a Dutchman who held strong opinions for which he was imprisoned, and only escaped with the help of his wife who succeeded in getting him carried out in a linen chest. He wrote an influential work, *De Jure Belli et Pacis*, which outlines matters of public rights, and many theological topics. Grotius was assured that Christ came into the world to make evident the enormity of human sin and to make atonement so as to allay future transgressions. Through Christ's atonement salvation is possible for everyone. God, declared Grotius, is the supreme moral ruler and all sin is an offence against his moral order.

God pardons whoever he wills, but the death of Christ was not a satisfaction for sin but was a tribute to the moral law of God that had been offended by sin. God chooses the terms on which his forgiveness is given, provided the terms are accepted, namely, faith and repentance.

The theory of Grotius was innovative but it did not gain approval. It was thought to be too artificial, even theatrical. There is another contribution of Grotius to the development of theological thought and its spiritual tradition that merits mention. Christians claim to be united in an "invisible" spiritual unity yet they give allegiance to divided churches (Protestantism was in the process of fragmenting into a number of sects), but why should they not make their "invisible" unity a visible reality? Grotius seemed to advocate such a move. Christian doctrines consist of those that are indispensable and necessary for redemption and those which are optional or marginal. The former are the prescribed conditions for Christian salvation. To ensure that they are observed the Church must expand and project those vital doctrines in a manner that makes them accessible to all Christian believers.

The controversy between free will and determinism persisted. Thorough and powerful though Calvin's doctrine of predestination was, it raised issues of human rights and freedom that many people could not reconcile with the world of real experience or with the new movement of thought that was captivating the contemporary mind. How is it possible to harmonize the view that everything that happens in the world is pre-determined by divine decree with human free will? Is everything that happens on the stage of history a pre-arranged plan conceived in all its detail by the divine artificer from all eternity? If this is so it leaves no place for human initiative or the freedom to pursue objectives to their conclusion. It reduces the human will to no more than a part of an almighty process of causation initiated and controlled by an omnipotent divine mind. Such views created a spiritual restlessness as their spread seemed inevitable and their impact irresistible. To comply with the doctrine of predestination would be to diminish the precious gift of freedom and the exercise of natural faculties. Does not the Spirit of God operate through human beings, raising them to a higher level and predisposing them for the higher life of free and willing obedience to his will? The human spirit is not passive but free to respond to the divine will of its own volition. And in truth the Spirit of God works through the human spirit in such a way as to reveal the affinity between God and the human being. Thus individuals are equipped to discover the meaning and intensity of human freedom, and realize their true selves by entering into union with God and living according to his purpose.

In this way they experience the reality of God not just as "first cause" but as fire, joy and peace. This was the view of Blaise Pascal (1623–62), a mathematician and scientist who is also well known for his theological writings. His spirituality is summed up in his famous saying, "the heart has its reasons, of which reason knows nothing". These words imply that existence consists in finding union with God, and the reasons the heart has open up realms of reality that are otherwise blocked.

Pascal had a penetrating insight into the means of arriving at a state of union with the living God. He discovered that the ultimate truth and meaning of existence is Jesus Christ, and so he turned his mind to the study of the Bible, the most significant study in which the human mind can engage. He expounded the unique character of the Bible, and especially how God is to be discovered therein. The God of the Bible is related to human beings, but he can only *be known* by those who seek him. As they earnestly seek God they discover how Jesus becomes luminous to them and provides answers to life's profoundest questions and deepest needs. The study of the Bible can bring about the transformation of the heart and become a rule of life. Only by the ways taught by Christ in the gospel is it possible to "keep hold of him". For this purpose there must be, "Total submission to Jesus Christ as my director." Pascal was a devout member of the Catholic Church and hated being separated from it. He declared:

> We know all the virtues, martyrdom, austerities, and all good works are useless outside of the Church, and the communion with the head of the Church, who is the Pope.

He rejoiced that he had no bond on earth but to the Church, and he was determined to live and die in communion with the pope, for there is no salvation outside the Church. He prayed for grace to remain for ever within the Church, for he would be lost without it. The Church appeals to that quality that transforms the soul and makes the individual the child of God. He wrote his profession of faith in his will, which was read after his death:

> First, as a good Christian, Catholic, Apostolic, Roman, the suppliant has recommended and recommends his soul to God. Who through the merits of the precious blood of our Saviour and Redeemer Jesus Christ may it please him to pardon his faults and to join his soul, when it shall leave this world, to the number of the blessed, imploring to this end the intercessions of the glorious Virgin Mary and all the saints of paradise.

Natural and revealed religion

Some prominent churchmen endeavoured to come to terms with the Enlightenment and its view of man as the centre and measure of all things, or with what Kant called the "Copernican revolution in philosophy", and the new scientific theories about the universe with the sun, not the earth, at the centre. Foremost in this connection is the work of Bishop Butler (1692–1752), the author of the justly famous work *Analogy of Religion* (1736). Butler was successively Bishop of Bristol and Durham and addressed his *Analogy* to enquirers who found it difficult to reconcile the doctrines of the Church, especially of revealed religion, with the laws of nature. In response Butler developed his thesis of analogy between "natural" and "revealed" religion. At the same time he answered the arguments the deists had advanced against the reasonableness of revealed religion. Bishop Butler provided a defence of Christianity by means of rational argument and the logic of probability. Human beings live by probability, they live on assumptions that cannot be proved with mathematical certainty. The world is such as to make the doctrines both of natural theology and of Christian revelation probable. Butler insisted:

> Probable evidence, in its very nature, affords but an imperfect kind of information, and it is to be considered as relative only to beings of limited capacities . . . to us probability is the very guide to life.

This must mean that religious belief (probability) is universal, even though total mathematical proof is out of the question. Nevertheless, belief can be shown to be reasonable. Human beings are endued with capacities of action, happiness and misery, and it is "indeed a probability of it abundantly sufficient to act upon unless there be some positive reason to think that death is the destruction of those living powers".[9]

In respect of spirituality Bishop Butler expounded a high doctrine of moral duty. In the course of his work called *Fifteen Sermons* he expounded conscience as the voice of God making itself heard in human affairs. He dismissed any thought of discrepancy between the voice of conscience and rational thought. Human beings, he declared, are capable of reflecting rationally on their behaviour. It is conscience that determines whether an action is good or not good; human beings have the capacity to approve or disapprove of what they do. They should have a proper self-regard for the way they behave, for this is reasonable, and those who have such regard know that conscience directs them to do what is right. Conscience is a rational faculty that inspires positive motivation for doing what is right. This Bishop Butler believed to be all-important. He deplored the tendency to allow matters of ritual and Church government to take precedence over attention to a life of goodness, pure morals, and spiritual discipline. This would be to tear Christianity from its roots and mar the purity of the Church. If conscience were to be obeyed then morality would rule the world. Bishop Butler would have approved of the *Natural Theology* of William Paley (1743–1805) and his well-known definition of virtue, "doing good in obedience to the will of God for the sake of everlasting happiness". Both churchmen urged the infusion of genuine Christian piety into popular religion, both believed morality to be of prime importance, and both preached the urgent need of spiritual revival.

A way of holiness

Alongside the moral earnestness of Bishop Butler we must refer to the work of William Law (1686–1761), a man of mystical tendencies who was influenced by Jacob Boehme, but whose originality of thought and extraordinary intellectual power marks him out as one of the most influential Christian thinkers of his age. Law was a high churchman, a man of saintly character and deep spiritual fervour. It has been said of his spiritual classic, *Serious Call*, that with the exception of *Pilgrim's Progress* there is no religious book in the English language that has had a stronger influence.[10] The book consists of twenty-four chapters, but it is only possible here for a few samples to give a flavour of his religious fervour and intellectual power. Living in a rationalistic age, when moral behaviour often fell short of the holiness and standards of pure Christianity, Law enquired into the reason why the principles of Christian living were so much neglected. He exposed the incidences of lax morality seen in the prevalence of swearing, sports and gambling, intemperate pleasures and high living. He attributed this laxity to the neglect of the Christian spirit and the lack of inner intention to please God. He wrote of the behaviour of people who "acted strangely contrary to the principles of Christianity", and declared that this is so because they "have not so much as the intention to please God". He insisted on the paramount importance of cultivating right motive and intention and maintained that:

> when you have this intention to please God in all your actions, as the happiest and best thing in the world, you will find in you as great an aversion to everything that is vain and impertinent in common life, whether of business or pleasure, as you now have to anything that is profane. You will be as fearful of living in any foolish way, either in spending your time, or your fortune, as you are now fearful of neglecting the public worship.

If this were to be the case then the whole world would be revolutionized:

Now, who that wants this general sincere intention, can be reckoned a Christian? And yet if it was among Christians, it would change the whole face of the world; true piety, and exemplary holiness, would be as common and visible, as buying and selling, or any trade in life.

William Law expounded at length on the nature and content of Christian devotion, and showed how a life of devotion can bring the greatest peace, happiness and enjoyment of life. But the secret of this is devotion to God, which is shown especially in the practice of prayer at regular times, the singing of psalms, in private devotions, cultivating a spirit of humility, showing universal love, and living contrary to the world. He declared:

> He, therefore, is the devout man, who lives no longer to his own will, or the way and spirit of the world, but to the sole will of God, who considers God in everything, who serves God in everything, who makes all the parts of his common life parts of piety, by doing everything in the Name of God, and under such rules as are conformable to His glory.

An upsurge of interest in spirituality resulted from the labours of influential theologians who are known collectively as the Caroline Divines. They were active during the reign of Charles I (1600–49) and held many views in common, especially on the continuity of the Christian Church from the beginning. In some respects they were the product of the Protestant Reformation but in others they clung to traditional Catholicism. They recognized the Elizabethan Settlement but wished the Church of England to retain its Catholic character. They sought to maintain a balance between the sacramental life of the Church and the Scriptural emphasis of the Protestant reformers on the Bible as the Word of God. They felt themselves bound to both aspects and believed this to be perfectly reasonable.

Their commitment to the Church of England was real but they coveted a form of Church government that embraced the best in Catholicism and Protestantism. The Caroline Divines were men of learning and interpreters of history, they were theologians who used the power of reason in their expositions, and who were skilled in the use of evidence in defence of their beliefs.

One of the Caroline Divines was William Laud (1573–1645), Archbishop of Canterbury. In theology Laud was anti-Calvinist but his main contribution to spirituality is in the field of liturgy. He was attracted to the pre-reformation liturgical practices of the Church and wished to see these implemented in the liturgy of the Church of

England. To this extent he was a devoted conformist who believed that the whole Church should conform to a common liturgy. He sought to impose his own liturgy in Scotland and also to compel people to uphold the government of the Church of England without any alteration. This roused hostility from the Puritans, and when the formula of conformity to Church government was suspended by the king, Laud was imprisoned and found guilty and executed.

Laud was a supporter of the established church and of the authority of its official position within the state. He upheld its privileged protection by the state as essential to its growth and influence. Scripture and tradition gave support to the logic of this position and Laud called for a reasonable examination of the evidence. Laud reflected on the time when the Church very largely dominated daily life and he sought the support of the state in realigning Church discipline with social reform. Church and state were allies in a common cause. Laud had a passion for orderly and dignified worship that expressed the grandeur of Christian faith. He brought to the defence of Anglicanism evidence drawn from early Christian tradition, including the Church Fathers. Such activity enhanced respect for the Church of England and ensured for it a dominant hold on the majority of English churchmen.

Along with William Laud, reference needs to be made to Lancelot Andrewes (1555–1626), a distinguished scholar who became dean of Westminster, and afterwards Bishop of Ely and Winchester. He was committed to belief in the continuity of the Christian Church from its inception and considered that division between Catholicism and Protestantism was more a matter of outward governance than of essential faith. Andrewes was an able preacher and in lengthy sermons he expounded the character of divine revelation, as contained in the Bible, and his commitment to the proper government of the Church as it had been handed down from the earliest times. He preached a high view of the Church's sacraments, especially of the eucharist, and this emphasis on a sacramental religion was expressed in the introduction of adornments and ceremonial to the worship of the Church. At the same time he cultivated a deeply personal religion with private prayer at its heart. He was respected for his piety and holy life, and his book of prayers, *Preces Privatae*, is one of the gems of devotional literature. His prayers mirror his personal faith and his deep spirituality. He addressed God as the "Being beyond all being, Existence uncreate, framer of the Universe", and believed that before such a Being humility and submission to his mercy in earnest petition for forgiveness is appropriate. He prayed:

> I stretch forth my hands unto thee;
> my soul graspeth unto Thee as a thirsty land.
> I smite upon my breast and say with the publican,
> God be merciful to me a sinner altogether,
> the chief of sinners,
> to me, a sinner greater than the publican,
> be merciful as to the publican.

This forgiveness Andrewes pleaded for had been made possible through the death of Christ, the Saviour of sinners. It is the gift of Christ and of divine grace that strengthens the inner life and brings the Christian to the end of life without sin. The Spirit of God is the mediation of this forgiveness, and belief is characteristic of his prayers:

> And Thou, all holy, good life-giving Spirit,
> despise me not;
> Thy breath, Thy hallowed thing, despise Thou not;
> But turn Thee again, O Lord, at the last,
> And be gracious with Thy servant, and visit him.

Andrewes laid much emphasis on the cultivation of personal piety, and there are many indications of this throughout his prayers. He willed to preserve the divine image in himself pure and holy; he longed that God would do good to his soul so that he might do whatever pleases God. There are echoes of the spirit of the age in some of his prayers as he acknowledges the gift of reason and education given to teachers and intelligent learners. Along with this no one can deny his all-embracing spirituality. This extended to every part of his being and he expressed this very devoutly in the range of his prayers. He included in his prayers "all who have profited me", and prayed for good and honest parents, gentle preachers, congenial companions, sincere friends and faithful servants. He willed for himself and others that "we may accomplish the rest of our life in repentance and godly fear, in health and peace".

The crux of Andrewes' theology is embedded in his prayers, and this is particularly so when we consider his Christology. He believed in Jesus who was conceived by faith and anointed as Christ (Messiah). He was the only begotten Son who suffered and was put to death on the cross, yet he was raised and ascended to God, but he will come again as judge. The benefits for the Christian of the life and ministry of Christ include the assurance of salvation, the renunciation of sin, the mortification of the flesh, newness of life, meditating on the unseen world and seeking those things that are at the right-hand of Christ. Through the breath of the saving grace of Christ, the Church is assured of its election, sanctification, and communion in the holy means of grace. It has been said that Andrewes' theology is one of the main planks in the formation of the theology of the Anglican Church.

Another of this band of able theologians is George Herbert (1593–1633) who is best known as a devotional poet. He received his university education in Cambridge where he won his laurels as an outstanding scholar who became the university's public orator. He trained for the priesthood but was diverted from this to becoming a member of parliament. Later, however, he became rector of Bremerton where he remained until his death. He soon became widely known for the quality of his ministry, especially for his care of souls. This is the core of his well-known book called *The Country Parson* which was published nearly twenty-five years after his death. It made a considerable impact on other clergy as a guide for pastoral care.

Herbert was a devoted churchman who believed deeply in the corporate nature of the Christian faith. He saw himself as a priest looking out over his people, but he also saw the beauty of union between priest and people when they were together in the community of worship. The *Book of Common Prayer* is a focus of this union and Herbert followed assiduously its liturgy of morning and evening prayer and the eucharist which he celebrated weekly. He described the relation of the priest to the people as that of the "deputy of Christ" charged with aiding the obedience of the people to God. The work of the priest is all-consuming, and in *The Country Parson* Herbert described the aspects and attributes of his work.

The practical spirituality of George Herbert is well represented in his poetry. The poetry exudes a spirit of deep emotion and is distinguished by many impressive images. Many of his poems are sung as hymns today. They are taken from his collection of poems entitled *The Temple*, and those in current use include:

> The God of love my Shepherd is,
> And he that doth me feed;
> While he is mine and I am His,
> What can I want or need?

> Let all the world in every corner sing
> My God and King! . . .

In the spiritual tradition of England the contribution of Jeremy Taylor (1613–67) is frequently associated with that of Lancelot Andrewes. This is an account of his personal holiness and especially his commitment to a life of prayer. He and others formed "religious societies" for regular devotion and sacred study. Taylor is the author of some of the greatest prayers in the English language. He also wrote two works of practical devotion, namely, *Holy Living* and *Holy Dying*. In both works Taylor drew heavily on the teaching of the Bible and the writings of the Church Fathers. He was an able scholar and a high churchman who after the Restoration in 1660 became Bishop of Down and Corron. We get a sense of Taylor's spiritual passion and some intimations of his theology and beliefs in his poetic prayer *Athirst for God*:

> My soul doth pant tow'rds Thee,
> My God, Source of eternal life:
> Flesh fights within me,
> Oh! end the strife,
> And part us, that in peace I may
> > Unclay
>
> My wearied spirit, and take
> My flight to Thy eternal spring,
> Where, for His sake
> Who is my King,
> I may wash all my tears away,
> > That day.
>
> Thou conqueror of death,
> Glorious Triumpher o'er the grave,
> Whose holy breath
> Was spent to save
> Lost mankind, make me to be styl'd
> > Thy child.
>
> And take me, when I die
> And go unto my dust; my soul
> > Above the sky
> > With saints enrol,
> That in Thy arms, for ever, I
> > May lie.

Taylor's spirituality is a well-ordered piety coupled with a stress on moderation and temperance.

A new birth

By the beginning of the eighteenth century the standard of living for more people was more favourable and less subversive. The nation was more at ease and there was, ostensibly at least, a greater unity and fairer distribution of wealth. The Church of England developed closer ties with the state and allied itself more closely with the political establishment. But religion was still a divisive force and rivalry continued between its various factions. Yet there was a renewal, which A. H. Francke (1663–1727) described as "a new birth", a new wave of pietistic fervour, a recoil from the coldness of rationalism. The new piety was a spiritual reaction to the restrictions of the "age of reason", and an upsurge of spiritual vigour began to manifest itself, in, for example, "Quietism" in France, "Mysticism" of Spain and Holland, and the "Pietism" of Germany. These movements were the harbingers, as we shall see, of the eighteenth-century religious revival in England. A fresh spiritual culture began to take shape that found embodiment in England in the influential Wesleyan revival. It attached considerable importance to those spiritual principles that lie at the heart of the religious life, especially the dominance of the love of God. The evangelical revival of Wesley in the second half of the eighteenth century was the culmination of the mystic and spiritual activities which received much decisive impetus from the works of such spiritual giants as George Fox, William Law and others, whose spirituality has been mentioned earlier.

The influence of pietists such as P. J. Spener (1635–1705) of Germany, and the theology of grace propounded in France by Cornelis Jansen (1585–1638), Bishop of Ypres, and the teaching of Quietism, such as that of François Fénelon (1651–1715), Archbishop of Cambrai, with its stress on complete abandonment to God, infiltrated to England and cradled an urge for religious revival. Spener was a passionate champion of pietism who advocated the practice of meditation and the cultivation of spiritual practices in the hope that this would eradicate the acrimony and the contentiousness that had surrounded so much theological discussion. Spener believed in the primacy of spirituality and its nurture as the supreme element of the Christian life and he worked assiduously for its revival. He was committed to Martin Luther's doctrine of "justification by faith alone", and deplored its neglect, striving to restore it as the centrepiece of Christian theology.

In 1675 he completed his work *Pia Desideria*, which specified his particular religious interests and the educational methods he employed, as well as guidance on Bible study and the nature of the devotional life. Spener, along with A. H. Francke, founded the University of Halle in 1694 and established it as a leading centre of Pietism. In France the Jansenists contended for more freedom in the interpretation of divine truth and stressed the importance of personal communion with God. They laid much emphasis on inner purity rather than intellectual prowess. Inner purity is the work of divine grace which is experienced through the operation of the Holy Spirit. The primary emphasis of the Quietism of Spain was the complete surrender of the self to God. This surrender is achieved by voluntary withdrawal from worldly pursuits and interests. The Wesleyan revival in England crystallized these principles in an unprecedented spread of evangelical fervour and missionary purpose.

The evangelical revival

It has been said of the evangelical revival that

> the movement was not built on startling conversions, as its preachers sometimes implied. It initiated the methods and drew on the personnel of the multitude of religious societies for meditation and mutual edification which were proliferating in England, not least within the established church, from the end of the seventeenth century, and it appealed to the hard-working and respectable families of tradesmen and artisans who wanted to find in their religion a deeper sense of "belonging".[11]

John Wesley (1703–91) is the name most closely associated with the evangelical revival, often called the Methodist revival. John Wesley was born in Epworth into a family of high churchmen and remained a member of the Anglican Church throughout his life. He was educated in Oxford and went on to serve his father as his curate. He returned to Oxford in 1729, where his younger brother Charles formed a society called the Sacramentarians. The aim of the Society was to improve the moral and spiritual condition of the members and live a strictly religious life. Their activities included meetings for prayer, reading and pious conversation, visiting the poor and prisoners, and supporting charitable works.

The society became known as "the Holy Club", but its members were described as "Methodists". According to an entry in his *Journal*, John Wesley had a transforming conversion experience on 24 May 1738:

> About a quarter before nine while he was describing the change which God works in the heart through faith in Christ, I felt my heart strongly warmed. I felt I did trust in Christ, Christ alone for salvation; and an assurance was given me that He had taken away my sins, even mine, and saved me from the law of sin and death.

In his theology, John Wesley professed the doctrines of the Church of England, and he coupled this with relevant sources drawn from the works of Thomas à Kempis, Martin Luther, John Calvin and William

Law. He preached a doctrine of human depravity, and believed that "the fall of man is the very foundation of revealed religion". Being in this condition of depravity made redemption imperative, and this had been assured through the atoning work of Christ. At the heart of the death of Jesus on the cross there is great mystery but there is no denying its saving power. Salvation is the rescue of the soul from the grip of sin. In a sermon preached in 1738 Wesley declared that present salvation is something that is attainable through faith. Faith is not an opinion, but a vision of the soul; it is the power by which spiritual things are apprehended, faith is "the eye of the soul whereby the believer sees Him who is invisible". The experience of salvation through faith restores the soul to divine purity:

> He that is, by faith, born of God sinneth not, by any habitual sin; for all habitual sin is sin reigning. But sin cannot reign in any that believeth. Nor by any willful sin. For his will, while he abideth in the faith, is utterly set against all sin, and abhoreth it as deadly poison.[12]

Wesley also taught the regenerative power of the Holy Spirit. He preached about the Spirit as not only promised but actually conferred, "which should enable Christians now to live with God". The Holy Spirit enables the believer to fulfil all spiritual precepts, and the preaching and death of Jesus Christ were designed "to represent, proclaim, and purchase for us this gift of the Spirit". The Lord Christ is that Spirit. Another key concept of Wesley's theology is his insistence on grace as a free gift of God. Grace is the free unmerited favour of God, the divine influence that regenerates and sanctifies. The life of the Christian is grace-given, for, according to Wesley:

> All the blessings which God hath bestowed upon man are of his mere grace, bounty, or favour; his free, undeserved favour; favour altogether undeserved; man having no claim to the least of his mercies . . . The same free grace continues to us, at this day, life, and breath, and all things.[13]

This stress on grace as unmerited favour gives insight into Wesley's doctrine of sanctification. For him sanctification follows justification and produces perfect love. Sanctification is entire, an experience that embraces the whole of life. Hence his doctrine of Christian perfection, "It is the giving God all the heart . . . it is all the mind which was in Christ enabling us to walk as Christ walked . . . It is the renewal of the heart in the whole image of God." This doctrine of sanctification is one of the contentious elements in Wesley's theology. He stood firmly against the Calvinists, as had his father who rejected the doctrine of election. John Wesley believed in the whole gospel for all people who through grace are sanctified.

These are some prime aspects of the theology of Wesley, but his interests were also practical and ethical. He applied his doctrine as a means to an end, namely, to preach repentance and combat the spirit of fatalism that characterized Calvinism, and to counter the apathy of the age. His spirituality was distinctive, he was a sacramentalist, and regular celebration of the eucharist was important to him. So also was reading the Bible, which he reverenced greatly, to the extent of reverencing every letter in it. The power of Wesley's preaching was an important part of his spirituality. Through his preaching he pronounced his strong belief in the love of God as God's supreme gift to the whole world. Wesley claimed the world as his parish, and he journeyed on horseback to many parts of the country and is reputed to have preached more than forty thousand sermons. Their prime theme was love and the joy of the good news of the Christian gospel which offered to everyone hope and a new way of life, sanctification and perfection. His preaching aroused great enthusiasm, but this was controlled by theological considerations. He preached extensively to the poorer classes, to artisans, weavers and miners, and it is said that his preaching brought tears to the eyes, women fell down in convulsions and men responded with frenzied cries.

Wesley had a genius for organization, he organized membership of the Methodist Society through membership of Band-Societies, that is, regular meetings for open confession and meditation, and smaller classes for exercising pastoral care and mutual edification. The membership was reviewed quarterly, and members were judged according to their spiritual progress and good behaviour. Each class had a leader, who worked alongside the steward whose task was to manage the day-to-day affairs of the Society. A final characteristic of Wesley's spirituality is his philanthropic and social work. Wesley designated Christianity essentially a system of personal relationships linking believers together:

"The gospel of Christ," he declared, "knows no religion but social, no holiness but social holiness."[14]

No form of injustice or oppression escaped his attention, and his last surviving letter was one to the anti-slave trade reformer William Wilberforce, offering support and encouragement in his campaign against slavery. Wesley sought to practise the positive teaching on charity in the New Testament – he displayed a keen sensitiveness to the needs and sufferings of the poor and a genuine humanitarian spirit. His ethical code was based on Christian doctrine as a rule of life that secured a real advance in improved social conditions. Towards the close of a sermon he preached in 1770 Wesley expressed what he meant by being a follower of Christ:

> Let brother no more lift up sword against brother, neither know ye war anymore. Rather put ye on, as the elect of God, bowels of mercies, humbleness of mind, brotherly kindness, gentleness, long-suffering, forbearing one another in love. Let the time part for strife, envy, contention, for biting and devouring one another.

The earnestness which John Wesley felt in his concern for the practical application of Christian faith is reflected in this prayer of his:

> But that I may assist all my brethren with my prayers where I cannot reach them with actual services. Make me zealous to embrace all occasions that may minister to their happiness, by assisting the needy, protecting the oppressed, instructing the ignorant, confirming the wavering, exhorting the good, and reproving the wicked. Let me look upon the failings of my neighbour as if they were my own; that I may be grieved for them, that I may never reveal them but when charity requires, and then with tenderness and compassion.

John's brother, Charles Wesley (1707–88), was an active associate in the work of evangelism, and he too is a notable figure in the religious life of his time. Charles is chiefly remembered for his hymns, although we should note his staunch attachment to the Church of England and his robust Christian faith. He, along with other hymnologists to whom we shall refer, enriched the worship and spiritual life of the Church, and his hymns expressed a depth of personal and collective religious experience that enlivened the Methodist revival. They suited the mood of personal commitment and evangelical fervour that was generated by the religious revival. The emotional power and rich biblical imagery and poetry of Wesley's hymns shaped the piety, wholesome spirituality and evangelical zeal of the revival. Wesley was skilful in his use of assonance and alliteration and he made good effective use of repetition to ensure that the thought of the hymns was carried forward and made emphatic. But the dominant message of his hymns is the love of God as revealed in Jesus Christ. This is so in the hymn whose setting is firmly in the revelation of Christ:

> Love Divine, all loves excelling,
> Joy of heaven, to earth come down . . .

This love evokes a response of praise. The rendering of praise is another aspect of the spirituality of Wesley's hymns:

> O for a thousand tongues to sing
> My great Redeemer's praise . . .

The praise issues in personal commitment:

> Jesus, the first and last
> On thee my soul is cast . . .

In the fervent revivalism of the time, hymn singing displaced the metrical versions of the psalms in popularity and became a way of expressing collectively an unalloyed love and devotion to Christ.

Hymns, therefore, made an important contribution to the spirituality of the eighteenth century and many of the most notable English hymns writers contributed to this. Isaac Watts (1674–1748) is one such pioneer of English hymnology. He was born in Southampton to a dissenting family and began at a young age to compose verses, especially for children, and later became a tutor to the family of Sir Thomas Abbney. During this time he wrote a number of textbooks and poems, but it is as "the father of English hymnology" that he is best remembered. It is said that "To Watts more than to any other man is due the triumph of the hymn in English worship. All later hymns written, even when they excel him, are his debtors."[15] Watts maintained that hymns should express personal address to God and personal concerns and that the language should be adapted to the general needs of the worshippers. The focus of many of his hymns is the life and ministry of Jesus Christ, in which he displayed especially Christ's compassion and grace, as in the hymn:

> With joy we meditate the grace
> Of our High priest above . . .

Or the suffering of Christ on the cross in the hymn,

> When I survey the wondrous cross,
> On which the Prince of Glory died . . .

Or the resurrection of Christ in the hymn,

> Blest morning, whose first dawning rays
> Behold the Son of God . . .

Watts conveyed his joyful response to the work of Christ in a call on all creation to bless him:

> Come let us join our cheerful songs
> With angels round the throne . . .

Isaac Watts became involved in the theological discussions surrounding
the doctrine of the Trinity which brought the Unitarians into prominence in the eighteenth century. Watts' position in the controversy is
ambivalent, some of his protagonists claimed that he sided with the
Unitarians, although he would not have subscribed to this view, and it
is unlikely to have been the case when we read this verse from his hand:

> Almighty God, to Thee
> Be endless honour done,
> The undivided Three,
> And mysterious One . . .

Watts described the Church as a fellowship of believers assembled for
worship. He held to the congregational view of the Church as a fellowship of the redeemed united and guided by the Holy Spirit. The
fellowship met in a spirit of joy and seeking, as Watts expressed in the
hymn:

> How pleased and blest was I
> To hear the people say,
> Come, let us seek our God today . . .

In line with the spirit of the age of mission and Christian expansion,
Watts conveyed the vision of the coming universal reign of Christ in the
triumphalist hymn:

> Jesus shall reign where'er the sun
> Doth his successive journeys run . . .

The eighteenth century bequeathed to posterity a wealth of tradition of
Christian spirituality in the hymns of Watts and Wesley, but others too
contributed handsomely to this. Their hymns became embedded in the
worship and devotion of the Church and in the consciousness of individual Christians. To this tradition Philip Doddridge (1702–51), a man
of great learning who wrote a theological work entitled *The Rise and
Progress of Religion in the Soul*, contributed the hymn "O God of
Bethel, by whose hand, / Thy people still are fed", and "Ye servants of
the Lord . . . ". William Cowper (1731–1800), the son of the chaplain to
George II, was a poet who also wrote hymns, many of them of an intimate and personal strain. They express Cowper's own religious mood
and his deep longing for faith. His hymns include "God moves in a

mysterious way", and "O for a closer walk with God . . . ". Another worthy of mention in this context is John Newton (1725–1807), who was converted to Christianity after reading Thomas à Kempis's *The Imitation of Christ*, and who came under the influence of John Wesley. Newton wrote his hymns to promote the faith and bring comfort to sincere Christians. He also wrote hymns "designed for public worship and for the use of plain people". Among his hymns are, "How sweet the name of Jesus sounds . . . ", and "Rejoice, believer in the Lord . . . ".

It is clear that hymnology played a key part in the religious revival of the eighteenth century. Hymn singing inspired evangelic fervour and focused the heart and spirit on the central purpose of worship and piety. This enhanced the part of the congregation in Church worship. Hymn singing was essentially the people's part in the liturgy, but also, in the avoidance of a set creed, it enabled the people to sing their belief. The enthusiasm this engendered meant that hymns were sung "with the spirit", whilst their theology expressed the primary themes of the Christian faith. The hymns that have accrued from the evangelical revival provide insight into the spirituality of their authors, but they also reflect how the Christian faith was taught and communicated in song and in ways that touched the heart and conscience of ordinary people.

Spiritual outreach

Enough has been said to show that the eighteenth century in England developed its own style of Christian spirituality. A spirituality based on Christian doctrine became a rule of life to a much larger proportion of the population as they came under the influence of the evangelical revival. Indeed, the age of Wesley and Watts, Doddridge and Cowper was arguably as "spiritual" as any, where there was restrained tolerance of theological divergencies and a broadening of spiritual activities. The religious landscape was dominated by the Methodists or Evangelicals and the "broad" churchmen or Latitudinarians. They performed functions of their own choosing and pursued their own way of developing spirituality. Methodists displayed a fervent spirit of enthusiasm and philanthropy, whereas Latitudinarianism stood for more reason and logic as the criteria for interpreting Christian doctrines. Taken together the Evangelicals and the Latitudinarians kept religion permanently as a powerful force before the nation. Considerable emphasis was placed on morality with an appeal for good behaviour as being reasonable and a matter of sound common sense. The appeal to social duty stirred the conscience and led to an increase in good works and to the practice of charity and philanthropy. Of course we should not assume from this that all forms of social neglect were overcome or that all spiritual laxity was obliterated, but the philanthropic and humanitarian spirit led to many benefits that enriched the quality of life. One was the improvement in medical care and another the provision of education through the founding of Charity and Sunday Schools. These schools were the first organized attempts to provide education for the mass of ordinary people. This was directed particularly at young people.

Education

The man responsible for instituting the Sunday Schools as a structured system was Robert Raikes (1736–1811), the son of a Gloucester newspaper proprietor. Of particular relevance to this study of spirituality is Raikes' concern for procuring some kind of moral and religious instruction for ordinary people. Many of these suffered from poverty and lack of employment; they were destitute and crime among them was rife. Raikes allied himself with the prison reform movement of the time but was intent on dealing with the cause of crime and not only with its symptoms. He considered ignorance to be the cause of the moral malaise and believed that education would obviate this cause. So in 1780 he opened the first Sunday School, in Gloucester. As well as providing instruction the schools included a church service, and after an uneasy start the Sunday School movement was consolidated and spread. Education and religion must go together, so Raikes contended. Education is a means of filling the mind with what is good, and this will lead to reflecting on God who is wholly good and the source of all goodness. The aim Raikes set for the schools was the promotion of high moral standards. The Sunday Schools were mainly supported by Dissenters. Other Dissenters, like Hannah Moore (1745–1833), became earnest supporters of the aims of the Sunday School movement, especially as a means of combating drunkenness, crime, ignorance and atheism. The teaching given was Bible-centred, and the catechism and good works were also prominent in the curriculum.

In general terms it can be said that the movement raised the moral standards of the poorer classes, but without producing a revolutionary social change. Nevertheless, this movement contributed to the education of the spirit in an age of social transition.

Abolition of slavery

Along with the humanitarian work of Raikes and Hannah Moore we might mention the movement associated with William Wilberforce (1759–1833), whose work led to the abolition of the trans-Atlantic slave trade. Wilberforce belonged to the fellowship of evangelicals known as the Clapham Sect. The members of the sect met in conclave to consider spiritual matters and the cultivation of the life of devotion. Wilberforce spent long hours in prayer and self-examination, and was deeply conscious of his sin. As a spiritual son of the evangelical revival he sought for the means of inner peace and found it in the grace of God. He may well be described as a practical evangelical who carried his faith into his political activities. In his political life he championed the weak and poor, but his main endeavour was to win freedom for slaves. His spiritual advisor was John Newton who himself had experience of this pernicious trade. His theology was evangelistic, he believed in original sin, in the condemnation of the sinner to the judgement of hell, and at the same time he proclaimed the grace of God that was available to all people. His religious devotion was deeply earnest and he deplored those who only paid it lip service. He urged Christians to show a spirit of liberality and beneficence and act towards all people as the children of God, the heavenly Father.

In 1807 an Act was passed to abolish the slave trade, in the face of powerful opposition, but this proved a decisive step towards the freeing of all slaves in the British Empire. Wilberforce had worked persistently in the pursuit of this humanitarian ideal and was ready to join forces with any persons of goodwill who were willing to work with him. He was a man of enthusiasm but also of sagacity, a skilled agitator and tireless advocate. Wilberforce achieved something entirely new in humanitarian reform through the abolition of slavery; he pioneered new methods of moulding public opinion and public agitation in a humanitarian cause. His methods were widely adopted with the result that public debate and openness in discussion of important issues became more normal. At the same time he diverted his energies into other areas, including support for prison reform, opposition to child exploitation and child labour as chimney sweeps, and support for the missionary societies that were being formed towards the end of the eighteenth century (the Baptist Missionary Society in 1792 and the London Missionary Society in 1795).

Nevertheless, it is for his endeavours on behalf of slaves that Wilberforce is best remembered, and this was rooted in his evangelical

Christianity, his personal commitment to Christ that led him to involve himself in political action on behalf of the least privileged of all humankind. Can any man, he asked, "contradict the principles of his own conscience, the principles of justice, the laws of religion, and of God?"[16]

Missionary expansion

Earlier we referred to the missionary societies which were founded in the 1790s. Their founders merit a place in the galaxy of those who contributed to the Christian spiritual tradition of their age. The Church, of course, from the days of the first apostles, had an impressive tradition of missionary expansion, and in the period after the Protestant Reformation the tradition was considerably enhanced. The Lutherans and the Moravians began to send missionaries overseas in the late sixteenth century, and the Jesuits were also active in missionary work.

William Carey (1761–1834), a Baptist shoemaker of Nottingham, felt very strongly that God was calling him to carry the Christian message to the people of India. It was in an evangelical prayer meeting that the call came to him and this led to his being baptized. From then on he spent much time in studying the Scriptures, and this led him to prepare to found a missionary society. Prayer was a powerful force in Carey's life and this infused a new spirit of fervour for missionary expansion. Carey thought of mission in world-wide terms and was inspired by a vision of "The world for Christ". He brought to the Church a notable vigour and passion for evangelism, a concern for education in the Christian faith, and a zeal for its world-wide propagation.

The work of Carey and the founding of the Baptist Missionary Society in 1792 may be coupled with the wave of Protestant missionary zeal that characterized the last decade of the eighteenth century and led to the founding of the London Missionary Society in 1795. In that year a group of Protestant ministers resolved to meet and "at the first meeting of every month, at seven o'clock in the evening, be a session for united prayer to God for the success of every attempt made by all denominations of Christians for the spread of the Gospel." The outcome was the formation of the London Missionary Society with the purpose of sending overseas the message of "the glorious gospel of the blessed God". The Society was non-denominational at its foundation, and missionaries were commissioned and sent to Africa and India and further east. Other societies proliferated at this period all of whom thought of their work in global terms. This initiative infused new life into the churches and anchored them to new spiritual vigour, and support for the world mission of Christianity increased. New countries were opened up to the Christian message and Christianity was expanded as a world faith. The missionaries were mostly ordained ministers, but the activities included teaching and translating the Bible, medical work and raising the standard of living of poorer people. The missionaries pioneered a nobler way of life for the people they served and opened to them the means of spiritual enrichment.

Spirituality, literature and music

We need to supplement this account of the bearing of the "age of reason" and evangelism on the development of Christian theology and its spiritual tradition with reference to the artistic or aesthetic factor in literature and music. This contributed richly to the development of the finer spirit that emerged during the eighteenth century. This, as much as theological affirmations, fostered a broader spiritual awareness and cultivated new insights of spiritual enlightenment. A number of poets and musicians composed works of quality that expressed the wealth of spiritual experience and induced in those who read and heard them a fresh impulsion to explore for themselves the unplumbed reaches of spirituality within and then nurture its potential. We can here only illustrate this briefly.

William Wordsworth (1770–1850) expressed a view of poetry as "the breath and finer spirit of all knowledge"; it is "the impassioned expression which is on the countenance of all science". Wordworth's poetry breathes the atmosphere of the age and reflects the spiritual aspirations that inspired him; his poetry is pregnant with prophetic visions and broad thoughts, as well as expressing human instincts and yearnings. His poems are resonant with a sense of wonder, without which there can be no real worship, and many are couched in the language of the spirit.

Images and symbols drawn from nature and human experience abound and the range of imagination draws into its vision distinct religious and spiritual ideas. The spirit of romanticism that spread during Wordsworth's lifetime permeated his thought and experience. He was immersed in its appeal to nature, but at the same time his poetry expresses something of his own beliefs, as in this stanza:

> Our birth is but a sleep and a forgetting:
> The soul that rises with us, our life's Star,
> Hath had elsewhere its setting,
> And cometh from afar:
> Not in entire forgetfulness,
> And not in utter nakedness,
> But trailing clouds of glory do we come
> From God, who is our home.

Wordsworth, as is well known, loved nature passionately and much of his poetry springs from this love. It is the key to his spirituality which blossoms in some of his memorable verses, as:

> Sweet is the lore which Nature brings;
> Our meddling intellect
> Mis-shapes the beauteous forms of things: –
> We murder to dissect.
>
> Enough of Science and of Art;
> Close up those barren leaves;
> Come forth, and bring with you a heart
> That watches and receives.

Wordsworth's poetry is for the most part infused with joy and a sense of dignity, he saw beauty oozing in all around him, he had a passion for freedom and truth, and many moral maxims are woven into his poetry. He cared greatly for his art, and we get an inkling of his spirituality in these words:

> He looked for no escape from reality in pageantry. He did not senti-mentalize, nor affect poetic gloom. He claimed no wilful code of morality as the poet's preserve ... He sought no calm as a conditional essential to veracity, so that he might report faithfully the passion and the exaltation with which he viewed the world.[17]

During the period covered by this chapter, as well as the wealth of hymnology that was produced, there was a great flowering of sacred music. This was the period of the birth of the oratorio and the chorale, which had a remarkable impact and a wide appeal. Their composers were men of deep Christian spirituality and their oratorios and passion music have retained their appeal up to this day. Some of the greatest names in the world of sacred music were active in this period, G. F. Handel (1685–1759), whose oratorio *The Messiah* is probably the best known of all religious compositions; J. S. Bach (1685–1750), arguably the most eminent of all composers; F. J. Haydn (1732–1809) who composed the well-known oratorio *The Creation*; W. A. Mozart (1756–91) whose *Requiem Mass* is a work of deep feeling and great skill.

These composers found their inspiration in Christian faith and doctrines, and they had a riveting impact on Christian liturgy and devotion. The music of J. S. Bach, for instance, became an integral part of the musical and spiritual provision of many Christian churches, as it is to this day. Bach's music is a personal testimony to his faith and spirituality. His passion music may be compared to the ancient passion play tradition (see chapter 4) which had established such a firm hold on popular religion, but most emphatically Bach ensured that his music conveyed a sacred spiritual ethos. He expressed through his music his religious and mystical feelings, which were made resonant in moving dramatic musical forms and styles. His masterpiece, *St. Matthew's Passion*, is a remarkable musical setting for the gospel narrative of Christ questioning his disciples about his identity, the scene of Christ washing the feet of the disciples and the prediction of his betrayal. Bach used the full range of musical techniques at his disposal in order to convey faithfully the feelings and thoughts that animated him as he confronted these scenes in the gospel, and how his music might impact on those who heard it. His music evokes most powerfully the mood of the mystery and elation of the spiritual life, and to achieve this impact Bach engaged skilfully all the musical power at his disposal. This included the dramatic highlighting of certain musical forms for emphasis and the repetition of others. This may be illustrated by the well-known Passion Chorale set to the words by Paulus Gerhardt (1607–76).

> O Sacred Head! sore wounded,
> With grief and shame weighed down,
> How scornfully surrounded
> With thorns, Thy only crown . . .

At the end of the scores of his musical compositions Bach added the inscription *Soli Deo Gloria* (To God be the glory). He used his musical talents for the honouring of God. Frequently he incorporated non-biblical texts along with the biblical texts into his music, some of his music was composed for devotional and meditative purposes, some for different liturgical functions, but the purpose was constant, all was for the sole glory of God. It has been said that "no composer of the first rank has devoted all, or even the greater part, of his creative energies to church compositions . . . he devoted himself naturally to the saviour of the faith in which he had been reared".[18]

During the period we have considered in this chapter there was no intention to wipe out the concept of spirituality. In the Age of Reason, religion was displaced from being the central core of ultimate knowledge and truth to being a contributing factor. Reason stated its claim to be heard – yet reason alone could not satiate the unquenchable spiritual quest for wholeness. In the eighteenth century powerful testimony was borne by the evangelical revival to the spiritual aspirations and hopes of masses of people.

What Luther had achieved in the sixteenth century through raising the level of theological debate and initiating spiritual reform, John Wesley did for the eighteenth century through his evangelical preaching and kindling of a new kind of spiritual fervour. This was accompanied by a fresh upsurge of religious enthusiasm, spiritual earnestness, and moral action that extended to social as well as personal life. The spirit of beauty and devout passion expressed in the art and music of the age ventilated a response of untapped energies that lie deeply embedded within the human psyche. It may be said that as the eighteenth century drew to its close the spirit of missionary expansion that emerged was the consequence of the outworking of the inner spirit of religious revival and social reform that had characterized so much of its action. How well these events equipped Christian theology and its spiritual tradition to confront the challenges of the following century remains to be seen.

The Victorian Era

This cameo by the historian Halévy of the early nineteenth century provides a base from which to consider the theology and spirituality of the overtly religious Victorian era:

> Men of letters disliked the Evangelicals for their narrow Puritanism, men of science for their intellectual feebleness. Nevertheless during the Nineteenth Century, Evangelical religion was the moral cement of English society. It was the influence of the Evangelicals which involved the British aristocracy with an almost strict dignity, restrained the pluto-crats who had risen from the masses from a vulgar ostentation and debauchery, and placed over the proletariat a select body of workmen enamoured by virtue and capable of self restraint. Evangelicalism was thus a conservative force which restored in England the balance momentarily destroyed by the explosion of revolutionary forces.[1]

The vision of the global expansion of Christianity inspired by Protestant missionary fervour at the end of the eighteenth century continued to capture the imagination and enthusiasm of evangelical Christians. Christianity was central to the beliefs and aspirations of the mass of the population. Evangelical religion was a force in the land; the preaching and message of John Wesley and his fellow revivalists continued to "warm" the heart and give people direction for life in this world and the hope of bliss in the world to come. To be holy was a condition of success in all human endeavours; moral uprightness went hand in hand with personal prosperity and social welfare; the practice of godliness restrained the "revolutionary violence" that might other-wise have erupted in the face of social neglect, economic injustice and industrial unrest. On the continent of Europe also:

> The Pietist or evangelical movement in Western Europe and Protestantism was at its strongest during the first thirty or forty years of the nineteenth century, it conditioned the earnestness of what in England

was called the Victorian ethos. It was very biblical; puritan in behaviour; and dedicated to the propagation of the gospel at home and abroad.[2]

Moral stimulation and attitudes that were "puritan in behaviour" worked for the improvement and reform of social conditions. The gains and losses of industrialization were measured by the canons of morality which assessed their impact on the quality of life, on social attitudes, and on political and cultural ideology. The new culture of mechanism and industrialization needed to be controlled by the vitality of moral incentives if the practices of "the nobleness of work" were to become a creative and not a debilitating force in the new age of mechanization. The observance of whatever was "puritan in behaviour" by the work force was a certain way of keeping alive the idea that "work is of a religious nature". The pressures of industrialization should not submerge the cultivation of spirituality as a means of enjoying a rich and self-fulfilling life. Education was the factor that should contribute to this enrichment of the quality of life. Cardinal Newman assumed as much in this excerpt from his *Apologia*:

> Virtue is a child of knowledge; vice of ignorance; therefore education, periodical literature, railroad travelling, ventilation, and the art of life, when fully carried out, serve to make the population moral and happy.

So there developed what has been called the "work ethic", that is, what makes work purposeful is its moral incentive stimulated by spiritual discipline. Only the impious could fail to discern a moral purpose in work. Christian theology expounded a doctrine of the dignity and godliness of work, whilst Christian socialists crusaded for the protection of the worker against exploitation and social injustice. The moral crusade was broadened to include education, which received a fresh impetus during the industrial revolution, and the condition of children in factories, and the employment of women. In this respect religion was "the moral cement of English society". It provided the context and the text for developing partnership between goodness and honest labour, virtue and material prosperity, holiness and social progress. The "explosion of revolutionary forces" was unproductive whenever it destroyed the balance between morality and right action or goodness and progress. The tried and tested principles of Christian morality were bound to inject self-confidence and determination into any movement for reform and ensure that it achieved a positive outcome. The Bible provided the text for such confidence, it contained and set out all that needs to be known about the right ordering of life and how human behaviour and interests might be elevated to a higher plain. The Bible provided a blueprint for establishing a just and stable social order. Of this emphasis on the moral imperative and outcome of right living it has been said:

> Moreover its particular type of Christianity laid a particularly direct emphasis upon conduct; for, though it recognized both grace and faith as essential to salvation, it was in practice also very largely a doctrine of salvation by works.[3]

In consequence of this emphasis on "salvation by works", Christian theology was directed towards expounding a pragmatic idealism. Theology and praxis were wedded in theory, although the application of the ideal was not as swift or universal as might have been hoped. The vein of the rationalism that had diverted the attention of theologians in the preceding two centuries now posed an irresistible fascination as theologians grappled with the complexities of the new science and industrialization. The discoveries and implications of new scientific theories and experiments posed many searching human questions that theology had to take on board. The range of these questions spread over the origin and age of the universe, the operation of natural law, the role of the divine creator, the beginning of human life, and natural selection, questions which previously had been thought to be the prerogative of religion. They were now debated openly between churchmen and those who professed no religion. The traditional wisdom on these matters postulated by indigenous doctrine had to seek new means of asserting its claims and of defending its truth. The advances of scientific and technological progress opened up a whole new world and hitherto undreamed of possibilities for humankind.

At the same time progress in social improvement and human welfare did not keep pace with the advances in science. Towards the end of the century there was growth in the population and life expectancy was longer,and many changes tended to destabilize society. Society was in danger of being swept off its feet and losing all sense of direction unless a stabilizing factor was injected into the whirlwind changes that now threatened it. Many of the old and tested social stabilizers were less safe and reliable and the search was on for new and trustworthy certainties that would provide the necessary anchor of stability and confidence. Theology sought to address this need. Christian faith provided the stability that kept social progress on course; the values taught by Christianity were the foundation of social well-being; the practice of Christian virtue in personal and social life ensured social cohesion.

Faith, therefore, offered a bulwark of security and stability: it is personal and is available to all, it is the creation of the Holy Spirit, it is nourished by the teaching of the Bible, it ensures reward for faithfulness in the present and the hope of the glory of life hereafter.

Theology of consciousness

Friedrich Schleiermacher (1768–1834) has been called the father of modern theology; his definition of religion as response to God's saving love and the feeling of absolute dependence won wide acceptance. Schleiermacher gave a fresh impetus to the study of theology in the early years of the nineteenth century. His definition of religion as "absolute dependence" met the mood and need of the age. His theology is based primarily on the historical revelation of Christ and the divine government of the world. Schleiermacher regarded Christ as the centre of divine revelation and Christianity as an absolute and totally comprehensive religion. He viewed the world as having a unity of purpose conceived and activated by God, with the subordination of the natural to the spiritual world.

Schleiermacher came under the influence of the Moravian Brethren and became professor of theology in Berlin. In 1821 he published his magnificent work *The Christian Faith*, whose central theme is that every being is a direct recipient of the redemption which Christ accomplished. Redemption is mediated through the personal work of Christ, who is also the mediator between God and humankind. There is within everyone an irresistible craving for dependence on an absolute external power, and this constitutes the longing for God and awareness of him that pervades human life from beginning to end. Christ is the revelation of God and the relationship with him satisfies this longing. The experience of this relationship is tantamount to redemption, and the grace that is manifested in Christ is the seal of redemption. Christ is the source of the spiritual life and relationship with him assures it is satisfied. But this relationship is not complete unless it shares in the spiritual community of the Church which Christ founded. Only then is the consciousness of redemption complete. This redemption is perfected by Christ in whom dwells the Holy Spirit in perfect unity. God wills that everyone should be united in Christ in the same way in order that they may abide in him. In the Church, Christ is present to bring this relationship to fruition.

The community of the Church exists to bear witness to its consciousness of the presence of God through the presence of Christ. Therefore, stated Schleiermacher:

> The work of Christianity, in short, consists in this – that by him are created the experience of peace with God, and deliverance from sin. Christianity refashions those who come into contact with him with the receptivity of the believing heart, and communicates to them an inner experience and relation towards God which are akin to his own.

Schleiermacher's theology has been called "the theology of consciousness", and when applied to the English scene we see how apt it is. As we observed earlier, the need to cultivate the religious consciousness in the circumstances of the age was paramount. Christians felt the need to refurbish this consciousness in relation with Christ, and Schleiermacher asserted that Christ and the Christian religion are inseparable. In England in the early nineteenth century it was left to the Nonconformists to provide the impetus for social reform and invigorate society with a greater sense of moral purpose by revitalizing the religious consciousness. At the same time there was much stress on the development of personal spirituality and its moral outreach, whilst keeping in view the importance of belonging to the spiritual community (the Church), as Schleiermacher had emphasized.

The Church of England

The Church of England in the years before the 1832 Reform Act was by and large immersed in a mood of conservatism, if not of complacency towards social reform. There were certain anomalies within the Church which were an irritant to those outside. The glaring economic discrepancy between the stipends of bishops and of ordinary clergy was an impediment to any real desire to work for a more just and equitable society. Their social standing was also very unequal, and this, and much else, aroused strong feelings against the established church on the part of Nonconformists. Along with this there was a suspicion on the part of Evangelicals that the Church of England clung too closely to certain doctrines of the Roman Catholic Church. These are some of the symptoms which account for the plurality of Christianity in form and doctrine during the nineteenth century, and why the churches sometimes seemed to be locked in a deadlock of polarization.

Despite the glaring need for reform, the Church of England remained stubbornly conservative. It stood out against the Reform Bill, it opposed Catholic Emancipation, it turned a blind eye to social abuses and lack of moral rectitude. The Church of England was class ridden, many bishops enjoyed rich livings, and the Church of the early decades lacked leadership of high calibre. Political patronage was sought and coveted, but spiritual energy and moral idealism were on the ebb. Medieval abuses and sinecures continued to invade the Church. No bishop of stature arose to give the invigorating spiritual vision and leadership so much needed during the first decades of the century.

Some prominent churchmen did voice their dismay at the lethargy of the Anglican Church, such as Dr Thomas Arnold (1795–1842), headmaster of Rugby, who is said to have written in desperation, "the Church, as it now stands, no power can save". And Jeremy Bentham (1748–1832), a law reformer, declared more categorically, "The Church of England is ripe for dissolution." Reform could only do the Church good, but no move was made to bring this about. In 1835 prime minister Peel appointed an Ecclesiastical Commission with a brief to investigate the use of Church property. The commission received the support of Bishop Bloomfield, and Acts were passed on the advice of the commission in 1836 and 1840. These forbade pluralism among the clergy, the wealth and numbers of the cathedral clergy were reduced, and diocesan boundaries were revised. Some felt that the effect of these measures was minimal, and it was around this time that the internal vigour of the Church of England began to stir.

An evangelical spirit began to manifest itself more evidently than in the earlier decades of the century, and at the same time the Church of England began to develop more as what is called today, "a broad Church", that is, it became tolerant and receptive to different ways of expounding the faith of the Church, the interpretation of its teaching and the performance of its rituals. Against this background the most transformative movement in the theology and spirituality of the Church of England and its liturgy in the nineteenth century has to be assessed. In 1841 John Henry Newman (1801–90) compiled a pamphlet or tract in which he argued that the Thirty-nine Articles of the Church of England could be interpreted in a Catholic and not merely a Protestant sense. This was a powerful argument that stirred the Church of England to its roots, and the Tractarian or Oxford Movement, as it became known, became a marked feature of the Church of England from then onward. The ethos of the Oxford Movement was clerical and its thought and practices soon spread throughout the Church.

The Movement got underway, so it is assumed, as early as 1833 after John Keble (1792–1866) had preached a sermon on national apostasy and publicized the dangers facing the Church. The Church must assert its divine origin, and the authority of its clergy as received direct from God through the apostolic succession. These views were received with sympathy and approval by liberal-minded Roman Catholics. They saw the door being opened for a return to unity with the Roman Catholic Church that had been severed at the time of the Protestant Reformation. The evangelical wing of the Church of England adhered mainly to scriptural authority in theology and proclaimed the death of Christ as an atonement for sin; it preached the importance of conversion in a way that appealed to many parishioners. What the low church (evangelical) party lacked, so it was argued, was a high doctrine of the Church as a holy, catholic and apostolic body. The Tractarian Movement was determined to redress this omission by confidently asserting a "high church" doctrine, that is, the belief that the Church is established in history by God as a divine society; by declaring that authority within the Church has been transmitted from age to age through the apostolic succession of bishops and priests; and by proclaiming that the Church is a sacramental community of believers who regularly participate in the sacraments administered by the clergy.

The Oxford Movement in its essentials was a restatement of the Church as a visible, sacramental, hierarchic society whose ministry and mission could be traced back to Christ himself. It derived its view of the Church and its authority from the teaching and discipline of the apostolic age, and sought to create a renewed sense of the "catholicity" of the true Church:

> There is no fair observer who denies that Anglo-Catholicism is succeeding in making the Church of England aware of the "Catholic" climate in its heritage, so that it is no longer, as a hundred years ago, a Protestant Church in which some reminiscences of Catholicism have survived, but rather a Catholic Church which retains certain emphases of the Reformation.[4]

The men who steered the Oxford Movement and marshalled its creative forces displayed notable gifts of leadership as well as theological literacy and deep spirituality. Their collective influence on the life of the Church of England in every aspect can scarcely be overstated.

Spirituality and sacramentalism

John Keble and John Henry Newman along with Edward Pusey (1800–82) were responsible for giving a new direction to the Anglican tradition in Christian theology and spirituality. In respect of episcopacy, priesthood and liturgy, they sought a revolution, but only for the sake of attaining and operating the highest standards of churchmanship. In particular, they aimed to construct a dignified pattern of worship wedded to an orderly ritual carried out with dignified ceremonial. The leaders of the Movement claimed not to be innovators but rather restorers of the primitive apostolic ways, upholding the Church as a divine institution that had been ordained by Christ. The Church must be committed to apostolic succession, devout in its observance of the sacraments, steadfast in its doctrine, pure in its ritual, and so vindicate and then exercise the authority and mission committed to it by Christ himself.

The outward manifestation of the impact of the Oxford Movement was seen most notably in the reform of the liturgy. Worship was conceived as the movement of the whole person in response to God the creator and redeemer, and this movement is of the body as well as the mind and spirit. Every movement or gesture in worship is a focus of devotion, every action is meaningful and conveys the purpose of the liturgy as that which unites the worshipper more closely with God. This movement as it proceeds through dignified ritual and ceremonial concentrates the mind and heart on the object and purpose of worship. Its motivation is faith and response to the divine revelation in Christ as God's supreme gift of redemption to the world. Worship of this order strengthens the link between the worshipper and Christ; thereby the worshipper receives and participates in the faith delivered to the apostles by Christ himself. As this takes place so the tradition becomes more visibly absorbed into the liturgy and thereby enhances its authority. The authority of the Prayer Book was received as the authentic source of liturgical form and performance.

The influence and advance of the Oxford Movement was rapid and seemed at the time to be inevitable. The reform of the liturgy and sacramental life of the Church reinvigorated its worship, and some went so far as to say on reflection that it saved the Church from oblivion. The movement counteracted the growing spirit of liberalism and brought to the Church a sense of order and stability. It affirmed the status of the Church as a divine community and God's appointed instrument for salvation. Spiritually it injected a revived sense of holiness into the Church, and it was this emphasis on personal holiness as much as anything that gave the Oxford Movement its character and power. The leaders worked for a more structured devotional churchmanship, a deeper commitment to the sacramental community of the Church, with the eucharist at its heart, the strict observance of Christian standards in personal behaviour, and adherence to the orthodox Christian faith as a guide for life.

However, the Oxford Movement left large numbers of churchmen unmoved. It had its critics, especially on account of its revival and insistence on past tradition. They saw the Movement as one that clung to the past for solutions to modern questions. The critics, therefore, sought to dismiss Tractarianism as irrelevant and unnecessary. But the leaders of the Movement were men of strong passion and high idealism and were not easily diverted. Their object was to restore the Church to its historical position and authority and to win the hearts of the people in allegiance to it. In order to habilitate the Church in the life of the nation, they believed that it should be made attractive in all respects, in its ritual and ceremonial, its music and architecture, its language and liturgy.

It required, too, that it should be spiritual and ethical, appealing to the intellect and conscience, and have a firm theological basis. The vindication of the Movement is to be measured by the extent to which these objectives were realized and provided a new forward movement for the Church of England. In order to discover whether this is so we need to look more closely at the theology and spirituality of the men who were the stalwarts of the Oxford Movement, and who are among the notable spiritual leaders of the nineteenth century.

John Keble   John Keble was appointed vicar of Hursley in Hampshire at the age of forty-three. He was a contemporary of Newman and had considerable influence on him during his term as professor of poetry at Oxford. Keble himself lacked the practical wisdom for dealing with people sensitively, and he was unsympathetic towards those who did not measure up to the moral and intellectual standards he expected of them. He contributed to the publication of the Tracts for which Newman is better known. He believed, as did Newman, that alignment between the Thirty-nine Articles and the doctrines of the Roman Catholic Church was feasible, and he endorsed the view of the underlying agreement between them.[5] John Keble was at the heart of the Oxford Movement, and was active in consolidating its theological assumptions and in the defence and spread of its intentions. He was influential in the reshaping of the pattern of the liturgy and in expounding the nature and aims of Christian worship. He held tenaciously to the doctrine of a "high church" based on its divine origin and authority; he believed it was the duty of all members of the Church to submit to this. This included recognition of episcopacy as the *esse* and not just the *bene esse* of the Church. It was decreed from the beginning so that all clergy must be episcopally ordained into the apostolic succession. This view of episcopacy has prevailed ever since in the Church of England as being "essential to the Church's fullness".[6]

In theology and spirituality Keble maintained that the only certain way to salvation is through the body and blood of Jesus Christ administered in the eucharist. The eucharist is the supreme treasure of the Church, and it must in every respect be observed in purity and holiness and according to the manner of the apostolic church. Likewise the Church must be restored to the unity and purity of the apostolic age.

It is arguable that Keble is remembered above all else for his literary work and the book of poems entitled *The Christian Year* published in 1827. These poems are based on the *Book of Common Prayer* and had a very wide appeal. Each poem is devoted to a Sunday or Saint's day or the gospel or epistle for the day. Being closely aligned with the *Book of Common Prayer*, echoes of Cranmer's prose are evident in them. They also echo Keble's innermost feelings, his private devotion and spirituality. God, he felt, had taken hold of his poetic gifts, and his compositions were a humble offering in gratitude and devotion to God. We have an example of his humble devoting of his gift to God in this verse:

> Lord, by every minstrel tongue
> Be Thy praise so duly sung
> That these angels' harps may ne'er
> Fail to find fit echoing here:
> We the whole of meaner birth,
> Who in that divinest spell
> Dare not hope to join on earth,
> Give us grace to listen well.[7]

Keble also wrote hymns, some of which are still in use. Among those which are often sung are:

> Blest are the pure in heart
> For they shall see our God ...
>
> New every morning is the love
> Our waking and uprising prove ...

Edward Pusey   Pusey was an outstanding scholar and distinguished regius professor of Hebrew at Oxford. His influence was such that members of the Oxford Movement were sometimes called "Puseyites".

He was learned in the works of the Greek and Latin Fathers of the early church and edited a series of translations of their writings. He too was devoted to the orderly administration of the sacraments, and he revived the practice of sacramental confession as a vehicle of movement towards God and a life of holiness.

Sacramental confession can call out from the soul penitence and contrition; sacramental confession also leads the penitent to the altar where confession and the repudiation of sin are rewarded by the sinner being reconciled to Christ. This reconciliation, according to Pusey, is the meaningful heart of the eucharist.

Pusey was active in founding Anglican religious orders, parallel to those of the Roman Catholic Church. The theological foundation and idealism of the Benedictine Order had a special appeal for him. From 1842 onward he became the spiritual director of an order of nuns, who came together as groups of women who dedicated themselves to teaching and ministering to the sick and elderly. The women lived together in community under the jurisdiction of a mother superior. The first nunnery set up within the Church of England was in 1842 in London, and the first male order was founded in Cowley in 1866. Pusey's deep spiritual care and concern for the men and women of these orders comes through in his prayer for religious communities:

> Bless these, whether men or women, whom Thou hast already gathered together in one to serve Thee alone with a devoted heart; guard, guide, and bless them within and without, that they may grow in all spiritual graces, and that Thy light within them may shine on those without. Give them fervour in devotion, diligence in labour, singleness of heart in action, burning love for Thee . . . [8]

Pusey contributed three tracts to the series which Newman initiated, although his writings were technical rather than philosophical in tone. He practised a strict self-discipline and developed an inflexible attitude that tended to isolate him from human company. He immersed himself in his work. He was deeply disturbed by fear of the wrath of God which he believed was punishing him for his liberal beliefs in earlier days. He repented of this and demonstrated his penitence by devoting himself to a life of strict orthodoxy, as he perceived it, to the practice of holiness and the dutiful observance of the eucharist. He had a charismatic gift for influencing others and of counselling them in matters of faith and spirituality. Pusey was a ritualist and a sacramentalist who set the celebration of the eucharist at the centre of the Church's worship. It should be celebrated weekly and observed in the tradition of the early church, to which he was committed. He believed the Athanasian Creed should be recited at Christmas and Easter and during the major Christian festivals. He was devoted to the Bible and its authority, and was confident that the Vatican Council of 1870 would provide a bridge of meeting between Roman Catholicism and Anglicanism. This confidence arose out of the depth of his regard for the sacraments and episcopacy and his reverence for the tradition of the early church. His attitude to the changes currently taking place was conservative, but he proved a doughty apologist for Christianity wherever its beliefs were under threat. His defence of the faith was implicit in his definition of holiness as centred on the two sacraments, the episcopacy as God's ordinance, the Church as the visible body of Christ, devotion and spiritual discipline, and viewing the early church as the model for the Church of England.[9]

John Henry Newman   Newman is the most eminent and productive of the leaders of the Oxford Movement, and, arguably, the most influential figure in English Christianity in the nineteenth century. Whilst Pusey and Keble promoted the Anglican Catholic wing of the Church of England, Newman's theology and energies were also conducive to the renewal of the Roman Catholic mission in England. Pope Pius IX (1792–1878) decided to revive the Roman hierarchy in England. Newman's spiritual fervour, coupled with his massive intellectual powers, his unshakeable faith rooted in resolute conviction, enormously increased the profile of the Christian religion in his day. He expressed his unswerving commitment to the cause of Christian renewal in these words:

> I had supreme confidence in our cause, we were upholding that primitive Christianity which was delivered once for all by the early teachers of the Church, and which was registered and attested in the Anglican formularies and by Anglican divines.

Newman was an able communicator, somewhat devious in argument but a gifted author who expounded and propagated his views in a series of pamphlets or tracts that were widely circulated and discussed. The prime theme was the true essence and nature of Christian faith and the need to hold tenaciously to it. He was conversant with the current developments in science and the questions which these posed for religion. Where the new scientific knowledge was consistent with his religious beliefs he was ready to accommodate it. This earned him the title of modernist in his religious stance. Many liberal Roman Catholics were also open to receive the impact of science on religion and they were to this extent in tune with the thought of Newman. Younger people were attracted to his teaching for this reason. They saw that it broke the mould of insularity and isolationism in religion and replaced with a refreshing openness the iconoclastic method of treating religious issues.[10]

Even so, Newman's hold on his personal faith remained as firm as the rock: "I know that I know," he declared. His faith was uncompromising and unpurchaseable. In early life he came into contact with evangelical religion, but he never embraced it. There are strains of Calvinist doctrine in some aspects of his theology, especially in his exposition of God's predisposed compassion and care, that suggest that he saw the Church of England as a bridge between Protestantism and Catholicism. Yet the balance was tilted towards the Catholic Church. He confessed, "I believe in the Holy Catholic Church," but elaborated, "I have even kept before that there was something greater than the Established Church, and that was the Church Catholic and Apostolic, set up at the beginning, of which she was the local presence and organ." In 1845 Newman converted to Roman Catholicism. The Protestant Reformation had severed the Church from its roots, and Newman's churchmanship rediscovered its rootedness in early catholic and apostolic faith. In theology Newman expounded the principle of continuity. He discerned in Christian theology a legitimate process of development, not merely a restatement of the dead past, that is, "the preservation of type, continuity of principle, power of assimilation, logical sequence, anticipation of its future, conservative action on its past, chronic vigour". Here the words of Pope Paul VI spoken of Newman in 1964 are apt; he declared that Newman:

> guided solely by love of truth and fidelity to Christ, traced an itinerary the most toilsome but also the greatest, the most meaningful, the most conclusive, that human thought ever travelled during the last century, indeed one might say during the modern era, to arrive at the fullness of wisdom and of peace.[11]

Newman sought to establish a balance between theology and ecclesiology and to interpret the important Protestant doctrine of justification by faith in relation to the efficacy of the Christian sacraments.

At the heart of the sacramental life of the Church is the eucharist, which truly and substantially contains the body and blood of Christ, and imparts the grace of God through the action of the Holy Spirit. Christ offered himself in sacrifice to God to procure eternal salvation once and for all time. Humanism is rebellion against God and is "the mortal enemy of the All-Holy". God and sin cannot co-exist, so, there-fore, God banishes sin into outer darkness. The guilt of original sin is remitted through the grace of Christ. God has invested his Church with divine authority and it is the duty of its members to submit to its creed and laws. Obedience to the bishop is obligatory as the bishop is the medium through whom the apostolic succession is made visible. All clergy must be episcopally ordained, and only those so ordained can administer the sacraments. The Christian religion generates a lively spiritual awareness, it propounds high ideals and fosters holiness in personal life and in the life of the Church. Devotion to the sacraments is a primary requirement, and God wills the cultivation of a life of devotion. Vocation to the religious order is a mark of holiness and directs life in commitment to God. Newman disapproved the control of the Church by the state, and rejected the Thirty-nine Articles as the productions of an uncatholic age, which were constituted to accom-modate diverse religious opinions. Newman's views were not well received by many within the Church of England, including the Bishop of Oxford, but his departure to Rome left a considerable intellectual and spiritual vacuum in the Anglican Church.

After his secession from the Church of England Newman continued his literary work and produced *The Development of Christian Doctrine*, which has been acclaimed as one of those works of genius "in which a man's whole store of learning is mobilised under great essential pressure".[12] At the heart of Newman's theological and literary activity is the pre-eminence he afforded to cultivating the spiritual life. The pre-eminence of Christ and his living presence is mediated to the believer who comes into life-giving union with him. Newman brought to the Church a spiritual enrichment through his experience of the Church as "a great spiritual society extending through all Christian ages, living by its own truth and life". His personal piety is reflected in his prayers, and those which are extant convey his deep yearning for inward peace and virtue, as in this prayer:

> Teach me, O Lord, and enable me to live the life of saints and angels . . .
> Breathe on me with that Breath which infuses energy and kindles fervour
> . . . In asking for fervour I am asking for faith, hope and charity . . . I am
> asking for that loyal perception of duty . . . I am asking for sanctity and
> joy, all at once . . .

Newman was gifted as a poet and hymn writer, and some of his hymns are well known amongst churchgoers, especially the hymn:

> Praise to the Holiest in the height
> And in the depths be praise,
> In all his works most wonderful
> Most sure in all His ways.

This hymn appeared in *The Dream of Gerontius* (1865). The theme of the hymn is the mystery of the Incarnation and it has been called a hymn of "austere and splendid advocation". The line in the hymn, "a higher gift than grace" has sometimes been taken to refer to the Catholic mass and the doctrine of the real presence of Christ, but this is unclear. Equally well known is the hymn:

> Lead, kindly light, amid the encircling gloom,
> Lead, thou me on . . .

Newman told how he wrote this hymn whilst on a voyage in the Mediterranean when he fell ill and his servant thought he might die. It was when he caught a boat bound for Marseilles that he wrote the line, "Lead, kindly light." The words "kindly light" have been variously interpreted to mean either "the light of conscience" or "the light of the guiding hand of God".

Christian socialism

Frederick Denison Maurice (1805–72)

As the Oxford Movement continued with its reforms many churchmen were tackling the question whether "the church's only duty is to convert individuals and leave politics to the politicians, or whether if society is unjust it is the duty of churchmen to change society".[13]

Some eminent churchmen resolved the dilemma by actively promoting the cause of social justice for all people. Christianity, they believed, imposed on them the duty to change society and secure justice for everyone. Those who became actively engaged in this crusade became known as "Christian Socialists".

The most prominent leader of this movement is Frederick Denison Maurice, who was also one of the notable Christian theologians of the century. He was the son of a Unitarian minister but he became a communicant of the Church of England and a trinitarian in theology. His two best-known works are *The Kingdom of Christ* and the *Doctrine of Sacrifice*, which both treat his prime spiritual belief that Christ is present in every person. Christ dwells in everyone and everyone is therefore by nature a child of God. As Christ dwells in everyone so all people belong to each other and he forms the bond of union between them. The experience of Christ within is the realization of salvation. Sin is the refusal to acknowledge the Christ who dwells within, but he has secured forgiveness and reconciliation through his death. Christ has presented himself before the world as "the image of Divine holiness and love".

Christ, Maurice declared, "is the sinless root of humanity", and the Church is the noblest sign of the Kingdom of Christ already established in the world.[14] Furthermore, Maurice asserted that the "root of righteousness is in everyman". This is tantamount to saying that the Kingdom of God is within everyone. Baptism is a sacrament of union with God, and the Church is a sign of what the world could become. Maurice deplored sectarianism of any kind and wove his theology around the Fatherhood of God, the brotherhood of man, the sanctity of human personality, and the significance of the Church as a focus of unity. When these factors are set within the framework of God's revelation in Christ then their true meaning becomes incontrovertible. Interpreting them in this way is God's manner of directly speaking to the human spirit. There is within everyone that to which Christ can appeal and evoke a positive response. Unity between all people is then assured.

A vein of mysticism permeates Maurice's thought, but this has to be set alongside a strong practical career which led him to ally himself with the activities of the Christian Socialists. Maurice threw in his lot with the working classes and championed their just cause. As a leader of the movement, he denounced all forms of social injustice and political exploitation. Christ, he maintained, made the human rights of individuals sacrosanct through his teaching, and sealed his love for all people by the sacrifice of his own life. The mission of social justice unites people in a common crusade and mobilizes them in the service of social improvement. Christ approves them for such service, although Maurice was prepared to face the consequences of active engagement in the pursuit of social justice for everyone. He said they should work

for their less fortunate brethren, the mass of people without roots, thrown up by the industrial revolution and infesting the slums of every large town. Society itself must be changed and based upon mutual love not selfishness, "a society in which the chief of all must become the servant of all".[15]

Maurice's theology may be described as fundamentally a spur to Christian action. A vital dimension of his theology, notwithstanding its intellectual vigour, was how to overcome the divide between theological literacy and intellectual understanding, and the practical expression of religious faith. As well as answering the question whether theology and social practice relate to each other, Maurice sought a methodology of how they do so. He wove his theological beliefs into the fabric of his life. This made explicit what was always present implicitly, and was modelled on the example of Christ. Relationship with Christ is the stimulus for this wholeness of belief and practice. For Christians this relationship requires belonging to the Church, whose fellowship and worship express the union of faith and action and where the power to implement the unity is found. Accordingly, "To the Church, he (Maurice) preached richer fellowship, to the Socialists he preached the necessity of Christianity."[16]

Maurice's ideas did not commend themselves to the more conservative churchmen of the time, and his position was misunderstood and misrepresented, especially his views on eternal life. Whereas he used the word eternal in a spiritual or supra-temporal sense, some took it to mean something different. It has been said that Maurice wrote too much and too rhetorically, that he never thought through thoroughly his ideas or really listened sufficiently to his critics. Yet "he was a reconciler. He bequeathed to thoughtful Anglicans a hunger for a more comprehensive Catholicism," and "He also deserves to be remembered as a man who did what he could to end the class war which Karl Marx was sure would intensify." A fitting postscript are his words to his son:

> The desire for unity and the search for unity both in the nation and in the Church has haunted me all my days.[17]

Nonconformity

We have observed earlier how separatist groups developed within Protestantism that broke away from the Established Church. The reasons for these divisions are various but during the nineteenth century they were exceedingly active and won a large following. Many of these Nonconformist groups developed their own organization and system of church government, but they were united in their rejection of the control of the Church by the state. They all proclaimed the sovereign leadership of Christ as the head of the Church. In the early years of the century these groups suffered many disabilities, Nonconformists were not allowed to enter the universities of Oxford and Cambridge and they were saddled with compulsory church rates. But the Nonconformists were free to develop their own styles of worship and church governance. The variety of styles of worship and organization proved to be a stumbling block to some devout Nonconformists, and Edward Irving (1792–1834) voiced the disillusionment of many with the divisions within Nonconformity. He wrote:

> The number of our sects is our shame: for the Christian Church is intended to be one: and of which the evil is, that we are all as full of our own peculiarities, and so nourish them in secret . . . that it is hardly possible for anyone born in their bosom not to be reared up with a great pride and fervour for this which is our fame.[18]

Edward Irving

Edward Irving was a minister of the Church of Scotland and prominent in the Catholic Apostolic Church. As a young minister he worked among the poor in Glasgow and later in London. His activities substantiate the view that the Christianity of the nineteenth century placed "a particularly direct emphasis upon conduct; for though it recognized both grace and faith essential to salvation, it was in practice also very largely a doctrine of salvation by works".[19]

In his theology Irving became immersed in the doctrine of the second coming of Christ. Of this he wrote with great passion and conviction:

> There is no question nor ever has been, nor ever can be, concerning Christ's personal reappearance in human form upon the earth . . . In all Scripture, it is the grand object of faith and hope, ever present, ever useful, to the holy apostles and prophets of the Lord.[20]

This hope, he declared, liberated him from worldly cares and attachments but also filled him with watchfulness and patience. Irving expounded the offices of Christ as prophet, priest and king, and through the action of the Holy Spirit these work for the redemption of the believer. Christ came to earth to be the sacrifice for sin, he was conceived of the Virgin Mary and he himself was wholly pure and separate from sin. Through his work of redemption Christ sanctifies the whole person, body and spirit, and prepares it for eternal glory.

The office of the Church is given by the Holy Spirit so that it is enabled to understand and explain the prophetic word of God and declare it to the world. The Church exists also to intercede as priest for the world, and exercises the kingly office of forgiveness and ex-communication.

As was mentioned above, Irving had close connections with the Catholic Apostolic Church and his spirituality was nurtured within its fold. One of its main elements was prayer and seeking out the Holy Spirit, which frequently began early in the morning and lasted many hours. Irving wrote:

> We cried unto the Lord for apostles, prophets, evangelists, pastors and teachers, anointed with the Holy Ghost, the gift of Jesus, because we saw it written in God's Word that these are the appointed ordinances for the edifying of the body of Jesus. We continued in prayer every morning, morning by morning, at half past six o'clock, and the Lord was not long in hearing and answering our prayers.[21]

Thus the Catholic Apostolic Church was born. It believed that the worship of the Church must be in accord with Scripture and under the guidance of the Holy Spirit. The authority of the Bible is paramount. The Catholic Apostolic Church became a Bible, sacramental and liturgical church, but it did not form an organization separate from other churches; it existed as a unitary fellowship within the universal church. It bore witness to the charismatic nature of the Church and to the phenomenon of speaking with tongues. The eucharist received a central place and was observed every Sunday. Irving had notable theological gifts which in his day were seen to be misapplied. He was accused of heresies and his ministry in the Church of Scotland terminated. Yet he claimed the inspiration of the Holy Spirit for all his activities and believed that God the Father lived in him and sustained him.

The Catholic Apostolic Church is one example of the evangelical fervour that swept through the country during the Victorian age. Movements and groups came into prominence and organized themselves into separate crusading communities with their own axe to grind. They were the champions of one strand or another of the rich diversity of Christian theology and spirituality. When these varied groupings are brought together and their basis defined, and their activities and ideals described, we see how in theory and practice the Christian religion wove a rich and intricate tapestry of beliefs and activities that ranged over the whole spectrum of human spiritual concerns.

Here we can only select two examples of this variety that shaped Victorian spirituality, namely, the power of preaching and the impact of social reform.

Proclaiming the gospel

Two of the most publicized and powerful Nonconformist preachers of
Victorian England were Joseph Parker (d. 1902) and Charles Hadden
Spurgeon (1834–92). Both attracted large congregations by the power
of their preaching and both possessed a gift of magnetic oratory; both
were conservative in their theology and both were elegant in writing as
well as speaking.

Joseph Parker

Joseph Parker ministered in the City Temple in London where thousands were attracted on Sundays and on Thursdays to hear him preach.
He reckoned himself to be an evangelical, but he also aimed to present
the Christian faith in a modern guise and to interpret the Bible in such
a manner that the most simple people could understand it. He published
a *People's Bible* in twenty-five volumes, and from this we can sample
the dramatic style and content of his preaching. His thought of God
finds expression in his expository sermon on *The Works of the Lord*.
God's method of working is to keep everything in his own hand so as
to ensure that there is order in creation, a place and a time for everything. God allows humankind wide choices, freedom and privileges, but
no one can know or find the Almighty God to perfection. When life
reaches a tragic point people cry out for God, the living Father. The
cross of Christ is also the throne of judgement, and Parker pictured
everyone standing before it and giving an account of themselves to God.
The cross and the judgement depict the relation of God to humanity
and humanity's relationship with God. A basic theme of the preaching
of Parker is divine purpose. The divine purpose has been in being since
time began, but it came to fulfilment in the incarnation of Jesus Christ.
God then proposed to create an idealized humanity, and Jesus
Christ, through his zeal for God, aimed to perfect the divine purpose.
Christ is Lord of Lords and King of Kings, and through his incarnate
life he has implanted God's purpose in the world. Christ has come into
the world and is destined to conquer it. It is fitting to rest in this faith
and love, and to pray the prayer of Christ. "Thy Kingdom come; Thy
will be done on earth, as it is in heaven."

Charles Hadden Spurgeon

Spurgeon also ministered in London in the Metropolitan Tabernacle.

He was a native of Essex and had adopted Baptist views by the time he settled in London. He is known for his eloquence, his moral passion and intense conviction. His style was unconventional but he attracted large numbers to his services. He was forthright in defending his beliefs and vehement in his judgement of those who did not carry them out. "I impeach before the bar of universal Christendom," he declared, "these men, who, knowing that baptism does not regenerate, yet declare in public that it does." This was an attack on evangelical clergy. Spurgeon was active in other directions also. He founded the Stockwell Orphanage in 1867 and also a college for the training of pastors. Spurgeon believed that baptism was for adult believers only. In theology he was closest to Calvin, although he was never an out and out believer in predestination.

He could not believe that a child who died unbaptized was destined for hell. Yet when the Metropolitan Tabernacle was opened in 1861 he got visiting preachers to expound the five points of classical Calvinism – human depravity, election by God of those to be saved, particular redemption, effectual calling, and final perseverance.[22] In respect of the Bible, Spurgeon was a literalist who regarded it as the literal word of God from cover to cover. He believed profoundly in prayer, in the atoning death of Christ, in the power of the Holy Spirit and in the resurrection of Christ. He believed that people are saved or unsaved, but those who are saved are saved by grace and in no other way. Salvation must be by grace. In a sermon on the subject he proclaimed:

> Salvation by grace through faith, is not of ourselves. The salvation, and the faith, and the whole gracious work together, are not of ourselves.

Salvation is the gift of God, and therefore it does not pass away as the gifts of others. God does not take back the gift of salvation. Spurgeon held very definite views about conversion. There is no hope of forgiveness without conversion. How, he asked, could it be consistent with the holiness of God for him to put aside past sin, and allow people to go on sinning as they did before? Christ came to save sinners, but nowhere in Scripture is there promise of forgiveness without renouncing iniquity. No one can be pardoned and not changed. The wicked is to forsake "his way", that is, the natural way, the way of the flesh. But God prepares the way for all people to turn to him. He gives the Holy Spirit to sinners, and this turns the sinner to God. God sent him to offer full and complete atonement for sin. Christ bore the penalty that sin deserved, "and the effect of that atoning sacrifice upon everyone who truly trusts to it is that he finds himself so changed that he hates the sin he formerly loved".

Along with Parker and Spurgeon we must include R. W. Dale
(b. 1829) of Birmingham, another of the princes of the English pulpit in
the nineteenth century.[23] He was a leader of the Congregational
churches and exercised a formidable influence on life in Birmingham in
educational, municipal and political affairs. He combined his religious
attitude with intense moral fervour and crusading zeal. Dale held a high
view of the Church, but not in the sense of the Oxford Movement.
Believing in the presence of Christ in the Church as a gathered community of believers, Dale expounded the nature and authority of the
Church as received directly from Christ himself. With Christ as the sole
authority it is intolerable that the Church should be subject to
the authority of the state or any clerical hierarchy. This he believed was
contrary to the Bible. Dale was a prolific author, but his best-known
work is *The Atonement*. All who repent will be saved from the condemnation of sin; this applies not only to the elect but to everyone. The
atonement is a positive act on the part of Christ performed for humanity, and thus it opens the way and permits a willing human response to
God on the part of all people. Christ endorsed the penalties of sin and
made his own submission to suffering for the salvation of the world.
Only he could have done this, for he alone is the agent of salvation, and
through union with him it is possible to live a life of submission to God.

The primary theme of Dale's preaching was the living Christ, whose
resurrection he celebrated every Sunday. As Christ is alive he rules over
his Church, he offers salvation to everyone, including infants who were
baptized, and to all who participate in the eucharist. This sacrament is
central as the act of God and its observance cements the fellowship of
the Church and matures and sustains it. The eucharist provides experience of the redemption Christ had procured through his atoning death.

Social revival

The Salvation Army

In 1877 one of the most powerful and charismatic ameliorative movements of the modern era was organized. The movement was inspired
by Christian idealism and directed to those whose condition was
considered to be desperate and who were rejected by society at large.
The movement is known as the Salvation Army, founded by a
Methodist preacher, William Booth (1829–1912), and his wife
Catherine. Together they worked out a scheme that they hoped would

appeal to the most needy people in East London. The Army was organized along the lines of "soldiering", but most prominent in its purpose was its spirituality. It achieved a striking impact almost from the beginning, in spite of its unusual methods and strange nomenclature. Its government was autocratic but from the start its missionaries were active in every part of the United Kingdom and its rescue work spread to the continent and world-wide. It was a bold and unprecedented experiment in social regeneration and its aims received wide support. The Salvation Army constituted the last great evangelical revival of the modern period with enthusiasm for conversion reminiscent of the evangelical revival of John Wesley, but its methods were more sensational. It linked social work and care for the physical and material welfare of the underprivileged classes with evangelistic zeal for conversion, and practised this union as the epitome of Christian mission. To create music corps and street bands, to use military terms to describe the "ranks" of members, and to wear distinctive colourful uniforms, was something new in the religious life of the time. Prayer was called "knee-drill", the meeting place was called "barracks", and the "soldiers" marched in military formation.

In 1890 General Booth published his influential book called *In Darkest England*. The title was borrowed from the book by H. M. Stanley, *Darkest Africa*, it drew attention to the victims of social neglect and appealed for larger sums of money in order to alleviate their desperate condition. In his book Booth described vividly the condition of those who were "excommunicated by humanity" and the "enormities, callously inflicted, and violently borne by these miserable victims". He made an impassioned appeal on their behalf:

A population sodden with drink, steeped in vice, eaten up by every sound and physical melody, these are the denizens of Darkest England amidst whom my life has been spent, and to whose rescue I would now summon all that is best in the manhood and womanhood of our land.

The Salvation Army distanced itself from the mainstream churches by reducing the status of the sacraments as not being necessary to salvation.

The arts and spirituality

A major aspect of the religious culture and spirituality of the nineteenth century is expressed through the poetry, literature and music

of the period. We can point to a number of reasons why the arts
provided a fruitful source of spirituality in Victorian England. They
often exude a new kind of religious consciousness and their works
are dominated by issues of spirituality. The culture of the time had
its impact on spirituality, particularly on the new humanism and
interpersonal issues born of the cultural and intellectual changes
whose origins can be traced to the rapid changes in science and technology. This produced an increasing interest in human, moral and
religious questions, and these affected individual subjectivity and personal feelings. The works of poets and novelists reflect the overall
piety and the evangelical, spiritual and social reform movements. We
can only here refer to examples chosen from each of the three areas
mentioned, which in different ways shed light on the spiritual
perspective.

Poetry

The strands of religion and spirituality are intricately interwoven in the
works of many eminent Victorian poets. This is a feature of the poetic
splendour of Robert Browning (1812–89) who described the poet-seer
as one who seeks to present imaginatively his conception of truth.
Browning conveyed a prophetic image and message through his poetry,
the image is a vision of meaning "within" that reflects that blatant truth
that is embedded in everyone. Browning was also a keen observer of
nature and his poetry is resonant with exquisite images of natural
phenomena, of flowers and birds, that create a kaleidoscopic picture of
the created world and the joy in the heart of the Creator who rules over
and above the world in majestic spendour:

> His presence on all lifeless things: the winds
> Are henceforth voices, wailing or a shout
> A querulous mutter or a quick gay laugh,
> Never a senseless gust now man is born.
> The herded pines commune and here deep thoughts
> A secret they assemble to discuss
> When the sun drops behind their ranks which glare
> Like gates of hell . . .
>
> (from *Paracelsus*)

Browning's poetry is shot through with deep religious feelings, and,
according to one opinion, he discerned unquestionably in the incarnation the climax of history, the crown of philosophy and the
consummation of poetry.[24] In this respect he embraced and portrayed

the higher intellectual reaches of religious thought, although none of this is compressed into cold logical or dogmatic phrases. He was aware of the searching and intransigent questions raised by Christian faith and he was frequently fearlessly forthright in expressing his personal beliefs. In his poem *Christmas Eve* Browning expressed how Christ revealed the divine love, whose power Browning believed was obvious:

> That He, the Eternal find first and last,
> Who, in His power, had so surpassed
> All man conceives of what is might
> Whose wisdom, too, showed infinite
> – Would prove as infinitely good . . .

Browning believed that love is the ultimate truth about God and religion; and his poetry depicts its anguish and travail as well as its triumph. But through it all is to be heard the clear voice that calls on conscience for courage and duty, and the quest for God:

> What is that I hunger for but God,
> I not plead my rapture in Thy works
> For love of Thee, nor that I feel one
> Who cannot die; but there is that in me
> Which turns to Thee, which loves, or which should love.
>
> (from *Saul*)

The poetry of Browning also radiates a spirit of love. This is not a facile superficial optimism but hope that is earthed in truth as reliable as is the evidence for Jesus. He was sensitive to the difficulties and stumbling blocks of Christian faith and was perplexed by questions that arise about the nature of religious belief and the practice of Christian morality and ethics. Nevertheless, Browning was firm in the belief that goodness is superior to evil, faith to doubt, and truth to falsehood. Hope means facing the future with confidence, it is the certainty of the triumph of right.

> Never doubted clouds would break,
> Never dreamed, though right were worsted, wrong would triumph,
> Held we fall to rise, are baffled to fight better,
> Sleep to wake.

Spiritually Browning disclosed "the God within the soul". This is the assurance of the presence of the ever-living Christ, whose love is the active secret of communion with God. Love is the meeting point between God and the self and the self and God. Browning affirmed belief in the historical Jesus but he also cultivated the spiritual Christ whose Easter resurrection is the earnest of his continuing presence:

> But Easter-Day breaks! But
> Christ rises! Mercy every way
> Is infinite – and who can say?

Literature

Many a Victorian novel provides an image of the beliefs and spirituality of the novelist and of the age. Victorian novelists often had the leisure and the background for creating lengthy novels which are living encounters with spiritual, religious and moral issues, drawn from complex situations and interpersonal and social relationships. These not only reflect the novelist's own perceptions but also mirror the spiritual concerns of their age. Religion may suffuse parts of the novel, be the subject of the dialogue, be expressed implicitly or explicitly in encounters between the characters when facing human dilemmas, or in engaging speculations about the present or the future. The spiritual perception of the meaning of life, or the experience of conflict and doubt, or joy and anguish or even the search for God, inner peace and reality, may all be overtly or inovertly present.

The novels of Thomas Hardy (1840–1928) may be cited as works that frequently reflect the author's own religious views and spiritual concerns. Take for example this poignant scene in Hardy's novel *Tess of the D'Urbervilles*, which describes Tess's anguish over the baptism and burial of her baby Sorrow. When Tess reached home one night she learned that her baby was seriously ill. She was plunged into misery, realizing that her child was not baptized. Her child was about to die, without the assurance of salvation.

And the novel continues, "I must get the parson!" she cried, but her father, drunken and obstinate, locked the door. The night wore on; the infant was rapidly sinking. Distracted, she murmured incoherent prayers; she lit candles, woke the other children, arranged the water-stand as a font, and stood by it with the baby in her arms. A name suggested by a phrase in the book of Genesis came into her head. "Sorrow, I baptize thee in the name of the Father, and of the Son, and of the Holy Ghost." A child unbaptized and illegitimate was destined to damnation and Tess's father is depicted as bad and obstinate; he would not permit any prying into his house and affairs (by the parson), and locked the door. Between the father and the parson there is a great divide. The episode is fraught through with suffering; even the child's name, Sorrow, is indicative of this. Suffering in life is inevitable, and Hardy made no attempt to brush this aside, but is the answer to the problem of suffering found in religion? The parson did not perform the baptism nor did he bury Tess's child, for he was steeped in formal convention.

Hardy portrays Tess, the heroine of his novel, as "a pure woman". She was obedient to her mother, she acted for the best, she applied herself diligently to her work, she loved passionately. These phrases describe her character, as though the author wished to show that her misfortunes did not happen on account of her wickedness. The evil of the world is not resolved by reference to human evil. Indeed, the novel is threaded through with a mixture of misfortune and happiness. Tess loved Mr Angel Clare "so passionately, and he was so godlike in her eyes". But she felt she could not marry him. The affair with D'Urberville haunted her, and only after Clare had implored her, because he knew she loved him with "all heart and soul", did they marry. But the tangled web of human relationships is shown to be woven more tightly when Alec D'Urberville and Tess meet up, and Alec knew that his desire for her was not dead. He said that she had knocked out his faith and was her "slapdash" lover again. He offered to marry her, but the outcome was that she killed him. This she confessed to Clare on his return, but his response was, "I cannot ever despise you."

Behind the portrayal of the relationship between Tess, Alec and Clare there is a sort of realism that fathoms the essence of the tensions of love. This includes the notion of interpreting the inner passions as well as describing what appears to happen. Hardy unravels the innermost feelings of his characters, not merely their actions. In other words, he penetrates the truth of the situation to reveal the motives as well as the tensions. In telling the story of Tess the novelist reveals its underlying spiritual significance. The importance of recognizing individual feelings and the necessity of love comes through the novel strongly. Tess could be viewed as a model of someone facing and being influenced by entities that allowed her to explore the idea that love can never be understood by recourse to set rules and conventions. The higher reaches of love can only be fully appreciated through the interplay between individuals in their creative encounters with each other. Clare and Alec operate on different levels. Hardy points beyond the deeds of these two so as to project the view that no human being should be used only as a means to satisfy another person's end. Both characters acquit themselves nobly in their attitude to Tess. But the novel leaves us with a question that is not resolved. Is it fate that led Tess to kill Alec or was it chance? The novel ends with the hanging of Tess and the picture of the black flag extended in the breeze. "Justice" was done. The gazers bent in prayer; the flag waved silently. But to whom was justice done?

Music

Music was a great part of the cultural life of Victorian England. Singing classes, choral societies, factory bands and the music hall were some of the chief leisure activities of the masses. Congregational singing was prominent in Protestant worship. The great works of Handel, Haydn, Beethoven and Mozart were popular and much heard. A large part of the music heard and sung was "religious" and there was much eagerness among ordinary people to hear it. It provided experience they could all appreciate and created a sense of spiritual elation and harmony. Music was a great social leveller, and as the century wore on more people were prepared to spend their money and leisure in its enjoyment. Choral music and music festivals became very fashionable, and church music by well-known composers – Handel, Mozart and Beethoven – became a feature of worship once it had been provided with English words. In some places the congregational singing in church was accompanied by the local band, but as the Oxford Movement proceeded, surpliced choirs were trained to lead the singing from the chancel. In 1829 Mendelssohn (1809–47) came to England. He was one of the influential talented musicians who gave a fresh direction to choral music. Felix Mendelssohn was a member of a highly respected and prosperous German family without any deep religious convictions, but he was baptized into the Christian faith. He was an emotional person who developed deep religious convictions and an interest in the mysteries of medieval Christianity. He was a serious composer of church music. He also became attached to the music of Bach and endeavoured to bring about a revival of interest in this. Mendelssohn's performance of Bach's *St. Matthew Passion* in 1829 was a notable occasion. This promoted the revival of Bach's music, which it was said interpreted and promoted the "rare states of the soul" and was "the embodiment of eternal laws". The impact of music on the promotion of spirituality is considerable, and some would say it is compelling. Music stirs the emotions and engages the mind, it soothes and arouses spiritual feeling and creates enthusiasm. Religious and devotional music minister to the spirit and have an edifying and devout effect on the practice of spirituality.

By its very nature, its variable style and its contrasting moods of rapture and joy, solemnity and pathos, music, performed or listened to, embraces all aspects of spirituality in subtle and creative ways. Some of the hymn tunes composed by Felix Mendelssohn continue to be sung, among the best known being the tune to the words of Charles Wesley's Christmas carol, "Hark! the herald angels sing, Glory to the new born King", and the tune to Martin Luther's setting of Psalm 130, "Out of the depths I cry to Thee, Lord hear me. I implore Thee."

The publication of *Hymns Ancient and Modern* in 1861 was a landmark as it extended the range and practice of hymn-singing in public worship beyond what had previously been, in the main, characteristic of the worship of Nonconformist churches. This publication included hymns which were composed originally as poems but were adapted for public devotion. Metrical versions of the psalms continued to be sung, but there was a notable upsurge in hymn-singing, many hymns becoming popular almost to the extent of being sung as folk-songs. The compilers of this collection of hymns and tunes asserted "they have endeavoured to do their work in the spirit of the English Prayer-book, and in dependence on the grace of God".

This glance at certain aspects of the theology and spiritual tradition of the nineteenth century will have shown how spiritual forces were deflected by the upheavals and changes in society, especially by the advances in science and technology. The impact of these changes was such as to determine the spiritual values and moral direction of the age. The legacy of these changes spilled over into the twentieth century, and the evolution of ideas and the theories of science, that were so much part of the mind and culture of the nineteenth century, continue to exercise an influence in philosophy and religion.

We may sum up the Victorian era as a self-conscious religious world that was served by able pioneers of religious thought who propounded ideals and a path to the future that was often only dimly perceived and only partially followed. They created a complex world of thought fraught with many intractable questions that have yet to be unravelled. Advances in industrialization and scientific discoveries, along with increased wealth and material prosperity in a world of expanding trade and conflicting commercial interests, constituted for religion an unprecedented challenge and tested to the uttermost the relevance and integrity of its moral precepts. The Church needed to make adjustments and to re-evaluate its beliefs and realign its practices in order to affirm and maintain its ascendancy as the guardian of the nation's conscience. New questions arose and new factors emerged that complicated the traditional teaching and authority of the Church. Christian theology and spirituality needed to rise to the challenge of the age in order to retain its position. Christianity was in some respects thrown onto the defensive and made to reconsider its first principles. As far as these principles are concerned they are still the subject of theological investigation and of spiritual implementation.

8

The Contemporary World

A century of cyclonic changes. At the dawn of the twentieth century "a certain buoyancy of spirit was evident in most schools of thought",[1] and the channels of progress that flowed in so many directions were confidently expected to rumble on unabated. A spirit of optimism prevailed, the leisurely rhythm of life was punctuated by regular church attendance, when "the Edwardians would sing the psalms and hymns with reverence, would listen to stories from the Old Testament", before they departed "as the final benediction descended on bowed heads".[2] A different consciousness prevails today, and confidence in inevitable social, moral and religious progress has evaporated like the dew of the early morning. A radically contrasting life-style and social organization have developed that make the overt optimism of the early years of the century seem light years away. The intellectual understanding of the world and human life has been turned on its head; the revolution in technology and science has transformed the outlook, habits and life-style of people all over the globe. Where does this leave Christian theology and its spiritual tradition at the turn of the century?

As we began this excursus into Christian theology and spirituality we observed that all life is spiritual and that theology is suited to serve the whole of experience, so as we come to the concluding phases we ask, What are the forces that have shaped and fashioned Christian theology into being what it is today?

Ecumenical theology and spirituality

The concept of globalization received a fresh impetus as new lines of mass inter-continental communication and accelerated transport began to change the shape of the modern world. Today life is consciously and inevitably lived against a global backcloth; events in one part of the world have an instant impact on every other; a local crisis in one continent sends ripples world-wide; achievement or advancement in one place reverberates in every other. Life in "the global village" has an upside of hope and a downside of despair, and in the profoundest sense Christian theology and spirituality have to take cognizance of this. Experience in the "global context" is the immediate context of theology and spirituality.

Human experience world-wide is a mixture of hope and despair, and this, at the profoundest level, projects a vision of the global condition of humanity. Humanity is the same the world over. The term ecumenical (= the whole inhabited world) carries the image of the reality of the unity of all people at the deepest level of their humanity. Ecumenical theology explicates the rationale and the implications of this truth, and spirituality traverses the way for this unity to be harmonized for the sake of the good and survival of humankind. The ecumenical movement in Christianity during the past century has pioneered the way for the promotion of global harmony between all people. It has demonstrated that all human questions are ecumenical questions, and that harmony between all peoples the world over is the heart of spirituality.

Ecumenical mission

In Edinburgh in 1910 a flame was lit that has burned more or less throughout the century. Churchmen gathered from Britain, Europe, the USA, Africa and Asia to pray together and discuss the theme "the world for Christ". The theme arose out of the prayer of Jesus that his followers might "all be one". The unity of Christians, it was believed, would promote the Christian mission more effectively and this would prepare the way for the wider unity of the whole human race. This goal has been pursued in various ways throughout the last century and attempts have been made to formulate an ecumenical theology that justified it. This has been the hope of churchmen of different traditions and different continents, and whilst we cannot specify any officially approved ecumenical theology, ecumenical cooperation between churchmen has been fostered and increased. The Edinburgh Conference did not produce a theological statement or blueprint, but the chairman, J. R. Mott, an American ecumenical statesman, voiced the conviction of those present:

Our movement stands pre-eminently for the emphasis of the belief that by a great enlargement of the agencies employed by the missionary societies today, the Gospel can and should be brought within the reach of every creature within this generation . . .

The issues raised at the Edinburgh Conference have been the subject of debate throughout the century. What is the relation of evangelism to conversion? Must evangelism aim at conversion? Is Christianity the sole vehicle of salvation? What about the truth claims of non-Christian religions? The discussion of these and related questions has broadened as the global society has developed and they remained the Church's unfinished agenda at the end of the century. The moral supremacy of Christianity, as associated historically with the west, is suspect to some eastern religionists, having regard to its involvement in two world wars. Nevertheless, the question of what Christianity has *uniquely* to offer to the promotion of global human harmony is still being pursued. The concept of evangelism as the promotion of this harmony, as against the aim of conversion, is one that appeals to many Christians in this multi-religious global age. It is conjectured that the spirituality Christians practise serves to promote the harmony of all people, who are equally made in the image of God. Even so, the ecumenical movement has kept its sight firmly on the promotion of union between separated churches, and the Church of South India, the United Church of Canada, the Uniting Church of Australia, and the United Reformed Church in the United Kingdom, are examples of what has been achieved.

Churches together

A series of world-wide ecumenical gatherings were held during the two decades following the First World War with the result that action was taken to form a new inter-church organization, the World Council of Churches. This Council of Protestant churches was intended to bring together churches from all over the world so that they could fulfil their common mission through collaborative action. Such a Council was mooted soon after the 1914–18 war ended, and its formation was advocated in 1919 by Archbishop Söderblom:

What I advocate is an Ecumenical Council of Churches. This should not be given external authority but would make its influence felt so far as it can act with spiritual authority. It would not speak *ex cathedra*; but from the depth of Christian conscience.

A decisive decision was taken to create a World Council of Churches in 1937, but it was not until three years after the end of the Second World War in Europe that the Council was formally constituted at Amsterdam. Between 1937 and 1948 the decision to form the Council was kept on the boil by a Provisional Committee which was charged with responsibility for planning the pattern of the organization. The committee eventually became known as "The World Council of Churches in process of formation". Member churches from across the world were able to keep in touch with each other during the years of the Second World War, and a number of them won admiration for their witness and courage, and service to the cause of reconciliation. They provided help for refugees and prisoners of war, they laid plans for Christian reconstruction after the war, and they strove to keep alive the witness of the churches in countries that were at war with each other. The World Council of Churches was finally constituted at Amsterdam in 1948. One hundred and forty-seven churches joined the Council, including some of the oldest churches of Christendom, such as the Church of Ethiopia and the Syrian Orthodox Church, and some of the youngest, such as the Presbyterian Church of Korea. The member churches agreed to transmit the Amsterdam Message to the world:

> Here at Amsterdam we have covenanted ourselves afresh to Him, and have covenanted with one another in constituting this World Council of Churches. We intend to stay together.

The faith affirmation of the Council, also agreed at Amsterdam, reads:

> The World Council of Churches is a fellowship of churches which accept our Lord Jesus Christ as God and Saviour.

This formula has been the subject of discussion at subsequent meetings of the Council, and has since been amended. The Council aims to perform three main functions: to be an instrument of service of the churches together, to cooperate in witness together to the world, and to indicate the range of the fellowship between the member churches. The Council intended to present a united Christian viewpoint on important moral, political, educational and intellectual issues facing the world. Since 1948 the World Council of Churches has met in assembly in different countries, the latest being in 1998 in Harare, but it is still faced with the question of how to accomplish the overall purpose of the Christian mission in a pluralist world. The possibility of the conversion of people of all nations and religions to Christian faith as an ideal is questioned. So it is asked: is this the time when Christian theology and spirituality should take the initiative of structuring a theology and spirituality whose focus is not the union of churches but the unity of humankind? The goal would be the unity of the whole human race, on the basis of its common humanity. Is this century's ecumenical action and spirituality pointing in this direction and presenting a fresh challenge?

> If within the coming century world-wide Christianity is compelled to embrace such a degree of diversity and provisionality and, indeed, to welcome this as intrinsic to its true nature, its pursuit of Christian unity will have to change direction.[3]

Global spirituality

Christian theology has had to face many challenges during a century of rapid change, but it has also been enriched by the interaction of theologies from different continents in this age of globalization. This development is one of the factors that has made Christian theology what it is today. We may refer to three key areas in illustration of how Christian theology and its spiritual tradition have developed in recent times.

Spiritual liberation

We turn first to Latin America where Christianity infiltrated some five hundred years ago. The majority of Christians today are Roman Catholic, although there is a flourishing Pentecostal charismatic movements.

About fifty years ago "base Christian communities" (*communidades eclesiasles de base, CEBS*) began to spread and involve poor people in group meetings for learning the Bible, learning about the faith, and discussing social, political and economic questions. The poor gained much comfort and hope from these meetings. They were able to share their troubles and ventilate their grievances, they prayed together and learned to read and how to analyse their problems. This gave them a sense of identity and self-esteem; it developed their self-confidence and they were helped to understand their personal and social conditions better. This encouraged and emboldened them in their struggle against social evils and economic depression, and, equally important, how to handle misfortune and stress positively. The meetings helped to mobilize them for social and political action and to work to bring about change. Out of this movement there grew what has been known world-wide as liberation theology.

Liberation theology makes use of Marxist concepts, especially of praxis, in enlisting the active participation of the poor in the process of change. This is related to the biblical teaching on liberation for the oppressed and the Christian doctrine of hope. To this extent liberation theology is hopeful, it sees the world moving towards an ultimate goal over which God has control. This belief shapes events and confronts issues of oppression, poverty, injustice and exploitation from the perspective of the Bible. It derives its models from the teaching of the Old Testament prophets and John the Baptist. The teaching of Jesus and how he championed the oppressed and the downtrodden is used as a model. So the Bible is read in the light of the prevailing socio-economic–political conditions, especially that part which tells of God acting as the liberator of his people from the slavery of Egypt or from captivity in Babylon. The current social conditions provide the context for learning the Bible. It speaks directly to the poor. It reveals God's preferential option for the under privileged.

Liberation theology aims to be holistic. A leading exponent, Gustavo Gutierrez, in his work *A Theology of Liberation*, considers traditional spirituality as being too individualistic and introspective. For spirituality to be true to the Bible it must be available for all people who live in community not in isolation. Spirituality must be directed to social change and work for a just social order. Both theology and spirituality exist for the sake of the world – they can't be divorced from it. Their proper home is the market place. Liberation theology takes seriously the Bible view of incarnation: it aims to fulfil the purpose of the incarnation by carrying its message to everyone, and by enriching the poor. To do this is to encounter Christ, to walk in the Spirit and to journey to the Father. As they do this, people experience the free grace of God, they find joy in the struggle for liberation, they foster their commitment to the poor and they take a full share in the life of the community. The foremost champion of the poor in San Salvador in recent times was Archbishop Romero (1917–80), who was committed to the aims of liberation theology. He refused to cooperate with the state whilst the poor were neglected, and he condemned outright the "mysticism of violence". He made a public stand against injustice and violence, and in his last sermon before he was shot before the altar of his church he declared:

> We must not love ourselves so much that we refrain from plunging ourselves into those risks history demands of us, and that those wanting

to keep out of danger will lose their lives . . . We know that every effort
to improve socially, above all when society is so full of injustice and sin,
is an effort that God blesses, that God wants, that God demands of us.

African Spirituality

It is appropriate to refer here to theology and spirituality in Africa
alongside Latin America for the reason that "black theology" and
"liberation theology" become more and more interwoven, and this will,
in all likelihood, happen without either of these labels permeating the
thought of African Christianity.[4] Today African theologians engage
more than in the past with questions that relate to their own indigenous
culture and ask what can Christianity contribute to the progressive
understanding of this. African spirituality is of necessity orientated in
style and content to native African culture. Therefore such questions as
celibacy, polytheism, polygamy, exorcism, cosmology, rites of passage,
liturgy, worship and church organization give spirituality a wide base
indeed. The search continues for a credible cultural autonomy and for
an active indigenous theology. Such a theology will need to be contex-
tual, expressive of native African concepts, and thought and ideas. Some
of the characteristics of this enculturation are the focus on the Bible and
its message about poverty, destitution and hardship. The message of the
Bible creates an inner yearning for the promised freedom from
privation and suffering and for the means of growth to a nobler life of
freedom, dignity and self-fulfilment. The Bible has a message for the
victims of corruption and exploitation that are endemic in African
society. It points to sin as the root cause of all evil and "the underlying
cause of all things that do not work".[5]

If all things are to work together for good then sin must be uprooted.
But uprooting sin has to go hand in hand with the promotion of social
justice and the elimination of potential corruption. Polarization, the
curse of African society, is the result of sin, but the forgiveness of sin is
for the sake of securing justice for everyone. It has to be said that African
theology is in a state of fluidity. A good deal of what we may call African
"theological output" has only been transmitted orally through sermons,
teaching, prayers and oral communications. The expectations which
theologians have of the direction African theology may take are various:
some expect it to be "evangelic, erecting bridges between the Gospel and
African thought forms", or "to emerge at the point where Christianity
meets the traditional African Religion", or relate to the "African
peoples' experience of their God", or "the adaptation of Christian

doctrine to the mentality and needs of people", or "to engage in a dialogue with the Black People who feel that somehow theology has not taken them into consideration".[6] Professor John Mbiti, who has listed these various expectations, has also listed six major concerns that engage African theological reflection at the present time, namely, biblical theology, pastoral theology, political theology, cultural theology, theology of dialogue, and missiological theology. Professor Mbiti also refers to the necessity of finding an answer to the question: What is the Church in African understanding?[7] The search for an answer to this question continues, but its challenge to African spirituality is twofold. When it comes, will the answer given encapsulate the true spirit and aspirations of African Christians? Will it mirror the great diversity of Africa and serve as a focus of spiritual and moral unity? An African Christian spirituality will need to reflect the complexities of the vast diversity and be expressive of the African psyche in its manifold manifestations.

Christian theology aspires to expound and highlight the particular African insights and experience of Christian faith. Many basic elements of Christian practices and traditions appeal to the African mind and spirit and are experienced in characteristic African style, notably, its charismatic phenomena, its love of community gatherings, its lively and joyous worship, rhythm and dancing, its love of biblical stories of dreams, its interest in divinities and the supernatural. In some ways these characteristics reflect the ethos and practices of the early Christians. As global spirituality evolves, the role of African theology is bound to be influential. If spirituality in the modern world is to develop global dimensions and achieve theological maturity it must permit the current indigenous approaches to be genuinely free to have a stake in this.

Undoubtedly Archbishop Desmond Tutu (b. 1931) is the most charismatic representative of African Christian spirituality of recent times. Theologically it is difficult to associate him with any particular school. From time to time he has displayed radical and conservative tendencies, but he has consistently voiced eloquently how faith expresses itself in openness and inclusiveness, in vulnerability and compassion for all people. This faith has sustained his vigorous protests against racism and apartheid, but always with the positive purpose of securing for the victims of racial oppression their rightful citizenship in their nation and the world. Tutu has followed the vision of reconciliation as an architect of the unity of all people irrespective of colour, and the right of all to live within the relatedness of the human family and the relatedness of the whole creation.

Tutu cannot be classed with liberation theology or theological contextualism, for he has displayed in his utterances a single-minded independence that drives him on in the search for authentic reconciliation and healing in personal life, in the Church and in society. His spiritual leadership won him the Nobel Peace Prize, but at the centre of his spirituality is a deep commitment to a life of prayer and communion with God. This is mirrored in his book *An African Prayer Book*, where his passion for social justice and reconciliation are expressed in his prayers. Here is part of his prayer for reconciliation and peace:

Lord, let your spirit of reconciliation blow over all the earth . . .
Lord, we thank you that we have brothers and sisters in all the world,
Be with them that make peace.

Tutu's unwavering confidence in the triumph of goodness radiates through these lines:

Goodness is stronger than evil;
Love is stronger than hate;
Light is stronger than darkness;
Life is stronger than death;
Victory is ours through Him who loves us.

His empathy with the victims of injustice and his anguish at the world's suffering are expressed in this prayer:

God, my father
I am filled
With anguish and punishment.
Why, Oh God, is there so much suffering?
Everywhere we look there is pain
And suffering . . .
In Nicaragua . . .
In Guatemala . . . [8]

Asian Spirituality

According to received knowledge Christianity was transmitted to India in the age of the apostles by the Apostle Thomas. It has had a continuous presence in some of the main countries of Asia for many centuries, but Christianity has also faced some of its most testing challenges in the nations of the East. We can only here refer to a few highlights of Christian theology and spirituality in the East.

Earlier reference was made to the Church of South India as a signal example of the union of churches in the twentieth century. The churches, which covenanted to form the Church of South India in 1947, believed the union to be an answer to prayer. At the inaugural service the prayer was said, "Thou hast heard the prayers of Thy people and blessed the labours of Thy servants, and hast brought us to this day for the glory of Thy name." The churches then declared their union and the Church of South India was born.

There was unification of ministry, and three and a half thousand communicants took part in the eucharist. This moulding of different church traditions in one church has been a model for inter-church amalgamation in the twentieth century. The primary emphasis is on spirituality as the cement of union between churches of different tradition and organization. The eucharist is open to all members of the uniting churches; the grace of God is bestowed equally on all members.

The formation of the Church of South India is a model of a new creative form of spirituality which at the same time conserves the best in the spiritual and religious tradition of the uniting churches. In a commemorative book issued by the Church of South India there appears the name of Pandita Ramabai (1858–1922), who was born into an orthodox Hindu family but who became a Christian and is honoured today as one of the spiritual saints of the last century. Like some other Hindus, Gandhi among them, she revered Jesus as a prophet and teacher but could not believe in him as the Son of God. She attributed her conversion to the influence of an Anglican Sisterhood in Berkshire during a visit to England. Here she heard of Christ's meeting with the woman of Samaria and she then realized "that Christ was the divine saviour", and that he could uplift the downtrodden women of her own country. She was baptized and confirmed, but was bewildered and disillusioned by the many different church denominations, yet she did not lose her faith in Christ. She worked to establish a home for high-caste child widows in Bombay. She continued to wear Indian dress but her life-style was completely devoted to Christ. She campaigned for the relief of famine victims and victims of bubonic plague. She believed passionately in the power of prayer to supply her needs. She spent much time in meditation and fasting and as an ardent evangelist. She also sent her helpers out to preach in the nearby towns and villages. To spread the gospel of Christ to her fellow countrymen was a consuming passion of her life.

Another notable Indian spiritual leader of the twentieth century is Sundar Singh (1889–1929). Sundar was born into the Sikh religion and was deeply touched by Sikh spirituality as a youth. However, he rebelled against this, and publicly burned a copy of the Christian gospels that he had been compelled to study at a Christian mission. He felt great remorse for this wanton act, and after three days prayed earnestly that God would reveal himself to him, until he eventually confessed, "as I prayed and looked into the light, I saw the form of Jesus Christ . . . I heard a voice saying in Hindustani: 'How long will you persecute me? I have come to save you; you were praying to know the right way. Why do you not take it?'" Thus he was led to the Christian faith and was baptized in 1905. Asked about Christianity in India, Sundar replied, "Only when it is given in an Eastern bowl will it be accepted by simple men and women who seek the truth." Christianity, he maintained, is the fulfilment of Hinduism and brings to everyone the greatest gift of light. He joined a Franciscan Community, and like the early friars, travelled around preaching the message of Jesus. He made skilful use of parables in his preaching and emphasized the need of grace to live the life of Christ and to be the agent of bringing others to him. He had strong mystical tendencies and believed that the fire of the Holy Spirit would quench the thirst of spiritually parched souls. He spent long hours in prayer and meditation.

Christianity in Japan has had a somewhat chequered history. Christian missionaries have made fewer inroads into the country, but in illustration of the Christian spirituality, tenuous though it is, we may refer to the non-church movement, the creation of a Protestant Japanese Christian, Uchimura Kamzo (1861–1929). He was active in the early years of the twentieth century and is remembered for his great courage and liberal tendencies. He rejected the organized structures of the Christian Church with their hierarchies and formalities. Instead he concentrated on teaching the Bible in informal groups, modelled on the Asian method of student–teacher participation. Thus the Bible was studied and its message taught in intimate groups where friendly personal relationships fostered a real sense of spiritual community.

Uchimura aimed to keep the balance equal between being a good patriot of Japan and a practising Christian. His courageous and un-compromising moral stand on political issues won him great respect. He visited the USA for further study, and when once overcome by a mood of depression he was asked by the president of the college, "Why don't you stop looking inside yourself and look up to Jesus who bore your sin on the cross?" This proved a defining moment in Uchimura's life, for he confessed, "This is the most important day of my life. The power of Christ's redemption was never so strongly revealed as today. Christ has paid all my debt and can take me back to the purity and holiness which humanity enjoyed before the fall of Adam."[9]

Another notable Christian of Japan who has made an impact on Christian theology and spirituality is Toyohiko Kagawa (1888–1960). When Japan began to develop its industrial potential towards the end of the nineteenth century and the early years of the twentieth, many people suffered as a result of the rapid industrialization. They were impoverished and ostracized without having any share in the nation's new prosperity. Kagawa turned his attention to these people and set about striving to improve their lot. In 1936 he wrote a book called *The Thorn in the Flesh*, which mirrors his experience of adversity and suffering, and the victory that he eventually achieved through faith in God. He wrote:

> Personally I always think of religion as a means of getting the better of our weaknesses and deformities; this is the real goal of loving. It is as if a man should take himself as a whole, chiselling out both soul and body into the pattern of beauty set by God himself . . . [10]

Kagawa fashioned much of his theology and spirituality on the teaching of St. Paul, especially Paul's faith and ability to be joyful in the face of tribulation. He wrote, "We can see in Paul, even when he was in want, the secret of a great joy-giving faith. I myself am frequently in want. What with my various enterprises in Tokyo, Osaka and Kobe; what with farmer unions and labour unions and all the numerous problems arising from them, I am at a loss to know how to proceed. At such times I should like to look upon these 'thorns in the flesh' as so many blessings from God."[11] We gather from this excerpt how committed he was to the work of economic and social improvement; he saw this as advancing the Kingdom of God on earth. This is a kingdom of love, and this, Kagawa confessed, is what Jesus taught and what he himself believed. Love, he said, is the ultimate religion.

The distinctive contribution of the liberation theology of Latin America, and the theologies of Africa and Asia, along with their spiritual practices, testify to the universal appeal of Christianity. This hardly needs further justification in the light of the final commission of Jesus to his disciples, "Go unto all the world and make disciples of all nations." Christian theology is for ever theology in the making and the final shape of a global theology has yet to be formulated. But the theologies that have been referred to mirror the religious and cultural complex of their place of origin, as well as the living social and political issues they seek to answer. In all theologies there are elements of eternal truths, but these need to be communicated and applied in ways that are within the reach of the people to whom they are addressed. The focus has to be on how to nurture an ecumenical spirituality that intimately involves the realities of contemporary living in a rapidly changing world.

As the physical distance between continents and nations shrinks, will there develop a global theology adequate for the task of promoting universal harmonization at every level of human existence? And will this harmonization be achieved as the different theologies share together those insights that they have made so much their own?

Theological foundations

The norms of Christian theology remain fundamentally the same from age to age, and the developments in Christian theology and spirituality in the twentieth century have also to be assessed in relation to the Trinity of Father, Son and Holy Spirit. The century can boast a succession of theologians and philosophers who have produced many fresh insights into understanding religious thought and practice in a world of increasing secularization. The insights and theories have at times been startling and the subject of great public interest, as, for example, when *Honest to God* was published in 1963. John Robinson and other theologians of high calibre have adorned the age with their interpretations of fundamental Christian beliefs, but without exception they have all faced the problem of communicating theological truth effectively to the modern scientifically conditioned mind. This will become clear from an account of some of these leading theologians.

Absolute idealism

In the early years of the century the philosophy of idealism was reflected in the approach of some theologians to their task. J. R. Illingworth (1848–1915), a philosophical theologian and rector of Longworth, near Oxford, taught a philosophy of absolute idealism and linked this with experiential religion and the nurture of spirituality.[12] His theology was mainly orthodox, with an emphasis on the practice of Christianity as a living faith. Everyone is conscious of the divine within, but spirit and matter are distinct; yet religious experience is of wholeness in which spirit and matter combine. These two constituent components of the human self, Illingworth elucidated in his book *Divine Immanence*, whilst at the same time exposing the supremacy of the spiritual. Both matter and spirit are present within but the spiritual takes preference and directs matter for its own purposes.[13] The natural world is also interfused with the spiritual, and this led Illingworth to define his doctrine of divine immanence. It is a key to Illingworth's philosophy of life, for belief in divine immanence makes for the right ordering of life, and accounts for its unity.

The spiritual indwells the material but it also transcends it. God is transcendent and immanent and he is the source of the spiritual life, as he made known in the revelation of himself in Jesus Christ. Christ is the revelation of God, and the Spirit affirmed his filial relation to God; likewise as the same Spirit dwells within human beings they too bear a family relationship with God. God's revelation in Christ has assured that all may share the benefits of this relationship. Through Christ all may share a filial relationship with God the Father. This relationship unites human beings in thought, desire and will, and this reflects the unity of the Trinity between the Father, Son and Holy Spirit. This focus on the divine immanence is linked with the humanity of the historical Jesus who was himself the revelation of God. The human life of Jesus exemplified the infinite goodness of his physical nature and the unity of the physical and spiritual self.

The new theology

R. J. Campbell (1867–1956) was a Nonconformist preacher in London and one of the most controversial religious thinkers of his day. His views were both warmly supported and bitterly opposed. Campbell interpreted the biblical doctrine of the "Fall" as the descent of the life of God into the realm of finite beings. This descent or advent of God into the human domain was signally accomplished by Jesus. Jesus is, therefore, historically unique. Through his descent he represented to the world the highest ideals of morality and goodness. Through his advent the way is clear for human beings to ascend to living a life of moral perfection in perfect harmony with God. The awareness of God in every subconscious mind affirms the link between God and the self. The same awareness within every subconscious mind is a bond that unifies all people to be as one family. Campbell drew a distinction between the concept of divinity and humanity, but all beings have it within themselves to be as Christ was in character and behaviour. This potential for moral goodness is the consequence of the dwelling of the spirit of Christ within. Being partakers of the spirit of Christ, human beings can realize this potential to the uttermost. Jesus sacrificed his life on the cross out of love for all humankind so that the way is now open for them to enjoy communion with God. The Kingdom of God is also within and so is active in the present, but the Kingdom will be visible when everyone observes the standards of right over against wrong and works for justice in society.[14]

Campbell's teaching provoked much interest and public response, and there was wide discussion of this new rationalism. He came to be regarded as the leader of the modernist movement in theology. In this capacity he focused his attention on the modern critical and scientific approach to the study of the Bible. He rejected theories of verbal inspiration and literal truth. For this he was frequently credited with being a "progressive" theologian, especially when he propagated radical views and harshly attacked traditional conservative religion.[15] In the matter of church polity and worship, Campbell was seen as a rebel. He attributed a status and authority to rational and scientific knowledge that had previously been the prerogative of religion. He developed this liberalism in his book on *The New Theology* (1906), in which he wrote:

> The new theology . . . is primarily a moral and spiritual movement. It is one system of a great religious awakening which in the end will re-inspire civilization with a living faith in God and the spiritual meaning of life.

The "New Thought"

John Macquarrie includes in his trilogy of theological and religious writers of the early twentieth century R. W. Trine whom he describes as a theologian of the "New Thought". Trine was the author of works on religion and human behaviour, but his best-known work is probably *In Tune with the Infinite*. He equated God with the Spirit who is the great central fact of the universe and the power that is behind it, and that manifests itself in and through all. God is all-inclusive, all-sufficient, he wants for nothing, and his thought pervades the whole universe. Only in degree does God differ from human beings and they are able to partake of his divine life. Religion operates to bring people into harmony with God, and this conveys to the world a message of universal absolute idealism. This brings all people into a conscious unity with the infinite Spirit of God. It enables all people to approach and worship him, for God is everywhere present and active. Salvation works itself out for all people in this world, for the heart of the Christian message has a universal appeal. The theology of the "New Thought" has been described as "'translating' religion into terms of power available for daily use". This aptly conveys the practical rather than the philosophical outlook of Trine.

Reverence for life

This phrase sums up the spirituality of Albert Schweitzer (1875–1965), one of the most versatile figures of his age. Schweitzer was a distinguished German scholar, an accomplished musician, a medical doctor, theologian, philosopher and philanthropist. He served as a missionary doctor and was the founder of a hospital in Lambarene (now Gabor) in Africa. Here he developed his own style of spirituality, commonly known as "reverence for life".

In 1910 Schweitzer completed *The Quest of the Historical Jesus*, arguably the most provocative and productive work in theology of the time. Its main content is the author's doctrine of the person and work of Christ. Schweitzer tackled the question, *What can this Christ possibly have to do with the world of today?* He aimed to avoid the conventions of the past and the accretions of ecclesiological dogmatics and verbiage that have so clouded the true estimate of Jesus. Jesus was an enigma to his own contemporaries and lived among them as a stranger, but if he is to be comprehensible to modern people he has to be presented in contemporary language, concepts and thought forms. Christianity remains in the world as a robust and vital spiritual force and brings to it a stability that it would otherwise lack. The secret of this stability is dynamic love, which is the heart of Christianity. Schweitzer wrote:

> The essence of Christianity is world affirmation which has gone through an experience of world negation. In the eschatological world view of world negation, Jesus proclaims the ethic of active love.[16]

All life is lived in relation to the natural world and this may be in either an active or a passive way. An active relationship with the natural world influences it in positive ways, but a passive relationship is inactive and succumbs to things as they are. Human beings are endowed with the freedom and capacity to perform actions that are world transforming. The dynamic of such world-transforming action is love, and Christianity teaches that love is expressed through compassion towards all people and every living creature. This is the way of showing "reverence for life". Action of this order is the antidote that prevents civilization from disintegrating and saves morality from becoming moribund. The moral imperative of loving compassion gives dignity to human life and all living creatures, it respects everything that lives and does no harm to any living thing. Such compassionate action is the surest guarantee of the survival of civilization, and it is incumbent that human beings should perform such acts of this order, which they alone

of all living creatures are equipped to perform. Through the performance of acts of love and goodness people come to realize the nature of
truth and what it means. Truth is that which can be relied upon
absolutely. Whoever understands the nature and meaning of truth takes
up an active stance on the issues and problems that arise, and works to
resolve them. People of all conditions have an active involvement with
current issues and are equipped with the resources for dealing with
them. The engagement is global and the action inclusive of every living
thing.

The mandate Schweitzer claimed for this thesis was the teaching and
example of Jesus. Jesus displayed love and compassion for all people
irrespective of their status, and he also showed respect for the world in
which he lived. In other words, Jesus showed "reverence for life". He
nurtured the spiritual life in others and pointed the direction of spiritual progress to the goal of self-fulfilment. Jesus demonstrated that love
is world affirming; he projected love as the distinguishing quality of
civilization, and showed that love is the motivation of civilized advancement. He imparted his legacy of love as a means of fostering still further
civilized progress. Schweitzer discerned in the teaching and life-style of
Jesus universal love and reverence for life. This reverence was all-
inclusive of thought and emotion and the whole of human experience.
It permeated the spiritual and the natural realms.[17] Compassion of this
order is the pervasive dimension of all authentic action, and is equated
with the teaching of Jesus himself.

Theology of the Word

During the inter-war years, Karl Barth (1886–1968) towered above
others as Europe's leading theologian. He was a distinguished professor
of theology whose ideas had a profound effect on the testimony of the
German Confessional Church in its struggle against the Nazi ideology.
His theology came to be known as the theology of the "Word of God"
on account of its roots in the divine revelation of the Bible. The supreme
revelation of God is Jesus Christ in whom salvation alone is centred.
Christ is the revelation of God's grace, and grace is that which transforms lives and leads to faith. Human transformation is the work of
grace mediated through Christ, and only irrational thought rejects this
truth.

Barth's doctrine had a great influence on young church pastors, and
his twelve volumes of *Dogmatics*, the final part of which appeared in
1967, make Barth the most voluminous of the twentieth-century

theologians. He wrestled with many ethical issues and probed the profound theological problems which surround some of the most intractable questions human beings ask. Barth's deep sensitivity and spiritual approach to theological questions is the fruit of his years as a parish pastor on the frontiers of Switzerland. He challenged an easy-going Christianity to come to grips with the real significance of the moral and ethical dilemmas that people confront; he denounced the facile optimism that only treated superficially life's deepest questions. He took a sombre view of humanity's plight and dilated on the fragility and perilousness of human existence. From beyond the boundaries of this world there is transmitted the Word of God to bring to the world a new power, the power of salvation. Herein is the world's hope.

Barth identified himself with the German Confessional Church, but he was expelled from Germany when he refused to take an oath of allegiance to Hitler. Hitler deprived him of his university professorship, but in 1935 he accepted the chair of theology at Basle. He wrote numerous letters from Basle to encourage Christians in their struggle against Nazism, to impress on them how unequivocal allegiance to the faith would eventually triumph, and urged them to keep alive their Christian hope. Barth's theology was forged against a spiritually hostile world yet it dominated and sustained the faith and spirituality of vast numbers of believers. Barth expounded afresh the basic doctrines of Christian faith, especially the doctrine of creation and election, and the incarnation of the Son of God.

He presented Christianity as a genuine form of humanism. Human beings are precious and greatly loved because they are of worth to God and can be reconciled to him through the transforming operation of his grace. God enters into a personal relationship with humankind, as the Bible makes known, through his mighty acts of grace. Grace is uniquely the action of God, it requires no confirmation from whatever source there may be, philosophical or dialectical; the Word of God itself is self-sufficient:

> because it has been given us by God's revelation to know him, and what we previously thought we knew about originations and causes is called in question, turned around and transformed.[18]

Barth regarded the discipline of theology very highly; it is different from religion, for religion is something human, whereas theology is God talk, that is, the understanding of the nature of God. His spirituality is infused with joy, so that:

The special element to be noted and considered is that the glory of God is not only great and sublime or holy and gracious, the overflowing of the sovereignty in which God is love. In all this it is a glory that awakens joy and is itself joyful ... Joy in and before God ... It is something in God, the God of all the perfections, which justifies us in having joy, desire and pleasure towards him ... [19]

Barth fulfilled many roles, as prophet, professor, theologian, politician and patriarch. But he found spiritual refreshment in music and wide reading, and it has been said that no one could have a complete picture of Barth's spiritual nature without referring to his love for the music of Wolfgang Amadeus Mozart, about whose work he wrote in rapturous terms:

> Why is it that this man is so incomparable? Why is it that for the receptive, he has produced in almost every bar he conceived and composed a type of music for which "beautiful" is not a fitting epithet, music which for the true Christian is not mere entertainment, enjoyment or edification, but food and drink; music spelling comfort and counsel for his needs ... It is possible to give him this position because he knew something about creation in its total goodness ... Mozart enables us to hear that creation praises its master and is therefore perfect.[20]

Mythology reviewed

Among the notable Christian theologians of the twentieth century who have contributed also to the spiritual tradition we should mention Rudolph Bultmann (1884–1976), whose main contribution has been to the exposition of the New Testament and the message of the early Christian community. This, according to Bultmann, bore witness to the living Christ, resurrected and acting continually within the Church. The Church experiences the efficacy of the cross and resurrection of Christ by taking them into its own life. The experience continues to vitalize the life of the Church. Bultmann's work attracted considerable attention as he tackled the question of myth and reality.

The documents of the New Testament, Bultmann assumed, are not historical in the usual sense, but the records of the preaching of the primitive Christian kerygma in the language, conceptions, imagery and mythology of their own times. These images and myths are alien to the modern scientific mind and, therefore, if this primitive preaching is to be made meaningful, intelligible and relevant, it has to be stripped of its antiquated mythology. This will make clear and intelligible the real message of Jesus and the apostles, and show how the living Christ encounters people today. Christ can only be known through personal encounter, or in the context of existential thinking and experience.

Bultmann's views have exerted considerable influence in the west as a radical attempt to make the Christian message meaningful to contemporary people. But his views have also been contested as denuding the Christian revelation of its historical origins and marginalizing some of its basic concepts. His theories have brought into sharp perspective the question of Christian origins and the validity of the traditional presentation of the life of the historical Jesus and the preaching of the apostles. The controversy has centred around the historical Jesus of Nazareth and the Christ of faith. Other theologians have followed the Bultmann line or modified it in different ways.

Bultmann challenged the Church and theology with the personal question of making Christian faith accessible to the modern mind through stripping it of outmoded mythological thought forms and antiquated concepts. Too many of these have been perpetuated into modern and contemporary times. Directing his thought against the foibles of tradition, Bultmann's serious aim was to help believers correct their own projections. According to Bultmann this "existential" interpretation offers a new perspective on Christian belief without it being shackled by first-century imagery and mythology or being literally bound by ancient credal statements. Bultmann confronted the difficult question of the appropriate language for reinterpreting the Christian myth. He also expounded the nature of human life and how to conceptualize its form and structure in meaningful terms. Understanding the nature of human life needs to be related to the patterns of existential thought. Doing this presents everyone with a choice: to choose a way either of authentic or of inauthentic existence.[21] At the heart of the Christian story is the death and resurrection of Jesus Christ, and by taking the meaning of these into personal life their inner significance becomes known, and this is the ground of authentic existence. This assimilation is an "eschatological event", i.e., the moment when understanding and meaning become luminous. Such a moment isn't confined to past historical happenings but is the essence of every decision faith makes, every proclamation of the truth, and every celebration of the sacraments.[22]

The "depth of existence"

Paul Tillich (1886–1965) was born in Germany but became an American citizen in 1940 and later was a professor at Harvard University. He is among the theologians who have given a specific direction to Christian theology during the twentieth century. In particular, he endeavoured to relate theology to existential thought and depth psychology. In this context he discussed the truth and actuality of theological concepts and taught that God is "being itself", or is "the power to be". Tillich wrote about the "depth of existence" and moulded his presentation of Christian theology and faith into a comprehensive philosophical system. His method was that of "correlation", used as a method of stating Christian truth in answering questions that arise out of the conditions of modern culture.

Many testing questions are raised by the contemporary culture and there is no way to answer them satisfactorily except from the angle of divine revelation. When the question of God, for instance, is raised there is an answer to this in revelation. Revelation provides a meaningful answer, for God is not a projection in outer space or beyond the skies, of whose existence humans need to be persuaded or convinced, but rather God is "the Ground of our being". Asking the question of God inevitably makes the individual aware of being a finite being, yet with a concern to find the "ultimate ground of being". The name of this "ultimate ground of being" is God. The individual is only able to participate in what is ultimately real or what is beyond all existent objects through encounter with "the ground of our being", that is, encounter with God who is immanent. Everything else that may be said about God is symbolic; even to speak of God as personal, loving, just or living, means to traverse the realm of the symbols themselves. These symbols or qualities, together with joy, hope and truth, find their meaning in God.

God is known in Jesus through revelation as "the man from above"; Jesus is the "true man". In Jesus the distance and the forces that separate human beings from God are overcome. Jesus is the power from beyond who wipes out the superstition and the human sin that alienate people from God, and so he heals the conflicts and meets the human quest for discovering the "ultimate ground of being".[23]

Religionless Christianity

One of the Christian theologians who caught the public attention and who is acknowledged as an influential spiritual guru of the twentieth century is the revered Dietrich Bonhoeffer (1906–45). The story of his eventful life as a pastor, theologian, tutor, politician, opponent of Hitlerism, freedom champion, inmate of Flossenburg and martyr, is widely known. His writings have received wide circulation, and some of his memorable phrases such as the "God-shaped gap" in the make-up of modern persons, and "religionless Christianity", have been much publicized. He met Karl Barth for the first time in 1931, and his thought owed much to the seminal thinking of Barth. As a young man Bonhoeffer offered staunch resistance to the Nazi policy towards the Church in Germany and the appointment of a commission for church affairs. Along with Martin Niemöller and others he stood against the "nazification" of the Church, and demanded its reform. He served for a period as chaplain to the Lutheran Church in London and then returned to Germany in 1935 to become head of the seminary of the Confessing Church at Firkenwalde. However, the seminary was closed in 1937, and Bonhoeffer was banned from teaching. When the "Confessing Church" came into being in 1934, Bonoeffer soon became one of its most distinguished leaders. He subscribed to the articles of his church, which included:

> Jesus Christ, as he is testified to us in Holy Scripture, is the one Word of God which we are to hear, which we are to trust and obey in life and death. We refuse the false teaching that the Church can and must recognise yet other happenings and powers, personalities and truths, as divine revelation alongside his one Word of God, as the source of her preaching.[24]

He was arrested and imprisoned in 1943 on suspicion of having plotted against Hitler. On 8 April 1945 Bonhoeffer preached a sermon to his fellow prisoners on the text, "Through his wounds we are healed." After this he was ordered by the SS guards to follow them. As he did so he asked another prisoner to give a message to Bishop Bell of Chichester: "Tell him that for me this is the end but also the beginning." He was hanged the following day. Later the camp doctor wrote:

> I saw Pastor Bonhoeffer before taking off his prison garb, kneeling on the floor praying fervently to his God. I was most deeply moved . . . I have hardly ever seen a man die so entirely submissive to the will of God.

The foregoing reference to theological tendencies during the twentieth century gives some indication of the variety of matters treated. The treatment has sometimes received unprecedented publicity and won public interest on account of the sensational pronouncements made about belief in God. The public interest created by the publication of *Honest to God* (1963) by John Robinson, Bishop of Woolwich, which became an immediate best-seller, is evidence of how deeply religious topics stir the emotions. Robinson dealt with the same question as had agitated Rudolph Bultmann, namely, how to communicate the Christian gospel in a meaningful way to people today. The traditional and popular image of God as "a being out there" must go, contended Robinson, and, in the same vein as Dietrich Bonhoeffer, he pleaded for a Christianity relieved of the accumulated baggage of traditional forms and images that hindered its progress, and he aimed to formulate a theology and morality motivated solely by *agape* (love).[25]

Alongside the trend publicized by the *Honest to God* theology we may mention the radicalism of the theologians of the *Death of God* movement. This movement is ably represented by Paul von Buren whose book *Secular Meaning of the Gospel* (1963) contributed powerfully to current theological discussion. The work is a penetrating exposition of Christian belief expressed in contemporary language and thought forms. The author contended that in an age when many people have rejected belief in God and transcendence, or find such belief difficult, it is important to present a gospel that is "honest to God". Paul von Buren maintained that the secular gospel is a way of speaking about life in a contemporary idiom but also from the perspective of Jesus of Nazareth.[26]

As if to provide an antidote to the theologies of "religionless Christianity", the "Death of God" and the "secular gospel", which received much attention during the sixties, a series of theological works was produced which centred on the theme of hope as implicit within the Christian understanding of God. The works of J. Moltmann, *The Theology of Hope* (1967), and W. Pannenberg, *Jesus, God and Man* (1968), are among works that John Macquarrie has termed "Theologies of Hope".[27] Christian hope is not other worldly; it has a focus in the present world as it actually is, it applies both to the present and future of the world. The resurrection of Christ is an historical event that engenders realistic hope both for the present as well as for life beyond death. This hope has a powerful social emphasis and inspires engagement in the sphere of public and political action. The roots of Christian hope are in the revelation of the Bible; the dominant categories of the Bible are promise and fulfilment, and God's promise to his people fulfilled through his action on their behalf. The message inspires hope that what God promises he is sure to fulfil. These outgoing and communal components of Christian hope provide an alternative concept to the individualism of, for example, the eschatology of Bultmann. In fact, these theologies of hope are a break away from the individualism that is characteristic of much of twentieth-century Christian theology.[28]

Pilgrim of the future

In 1959 a formidable work of spirituality and philosophy by a French Jesuit was acclaimed as a "A landmark in thought. Possibly the book of the century". In the following ten years, more than fifteen hundred books were written about Teilhard de Chardin (1882–1955), who had spent most of his life exploring pre-history. The book that was received with enthusiasm by specialists and the public at large was *The Human Phenomenon* (*Le phénomène humain*), incorrectly translated as *The Phenomenon of Man*. Its author has been called "a pilgrim of the future", for he grappled with the question, *"How are we to think of what is emerging for the future and control it?"* In response he asserted, "that to progress towards God does not mean that one must turn one's back on the world".[29]

Teilhard has also been described by his biographers as a mystic, a naturalist of the open air, and a man of God. He tackled some of the major problems of our age, notably the conflict between science and religion, and although he never claimed to have resolved the conflict (he acknowledged, "I have gone astray at many points. It is up to others to do better"), nevertheless he pointed to the many parallels between science and religion. The one, he said, elucidates the other; reconciliation between them is a ground of hope for the future; the need to synchronize the one with the other is the way to secure the future of the human race and ally it with its ancient past, and prove to the world that science and religion each have a meaningful role that bears one on the other:

> Religion, science, reason – are not these the three teachers of humanity, the three persons that even today struggle for control of the moral world? And even today are we not asking ourselves which of these three is to overcome and subjugate the others – or whether they may be brought together in a lasting and beneficent harmony.[30]

Teilhard also taught a doctrine of man which developed from the experience of the child and its first vision of light. This vision provides a comparison with the vision of the past, which is often one of confusion and of unidentified objects. We see things all jumbled up, yet "To decipher the nature of man is to decipher the world." Human beings are migrants by nature but on a planet that is round they keep on meeting; there is "human convergence", inter-marriage, inter-breeding, a convergence of thought and desire, continuous communication; here human beings form tribes, communities and nations. A process of socialization is at work, and this is a means of drawing humankind and the world together in a single whole.

This signifies, for Teilhard, that everything has an inside and an outside, that deep within ourselves there is an "interior", and since nature also has an interior or "inner aspect at one point of itself" this makes possible a co-existence between the "within" and the "without" of things.

When the Christian understands "the inexpressibly wonderful work that is being carried on around him, and by him", the Christian is able to appreciate "the value of sacred evolution" and "the eternal hopes it contains". This eternal hope – bred of an inbuilt capacity to unite – is the product of love, the property of all forms of life, and the noblest quality the human being knows.

Amorization (Teilhard's term for expressing the capacity to love) depends on the coming together of all forms of life. In answer to the question, Who is to give direction to this process, or who is "the moving Principle and the all-embracing Nucleus of the World itself? Who is this God for whom our generation looks so eagerly?", Teilhard asserted, "Who but you, Jesus, who represents him, and bring him to us . . . Lord of consistence and union . . . 'evolver' and 'evolving' . . . are henceforth the only being who can satisfy us."

This view of Jesus, who represents God and brings him to us, expresses the purpose of revelation, but Jesus is not some added extra; rather, "He is the Alpha and the Omega, the Principle and the God, the foundation and the keystone . . . He is the one who consummates and the one who gives consistence to all things."[31] This is the evidence of the incarnation of Christ, for incarnation means making new, restoring all the universe's forces and powers. This meaning of the Christ event as the restoration of the forces and powers of the universe as they are intended to be, assumes that the world is progressing towards a destination, an "Omega point"; as the world had a beginning, so it also has an end. All that exists converges on that Omega point. This is the heart of Teilhard's spirituality, as he wrote to a friend:

> To love life so much, and to trust it so completely, that we embrace it and throw ourselves into it even in death – that is the only attitude that can calm and purify you: to love extravagantly what is greater than yourself. Every union, especially with a greater power, involves a kind of death of the self. Death is acceptable only if it represents the necessary passage towards a union, the condition of metamorphosis.[32]

Waiting on God

In the same year as the publication of *The Human Phenomenon* there was published a book that also contributed significantly to the moulding of twentieth-century Christian spirituality. Simone Weil (1909–43) was a French philosopher, who was equally proficient in literature and mathematics. Her short life of thirty-four years was varied and arduous. She worked on the land and in factories and took part in the Spanish Civil War. She was involved in social and political action, especially on behalf of the oppressed. Her outlook on life is summed up in the saying, "I am a human being, and I count nothing human as alien to me." Her view of Christianity is expressed clearly in her book, *Waiting on God* (1959):

> Christianity should contain all vocations without exception since it is catholic. Consequently the Church should also. But in my eyes Christianity is right by right and not in fact. So many things are outside it, so many things that I love and do not want to give up, so many things that God loves, otherwise they would not be in existence.[33]

Simone had a profound belief in God and especially in God's otherness or transcendence. God's sovereignty is unassailable and his supreme value is beyond the ability of anyone to demonstrate or define.

Those who claimed to know God are deluded, yet by a sort of miracle, God, the transcendent, can be known.[34] The miracle was Simone's discovery that in a time of suffering she experienced the presence of Christ, "a presence more personal, more certain, and more real than that of any human being". This did not mean that she embraced any particular form of Christian orthodoxy, indeed, talk of orthodoxies seemed repellent to her. Rather she saw the religious implications of all her concerns as being pregnant with value and purpose. But central to her religious awareness is the suffering of Christ. Deeply conscious of and moved by the brutality around her, Simone believed that Christ who suffered on the cross reaches out to all suffering humankind. If it were not for the cross, Christianity is no more than an empty dream. The cross brings the divine reality of love into the human soul at the point of greatest need. This is the essence of Simone's mysticism – the love of the cross of Christ transmitting itself to dwell within the human soul. In this sense Simone may be called a mystic, but she still remained active within the physical world. She speculated much on how the gulf between the God "within" and the need of the world could be bridged. Herein is a paradox (the holy and majestic God can only be spoken of in terms of paradox): God's presence is darkness, and yet he appears whenever human thought has reached its limits.[35] Being aware of this paradox leads to self-renunciation, the state wherein the soul becomes open to divine love:

> To empty ourselves of our false divinity, to deny ourselves, to give up the centre of the world in imagination, to discern that all points in the world are equally centres and that the true centre is outside the world, this is to consent to the role of mechanical necessity in matter and of free choice at the centre of each soul. Such consent is love.[36]

As we mentioned earlier, Simone Weil did not take kindly to Christian orthodoxy; she did not formally join the Church; yet she lived a life of devotion, she prayed, attended mass; she practised self-denial and fasted. She suffered much, but found love at the centre of her pain. Her God was a God of love who worked amidst and within the suffering of the world. She also worked tirelessly within and for the world, and it has been said of her that her theology was not a secular theology but a theology of the secular.

Spiritual guides

It has been the underlying assumption of this work that theology and spirituality in the Christian tradition belong indissolubly together. We need now to broaden the discussion further so as to include some notable persons and communities of the twentieth century who have enhanced the spiritual tradition by their teaching and practices. They can be no more than a representative few who nevertheless illustrate the major trends in recent developments in the concept and nurture of Christian spirituality.

Thomas Merton

Thomas Merton (1915–68) is best known for his book *Seven Storey Mountain* (1948), one of the classics of spirituality of our time. Merton was born in France but lived in America. In 1941 he entered a Trappist monastery in Kentucky, where the strictest of monastic rules are observed and the vow of silence is compulsory. Here the Benedictine Rule of prayer, sacred reading and labour is faithfully followed. Merton developed a deep love for the contemplative life but he also acquired a distaste for some elements. His autobiography describes the inner and outer friction he experienced and how he was led to becoming a hermit. He received permission to establish his own house, which he called Our Lady of Carmel.

Here he devoted himself to reading the lives of the Catholic saints, particularly the works of John of the Cross, Teresa of Avila and Julian of Norwich. He engaged regularly in meditation and began to explore the relationship between Buddhist and Christian meditation. This opened his mind to the special nature and content of eastern religions, and he devoted himself henceforth to examining what Christians might learn from these.

Merton described the nurture of spirituality as a long and exacting journey which leads slowly to discovery of the true self, the discarding of the mask of pretensions, and letting go and resting back in the security of love that gives and does not strive to get, that is always creative and positive. The two practices that dominate the spirituality of Merton are prayer and solitude. Prayer is the means of finding God, but there are no set techniques for doing this. Nor is there a set answer to the difficulties of prayer. Prayer is being humble and open in the presence of God and abandoned to the "life and death" question which God asks. Prayer is not a way of escape from the "tragic anguish" or the questions that are "like wounds that cannot be healed". Rather prayer unites the soul with God when the deepest self within is at one with the "Risen and Deathless Christ". As the self engages in the journey of prayer the self is lost, it becomes "the self in God, the self bigger than death yet born of death. It is the self the Father for ever loves."[37] This love extends to the whole person and the totality of relationships, it fashions the formulation of the true self and gives it its true identity. It represents the whole person before God; it is through prayer that the self discovers its "deepest reality", the self that really prays is the true self, and it has been said:

> The spirituality of Thomas Merton centers upon the fact that the whole of the spiritual life finds its fulfilment in bringing an entire life into a transforming, loving communion with the ineffable God.[38]

Everyone is engaged in the spiritual life and the quest for knowledge of the true self as a child of Adam, but they also struggle to find release from this self in order to grow into the life of Christ. Prayer is the turning away from the false self to God, for "Ultimately the only way that I can be myself is to become identified with Him in whom is hidden the reason and fulfilment of my existence."[39] The encounter with God takes place in the world, for this is where God meets persons in Christ.

Therefore Christians should cultivate respect for the world, the physical life, work, friends and everyday experiences.

The world is God's and everyone is part of God's world, but the world is not simply "out there", for Jesus took the world upon himself, he submitted to it in death on the cross, and now he calls Christians to share it with him so that they might share in his eternal life. Christ served the world in many ways, but supremely by his death, and prayer is a vital sharing of his death whereby the believer passes from death to life. To realize this requires faith, for faith is a bond that unites, it is the gift of the Holy Spirit given in Christ. Faith is also a gift of hope, and faith and hope find their fulfilment in love. The perfect union with God is not the fusion of two natures but a unity of love.

Along with his life of prayer, Merton lived out his life in solitude and silence. He wrote of solitude as the opportunity of disappearing with God, and conceived of this as the most forbearing silence. Silence is like a "sacramental force" calling from the midst of things: "be still and know that I am God". Spiritual discipline produces "something of the silence . . . if the inner self is to make some strong, unpredictable manifestation of his (God's) presence".

Through silence it is possible to discover the heart of the world and be drawn into communion with others. There is a silence within that hears only in silence, and which points to that self that speaks in silence and through which God grants that mysterious "something" that is born of silence. Silence makes possible being one with life and one with God. Yet to be silent is exacting, for silence is not a form of inertia.

Merton was convinced that God had called him to a life of prayer and silence. His spirituality is the story of a soul en route to an immediate, all-pervasive and direct experience of God. The words of Meister Eckhart might well apply to Merton, "Nothing in all creation is so like God as silence." Silence was essential to Merton's spiritual growth, but what went on in the silence was far more important. Silence is not the absence of noise, it is an absorbing personal quality, the inward seeking that finds God, the condition that makes accessible the inflow of God's power. The practice of silence requires nurturing and direction; it is on account of his guidance on cultivating the life of the spirit that Thomas Merton so perceptively set down in his spiritual autobiography that he is ranked as one of the outstanding spiritual guides of recent times.

Teresa of Calcutta

During her lifetime Mother Teresa of Calcutta (1910–97) was greatly respected for her spirituality and her sanctity. She devoted her life as a nun to the service of the poorest and most deprived people of India whom she cared for with loving devotion. She said she saw the image of Christ in the suffering of a child and in the face of a dying person. She declared, "In each suffering person you can see Jesus." Her work has been described as the most beautiful thing a person can do for God. Her action on behalf of the poor was not born of dismay or rage or distrust of political ideology, but out of something deep within herself, that is, from divine love which is the source of all genuinely compassionate action. Mother Teresa incorporated within herself the continuity between the devout religious life of the nun and that of practical service as a missioner to the world. She was equipped spiritually to take on the task of ministering to the poor in a predominantly non-Christian city. She answered, through her painstaking ministry to the sick and the dying, this question, *How does Christ relate to the people today?*

She pointed others in the direction of "doing something beautiful for Jesus". She wrapped this practical mission in the Catholic tradition of mystical prayer and complete obedience to her Church. Teresa was a tireless worker amongst abandoned children, rejected wives and the sick and dying in the streets, but she never visualized herself as a social worker or someone engaged in the work of social rehabilitation. She employed in the most efficient way the gifts she knew God had given her. She aimed to verify the gospel not in words and speech but by being ready "to love until it hurts". This she saw as the essence of Christianity, being attentive to God by spoon feeding a sick person or touching a leper or succouring a dying child. This was her vocation and she was not at liberty ever to relinquish it.

Mother Teresa founded the order known as the Missionaries of Charity whose work spread to a hundred countries. She lived a simple life and she and her nuns took no payment for their work. They followed the strict way of life of a nunnery – early rising, morning prayers, celebrating the mass, and then out among the poor and needy. As mentioned above, Teresa was devoted to the Catholic Church, was orthodox in her beliefs, obedient to the authority of the pope. She was a great inspiration to many people, and in 1979 she won the Nobel Prize for Peace, but she used the money this brought to carry on her work. Through her example she showed how the spiritual path she followed can be attained by others. In the service of love there are no restrictions. Through the performance of such service there is a great release of divine power. Her motive was conveyed in her own saying:

Let no one ever come to you without going away better and happier.

Basil Hume

In 1984 Basil Hume (1923–99), Cardinal Archbishop of Westminster, published a "spiritual notebook" entitled, *To Be a Pilgrim*, which the author declared was concerned with the spiritual life, its principles and practices. Basil Hume was a notable spiritual leader of the Roman Catholic Church in Britain, but his influence spread far beyond his own community. He was looked up to as their inspirational spiritual leader by people of many different beliefs. Hume was a Benedictine monk attached to Ampleforth Abbey who became Archbishop and a spiritual and religious leader of national importance. His motto was that faith should be lived openly as well as in private, and that everyone should aim to fulfil its moral implications and responsibilities.

The energizing force of Basil Hume's spirituality was prayer. Prayer, he said, is like being in a room in the presence of God. He defined prayer as, "trying to raise our minds and hearts to God". This involves being quiet, concentrating the mind on God and being aware of his closeness. He wrote:

> So praying is trying to be aware of God, and being aware of Him is to desire Him, to want Him. As I desire Him more and more then I become increasingly more aware.[40]

Along with this Hume offered guidance on ways to pray, on planning to pray, on the effects of prayer, and on the golden rules for prayer. He urged perseverance in prayer, conscious that sometimes there are periods when prayer is difficult, but that this is when God comes to give aid and encouragement. So perseverance is necessary. If there are distractions these too can be turned into prayer.

Observance of the sacraments also promotes spirituality. In the celebration of the mass the mystery of Christ's passion, death and resurrection is made real. But this belief comes from faith, "from the humility of mind to accept and to say 'yes' to what may seem to be unbelievable, namely, that the Body and Blood of Christ is present under the appearances of bread and wine". The mass should be celebrated with dignity, reverence and in a prayerful manner, so that there is created a sense of being in the presence of the holy.

A further aspect of Cardinal Hume's spiritual guidance is the cultivation of holiness. He asked, "How do we live out the full implications of being a son or daughter of the father, a brother or sister of Jesus Christ, a temple in which the Holy Spirit dwells?" The answer given is to become more Christ-like, to be sensitive to the promptings of the

Holy Spirit, to cultivate friendship with God, to live according to the values of the Kingdom of God, to make time for prayer and to be alone with God, to observe the sacraments as powerful means of satisfaction.[41]

As a spiritual guide Cardinal Hume counselled the pilgrim in the search for a right direction. There is in everyone something deep that drives them to search for spiritual wholeness. This is akin to hunger for God or a longing for meaning, for an explanation of existence, and an answer to life's diverse experiences. This is a search for God and is only one way of speaking of our response to God's search for us. God's search is evidenced in the incarnation of Christ, who showed what God means to those who seek him and what they mean to God. In the sacrifice of Christ, through which God made all things new, and through the power of his resurrection, those who seek him are assured of the defeat of death and the gift of eternal life.[42]

A final aspect of his spiritual guidance concerns suffering and eternal life. On this Hume wrote:

> When people are in great physical pain or mental anguish, they are unable to pray until they find out that in it all Our Lord is with them. I am sure that the only prayer a dying person is capable of is to kiss the wounds of Jesus Christ.

Death for the Christian is the moment of ecstasy which perfects the vision of God, the entry into ultimate union with that which is most loveable, namely, union with God, the unending "now" of perfect happiness.[43]

Guidance in prayer

Prayer is universally received as one of the essential elements of Christian spirituality, and the twentieth century has witnessed a succession of spiritual leaders who have provided guidance and given direction to the development of prayerful spirituality.

In 1974 Mark Gibbard published a small book called *Twentieth Century Men of Prayer*, which tells of twelve spiritual guides who have helped others to find their own way of praying and encouraged and instructed them in the practice of prayer.[44] Gibbard quotes the definition of Augustine Baker, "The spiritual guide is not to teach his own way, but to instruct others how they may themselves find out the proper way for them." We have already referred to the contribution of some of these twentieth-century men of prayer to our study of spirituality (Bonhoeffer, Teilhard, Merton, Weil), but we need to refer briefly to the guidance given by some other worthy spiritual guides. Friedrich von Hugel (1852–1925), "a convinced and open minded Christian", is a representative man of his age; his scientific, empirical outlook, along with his respect for the autonomy of secular studies, his practice of contemplation, and his faith in the transcendent, characterize him as a leading thinker of his day. He did not find it easy to analyse the meaning of the phrase, "the life of prayer", but he believed in the necessity of prayer and that prayer begins with God himself who is "a stupendously rich Reality". God is near, otherwise he is of no use; authentic prayer embraces and interprets the whole of life. Prayer is essentially a personal activity, an existential relationship with God; it should encompass all human interests and contain not only those that are religious; prayer is also a corporate act to be shared with others in the Church.[45] Prayer is the apprehension of the revelation of God and this is made possible through the sacraments and ritual of the Church.

Michael Quoist is the author of *Prayers for Life* (1954), a collection of prayers which received wide circulation mainly on account of their being prayers that arise out of the concrete situations of everyday living and contemporary life. The author contends that prayer should represent before God the ordinary and commonplace expressed spontaneously in personal rather than liturgical language. Prayer should be natural and not forced, there should be a time for prayer as much as for eating. Quoist described prayer as "dialogue with Christ", that is, meeting, talking, and loving him as part of daily activity. Every day should begin with prayer as this gives help to get through the day; at the end of the day all that has been done during the day should be reviewed, and this then should lead spontaneously to prayer. Such prayer is inclusive of four dimensions – praise, thanksgiving, penance and petition. Apart from this, there should be regular time for prayer so that a rhythm of contemplative prayer might develop, on the assumption that:

To contemplate God is to look at him and love him.[46]

Quoist's guidance has often been questioned, but it does guard against prayer being a mere formality or convention. It provides an alternative view of liturgical prayer and an approach that brings the act of praying into the arena of living concerns. It gives prayer a greater personal validity and vitality, and stresses the need to be more human in praying. By not being restricted to set liturgical practice, or to religious or churchy language, prayer can be more all-embracing of life's experiences. When the structures of prayer are related to live experiences, prayer assumes a greater relevance and necessity.

Anthony Bloom was ordained as a priest of the Russian Orthodox Church in 1948 and rose to be the Metropolitan of his church. In 1971 he published *God and Man*, which tells us how his real life of faith began. Prayer, he contended, can only be known from the "inside", "the experience of prayer can only be known from the inside and is not to be dallied with". Prayer is a serious matter, and even in personal prayers there should be the awe, wonder and beauty that characterize the liturgy of the Church. Prayer is an adventure, and the words used should be chosen with care and said with deep and real meaning. The words should express what is in the heart, otherwise the words are barren. Words should not break the intimacy with God: unless words have within them a depth of silence they are shallow and tiresome. Silence can give depth and reality to praying, it wraps it in the divine presence. Prayer is commitment, and no one can pray for others who is not willing to help, that is, prayer is offering the totality of life to God. The Jesus prayer ("Lord Jesus Christ, Son of God, have mercy on me, a sinner") is a revelation of the life of prayer, it focuses attention on the living God of love; through prayer the apprehension of Jesus Christ continues to grow, that is, "It is the living God, that every human soul from millennium to millennium is in search of," and prayer is engagement in this search.[47]

Communities of spirituality

Christian spirituality is both personal and social. Individuals cultivate their own personal spirituality, whilst at the same time having a part in the community of Christians where spirituality is perfected. From its inception the Church has sought to coordinate the development of personal and communal spirituality through the experience of community in which individuals can relate to each other as they relate to Christ. The early church of the apostles was a fellowship of "communionism" where its members "had all things in common". Throughout the centuries Christians have formed communities or orders or groupings for the purpose of promoting community spirituality through a common life of doctrine and service or through retreats or other means. The twentieth century has continued this tradition in a modern setting, as we see from two contemporary communities of spirituality.

Taize

Taize in France is the home of an ecumenical spiritual community which was founded by Roger Schutz and Max Thurien in 1949. Both Protestants and Catholics are members of the community, which is organized as a semi-monastic order. Christians of the Eastern Orthodox tradition also have contributed to the community and shared in its activities. It is the outstanding example of ecumenical community spirituality in the twentieth century. Roger Schutz became a convinced Christian as a young man, but he was also deeply disturbed by the divisions within the Christian Church. He had a vocation to the ministry of the Church and studied theology in Lausanne, but he was convinced that God had called him to revive the monastic life and establish a monastic community. He was attracted to the strength and force of the monastic tradition in Christianity and believed it could become strong again. He committed himself to restoring to the Church a vital resource of spirituality he believed it had lost or rejected.

But first he had to immerse himself in the essential principles and aims of monasticism and be prepared to translate and implement these in a modern ecumenical context. Such an order had to be open to Christians of all traditions from all over the world and also to both men and women. The order had to be truly ecumenical in spirit and organization where Christians could worship, work and live together and be a focus of reconciliation for the whole world. Prayer and reliance on the Holy Spirit was to be the driving force of the community. But it was not to be isolated from the world. The idea of founding such a community was in Schutz's mind as early as 1940, but as France was occupied by the Nazis, it was not until 1944 that he was able to return to Taize, in Burgundy, ready to lay the foundations of an embryonic, ecumenical spiritual community. Five members joined, made their vows, and professed allegiance to the community in 1949, and a "rule" for the community was formed in 1952–3 by Roger Schutz, who became prior of the order:

The Rule of the Community:

> We go to live with them in slums above all in order to ... turn a run-down shack into a place inhabited by a Presence. Immersing ourselves in slums means sharing the same conditions as they do and waiting with them for an event from God for their people. That Christ may grow in me, I must know my own weakness and that of my brothers. For them I will become all things to all, and even give my life, for Christ's sake and the Gospel's.

One of the aims of the Taize Community from the commencement is
to be an ecumenical community in its organization, administration and
work. Roman Catholics and Protestants have an equal involvement in
all aspects of the community's life. The local Catholic Church was used
for working until a new chapel was built in 1962 by young Germans of
a reconciliation movement, Cakon Subnezeichen. This was a gesture
of national reconciliation on their part after the divisions of the Second
World War, but also a tangible expression of reconciliation between
divided religious traditions. Roman Catholic, Protestant and Orthodox
Christians shared in its consecration.

The Church of Reconciliation is now open to all Christians and all
nations. The community is international in membership and the
brothers have active industrial missions throughout Europe and the
USA, and are active in serving churches in different parts of Europe and
in America. The members live among the people they go to serve,
support themselves by their labours, and form fraternities among the
local population. Their staying power is faith and prayer, their essential
vows are obedience to the prior, celibacy and sharing communal
possessions. The vows are binding for the whole of life. Those members
of the community who reside in Taize fulfil their calling by serving the
local people in a variety of ways, for example, in cooperative farming,
producing pottery, factory work, providing medical services, or as
pastors and theologians. They wear ordinary clothes during the day but
in chapel they wear a white habit. Worship in chapel is liturgical and is
held three times a day. Part of the worship takes place in silence, but the
atmosphere is generally one of joy and celebration.

Large numbers of people visit Taize annually for a variety of activities, but many come to enjoy a period of quiet and meditation.
Non-Christians as well as Christians are free to come for prayer and
relaxation, but also for study and learning. For the first time since the
Protestant Reformation, Catholics and Protestants are able to meet
together in a single community for the sake of cultivating a common
spirituality. There is a certain flexibility about the work of the community – there is real emphasis on practice, as its members wish to be
known "by their fruits". Their calling is to be active in the world and
not confined to a cloistered order isolated from the world's problems.
One of the members has said of their work, "It is our presence that
counts. We do not want to be too aggressive. We wait for an occasion
of conversation. We are conscious that this is an important ministry as
far as the church is concerned."

The Taize Community has developed steadily its own liturgy which is an attempt to rediscover the beauty and substance of the worship of the early Christian Church and adapt it to a modern setting. Its spiritual impact has spread to many other churches throughout the world.

Corrymeela

Another community whose aims are reconciliation in a divided nation is that of Corrymeela in Northern Ireland. The name is thought to mean "hill of harmony". The community was founded in 1965 by Ray Davey as an inter-church community of Protestants and Roman Catholics. It is dedicated to the work of reconciliation between divided communities as well as being a spur to ordinary people to promote the cause of peace by learning to live harmoniously. The community operates by developing strategies of friendship and cooperative activities, and by being actively engaged in the peace process. The members look upon the community as a divine instrument for achieving this purpose; all members here are equal in status and share in the organization, and they also share their material possessions equally.

The Corrymeela Community is housed in residential camps and a community house in Belfast, and is supported by groups in other parts of the United Kingdom and in Europe. The members aim to practise its ideals in daily life, in social activities and in formal worship. Included in the programme of activities is a monthly meeting for fellowship and planning, whilst membership of the community is renewed annually by reaffirmation of commitment to its ideals.

These ideals include allegiance to Jesus Christ and his call to his followers to be peacemakers. Worship is the heart of the community and the building in which it is held is called "Crio" (= heart). An important part of its work is to provide a sanctuary for victims of violence who come to Corrymeela for periods of rest and rehabilitation. Bereaved and handicapped people are catered for and given counselling; conferences are held on themes to do with peace and reconciliation, not always of a religious nature. The members commit themselves to a life of spiritual discipline, regular Bible study and prayer.

Two of the key words of the Corrymeela Community are "trust" and "cooperation", and these are built into the routine activities. These words are not only the antidote to suspicion and division, but also the seeds of confidence and security. Trust and cooperation are achieved and practised through sharing, serving and socializing.

Members share their goods, participate in a daily rota, and mix socially with each other, irrespective of age, sex, religion, class or background. In this way prejudice is overcome, political differences minimized, and personal relationships fostered. But all activities are related to Christianity. Bringing together people of different church traditions and social background ensures that trust is built up and co-operation promoted. This creates mutual respect and peaceful co-existence as essential steps along the road to reconciliation and peace.

The Pollen of Peace.

This song has become an unofficial theme song of Corrymeela:

O Christ has sown the seeds of love,
O Christ has launched the winged dove,
Let us make the flower grow,
And all the people know
That Christ has sown the seeds of love.

All it needs is our love to make it grow,
All it needs is our hopefulness to show
And tell those who are choked with fear
That the Prince of Peace is here,
All it needs is our love to make it grow.

O let us spread the pollen of peace throughout our land.

The appeal of communities of spirituality such as Taize and Corrymee, and others, like the L'Arche Communities, increases in the modern world as people seek refreshment and renewal of spiritual vitality. Here people are able to make contact with the theological roots of inner peace, catch a glimpse of their true humanity, and discover the depth of community relationships. Trust, confidence and sharing hold the community together and the roots of contemporary spirituality are discovered. Christian theology interprets the theological roots of such community as a "sign" of Christian spirituality. Individuals who discover the depths of their own humanity discover that of others also: they are answerable to each other and participate together in promoting community spirituality – practically, symbolically and prophetically. Then the wholesome divisions between sacred and secular become less as self-understanding deepens in the only way it can, through mutuality and communication in relationship:

What life have you if you have not life together?
There is no life that is not in community,
And no community not lived in praise of God.
(T. S. Eliot, *The Rock*)

Theology and spiritual issues

Pluralism

To be creditable today, theology has to be concerned with real questions and issues of modern life. *How does Christian theology shape up to the realities of postmodernism, a pluralist religious world, the impact of scientific theory and environmental issues? How do these issues impact on the concept of spirituality?* It goes without saying that today Christian theology operates in a religious, cultural and ideological pluralist world. It has to engage its multi-religious neighbourhood. Either it engages in dialogue with non-Christian religions, seeks to work with them and aims to make theological sense of their content and practices, or it insulates itself from them in order to promote its own partisan agenda. The Christian theological response to other religions has been varied, but three aspects of this response may be noted. The first is the response of *"exclusivity"*, that is, the theological affirmation of the uniqueness of the Christian revelation, the insistence that Christ alone is the world redeemer and the bearer of ultimate truth. He must be given pre-eminence. Christ is the one hope of the world, and all other religions lack the fullness of the truth and universality of Christ. The second response is that of *"inclusivity"*, that is, that the spirit of Christ is present in all faiths; this pervades all religions to give them validity and creditability. A Hindu may, therefore, identify with Christ as a spiritual guru and an authentic holyman with a message of redemption. The spirit and message of Christ pervades all religions universally and the whole of life. A third response is that of *"pluralism"*, the view that in all religions there is an element of revelation from God, but this has been transmitted in various ways to different faiths. Therefore all religions can lay claim to divine revelation and communicate this in their own way. All religions should learn from each other, and be ready to listen to the truth each proclaims. By so doing the integrity of all religions is preserved and the religious forms and the cultural environment in which they operate are respected. All religions manifest facets of divine truth.

It is not possible here to pursue these various approaches, but it is relevant when considering the spiritual tradition to keep in view the question voiced by Bede Griffiths, a Benedictine monk who has spent much time in India, who asks, "How can we reconcile . . . the cosmic revelation of the infinite, timeless being manifesting in this world of time and change, but ultimately unaffected by it, with the Christian revelation of God's action in history and bringing this world of time and change into union with himself?"[48]

The question goes to the heart of the matter, especially in the search for an answer to the question of a spirituality which is also a focus of universal harmonization. At present there does not seem to be an agreed answer that reconciles the Christian claim to be the ultimate authentic revelation and the claims of non-Christian religions to their redemptive authenticity. In this case the search for an answer has to continue. It will only continue positively through dialogue between Christianity and other religions in a spirit of openness and of genuine search for knowledge, understanding and truth. This encounter has to be between religions in their *wholeness* and not only selectively or partially. It will involve listening to the multifarious voices of other religions in a spirit of humility that is eager to learn.

Creative dialogue is not indoctrination but a genuine search for understanding the truth claims of other religions. Such encounter can be positive and productive, it is ready to learn in a spirit of tolerance. Inter-faith dialogue takes seriously the expanding experience of other religions and their claims to be of God. For such encounter to be productive, theology needs to develop a new language and a new mythology appropriate to the task of enabling religions to speak to each other across the divide of tradition and prejudice on the assumption that the Spirit has yet more light and truth to reveal on God's universal purpose for all people.

Science and spirituality

In the introduction to *Christianity at the Centre* (1968) John Hick stated, "It has become obvious that we are living at a turning point in the history of Christianity. This is mainly because the development of modern science has made incredible much of the content of Christian belief."[49] This is a salutary statement but a common perception, science and religion are often thought to be completely opposed and to make "incredible much of the content of Christian belief". Where does this leave Christian theology? Certainly science has changed the way people think about the world and human life. No longer can the origin and operation of natural phenomena be attributed to supernatural agencies without reference to the discoveries and interpretation of science. Far more is known about how nature operates its own system of laws without resort to the supernatural, and science gives its own explanation of the existence of the world, which sometimes supposes that the scientific world view and the religious are mutually exclusive, or indeed, that redemption is outmoded. But what are the issues?

Dr Arthur Peacocke, a biologist and director of the Ramsey Institute, has asserted, "There are various levels of complexity in the world, each with its own level of interpretation." No one will doubt the levels of complexity, but science has not solved the problems that arise from all the "various levels of complexity". Dr Peacocke has asserted that Christianity "has been in continuous dialogue with the scientists from the first, and it has faced up to the intellectual challenges in a way which enriches understanding of the creation". It is this "continuous dialogue" that engages theology and its spiritual tradition. In spite of the levels of complexity, this is a world in which things are interconnected, and this, according to Dr Peacocke, postulates "some supra-mind from which it derives its being". Keith Ward concludes from this that science increases the sense of the greatness of God, it demolishes some rather simplistic ideas of God, and allows it to be said that "God wills most events to occur in accordance with the laws of regularity he himself has instituted." Sometimes God acts concurrently with these laws, he directs them in accordance with his own purposes, or he acts beyond their actual powers altogether.[50] John Hick discerns how human life has emerged within such a natural environment as part of the world process and he states:

> This then is the new picture of the relation between science and religion, which theology offers: we exist by God's creative action as parts of a universe which constitutes an autonomous order; and the sciences are the activities in which we systematically explore and to some extent come to control this order from within it. There is no conflict between science and religion, for any development of scientific knowledge describing the natural order more and more fully without reference to God is compatible with the belief that God has deliberately created a universe in which he is not compulsorily evident but can be known only by a free personal response of faith.[51]

On the basis that "God has deliberately created a universe" it is fair to say that the material world is good because it is created by God, and there is order in the world as God is responsible for its creation. The same physical laws operate throughout the creation. These views are expanded in the Bible and many modern scientists have elaborated on this fact. They have written about the relationship between Christianity and science. This shows, according to these experts, that religion and science can be held together with integrity. Science does not prove the existence of God, but the relation of science and religion raises deep questions about God and the natural world. Scientists may say these are questions of faith, and science has no need of faith. But is this so? Christianity is grounded in interpreted facts and faith arises from these facts, the chief of which is the fact of Jesus. But does science have room for faith? Science is based on hypothesis and observation, and intuition undergirded by some element of faith. There are scientists and religionists who view science and religion as allies in the search for truth. Where this happens it is proper to speak of science and spirituality as having an ultimate common objective. Max Planck, who won the Nobel Prize for science, has expressed this idea succinctly:

> Religion and natural science are fighting a joint battle ... and the rallying cry in this crusade has always been, and always will be: "On to God".

Spirituality and the environment

It comes as little surprise that towards the end of the twentieth century Christian theology should discuss urgently the question of ecology and the environment. How is humanity to survive in a rapidly changing natural environment? A former Dominican priest, Matthew Fox, has developed a "creation centred spirituality". His teaching is focused on the creation theme, which he has developed in a tantalizingly attractive way, but which has also been much criticized.[52] Fox identifies the themes of creation spirituality as including the original blessing and the celebration of all things, the deification of humanity, and Jesus as a reminder of what it means to be God's child. He distinguishes between spirituality and "creation spirituality" in order to draw attention to the ecological and political dimensions of spirituality. In this respect he distinguishes between creation and redemption spirituality.

But this raises the question whether Fox thereby renounces Christianity's central teaching on redemption through the forgiveness of sin. Be that as it may, Fox has opened up an area of spirituality that is particularly relevant to today. All life is part of creation, but creation theology (or ecological theology) deals with more than just relationships between material phenomena in the physical environment, as we saw is the case with science. It has to be used in the broader sense to highlight the basic assumptions of Christian theology.

The first of these is that the natural world is the place allocated by God as humanity's dwelling place. The Bible is witness to this truth from the beginning. The world as creation is the sphere of human habitation and domination over all other creatures. Human submission in the exercise of this domination is the road to happiness in the natural world. Creation or ecological theology exemplifies this truth as a means of understanding creation and of ensuring human survival within it.

A second assumption is that ecological theology embraces the whole of nature and the physical components of human and natural life as originating with God. The concern of ecological theology is with the development of human wholeness within the natural world of time and space. Spirituality leads to self-fulfilment with God, self and the world; it is integrated with the life of the spirit *and* with the life of the universe. Therefore care for the environment and all things within it is of the essence of Christian spirituality, as "the earth is the Lord's and all that is therein".

A third assumption is that Christian theology affirms the inter-relatedness and the interdependence of everything that lives within the natural world. From this sense of interdependence there flows fresh perceptions of the self and the process of achieving spiritual wholeness. This is consistent with the creation perspective of Christian teaching, which orientates the human being toward a reverence for the natural world and the preservation and proper use of its resources. It assumes divine immanence, so that God can be known in the world. Ecological spirituality affirms that the world is home to the human being *and* the place where God is to be encountered. In this connection the words of Matthew Fox are apt: "Our story is in no way separate from the cosmic story. Earth is a child of the cosmos and we are children of the Earth. Trees, plants and flowers are offspring of the universe and our doctrines are intertwined with theirs, and this with the universe as a whole."[53] Christian theology would no doubt wish to add to this the divine equation in the relationship. From this there derives the passion for justice, truth and beauty.

Christian theology affirms the human need to live in concert with the natural world. At the same time it expresses the belief that the human destiny transcends that of the material world. It might seem that there is a contradiction in this, but, in fact, ecological theology offers a view of the unity and sacredness of life in all its dimensions. Yet within this there is a dilemma, for, on the one hand, this notion is world affirming, whilst Christianity also has within it an element of world renunciation. Can the theme of world affirmation *and* world renunciation be accommodated in the developing ecological theology? Can such correlation provide a blueprint of a spirituality that progresses to the goal of genuine wholeness? Christian theology is anchored in God the creator and in this world as his creation. Faced with the environmental problems of the present we have to ask: What are the implications of this belief? Pope John Paul II has asserted that:

> First, man must be reconciled with nature by carefully preserving the integrity of nature, its fauna and flora, its air and rivers, its subtle balances, limited resources and its beauty which praises the glory of the Creator.

This call for reconciliation with nature is a twentieth-century response to a theme that has often been in the forefront of Christian spirituality. We see this from the works of Hildegard of Bingen (1098–1179), a mystic, composer, poet, and visionary who wrote:

> All nature is at the disposal of humankind. We are to work with it. Without it we cannot survive.

The theme of survival has been sharpened by what is sometimes seen as evidence of a deteriorating environment that is stark and undesirable, and this presents a choice which a contemporary verse expresses:

> We cannot stifle knowledge or invention,
> The ways divide, the choice for ever clear;
> to drift, and be delivered to destruction,
> or wake, and work, till trust outmatches fear.

The choice either "to drift, and be delivered to destruction", or "wake and work" is the measure of the crisis of life on the planet, which is so threatening that it has been described as apocalyptic. But Christian teaching does not see destruction as inevitable, rather "There is no creation that does not have a radiance be it greenness or seed, blossom or beauty. It could not be creation without it." In the light of this confidence the crisis takes on a quite different perspective. Christian theology points in the opposite direction. It takes into account the fact that creation is the instrument of God's purpose, expressed in Christian tradition beautifully by Hildegard of Bingen, who wrote as a member of the Benedictine Community:

> Creation
> of course,
> was fashioned to be adored,
> to be shared,
> to be gifted with the love of the Creator.
> The entire world has been embraced
> by His kiss.
> God has gifted creation with everything
> that is necessary.

Christian theology sees, beyond and through the natural phenomena, the vast and sweeping images of eternity. Creation is destined for redemption.

Theology seeks to grasp and interpret the eternal truths underlying the visible and changeable, for the sake of elucidating and shaping the nature and meaning of the truth of what belief in God the creator of the world means today. This leads to other significant questions, such as, What of the human responsibility for creation? and, How are people globally to be equipped to fulfil it? Christian spirituality is being challenged to create the structures that will ensure effective dominion over the world and the means of survival within it. Ecological spirituality can never be merely a fringe effort or a marginal concern, but rather, should be the catalyst of a process of improvement, living creatively within, preserving and celebrating the natural world.

Christian theology and spirituality derives this mission from the biblical perspective of respect and protection of creation not its exploitation. The goodness of the creation is a powerful motive for positive action to control and limit the exploitation and pollution of it. Human dominion within the natural world is a trust from the creator to be exercised in the task of conserving and caring for the natural resources of the world by using scientific, technical and planning powers consonant with the divine purpose.

Spirituality and the arts

The variability of the spiritual tapestry of the twentieth century has been enriched by the contributions of many poets, novelists and artists whose works illumine and display the spiritual meaning and purpose of life as they seek to penetrate to the heart of human existence in a complex world. In their works there is frequently an openness to the experiences, demands and issues of present-day living that challenges in demanding ways deeper reflection on ultimate questions. Through the use of symbols and imagery drawn from contemporary life the poet or artist or novelist becomes the spiritual guide who stimulates thought and inspires participation in the spiritual quest of making sense of experience. It has been said that the artist "is the man who goes into the empty space between man and God, and takes the enormous risk of attempting to create in that vacancy a new fabric of connections between man and the divine power".[54] What is said of the artist is true of the poet and novelist.

One issue that has concentrated the mind most sharply on spiritual issues in the twentieth century is global war. Through the horrendous experience of two world wars, spiritual or ultimate questions have taken on new depth of meaning. The questions are real life and death questions earthed in concrete events and experience at a particular time and in tangible situations. Why war at all? Why the cruelty and carnage? Why the suffering? Why the untimely death? This poem from the First World War is rooted in the experience of war, in the horrific realities that surround war, and in the anguish, dilemmas and disillusion that it produces:

> If in some smothering dream, you too could pace
> Behind the wagon that we flung him in,
> And watch the white eyes writhing in his face,
> His hanging face, like a devil's sick of sin,
> If you could hear, at every jolt, the blood
> Come gurgling from froth-corrupted lungs
> Obscene as cancer, bitter as the cud
> Of vile, incurable sores or innocent tongues,
> My friend, you would not tell with such high zest
> To children ardent for some desperate glory,
> The old Lie: Dulce et decorum est
> Pro patria mori.
>
> (Willfred Owen, 1893–1918)

Bertolt Brecht (1898–1956) described in his poem *To those born later* the dark time of insensitivity that has challenged spirituality throughout most of this century and continues to do so:

> They say to me: Eat and drink! Be glad you have it!
> But how can I eat and drink if I snatch what I eat
> From the starving, and
> My glass of water belongs to one dying of thirst?
> And yet I eat and drink.
>
> I would also like to be wise.
> In the old books it says what wisdom is
> To shun the strife of the world and to live out
> Your brief time without fear
> Also to get along without violence
> To return good for evil
> Not to fulfil your desires but to forget them
> Is accounted wise.
> All this I cannot do:
> Truly, I live in dark times.

R. S. Thomas (1915–2000), a poet and priest, raises perplexing questions about belief, in his poem *The Lost*, a subject of great spiritual perplexity in the century of cyclonic changes:

> We are the lost people.
> Tracing us by our language
> you will not arrive where we are
> which is nowhere. The wind
> blows through our castles; the chair
> of poetry is without a tenant.
> We are exiles within
> our own country; we eat our bread
> at a pre-empted table. 'Show us,'
> we supplicate, 'the way home',
> and they laughing hiss at us:
> 'But you are home. Come in
> and endure it.' Will nobody
> explain what it is like
> to be born lost? We have our signposts
> but they are in another tongue.
> If we follow our conscience
> it leads us nowhere but to gaol.
> The ground moves under our feet;
> our one attitude is vertigo.
>
> 'And a little child,' the Book tells us
> 'shall lead them.' But this one
> has a linguistic club
> in his hand with which, old as we are,
>
> he trounces and bludgeons us senseless.

If we were to compile an anthology of twentieth-century authors whose works resonate with spiritual concerns and issues, room would have to be found for many of its important novels which unveil the experiences and situations that have been shaped by events in this contemporary, complicated and uncertain world. By awaking consciousness of the reality that lies beyond the visible, comprehensible and immediate experience we confront some of the spiritual dilemmas of our century. This is the case with regard to the works of D. H. Lawrence (1885–1930) about whom a recent estimate states:

> Lawrence's work emerges from a fertile religious soil. His writing is permeated by his spiritual cast of mind and is incomprehensible if this fact is ignored . . . he saw his upbringing in a positive light and was thankful that it gave him a "direct knowledge of the Bible". This knowledge informs his work on several levels: imagery and symbolism, use of

language, conceptualizations of the dilemmas facing humanity, intense apocalypticism.[55]

In his novel *The Rainbow*, Lawrence portrays the deeper levels of human relationships in a manner that exposes the inner feelings and thoughts of the characters concerned. He depicts the inner forces that mould and characterize personal relationships in a way that the reader is able to empathize with. The situations reflect the realities of life, and Lawrence uses metaphor and imagery expertly in order to convey the depth and reality of the thought. The symbol of the rainbow is a traditional Christian symbol of promise as well as variableness. At the heart of personal relationships, however distressful, there is promise. Will Brangwen – the male in the relationship – is seen to choose Eve as the subject of his wood carving, and both the subject and the creativity symbolize his love for Anna. The validity of love and creativity are heavily suggestive of spiritual values that underlie the vagaries of human relationships. The novel, in a really moving scene, describes the situation of Lydia during her stay in Yorkshire. There is concern about her state of mind after the death of her first husband, and the poignancy she feels as she becomes more and more withdrawn, morose, uninterested in everything, and hardly conscious of her surroundings. Yet she experiences a spiritual rebirth and this prepares her for her meeting with Tom Brangwen:

> There was green and silver and blue in the air about her now. And there was a strange insistence of light from the sea, to which she must attend. Primroses glimmered around, many of them, and she stooped to the disturbing influence near her feet, she even picked one or two flowers, faintly remembering, in the new colour of life, what had been. All the day long as she sat at the upper window, the light came off the sea, constantly, constantly, without refusal, till it seemed to bear her away, and the noise of the sea created a drowsiness in her, a relaxation like sleep. Her automatic consciousness gave way a little, she stumbled sometimes, she had a poignant, momentary vision of her living child, that hurt her unspeakably. Her soul roused to attention.
>
> Very strange was the constant glitter of the sea unsheathed in heaven, very warm and sweet the graveyard, in a nook of the hill catching the sunshine and holding it as one holds a bee between the palms of the hands, when it is benumbed. Grey grass and lichen and a little church, and snowdrops among coarse grass, and a cupful of incredibly warm sunshine.

*   *   *

Having cast the net broadly over Christian theology and its spiritual tradition in the twentieth century, we ask, by way of conclusion, What has it to hand on to the future? The legacy to the future must include the cumulative effects of past achievements. Developments in the future will require to continue the dialogue with the past, analysing its attainments, estimating its limitations, assessing its evolution. At the turn of the millennium, theology and spirituality are in the process of revision and renewal, to which past evolution, ideas and practices have made a contribution, but whose limitations also need to be considered. The ideal of a coherent, vibrant, global spirituality is ever a stimulus and challenge to theology and spirituality to locate those traces of confident progress that they alone can hold out to an uncertain and bewildered world. The key to unlocking the hope that this can be achieved is in humanity's most persistent and urgent quest, namely, *What is the real meaning of life?* A theology and spirituality that unlocks the answer to this question has to be shaped by those first principles which at the beginning gave them birth. A theology and spirituality that will meet this quest in holistic ways, and with evidence that is irrefutable, will inject powerfully a spirit of hope and stability that are the condition for living positively in the now.

The Seven Ecumenical Councils, 325–787

---

325   *Council of Nicaea*
Decreed Christ to be of one essence with the Father.
The Alexandrian and Roman dating for Easter agreed.
Decree of tax exemption for the welfare of the poor agreed.

381   *Council of Constantinople*
Adopted the Nicene Creed.
Holy Spirit declared equal with the Father and the Son.

431   *Council of Ephesus*
Reaffirmed faith of Nicaea.
Asserted the title of *theotokos* to the Virgin Mary.

451   *Council of Chalcedon*
Christ declared to be one person in two natures.

553   *Council of Constantinople (2)*
Christ is one incarnate nature.

680   *Council of Constantinople (3)*
Reaffirmation of Christ's two natures and two nature wills, a
human and a divine will.

787   *Council of Nicaea (2)*
Decreed the veneration of icons.

Notes

Note: M. Eliade (ed.), *Encyclopedia of Religion* (New York: Macmillan, 1987) 16 vols, is abbreviated throughout the notes to ER.

1 Christian Theology and Spirituality

1 Philip Sheldrake, *Spirituality and Theology*, p. 34.
2 Robin Gill, *Theology and Social Structure*, p. 1.
3 Geoffrey Wainwright, *Christian Spirituality*, ER, vol. 3, pp. 452ff.
4 Evelyn Underhill, *The Spiritual Life*, p. 36.
5 Elizabeth of the Trinity, *Complete Works*, [ET], Aletheia Kane, pp. 183–4.
6 Philip Sheldrake, *Spirituality and Theology*, pp. 25–6.
7 Hans Kung, *On Being a Christian*, p. 65.
8 Rowan Williams, *The Wound of Knowledge*, 121. See also John Hick, *The Fifth Dimension*, p. 83.
9 Thomas Merton, *Contemplation of a World in Action*, pp. 154–5.
10 Quoted by James Finley, *Merton's Palace of Nowhere*, p. 60.
11 Hans Kung, *On Being a Christian*, p. 163.
12 Jean-Noël Bezançon, *How to Understand the Creed*, p. 52.
13 Geoffrey Wainwright, *Christian Spirituality*, in ER, vol. 3, p. 453.
14 Quoted by Eric O. Springfield, ed. *Spirituality and Theology*, p. 8. For information of Evagrius see John Hick, *The Fifth Dimension*, pp. 145–6.
15 Karl Barth, *Evangelical Theology*, p. 160.
16 Rudolph Otto, *The Idea of the Holy*, p. 27.
17 Haleyon Bockhouse, *The Cloud of Unknowing*, p. 63.
18 James Finley, *Merton's Palace of Nowhere*, p. 56.
19 Thomas Merton, *New Seeds of Contemplation*, p. 1.
20 Geoffrey Wainwright, *Christian Spirituality*, in ER, vol. 3, p. 452.
21 Lucas Grollenberg, *A Bible for our Time*, p. 70.
22 A. J. B. Higgins, *The Lord's Supper in the New Testament*, p. 51.
23 John Hick, *The Fifth Dimension*, pp. 2–3.

2 After the Apostles

1 Clement of Rome, *[First] Epistle to the Corinthians*, in Henry Bettenson, ed., *The Early Christian Fathers*, p. 32. Cf. C. H. Dodd, *According to the Scriptures*.
2 Cyprian, *Ad Donatum*, in Henry Bettenson, ed., *The Early Christian Fathers*, p. 273.
3 Lactantius, *On the Anger of God*, in John Foster, *After the Apostles*, p. 54.

4　Irenaeus, *Against Heresies* (hereafter *AH*), in Henry Bettenson, ed., *The Early Christian Fathers*, p. 92.

5　Origen, *Matthaean Commentaries* Series 33, *The Early Christian Fathers*, p. 260.

6　*The Apology of Aristides*, in H. M. Gwatkin, *Selections from Early Christain Writers*, pp. 45–6.

7　Augustine, *Rebuke and Grace*, in W. Walker, *A History of the Christian Church*, p. 182.

8　Christopher Dawson, *St. Augustine and his Age*, quoted in *The Confessions of St. Augustine* by F. T. Steed.

9　F. T. Steed, ibid., p. 201. Augustine viewed the immaterial part of the self (the immaterial soul) as the highest of creaturely beings, as directly an image of God. Cf. Ian Hazlett, ed., *Early Christianity*, p. 215.

10　Owen Collins, *The Oral History of Christianity*, p. 76.

11　*AH* iv, xx.4, *The Early Christian Fathers*, p. 87.

12　Tertullian, *Apologeticus*, *The Early Christian Fathers*, p. 103.

13　Tertullian, *Adversus Praxean* 25, *The Early Christian Fathers*, pp. 129–30.

14　*The Early Christian Fathers*, p. 130.

15　Clement of Alexandria, *Stromateis, Pedagogus*, *The Early Christian Fathers*, pp. 170–1.

16　Origen, *De Principiis*, *The Early Christian Fathers*, p. 186.

17　*The Early Christian Fathers*, p. 226.

18　*The Early Christian Fathers*, p. 229.

19　Tertullian, *Apologeticus*, *The Early Christian Fathers*, p. 103.

20　*Stromateis*, *The Early Christian Fathers*, p. 169.

21　*The Early Christian Fathers*, p. 177.

22　*The Early Christian Fathers*, p. 178.

23　*Epistle to Diognetus*, *The Early Christian Fathers*, pp. 55–6.

24　*AH*, *The Early Christian Fathers*, p. 74.

25　*The Early Christian Fathers*, p. 281.

26　*The Early Christian Fathers*, p. 60.

27　Tertullian, *De Resurrectione Carnis*, *The Early Christian Fathers*, p. 113.

28　John Hick, *Christianity at the Centre*, p. 36.

29　*The Early Christian Fathers*, p. 288.

30　*The Early Christian Fathers*, pp. 75–6.

31　*The Early Christian Fathers*, p. 77.

32　Ignatius, *To the Trallians*, *The Early Christian Fathers*, p. 42.

33　Clement of Alexandria, *Protrepticus, The Early Christian Fathers*, p. 176.

34　Athanasius, *De Incarnatione*, *The Early Christian Fathers*, p. 291.

35　*The Early Christian Fathers*, p. 292.

36　*AH*, *The Early Christian Fathers*, p. 82.

37　Tertullian, *De Monogamia*, *The Early Christian Fathers*, p. 131.

38　Cyprian, *Ad Donatum*, *The Early Christian Fathers*, p. 272.

39　Athanasius, *Against Arius*, *The Early Christian Fathers*, p. 297.

40　*AH*, *The Early Christian Fathers*, p. 84.

41　Cf. Clement of Rome, *[First] Epistle to the Corinthians, The Early Christian Fathers*, p. 37.

42　Origen, *The Early Christian Fathers*, p. 237.

43　Origen, *De Oratione*, *The Early Christian Fathers*, p. 238.

44 Tertullian, *De Baptismo*, *The Early Christian Fathers*, p. 147. For further aspects of Tertullian's teaching, especially the need for public penance, *The Early Christian Fathers*, p. 153.
45 *AH*, *The Early Christian Fathers*, p. 94.
46 Origen, *Hom, in Leviticum* viii 2, *The Early Christian Fathers*, p. 247.
47 *Didache*, *The Early Christian Fathers*, p. 50.
48 Justin Martyr, *Apologia*, *The Early Christian Fathers*, p. 62. One may compare this with the discipline of Chrysostom (347–407), the Greek Father, who urged a spiritual understanding of the bread and wine, a stance taken also by Martin Luther who asserted that Chrysostom meant that "Just because humans cannot understand the concept of spiritual being, it does not follow that Christ's flesh, being spiritual, cannot be present in the eucharist." Irena Backus, *The Early Church in the Renaissance and Reformation*, in *Early Christianity*, ed. Ian Hazlett, p. 294.
49 W. H. C. Frend, *The Rise of Christianity*, p. 408. The epiclesis is an invocation for the reality of Christ to be made real in the community involved in the celebration. It is a eucharistic prayer for the communication of the blood and wine and for the sanctification of the faithful.
50 *AH*, *The Early Christian Fathers*, p. 69.
51 H. M. Gwatkin, *Selections from Early Christian Writers*, p. 5.
52 Tertullian, *Apologeticus*, *The Early Christian Fathers*, p. 166.
53 Clement of Rome, *[First] Epistle to the Corinthians*, *The Early Christian Fathers*, p. 31.

3 Eastern Christendom

1 Rowan Williams, *The Wound of Knowledge*, p. 93.
2 The words of Karl Barth quoted by Rowan Williams, *The Wound of Knowledge*, p. 94.
3 Philip Rousseau, *Christian Asceticism and the Early Monks in Early Christianity*, ed. Ian Hazlett, p. 112.
4 W. H. C. Frend, *The Rise of Christianity*, p. 576.
5 Ibid., p. 576.
6 See Vivian Green, *A New History of Christianity*, p. 67.
7 W. H. C. Frend, *The Rise of Christianity*, pp. 631f. Cf. the words of Basil: "The study of the Bible is the best guide to the discovery of one's duty. What with moral precept and the example of good men so abundantly set forth there, you hear all you want." Eric Routley, *The Wisdom of the Fathers*, p. 99.
8 See Henry Chadwick, *The Early Church*, p. 178, for further information on Basil's purpose. Also Basil's own confession: "The beginning of the soul's purification is tranquility – where the tongue takes a rest from gossip and the eye from licentiousness and the ear from buffoonery . . . Thus set free the mind can become occupied with the collection of all the virtues, and with the thought of the glory of God."
9 W. H. C. Frend, *The Rise of Christianity*, pp. 361f.
10 Frances Young, *The Greek Fathers, Early Christianity*, p. 141.
11 Paul Johnson, *A History of Christianity*, p. 100.
12 See Andrew Louth, *Mysticism, Early Christianity*, pp. 213–14.
13 Timothy Ware, *The Orthodox Church*, p. 195.

14 Ibid., pp. 198–9.
15 Kallistos Ware, *Eastern Christendom, The Oxford History of Christianity*, ed. John MacManners, p. 145.
16 Jeremy Johns, *Christianity and Islam, The Oxford History of Christianity*, pp. 131f.
17 Timothy Ware, *The Orthodox Church*, pp. 6–7.
18 For a catalogue of the chief doctrinal statements of the Eastern Orthodox Church, see Timothy Ware, *The Orthodox Church*, p. 203.
19 Quoted by Timothy Ware, *The Orthodox Church*, p. 209.
20 Cf. The description of the world by Gerard Manley Hopkins as charged with the grandeur of God; all creation is a gigantic Burning Bush, permeated but not consumed by the ineffable and wondrous powers of God's energies. Quoted by Timothy Ware, *The Orthodox Church*, p. 68.
21 Timothy Ware, *The Orthodox Church*, pp. 209–10.
22 Ibid, p. 119.
23 J. A. L. Riley, ed., *Birkbeck and the Russian Church*, p. 349.
24 On these elements of the eucharist, see Timothy Ware, *The Orthodox Church*, pp. 285–8.
25 Alvistos listed these reasons for divorce – treachery, adultery, bigamy, frivolous conduct, abortion without consent, disrupting the marriage union, luxury, leprosy. Herbert Waddams, *Meeting the Orthdox Churches*, p. 56.
26 Sergius Bulgakov, *The Orthodox Church*, p. 27.
27 A *hesychast* is one who pursues *hesychia*, utter silence or silence of the heart, in particular through the use of the Jesus prayer. This is a short invocation repeated, usually in the form 'Lord Jesus Christ, Son of God, have mercy on me.' Kallistos Ware, *Eastern Christendom, The Oxford History of Christianity*, p. 156.
28 S. W. Smithers, *Spiritual Guide*, ER, vol. 14, pp. 29ff.
29 See Knut Schaferdiek, *Christian Mission and Expansion, Early Christianity*, pp. 65ff.
30 Henry Chadwick, *The Early Church*, p. 212.
31 Kallistos Ware, *Eastern Christendom, The Oxford History of Christianity*, p. 155.
32 Ibid., p. 155.
33 Timothy Ware, *The Orthodox Church*, pp. 255–6.
34 See further, Timothy Ware, *The Orthodox Church*, pp. 73–7.
35 Ibid., pp. 129–31.
36 For additional information about the liturgical calendar and periods of fasting, see *The Orthodox Church*, pp. 300–3.
37 Owen Collins, ed., *The Oral History of Christianity*, pp. 99–101.
38 N. M. Vaporis, *Kosmas Aitolos*, ER, vol 25, pp. 441ff; vol. 8, pp. 376–7.
39 Basil Mitchell, *The Christian Conscience, The Oxford History of Christianity*, p. 625.
40 Paul B. Anderson, *People, Church and State in Modern Russia*, pp. 71–3.
41 S. Hackel, *Joseph of Volokolamski*, ER, vol. 8, p. 347.
42 See N. Gorodetzky, *Saint Tikhon of Zadonski, Inspirer of Dostoevsky*, p. 48.
43 Paul B. Anderson, *People, Church and State in Modern Russia*, pp. 53–7.

4 *Christianity in the West*

1 Robert Markus, *From Rome to the Barbarian Kingdom*, The Oxford *History of Christianity*, p. 96.
2 David Ayerst and A. S. T. Fisher, *Records of Christianity*, p. 23.
3 Ibid., pp. 26–7.
4 For examples of prayers from the early sacramentaries, see David Ayerst, *Records of Christianity*, p. 24.
5 Rowan Williams, *The Wound of Knowledge*, p. 104.
6 Vivian Green, *A New History of Christianity*, p. 31.
7 R. Kevin Seasolitz, *Benedict of Nursia*, ER, vol. 2, pp. 98–100.
8 Henry Chadwick, *The Early Church*, p. 183.
9 Vivian Green, *A New History of Christianity*, p. 45.
10 Henry Mayr-Hastings, *The West: The Age of Conversion*, The Oxford *History of Christianity*, p. 104.
11 Paul Johnson, *A History of Christianity*, p. 151.
12 Rowan Williams, *The Wound of Knowledge*, pp. 109–10.
13 Ibid., p. 111.
14 Bradley P. Holt, *Brief History of Christian Spirituality*, pp. 78–9.
15 Rowan Williams, *The Wound of Knowledge*, p. 112.
16 Ibid., p. 113.
17 Vivian Green, *A New History of Christianity*, p. 63.
18 John R. H. Moorman, *Saint Francis of Assisi*, p. 29.
19 Ibid., p. 33.
20 Zachary Hayes, *Bonaventura*, ER, vol. 2. pp. 281–4.
21 See David Ayerst and A. S. T. Fisher, *Records of Christianity*, pp. 185–9.
22 Oliver Davies, *God Within*, p. 37. References may be made to the extracts of Eckhart, especially of the controversial understanding of spirituality, pp. 30–65.
23 Ibid., p. 38.
24 Rowan Williams, *The Wound of Knowledge*, pp. 132–3.
25 Ibid., p. 113.
26 These aspects of Eckhart's thought are drawn from Rowan Williams, *The Wound of Knowledge*, pp. 135–7.
27 Ibid., p. 137.
28 Julian of Norwich, *Showings*, pp. 63ff.
29 Rowan Williams, *The Wound of Knowledge*, p. 126.
30 Ibid., p. 130.
31 Hannah Ward and Jennifer Wild, *Christian Meditation Collection*, p. 365.
32 Brian Stone, *Mediaeval English*, pp. 64–5.
33 Ernest Rhys, *Poetry and Drama*, pp. 154–82.

5 *The Age of Reform*

1 G. E. Duffield, *The Work of William Tyndale*, p. 4.
2 William Johnson, ed., *The Cloud of Unknowing and the Book of Privy Counselling*, pp. 162–3.
3 Clifton Wolters, *The Cloud of Unknowing*, pp. 60–1.
4 Ibid. This thought is reminiscent of the saying of Augustine about the heart being restless until it finds its rest in God.

5 Oliver Davies, *God Within*, p. 159.
6 Thomas à Kempis, *The Imitation of Christ*, ET, Betty J. Knoll, p. 54.
7 Bob Scribner, ed., *The Reformation in National Context*, p. 1. For a full list of Luther's theses, see Oliver Collins, ed., *The Oral History of Christianity*.
8 John Dillenberger, ET *Martin Luther: Selections from his Writings*, p. 76.
9 *Handbook to the Church Hymnary*.
10 Kenneth L. Parry, *Christian Hymns*, p. 28.
11 Vivian Green, *A New History of Christianity*, p. 132. See also G. R. Potter, *Zwingli*.
12 John Calvin, *Institutes of the Christian Religion*, ed. J. T. McNeill, Book i, chapters 5–6.
13 Ibid., Book i.
14 Ibid., Book ii.
15 Ibid., Book iv.
16 W. Bergsma, *The Low Countries*, in *The Reformation in National Context*, ed. Bob Scribner, pp. 70ff.
17 Vivian Green, *A New History of Christianity*, p. 154.
18 Paul Johnson, *A History of Christianity*, p. 261.
19 Ibid., pp. 261–2.
20 Hannah Ward and Jennifer Wild, *Christian Meditation Collection, Serving the Lord*, pp. 262–3.
21 Paul Johnson, *A History of Christianity*, p. 301.
22 Rowan Williams, *The Wound of Knowledge*, p. 164.
23 Bradley P. Holt, *Brief History of Christian Spirituality*, pp. 102–3.
24 Rowan Williams, *The Wound of Knowledge*, p. 168.
25 Ibid., p. 164.
26 Ibid., pp. 170–1. On the question of seeking God, John of the Cross taught that you should never desire satisfaction in what you understand about God, but in what you do not understand about him. Never stop loving and delighting in your understanding and experience of God, but love and delight in what is neither understandable or perceptible of him. God is the way of seeking him in faith. Hannah Ward, *Christian Meditation Collection*, pp. 149–50.
27 Bradley P. Holt, *Brief History of Christian Spirituality*, p. 97. The remark attributed to John Seldon is relevant also: "If you would know how the Church of England serves God, go to the Common Prayer Book, consult not this or that man." See A. T. P. Williams, *The Anglican Tradition in the Life of England*, p. 41.
28 Richard Hooker (1554–1600) in his *Laws of Ecclesiastical Polity* advanced the theory that in England there was an identity achieved between Church and state under one common law. He rested this justification of the Church of England on the threefold authority, Scripture, tradition and reason. His contention inspired self-confidence in members of the Church of England, but how far it truly represented the facts fully is debatable.

6 *From Reformation to Romanticism*

1 John McManners, *Enlightenment: Secular and Christian* (1600–1800), *The Oxford History of Christianity*, p. 278.

2 See further, G. F. Nuttall, *The Holy Spirit in Puritan Faith and Experience*, pp. 3ff.

3 N. H. Keeble, ed. *Pilgrim's Progress*, p. 9.

4 Ibid., p. 24.

5 Ibid., p. 62.

6 Ibid., pp. 126f.

7 Quoted from Doctrinal Statement of Evangelical Free Churches, F. G. Healey, *Rooted in Faith*, pp. 145ff.

8 John McManners, *Enlightenment: Secular and Christian, The Oxford History of Christianity*, p. 302.

9 Quoted from Antony Flew, *An Introduction to Western Philosophy*, pp. 149ff.

10 The full title of the work is *A Serious Call to a Devout and Holy Life*.

11 John McManners, *Enlightenment, Secular and Christian, The Oxford History of Christianity*, p. 303.

12 Quoted in Owen Collins, ed., *The Oral History of Christianity*, p. 278.

13 Ibid., p. 273.

14 John McManners, *Enlightenment: Secular and Christian, The Oxford History of Christianity*, p. 303.

15 Bernard Manning, *The Hymns of Wesley and Watts*, p. 24.

16 See further, Sir Reginald Coupland, *Wilberforce*.

17 Philip Wayne, *Selections from Wordsworth*, p. xxxvii.

18 Basil Smallman, *The Background of Passion Music*, pp. 116–17.

7 The Victorian Era

1 Quoted in G. M. Trevelyan, *English Social History*, p. 477.

2 Henry Chadwick, *Great Britain and Europe*, in John McManners, *The Oxford History of Christianity*, p. 351.

3 R. K. A. Ensor, *England 1870–1914*, p. 137.

4 W. A. Visser't Hooft, *Anglo Catholicism and Orthodoxy*, p. 28.

5 The Council of Trent in 1545 defined the doctrines of the Roman Catholic Church in a manner that showed how these differed from the Protestant doctrines of Martin Luther; then in 1570 the Thirty-nine Articles were added to the Prayer Book of the Church of England. It seemed from then on that reconciliation between the churches was remote, although complete neutrality between them was not feasible.

6 D. L. Edwards, *Not Angels but Anglicans*, pp. 40–2. Edwards also makes the point that Anglicanism has always been loyal to this estimate of episcopacy as the chief advocate and agent of the unity of the Church.

7 Percy H. Osmond, *The Hope of our Fathers*, p. 319.

8 Ibid., p. 333.

9 D. L. Edwards, *Christian England*, vol. 3., pp. 181–2.

10 Ibid., p. 190.

11 Ibid., p. 193.

12 Ibid., p. 190.

13 Henry Chadwick, *Great Britain and Europe, The Oxford History of Christianity*, p. 371.

14 D. L. Edwards, *Christian England*, vol. 3. p. 198.

15 Florence Higham, *Frederick Denison Maurice*, pp. 45–6.
16 Ibid., p. 125.
17 D. L. Edwards, *Christian England*, vol. 3, p. 200.
18 H. C. Whitely, *Blinded Eagle*, p. 56.
19 R. K. A. Ensor, *England 1870–1914*, p. 137.
20 H. C. Whitely, *Blinded Eagle*, p. 50.
21 Ibid., p. 74.
22 D. L. Edwards, *Christian England*, vol. 3, p. 259.
23 Dale has been described as "the finest and most spiritual nineteenth century representative of the Nonconformist ideal". H. W. Clark, *The History of English Nonconformity*, p. 415.
24 F. A. Iremonger, *Life of William Temple*, p. 46. For an alternative view of Browning's religion, see Hugh Martin, *The Faith of Robert Browning*, p. 42.

8 The Contemporary World

1 John Macquarrie, *Twentieth Century Religious Thought*, p. 19.
2 Harold Nicolson, *Small Talk*, pp. 73–81.
3 John Taylor, *The Future of Christianity*, *The Oxford History of Christianity*, p. 682.
4 Ibid., p. 665.
5 Jlunga We Bukole, *Paths of Liberation. A Third World Spirituality*, p. 136.
6 John Mbiti, *Some Current Concerns of African Theology*, Expository Times, pp. 164ff.
7 Ibid.
8 Bradley P. Holt, *Brief History of Christian Spirituality*, pp. 133–4.
9 Ibid., p. 139.
10 Toyohiko Kagawa, *The Thorn in the Flesh*, pp. 12–13.
11 Ibid., p. 92.
12 John Macquarrie, *Twentieth Century Religious Thought*, pp. 38–42.
13 Ibid., pp. 39–40.
14 Ibid., pp. 41–2. Campbell wrote in his book on *Christianity and the Social Order* that "the practical end which alone could justify the existence of Churches is the realization of the Kingdom of God, which only means the reconstructing of society on a basis of mutual hopefulness instead of strife and competition".
15 John Macquarrie, *Twentieth Century Religious Thought*, pp. 38–42.
16 Albert Schweitzer, *The Quest of the Historical Jesus*, p. 397.
17 See excerpts from the writings of Schweitzer in Victor Gollancz, *A Year of Grace*, pp. 9, 217–22.
18 Karl Barth, *De Kirchliche Dogmatik*, vol. 4 ET, (1977), p. 83.
19 Quoted by John Bowden, *Karl Barth*, p. 20.
20 Ibid., p. 118.
21 John Macquarrie, *Twentieth Century Religious Thought*, p. 363.
22 Ibid., p. 364.
23 Ibid., pp. 366–7. Tillich's main work is called *Systematic Theology*.
24 E. H. Robertson, *Christians Against Hitler*, pp. 48ff. For a clear view of Bonhoeffer's life and work, see André Dumas, *Dietrich Bonhoeffer, Theologian of Reality*, ET, R. M. Brown.

25 John Robinson, *Honest to God*, p. 5.
26 Paul von Buren, *Secular Meaning of the Gospel*, pp. 7ff.
27 John Macquarrie, *Theologies of Hope*, Expository Times, pp. 100ff.
28 Ibid., p. 105.
29 Vernon Sproxton, *Teilhard de Chardin*, p. 15.
30 Quoted by Sproxton, *Teilhard de Chardin*, p. 32.
31 Ibid., p. 89.
32 Ibid., p. 114.
33 Simone Weil, *Waiting on God*, p. 41.
34 David Anderson, *Simone Weil*, p. 28.
35 Ibid., p. 64.
36 *Waiting on God*, p. 36.
37 James Finley, *Merton's Palace of Nowhere*, p. 17.
38 Ibid., p. 19.
39 Ibid., p. 32.
40 Basil Hume, *To Be a Pilgrim*, p. 126.
41 Ibid., pp. 107–16.
42 Ibid., pp. 77–121.
43 Ibid., p. 230.
44 Mark Gibbard, *Twentieth Century Men of Prayer*, p. vii.
45 Ibid., pp. 12–23.
46 Ibid., pp. 80–8.
47 Ibid., pp. 89–98.
48 Quoted by Keith Ward, *The Turn of the Tide*, p. 151.
49 John Hick , *Christianity at the Centre*, p. 9.
50 Keith Ward, *The Turn of the Tide*, pp. 38–9.
51 John Hick, *Christianity at the Centre*, p. 96.
52 Matthew Fox, *Breakthrough, Meister Eckhart's Creation Spirituality in New Translation*, pp. 31ff.
53 Matthew Fox, *Sacred Origins*, Resurgence 61, p. 52.
54 Quoted in A. Ecclestone, ed., *Spirituality and Human Wholeness*, p. 25.
55 A. Gasiorek, *God and the Novelists: D. H. Lawrence*, Expository Times, p. 241.

Select Bibliography

Allen, Diogenes (1989), *Christian Belief in a Post Modern World*, Westminster, John Knox Press.

Anderson, David (1971), *Simone Weil*, London, SCM Press.

Anderson, Paula B. (1944), *People, Church and State in Modern Russia*, London, SCM Press.

Aquinas, St. Thomas (1903), *Summa Theologica* [ET], Fr Gilby Thomas, London, Eyre and Spottiswoode.

Ayerst, David and Fisher, A. S. T. (1977), *Records of Christianity*, Vol. ll, Oxford, Blackwell.

Backus, I. (1995), *The Early Church in the Renaissance and Reformation in Early Christianity*, ed. I. Hazlett, London, SPCK.

Barth, Karl (1963), *Evangelical Theology*, London, Anchor Books.

(1964), *Prayer and Preaching*, London, SCM Press.

—— (1956–69), *De Kirkliche Dogmatik* [ET], G. W. Bromiley and T. F. Torrence, Edinburgh, T & T Clark.

Becken, H. J. (1973), *Relevant Theology for Africa*, Durban, Lutheran Publishing House.

Bergsma, W. (1994), *The Low Countries*, in *The Reformation in National Context*, ed. Bob Scribner, Cambridge University Press.

Bettenson, H. (1956), ed., *The Early Christian Fathers*, Oxford University Press.

Bezançon, Jean-Noel (1987), *How to Understand the Creed*, London, SCM Press.

Blakney, Raymond (1941), *Meister Eckhart: A Modern Translation*, New York, Harper.

Bloom, Anthony (1971), *God and Man*, London, Darton, Longman and Todd.

Bockhouse, Haleyon (1985), *The Cloud of Unknowing*, London, Hodder.

Bockhouse, Robert (1989), *Ignatius, Spiritual Exercises*, London, Hodder.

Boff, Leonardo (1982), *Trinity and Society*, Abingdon, Orbis Books.

Bouyer, Louis (1963), *A History of Chritian Spirituality*, London, Burns and Oates.

Bowden, John (1977), *Karl Barth*, London, SCM Press.

Brown, G. F. (1910), *Boniface of Crediton and his Companions*, London, SPCK.

Brown, Peter (1967), *Augustine of Hippo, A Biography*, Princetown, University Press.

Bulgakov, S. (1935), *The Orthodox Church*, London, Harper Collins.

Buren, Paul von (1968), *Secular Meaning of the Gospel*, New York, Macmillan.

Butler, Cuthbert (1967), *Western Mysticism*, London, Constable.

Campbell, R. J. (1906), *The New Theology*, New York, Macmillan.

—— (1907), *Christianity and the Social Order*, New York, Macmillan.

Casaldaliga, P. and Vigil, J. M. (1994), *Spirituality of Liberation* [ET], P. Burns and F. McDonagh, London, Burns and Oates.

Chadwick, Henry (1990), *The Early Church*, Harmondsworth, Penguin.

—— (1998), *Great Britain and Europe*, in *Encyclopedia of Religion*, ed. M. Eliade, New York, Macmillan.

Chadwick, Owen (1958), *Western Asceticism*, London, SCM Press.

Chardin, Teilhard de (1959), *The Phenomenon of Man*, London, Collins; *The Human Phenomenon*, A New Edition and Translation by Sarah Appleton-Weber, Brighton and Portland, Sussex Academic Press, 1999.

Clark, H. W. (1911), *The History of English Nonconformity*, London, Chapman and Hall.

Clarke, W. K. L. (1913), *St. Basil the Great*, Cambridge University Press.

Collins, Owen (1998), *The Oral History of Christianity*, London, Harper Collins.

Corbishley, Thomas (1971), *The Spirituality of Teilhard de Chardin*, London, Collins.

Coupland, Sir Reginald (1945), *Wilberforce*, London.

Davies, E. (1978), *Three Byzantine Saints*, London, Mowbray.

Davies, J. G. (1952), *Daily Life in the Early Church*, Cambridge, Lutterworth.

Davies, Oliver (1988), *God Within*, London, Darton, Longman and Todd.

Dawson, C. (1944), *St. Augustine and his Life*, in F. J. Sheed, *The Confessions of St. Augustine*, London, Sheed and Ward.

de Cruchy, John W. (1999), *The Cambridge Companion to Dietrich Bonhoeffer*, Cambridge University Press.

de Waal, Esther (1995), *A Life Giving Way – Commentary on the Rule of St. Benedict*, London, Chapman.

Dillenberger, John (1961), *Martin Luther: Selections from his Writings*, New York, Doubleday.

Dodd, C. H. (1952), *According to the Scriptures*, Hitchen, Nisbet.

Duffield, G. E. (1964), *The Work of William Tyndale*, Canterbury Press.

Dumas, A. (1971), *Dietrich Bonhoeffer. Theologian of Reality* [ET], R. M. Brown, New York, Doubleday.

Ecclestone, A. et al. (1986), *Spirituality and Human Wholeness*, London, British Council of Churches.

Edwards, D. L. (1958), *Not Angels but Anglicans*, London, SCM Press.

—— (1984), *Christian England*, Vol. 3, London, Collins.

Eliade, Mircea (1987), ed., *Encyclopedia of Religion*, New York, Macmillan.

Ellis, Jane (1951), *The Russian Orthodox Church*, London, Croom Helm.

Ensor, R. K. A. (1936), *England 1870–1914*, Oxford University Press.

Evans, G. R. (1983), *The Mind of St. Bernard of Clairvaux*, Oxford University Press.

Finley, James (1992), *Merton's Palace of Nowhere*, Indiana, Ave Maria Press.

Flew, Anthony (1971), *An Introduction to Western Philosophy*, London, Thames and Hudson.

Foster, John (1951), *After the Apostles*, London, SCM Press.

—— (1965), *They Converted our Ancestors*, London, SCM Press.

Fox, George (1952), *Journal*, ed. J. L. Nickalls, Cambridge University Press.

Fox, Matthew (1980), *Breakthrough: Meister Eckhart's Creation Spirituality in New Translation*, New York, Image Books.

—— (1994), *Original Blessing: A Primer in Creation Spirituality*, Santa Fe, Bear and Co.

—— (1993), *Sacred Origins*, New York, Resurgence 61.

Frend, W. H. C. (1985), *The Rise of Christianity*, London, Darton, Longman and Todd.

Ganss, G. (1992), ed., *The Spiritual Exercises of St. Ignatius*, Chicago, Loyola University Press.

Gasiorek, Andrzej (1999), *God and the Novelists* 10, D. H. Lawrence, Expository Times, Edinburgh, T&T Clark.

Gibbard, Mark (1974), *Twentieth Century Men of Prayer*, London, SCM Press.

Gill, Robin (1978), *Theology and Social Structure*, London, Mowbray.

—— (1995), ed., *Readings in Modern Theology*, London, Mowbray.

Gollancz, Victor (1956), *A Year of Grace*, London, Victor Gollancz.

Gorodetzky, N. (1951), *Saint Tikhon of Zadonsk, Inspirer of Dostoevsky*, New York, Crestwood.

Greef, Wide (1993), *The Writings of John Calvin*, Leicester, Apollos/Baker Book House.

Green, Vivian (1996), *A New History of Christianity*, Stroud, Sutton Publishing.

Grollenberg, Lucas (1979), *A Bible for our Time*, London, SCM Press.

Gunton, Collin (1990), *The Promise of Trinitarian Theology*, Edinburgh, T&T Clark.

Gutierrez, Gustavo (1973), *A Theology of Liberation: History, Politics and Salvation* [ET], Caridad Inda and John Eagleson, Maryknoll, New York.

—— (1984), *We Drink from our Own Wells: The Spiritual Journey of a People*, London, SCM Press.

Gwatkin, H. M. (1937), *Selections from Early Christian Writers*, London, Methuen.

Hackel, S. (1987), *Joseph of Volokalamski, Encyclopedia of Religion*, ed. Mircea Eliade, Vol. 8, New York, Macmillan.

—— (1927), *Handbook of the Church Hymnary*, Edinburgh.

Hanson, Bradley (1990), ed., *Modern Christian Spirituality*, Atlanta, Scholars Press.

Hardy, Alister (1979), *The Spiritual Nature of Man: A Study of Contemporary Religious Experience*, Oxford University Press.

Harton, F. P. (1932), *The Elements of the Spiritual Life*, London, SPCK.

Hayes, Zachary (1987), *Bonaventura, Encyclopedia of Religion*, ed., M. Eliade, New York, Macmillan.

Hazlett, Ian (1995), ed., *arly Christianity*, London, SPCK.

Healey, F. G. (1961), *Rooted in Faith*, London, Independent Press.

Hick, John (1968), *Christianity at the Centre*, London, SCM Press.

—— ((1999), *The Fifth Dimension*, Oxford, One World Publications.

Higgins, A. J. B. (1952), *The Lord's Supper in the New Testament*, London, SCM Press.

Higham, Florence (1947), *Frederick Denison Maurice*, London, SCM Press.

Holmes, Urban T. (1981), *A History of Christian Spirituality: An Analytical Introduction*, New York, Seabury Press.

Holt, Bradley P. (1997), *Brief History of Christian Spirituality*, Oxford, Lion.

Hume, Basil (1984), *To Be a Pilgrim*, London, SPCK.

Iremonger, F. A. (1949), *Life of William Temple*, Oxford University Press.

Jeremias, Joachim (1965), *The Central Message of the New Testament*, London, SCM Press.

Jlunga, We Bukole (1988), *Paths of Liberation: A Third World Spirituality*, Abingdon, Orbis Books.

Johns, Jeremy (1993), *Christianity and Islam*, in *The Oxford History of Christianity*, ed. John McManners, Oxford University Press.

Johnson, Paul (1976), *A History of Christianity*, Harmondsworth, Penguin.

Johnston, William (1973), ed., *The Cloud of Unknowing and the Book of Privy Counselling*, New York, Doubleday.

Jones, Gareth (1995), *Critical Theology: Questions of Truth and Method*, Cambridge, Polity Press.

Julian of Norwich (1978), *Showings*, New York, Paulist Press.

Kagawa, Toyohiko (1936), *The Thorn in the Flesh*, London, SCM Press.

Kane, Aletheia (1984) [ET], *Elizabeth of the Trinity, Complete Works*, Vol. 1, Institute of Carmelite Studies.

Kavanaugh, Kieran (1979), ed., *The Collected Works of St. John of the Cross*, London, Thomas Nelson.

Keeble, N. H. (1984), ed., *Pilgrim's Progress*, Oxford University Press.

Kempis, Thomas à, *The Imitation of Christ* [ET], Betty J. Knoll (nd), London, Collins.

Kenneth, Brother (1987), *Saints of the 20th Century*, London, Mowbray.

Kung, Hans (1977), *On Being a Christian*, London, Collins.

Lakeland, Paul (1997), *Postmodernity: Christian Identity in a Fragmented Age*, London, Harper Collins.

Lash, Ephrem (1998), ed., *Orthodox Prayers*, London, SPCK.

Law, William (nd), *A Serious Call To a Devout and Holy Life*, London, Farron Brown & Co. Limited.

Lawrence, C. H. (1989), *Mediaeval Monasticism*, London, Longman.

Lawrence, D. H. (1915), *The Rainbow*, Harmondsworth, Penguin.

Lawson, A. Brown (1994), *John Wesley and the Anglican Evangelicals of the Eighteenth Century*, London, Portland Press.

Lincoln, Francis (1998), *The Message of St. Francis*, London, SPCK.

Llywelyn, Dorian (1999), *Sacred Place, Chosen People: Land and Nationality in the Welsh Spiritual Tradition*, Cardiff, University of Wales Press.

Lonergan, Bernard (1972), *Method in Theology*, London, Darton, Longman and Todd.

Lossky, Vladimir (1973), *The Mystical Tradition of the Eastern Church*, London, James Clarke.

Loughlin, Thomas O. (1999), *St. Patrick: The Man and his Works*, London, SPCK.

Louth, Andrew (1976), *Theology and Spirituality*, Oxford, SLG Press.

—— (1991), *Mysticism in Early Christianity*, ed. Ian Hazlett, London, SPCK.

Lowther-Clark, W. K. (1944), *Eighteenth Century Piety*, London, SPCK.

Macquarrie, John (1963), *Twentieth Century Religious Thought*, London, SCM Press.

—— (1971), *Theologies of Hope*, Expository Times, Edinburgh, T&T Clark.

—— (1998), *On Being a Theologian*, ed. John Morgan, London, SCM Press.

—— (1992), *Paths in Spirituality*, London, SCM Press.

Mayr-Harting, Henry (1993), *The West: The Age of Conversion*, in *The Oxford History of Christianity*, ed. John McManners, Oxford University Press.

Manning, Bernard (1942), *The Hymns of Wesley and Watts*, Peterborough, Epworth Press.

Marison, E. F. (1912), *St. Basil and his Rule*, Oxford University Press.

Markus, Robert (1993), *From Rome to the Barbarian Kingdoms in The Oxford History of Christianity*, ed. John McManners, Oxford University Press.

Martin, Hugh (1963), *The Faith of Robert Browning*, London, SCM Press.

Mbiti, John (1976), *Some Current Concerns of African Theology*, Expository Times, Edinburgh, T&T Clark.

McGinn, B., and Meyendorff, J. (1986), *Christian Spirituality: Origins to the Twelfth Century*, New York, Crossroad.

McManners, John (1998), ed., *The Oxford History of Christianity*, Oxford University Press.

McNeil, J. T. (1960), *John Calvin: Institutes of the Christian Religion*, Westminster, John Knox Press.

Merton, Thomas (1948), *The Seven Storey Mountain*, London, Harper Collins, Signet Books.

—— (1971), *Contemplation of a World in Action*, New York, Doubleday.

—— (1972), *New Seeds of Contemplation*, New York, New Directions Publishing.

Meyendorff, John (1974), *Byzantine Theology*, Fordham University Press.

—— (1975), *Christ in Eastern Christian Thought*, New York, St. Vladimir's Seminary Press.

Mitchell, Basil (1991), *The Christian Conscience*, in *The Oxford History of Christianity*, ed. J. McManners, Oxford University Press.

Moltmann, J. (1967), *Theology of Hope*, London, SCM Press.

Monk, A. (1998), *The Hermitage Within: Spirituality of the Desert*, London, Darton, Longman and Todd.

Montefiore, H. W. (1962), *Towards a Christology for Today*, in *Soundings*, ed. A. R. Vidler, Cambridge University Press.

Moore, J. R. (1998), *Religion in Victorian Britain*, Manchester University Press.

Moorman, John R. H. (1950), *Saint Francis of Assisi*, London, SCM Press.

Neill, S. et al. (1970), *Concise Dictionary of Christian World Mission*, Cambridge, Lutterworth.

Nicolson, Harold (1937), *Small Talk*, London, Constable.

Nineham, Dennis (1993), *Christianity in Mediaeval and Modern Europe*, London, SCM Press.

Nouwen, Henri J. M. (1998), *The Way of the Heart*, London, Darton, Longman and Todd.

Nuttall, G. F. (1946), *The Holy Spirit in Puritan Faith and Experience*, Oxford, Blackwell.

Osmond, Percy H. (1912), *The Hope of our Fathers*, London, Mowbray.

Otto, Rudolph (1923), *The Idea of the Holy*, Oxford University Press.

Pannenberg, W. (1968), *Jesus, God and Man*, London, Darton, Longman and Todd.

—— (1983), *Christian Spirituality and Sacramental Community*, London, Darton, Longman and Todd.

Parrinder, Geoffrey (1969), *Religion in Africa*, Harmondsworth, Penguin.

Parry, Kenneth L. (1956), *Christian Hymns*, London, SCM Press.

Peers, E. Allison (1934–5), *The Complete Works of St. John of the Cross*, London, Burns and Oates.

—— (1972) [ET], *Teresa of Avila, The Way of Perfection*, London, Sheed and Ward.

—— (1978), *Spirit of Flame*, London, Sheed and Ward.

Pegis, Anton (1997), ed., *Basic Writings of Saint Thomas Aquinas*, Indianapolis, Hackett Publisher.

Polkinghorne, John (1998), *Science and Theology: An Introduction*, London, SPCK.

Potter, G. R. (1976), *Zwingli*, Cambridge University Press.

Quoist, Michael (1963), *Prayers for Life*, London, Gill & Macmillan.

Rhys, Ernest (1920), *Poetry and Drama*, London, J. M. Dent & Sons.

Riley, J. A. L. (1917), ed., *Birkbeck and the Russian Church*, London, SPCK.

Robertson, E. H. (1962), *Christians Against Hitler*, London, SCM Press.

Robinson, John A. T. (1965), *Honest to God*, London, SCM Press.

Rousseau, Philip (1985), *Christian Asceticism and the Early Monks in Early Christianity*, ed. Ian Hazlett, London, SPCK.

Routley, Eric (1957), *The Wisdom of the Fathers*, London, SCM Press.

—— (1957), *The Music of Christian Hymnody*, London, The Independent Press.

Schmemann, A. (1978), *Ultimate Questions: An Anthology of Modern Russian Religious Thought*, London, Mowbray.

Schoferdiek, Knut (1991), *Christian Mission and Expansion in Early Christianity*, ed. Ian Hazlett, London, SPCK.

Schweitzer, Albert (1910), *The Quest of the Historical Jesus*, London, A&C Black.

Scribner, Bob (1994), *The Reformation in National Context*, Cambridge University Press.

Seasolitz, R. Kevin (1987), *Benedict of Nursia, Encyclopedia of Religion*, Vol. 2, ed. Mircea Eliade, New York, Macmillan.

Selman, J. (1994), *Saint Thomas Aquinas*, Edinburgh, T&T Clark.

Senn, Frank C. (1986), ed., *Protestant Spiritual Traditions*, New York, Doubleday.

Sheed, F. J. (1944), *The Confessions of St. Augustine*, London, Sheed & Ward.

Sheldrake, Philip (1998), *Spirituality and Theology*, London, Darton, Longman and Todd.

—— (1996), *Spirituality and History: Questions of Interpretation and Method*, London, SPCK.

Sherley-Price, Leo (1971), *Bede: A History of the English Church and People*, Harmondsworth, Penguin.

Smallman, Basil (1957), *The Background of Passion Music*, London, SCM Press.

Smithers, S. W. (1987), *Spiritual Guide, Encyclopedia of Religion*, ed. Mircea Eliade, Vol. 4., New York, Macmillan.

Sobrino, Jon (1988), *Spirituality of Liberation: Toward Political Holiness*, Abingdon, Orbis Books.

Spinks, Bryan D. (1999), ed., *To Glorify God: Essays in Modern Reformed Liturgy*, Edinburgh, T&T Clark.

Springfield, Eric D. N. (1998), *Spirituality and Theology*, Westminster, John Knox Press.

Sproxton, Vernon (1971), *Teilhard de Chardin*, London, SCM Press.

Stone, Brian (1963), *Mediaeval English*, Harmondsworth, Penguin.

Tantzen, Grace (1987), *Julian of Norwich*, London, SPCK.

Taylor, John H. (1999), *Pilgrim Spirit: An Introduction to Reformed Spirituality*, Canterbury Press.

Taylor, John (1993), *The Future of Christianity*, in *Oxford History of Christianity*, ed. John McManners, Oxford University Press.

Thornton, M. (1963), *English Spirituality*, London, Mowbray.

Thurston, Bonnie (1993), *Spiritual Life in the Early Church*, London, Harper Collins.

Tileston, M. W. (1925), *Great Souls at Prayer*, London, Allenson.

Tillich, Paul (1951–64), *Systematic Theology*, Vol. 1, London, Nisbet.

Trevelyan, G. M. (1946), *English Social History*, Harlow, Longmans.

Trevor-Roper, H. R. (1940), *Archbishop Laud*, London, Macmillan.

Tutu, Desmond (1995), ed., *An African Prayer Book*, London, Doubleday.

Underhill, Evelyn (nd), *The Spiritual Life*, New York, Harper.

Vaporis, N. M. (1987), *Kosmas Aitolos, Encyclopedia of Religion*, ed. Mircea Eliade, New York, Macmillan.

Vissser't Hooft, W. A. (1933), *Anglo-Catholicism and Orthodoxy*, London, SCM Press.

Waddams, Herbert (1964), *Meeting the Orthodox Churches*, London, SCM Press.

Wainwright, Geoffrey (1987), *Christian Spirituality*, in *Encyclopedia of Religion*, ed. Mircea Eliade, New York, Macmillan.

Wakefield, G. S. (1957), *Puritan Devotion*, London, SCM Press.

Wakefield, Gordon (1983), ed., *A Dictionary of Christian Spirituality*, Philadelphia, Westminster Press.

Walker, W. (1937), *A History of the Christian Church*, Edinburgh, T&T Clark.

Walsh, James (1981), *The Cloud of Unknowing*, London, SPCK.

Ward, Benedicta (1986), *The Wisdom of the Desert Fathers*, Oxford, SLG Press.

—— (1973), ed., *The Prayers and Meditations of St. Anselm*, Harmondsworth, Penguin.

—— (1976), *The Influence of St. Bernard*, Oxford, SLG Press.

Ward, Hannah and Wild, Jennifer (1998), *Christian Meditation Collection*, Oxford, Lion.

Ward, Keith (1986), *The Turn of the Tide*, London, BBC.

Ware, Kallistos (1993), *Eastern Christendom*, in *The Oxford History of Christianity*, ed. John McManners, Oxford University Press.

Ware, Timothy (1997), *The Orthodox Church*, Harmondsworth, Penguin.

Watts, Fraser (1998), *Science meets Faith: Theology and Science in Conversation*, London, SPCK.

Wayne, Philip (1932), *Selections from Wordsworth*, Aylesbury, Ginn.

Weil, Simone (1959), *Waiting on God*, London, Collins.

Wesley, John (1987), *The Journals of John Wesley, A Selection*, ed. Elizabeth Jay, Oxford University Press.

Whitley, H. C. (1955), *Blinded Eagle*, London, SCM Press.
Wildiers, N. M. (1968), *An Introduction to Teilhard de Chardin*, London, Fontana.
Wiles, Maurice and Santer, Mark (1975), ed., *Documents of Early Christian Thought*, Cambridge University Press.
Williams, A. T. P. (1947), *The Anglican Tradition in the Life of England*, London, SCM Press.
Williams, G. H. (1962), *The Radical Reformation*, Westminster, John Knox Press.
Williams, Rowan (1990), *The Wound of Knowledge*, London, Darton, Longman and Todd.
——(1991), *Teresa of Avila*, London, Chapman.
Wolters, Clifton (1978), *The Cloud of Unknowing*, Harmondsworth, Penguin.
Young, Francis (1991), *The Greek Fathers in Early Christianity*, ed. Ian Hazlett, London, SPCK.

Index of Names

Index of Subjects